THE PEOPLE
IN QUESTION

Citizens and Constitutions
in Uncertain Times

Jo Shaw

BRISTOL
UNIVERSITY
PRESS

First published in Great Britain in 2021 by

Bristol University Press
University of Bristol
1-9 Old Park Hill
Bristol
BS2 8BB
UK
t: +44 (0)117 954 5940
e: bup-info@bristol.ac.uk

Details of international sales and distribution partners are available at bristoluniversitypress.co.uk

British Library Cataloguing in Publication Data
A catalogue record for this book is available from the British Library

ISBN 978-1-5292-1042-2 paperback
ISBN 978-1-5292-0889-4 hardcover
ISBN 978-1-5292-0897-7 ePub
ISBN 978-1-5292-0890-0 ePdf

Cover design: blu inc, Bristol
Front cover image: Andrew Rogers, 'Individuals'

Contents

Notes on the Author

Jo Shaw holds the Salvesen Chair of European Institutions at the University of Edinburgh and is a part-time Professor at New Social Research, Tampere University, Finland.

Preface and Acknowledgements

To a much greater extent than I have ever encountered before, this book has involved the reconstruction of the ship while at sea. Citizenship and constitutions seem to be under assault from all sides.

As I prepared this book during the course of 2019 and into 2020, it was hard not to be regularly distracted by new constitutional outrages that impinged on the topics I was writing about. Donald Trump was a good source. First, he suggested that the US should buy Greenland as a 'real estate deal', taking no account of the self-determination of Greenlanders. Then, he argued that Jewish Americans could not vote Democrat without showing disloyalty. But he has not been alone. There were the increasingly hysterical manoeuvrings on the part of a British government determined to give effect to what it continued to insist was the 'will of the people', namely the conclusion reached on one day in June 2016, that the vague prospectus offered by the 'Leave the EU' camp sounded rather enticing ('Take back control', etc, etc). Until the decisive General Election of December 2019, which returned the Conservative Party led by Boris Johnson to power with a substantial majority, it was never clear how the issues raised by Brexit could be put through a deadlocked Parliament. At the same time, the daily communications of government have brought doubt into the lives of those citizens most affected by the legal and human impacts of the decision to leave the EU, in particular EU27 citizens resident in the UK and UK citizens resident in the EU.

Perhaps even more significantly, we have seen almost daily developments in two citizenship-related tragedies unfolding in South and South East Asia: the dispossession and oppression of the Rohingya in Myanmar in what seems to come close to an effort at genocide, and the mass denationalization of millions in India's north east state of Assam, who have been unable to prove that they are citizens and consequently face exclusion from the state. I partly blame this continued avalanche of fresh news for the fact that the book ended up much longer than originally intended.

Although the actual writing period for the book has been relatively short, the genesis of the research lies further in the past and, as ever with me, the ideas have evolved slowly over a long time. The book started life as a short essay on the same topic which I decided needed further exploration.[1] That essay was written while I was holding a EURIAS Fellowship at the Helsinki Collegium of Advanced Studies (HCAS) (2017–18), and the financial support of the EURIAS/Marie Curie Programme and HCAS is acknowledged with thanks; I am also grateful to the Law School of the University of Edinburgh for the necessary research leave. The arguments were further developed as part of a broader project on citizenship regimes, kindly funded by a Leverhulme Major Research Fellowship (2018–21). Looking to the deeper past, my reflections have benefited tremendously from the work done on the CITSEE project (The Europeanisation of Citizenship in the Successor States of the Former Yugoslavia), funded by the European Research Council (ERC 230239, 2009–14) and work funded by the Nuffield Foundation on friction between EU free movement law and UK immigration law, which has underpinned my reflections on citizenship post-Brexit. Without the support and funding of the European University Institute, as well as numerous other research funders including the European Commission and the British Academy, the Global Citizenship Observatory (GLOBALCIT) could not continue to thrive and to provide rich primary data and secondary analysis, on which I have drawn heavily throughout the book. The University of Sydney Law School, with a strong community of citizenship-focused researchers, was an excellent and conversational environment in which to benefit from a short research stay in 2018. My 'other employer', New Social Research at Tampere University in Finland, also offered a supportive research environment, and the opportunity to give a lecture to my colleagues planted the seed in my mind that this was a book I urgently needed to write. I am grateful to all of these funding bodies and academic institutions for their support. In particular, I would like to point to this book as a major output from my Leverhulme Major Research Fellowship.

Aside from institutions, I would also like to thank numerous individuals. At GLOBALCIT, I want to thank my co-directors Rainer Bauböck and Maarten Vink, and, since February 2020, Jelena Džankić. I had the opportunity to present part of Chapter 6 at the GLOBALCIT Annual Conference in November 2019 and to receive invaluable feedback. Within CITSEE, Igor Štiks contributed hugely to the development of my thinking about citizenship in the context of new states and post-conflict or transitional scenarios, as did our many other research fellows and assistants, whose career development during and after our collaborations I have

---

[1] J. Shaw (2018) 'Introduction', in J. Shaw (ed) *Citizenship and Constitutional Law*, Cheltenham: Edward Elgar (also published on the Edward Elgar website as a research review).

followed with pleasure and pride. Since starting that project, I have also been to three CITSEE weddings and cooed over quite a few CITSEE children. For reading, commentary and critique of all or parts of the text in draft, I want to thank Rainer Bauböck, Jelena Džankić and Igor Štiks (again), as well as Richard Bellamy, Alex Green, Helen Irving, Ashley Mantha-Hollands, Maarten Vink and Neil Walker. Many other colleagues have responded to queries with generosity, and supplied me with texts, ideas and new lines of enquiry. I am also grateful to Bristol University Press for their constructive review process, and for the generous and critical comments of their reviewers, as well as for their engaged and effective production and marketing procedures. In particular, many thanks for the design of the artwork for the cover, which was inspired by a photograph I took of an Andrew Rogers sculpture entitled 'Individuals' in July 2018. The sculpture, originally installed in Dag Hammarskjöld Plaza, gateway to the UN in Manhattan, New York City, now stands outside the University of Sydney Law School in Australia. The sculpture is intended to convey the complex relationships between individuals and community as well as the singularity of individuals.[2]

This book is heavily data-dependent, and it is not my data. I am massively in the debt of those many people who have collected and checked data about constitutions and citizenship and then made them publicly available on the internet for researchers like me to make use of. Throughout this book, I have used the English language versions of national constitutions made available via the Constitute project database.[3] In the minority of cases where there have been more recent amendments that have not yet been incorporated into the database (for example, the 2018 amendments to the Hungarian constitution), reference is made to official translations published on government websites.

As of 16 September 2019, the Constitute project database contained 193 constitutions in force. As of August 2019, 193 countries are members of the UN, but these are not the same countries for which Constitute contains constitutions. For example, the database contains constitutions for Palestine (which has observer status at the UN but is not a full member) and for Kosovo and Taiwan (which are not UN members but are recognized by at least one other UN Member State).

There are also three citizenship databases without which the research could not have been completed or this book written: see GLOBALCIT (2017a, b) and Vink et al (2015). These databases between them provide comprehensive information on modes of acquisition and loss of citizenship,

---

[2] See Andrew Rogers (www.andrewrogers.org/).

[3] See Constitute (www.constituteproject.org/search?lang=en).

and on global expatriate dual citizenship. In addition, other data sources on the GLOBALCIT website, such as the huge store of country reports and citizenship law timelines, have been invaluable for my research. My work has also benefited from the substantial resources and effective and responsive staff of the Library at the University of Edinburgh.

To stay sane during the writing process, I have been making regular visits to the gym. It's a winning combination if you can go to a class one morning, where an instructor (an ex-ballet dancer) tells you this is only 45 minutes out of your day and people lack discipline these days, and then follow it up the next morning with a spinning class, where your work is accompanied by strong motivational talk from the instructor telling you that each and every one of you is special. Academic research and writing nicely reflect that paradoxical mix.

Finally, I want to mention my family. I noted in the Preface to my previous book (see Shaw 2007) that its writing saw my son Leo develop from primary school child into university student. While I was writing this book, he has returned from a stint working abroad and got married, and I was happy that he mentioned my successes as an academic in his speech. His time working in Singapore gave me good reason to visit that region and to widen my interests in national citizenship well beyond Europe. He is obviously less of a daily presence in my life these days, but I know he has been out there, rooting for me to get this finished as scheduled. Alf Thomas has been very much present, and has been a hero in the domestic delivery department. I am very grateful to him for his support and forbearance in relation to a rather dull couple of months when I have been closeted away. Soups, salads, fresh bread and some absolutely epic homemade cheese straws have kept me going. Moreover, since it would not be most people's choice to have (planned) major surgery between completing the first draft and finalizing the manuscript, I want to pay tribute to the skill of the orthopaedic surgeons at Edinburgh Royal Infirmary, the excellent services of Lothian NHS supporting my recovery, and the dedicated care of Alf Thomas (again), while I have been slowly rehabilitating. Indeed, thanks to everyone who has been patient with me while I have been rather slow.

Legal and political developments have been closely tracked and reflected up to 16 September 2019, with outline coverage, so far as is possible, up to 11 December 2019 (and occasional references thereafter, for example, the UK General Election of 12 December 2019). I have accepted that by the time this book is published, some of the material may have dated, but hopefully I have written about the rapidly changing circumstances of citizenship and constitutions in a manner which avoids misleading the reader. Errors and omissions are, of course, my responsibility alone.

PART I
Setting the Scene

1

Introduction

CITIZEN: A member of a free city or jural society, (civitas) possessing all the rights and privileges which can be enjoyed by any person under its constitution and government, and subject to the corresponding duties. (Black 2004 [1891], 206)[1]

Why constitutional citizenship?

It has become rather fashionable to express negative views about citizenship and not to hold it in high regard. If states can put their citizenship on the market in return for what, to high net worth individuals, probably seems like only a relatively small charge or investment, why should everyone else treat citizenship with reverence? Surely, citizenship today is just a matter of passports and mobility, and not a lot else?[2] What is more, is it not a little odd to focus on something which is just a form of 'legalized discrimination' against aliens (Wimmer 2013, 74)?

The alternative view recognizes that citizenship has acquired a fundamental importance in relation to the organization of human affairs into polities. As such, it may be an empty vessel into which many different

---

[1] I should concede that the more recent editions of the classic work *Black's Law Dictionary*, edited by Bryan A. Garner, do not contain a definition of the citizen that quite so neatly fits my purposes: 'A person who, by either birth or naturalization, is a member of a political community, owing allegiance to the community and being entitled to enjoy all of its civil rights and protections; a member of the civil state, entitled to all its privileges' (Garner and Black 2009, 278).

[2] As a reflection on the anticipated 'drop' in the 'value' of UK citizenship, should a 'hard' or worse 'no deal' Brexit occur, see M. Skapinker (2019) 'Is French nationality worth more than British? A country's stability, freedom and opportunities count for a lot', *Financial Times*, 26 November (www.ft.com/content/f6a3402c-0d32-11ea-b2d6-9bf4d1957a67).

types of political aspiration can be poured, but its significance cannot be denied. It allows states to choose populations, but also to control them. Some of the most egregious crimes against humanity such as slavery, the Holocaust and apartheid have all involved the stripping and/ or denial of 'citizenship' (Lewans 2010). Citizenship has also played a role in the breakup of Yugoslavia and in the human suffering that followed thereafter (Štiks 2015), in the violence and persecution that the Rohingya in Myanmar have faced as a people (Parashar and Alam 2019), and in the continued oppression of minorities mainly identified by reference to religion in India, culminating – for now at least – in the denationalization of up to 2 million people in Assam (Jayal 2019a). Lacking or being refused the status of citizen has been part of a rhetoric of depersonalization applied in all of these cases.

Citizenship, as it is applied within states, is the legal mechanism for formal membership within the polity. There is an important external aspect of state-based citizenship, organizing individuals primarily by reference to the territorial and jurisdictional boundaries of states, and reinforcing the legally constructed character of that membership relation. This is widely seen as citizenship's 'Westphalian' core.[3] That is to say, as a legal marker, it helps to sustain the still dominant mode of political community in the modern world, namely the system of sovereign states which remain the most important actors within the international legal order (Farr 2005).[4] States are often quite instrumental in their engagement with citizenship, prioritizing certain groups over others. Citizenship laws pursue the task of setting the boundaries via rules on acquisition and loss, and, in many instances, this takes place against the backdrop of constitutional norms on citizenship and citizenship rights.

Citizenship also has an internal aspect that goes beyond the surface of legal norms and beyond the idea of citizenship as a bundle of rights. Most, if not all, (state) polities have some type of 'story of peoplehood' (Smith 2001), or even multiple competing stories. In these stories, the scope and practices of citizenship are treated – implicitly or explicitly – as a product of cultural and/or political processes of nation, or people formation, even if these are incomplete or contested. These aspects of citizenship are closely related to both the dynamics of self-rule and democracy, as well as

---

[3] See also Legomsky (1994, 299). The reference derives from the Peace of Westphalia in 1648, ending the Thirty Years War.

[4] In what follows, references to *national* citizenship and *state-based* citizenship (or constitutions) should be taken to be synonymous, despite the distinct 'nation' reference point of the word 'national'. This point will be clearer after the discussion of the distinctive usages of 'nationality' and 'citizenship' below.

to cultural and identitarian questions. Indeed, it is well established that the success of states/societies depends not just on the institutional regulation of citizenship but also 'on the virtues, identities, and practices of its citizens, including their ability to co-operate, deliberate, and feel solidarity with those who belong to different ethnic and religious groups' (Kymlicka and Norman 2000, 10). As regards both its external and internal aspects, citizenship is acknowledged to be one of the most important ties that bind communities together.

We cannot, in sum, ignore the importance of citizenship. Instead, we need to know more about it, and how it relates to other fundamental building blocks of modern polities both within and beyond the state, such as constitutions and constitutional law. This is the purpose of this book.

Beginning with an initial focus on states, the first question considered in this book concerns the scope and nature of state or national constitutional law and its relationship to citizenship laws and policies. What does it mean to buttress claims to the legitimacy and authority of state-based concepts of citizenship (a) by reference to a *constitutional concept* of 'the citizenry' and indeed 'the people' and (b) through the regulation of citizenship (directly or indirectly) via *constitutional law*? These two interconnected questions form the basis of the enquiry in Parts I and II of the book. The chapters in these two parts introduce and then examine in detail the many dimensions of 'constitutional citizenship' at state level. In Part III, we explore some of the issues that arise when 'constitutional citizenship' is put under pressure, by focusing on the challenges posed by populism and the de-territorialization of citizenship.

The enquiry undertaken in this book depends on isolating and exploring the idea of 'constitutional citizenship'. In what we now term the 'Global North', states have been including provisions on citizenship in their constitutions since the late 18th century. Examples include the first post-revolutionary constitution of 1791 in France, Spain's short-lived but influential Cádiz Constitution of 1812, and the Constitution of the United States after the adoption of the 14th Amendment of 1868 following the Civil War. As the era of modern states and constitutions dawned, constitutional provisions and laws adopted on the basis of those new constitutions started to build the structure of what we now recognize as a modern citizenship status. Thus, we can see that the linkage between citizenship and constitutional law has a long heritage. But to know more about what it might mean, we will need to dig a little more deeply.

One place to start is by looking at what judges say about this relationship. A good example of a resonant pronouncement about citizenship comes from Lord Justice Laws, when delivering in a judgment in the English

Court of Appeal on the scope of the UK's citizenship deprivation powers.[5] Despite the fact that these powers are stated in a *legislative* form, he noted that:

> The conditions on which national citizenship is conferred, withheld or revoked are integral to the identity of the nation State. They touch the *constitution*; for they identify the *constitution's* participants.[6]

From another (Canadian) judge, we hear about 'The intimate relation between a citizen and his [sic] country'.[7] In these statements from judges, we can see citizenship as an institution flowing into constitutional discourse, and constitutional norms flowing into citizenship discourse. At first sight, this seems to suggest that there may exist a smooth set of interconnections between the conditions of acquisition and loss of citizenship (and thus the task of identifying who the citizens are), 'the identity of the nation state' and the constitution as a political performance with 'participants'. These are the three key elements identified by Lord Justice Laws. All three elements are placed under close scrutiny in this book, both when we consider what might be termed the 'normal incidents' of 'constitutional citizenship', and later when we turn to examine what happens when constitutions are under stress.

The remainder of this chapter comprises the following elements: a synopsis of the whole book; an introduction to the existing literatures examining the interrelationship of citizenship and constitutions; some notes introducing the key terms of 'citizenship', 'nationality', 'constitution' and 'the people'; and an excursus outlining the principal methodological inspirations for the approach taken in the book.

---

[5] *G1 v Secretary of State for the Home Department* [2012] EWCA Civ 867; [2013] QB 1008, discussing the interpretation of s. 40 of the British Nationality Act 1981.

[6] Emphasis added. In UK (English?) constitutional terms, it is interesting to note that Jeff King (2016) believes this to be a 'remarkable passage' on the grounds that, if citizenship touches the constitution then so do many other issues such as residence. It is worth pointing out the context in which the statement was made, which demonstrated an antipathy on the part of the judges to the Court of Justice of the European Union (CJEU) having any jurisdiction in citizenship loss and acquisition cases. We return to this issue in a discussion of the constitutional context of (loss of) EU citizenship in Chapter 4.

[7] *Justice La Forest in United States of America v Cotroni; United States of America v El Zein* [1989] 1 SCR 1469 at 1480.

Synopsis of the book

There is one further 'introductory' chapter in Part I. Starting with the puzzle that explicit and detailed constitutional regulation of citizenship is actually quite rare across the globe, Chapter 2 presents some of the main ways in which citizenship and constitutions/constitutional law can and do iterate with each other at the 'top level' (that is, via the texts of the constitution and of constitutional law and in respect of constitutional principles and conventions). We then place these issues into a broader context, exploring issues such as the legacies of colonialism and understandings of citizenship beyond the so-called western world. The chapter also contests some of the presuppositions that lie behind the idea that 'citizenship of a (nation) state' could operate as the sole or even central model of citizenship. One short reflection focuses on whether the constitutional question is, in fact, an eccentric one to pose at the present time. This is because of the increasing shift towards treating citizenship as a matter of individual choice and elective affinity, in an ethos of strategy and instrumentalism (Harpaz 2015, 2019) rather than as a quasi-sacred gift of states (as some of the judicial statements quoted above come close to suggesting) or as a fundamental norm of democratic self-governance (Bauböck 2018a).

The next task for the book is to find an appropriate way to organize the main issues that emerge in those cases where citizenship and constitutions abut, in order to make sense of the different dimensions of the relationship between the two. To this end, Part II of the book 'unpacks constitutional citizenship' by exploring it from three angles: we look first at the constitutional ideal of citizenship, under which heading we can explore the proposition that the ideal-type of a citizenry is comprised of free, equal and sovereign citizens, underpinned by a notion of dignity; then we explore the direct and indirect impacts of constitutional law on the terms of citizenship as a legal status, including issues of acquisition and loss and the ever-present shadow of statelessness; and finally our focus falls onto the relationship between citizenship rights, constitutional rights and human rights. These discussions form Chapters 3 to 5 of the book.

In Chapter 3, we explore constitutional fundamentals such as constituent power, sovereignty and constitutional identity, and then examine how ideas such as equality and dignity can shape the constitution's engagement with citizenship. Chapter 4 turns the focus onto the main modes of acquisition and loss of citizenship, considering also associated topics such as dual citizenship. Furthermore, how do higher 'constitutional norms' such as equality shape citizenship as a legal status? Chapter 5 closes off this part of the book, with a reflection on how we understand rights in a constitutional context. The main themes here concern the scope and enforceability of rights, coupled with reflections on how rights can strain the relationships between majoritarian and non-majoritarian institutions in democracies (for example, between parliaments and courts).

Together, the chapters show that even though detailed regulation of citizenship within constitutions is rare, leaving key matters to be decided by legislatures, these texts none the less provide the discursive framework within which the ethics and often the practices of citizenship are debated at the national level. These discursive processes often play out in conflicts between different institutions of the state and the debates can include questions about what sort of 'link' between individual and polity is thought to be embedded in citizenship. Other issues recurring across the three chapters highlight the role of superordinate principles such as equality and dignity which are enshrined as constitutional rights in many countries. In sum, despite the apparent constitutional neglect of citizenship (and the puzzle as to why this is so), we can still learn a great deal once we explore the concept of 'constitutional citizenship' in detail.

This book aims not just to interpret the citizenship/constitution relationship, but also to place the insights so gained into a wider critical framework, and to exploit the current conjuncture in order to highlight *why* the work undertaken in Parts I and II of the book is important. Part III of the book accordingly looks at what we can learn from observing citizenship in a constitutional context when it is put under pressure. There are two apparently opposing movements which are put under the microscope. On the one hand, we can see the existence and, some might suggest, increasing prevalence at the national level, of 'populist' and exclusivist approaches to the boundaries of citizenship (and the rise of the phenomenon of 'populist constitutionalism'). Yet at the same time, and to an unprecedented degree, the governance of citizenship has become fragmented across transnational, supranational, international and subnational axes which place the state itself in question.

Chapter 6 explores the relationship between 'constitutional citizenship' and the rise of populism within political discourse and political practices. Is this leading to the erosion of modern citizenship as an ideal of equality and self-rule, or can we see an effective triangulation of the tensions between the rule of law and the 'rule of people' which, in fact, contributes to the ideals and effectiveness of both citizenship and democracy? The discussion focuses on how populist politics close down the discursive space within which 'constitutional citizenship' can function, leading to outcomes which tend to be exclusionary towards outsiders. It is interesting to note that many populist politicians make extensive use of constitutional amendment processes to reinforce their sense of identity with 'the people'.

Chapter 7 then turns to the phenomenon that Kristin Henrard (2018) usefully terms the 'shifting spatialities' of citizenship. It studies the impact on ideas of 'constitutional citizenship' of the dispersion of citizenship statuses and rights across vertical and horizontal axes. Under the influence of factors such as mobility and migration, the instability of state boundaries, subnational claims and movements, the creation of supranational/international institutions, including courts, such as the EU and the Council of Europe and cognates elsewhere in the world and the emergence of a body of international law that addresses many issues of citizenship and rights, we can discern a scheme of fragmented citizenship governance. This raises new challenges, for example, in relation to the legitimacy of how international law impacts on domestic constitutions. It cannot simply be assumed that the concerns with global justice and individual rights that stem from many of the international law sources that pertain to citizenship will, in fact, map comfortably onto citizenship in a constitutional context at the national level.

The sorts of tensions around 'constitutional citizenship' which emerge in these two chapters highlight that there are some substantial areas for further research that can only be hinted at in the brief Conclusions (Chapter 8) to the book. These also seek to reinforce how the two sets of issues explored in Chapters 6 and 7 articulate with each other, against the backdrop of the examples discussed in Part II and the framework for study elaborated in Part I. On the one hand, we live, many people have argued, in an age of populism; on the other hand, with unprecedented levels of mobility and migration across international borders, and the widespread liberalization of dual citizenship, it becomes ever more difficult to conceive of citizenship regimes operating solely within closed national borders. Practices related to constitution-building and citizenship are not exclusively confined to the (national) state level, but often occur above and below the state, in supranational and subnational institutions, as well as in the spillovers that occur transnationally between ostensibly separate citizenship and constitutional regimes. Citizenship and constitutionalism both operate within and between multilevel and complex transnational governance frameworks. Intersecting with constitutional frameworks both within and beyond the state, the phenomenon that Melissa Williams (2007) terms the 'citizenships of globalization' arguably offers the pluralist antidote to the potentially exclusivist conceptions that can emerge from the intersection of citizenship and constitutions at the national level, both as a matter of theory and a matter of practice. What is left hanging within this space, however, are two questions. One concerns how the various conceptions of citizenship fit together, and the other concerns questions of legitimacy and democracy 'beyond the state'.

What do we already know about how citizenship, constitutions and constitutional law relate to each other?

Echoing the words of Lord Justice Laws quoted earlier, Kim Rubenstein and Niamh Lenagh-Maguire (2011, 143) have suggested that 'the idea of citizenship, and the ideals it is taken to represent, go to the heart of how states are constituted and defined'. In similar terms, Michel Rosenfeld asserts that:

> The citizen is the constituent unit of the constitutional subject in all its multiple identities, chief among them, the *who* that makes the constitution, the *for whom* it is made, and the *to whom* it is addressed. The citizen is at the heart of modern constitutionalism and is the principal actor in its birth, deployment and continuing life. (Rosenfeld 2009, 211; original emphasis)

Yet despite the seemingly obvious relationship between citizenship, constitutions and constitutional law, there exists surprisingly little scholarship that attempts to analyse the relationship in more detail.

Such scholarship is lacking on both sides: both in constitutional studies and in citizenship studies. For example, a recent attempt to formulate an approach to constitutionalism via its constituent principles contains no systematic discussion of the place of citizenship or 'membership' within such a scheme, although citizenship is acknowledged to be central in particular to principles of democracy and to the rule of law (Barber 2018). Moreover, the UK provides an instructive example of a pedagogical framework for constitutional law in which nationality or citizenship laws are treated as specialized topics, along with immigration law (largely as issues of statutory interpretation, administrative law and the judicial review of administrative discretion), and not as part of the constitutional core that is covered in detail in the main textbooks and courses (Dummett and Nicol 1990, 1). Lest that point be thought just to reflect a UK-centric perspective, then the words of Marcus Llanque (2010, 162), a constitutional theorist working in a German and comparative tradition, can be used: 'Constitutions only hint at the role of the citizen, and the entire picture is revealed only through a mosaic consisting of legislative acts and executive orders as well as constitutional laws.'

In contrast, András Jakab's (2016) study of European constitutional language takes a broader approach to the identification of 'constitutional visions' that explicitly encompasses citizenship. In order to identify these visions, what is needed is an assessment of the relationship between nation(s) and the state, based on a review of materials including the 'constitutional preambles and other provisions, and also by citizenship laws (especially provisions on naturalization) and immigration laws' (Jakab 2016, 241). Together this comment and the methodology that Jakab puts forward suggest that citizenship law is for him by definition an important part of constitutional law.

In the domain of legal studies of citizenship, international law features as a meta-frame of reference much more often than constitutional law.[8] This is not surprising, as there is a rich corpus of norms of international law that serve a variety of purposes and that together build a picture of some of the most important elements of citizenship as a legal relation. Consequently, the standards set in measures such as the European Convention on Nationality[9] are quite commonly the reference points for scholarship on the scope and nature of citizenship laws (de Groot and Vonk 2016). There is a substantial body of scholarly work which examines in detail the implications of international law for the discretion of states in a sphere traditionally thought to lie within the domain of national sovereignty.[10] This has latterly involved a particular focus on international human rights law (von Rütte 2018), as well as on specific measures related to stateless persons, minorities and refugees (Vlieks et al 2017), although in earlier years the focus was more likely to be on those international law measures intended to assist in the suppression of dual nationality (Boll 2007). For the most part, however, those latter measures have now fallen into disuse, as the emphasis within international law has shifted towards an accommodation with individual rights away from a focus solely on states' interests. Both public and private international law make widespread use of the concept of nationality for the purposes of determining issues of jurisdiction (alongside concepts such as territory and residence) in areas such as family law, succession and commercial law.

Meanwhile, where citizenship law is studied within a national framework, we find many case studies that delve deep into the intricacies of national laws and into the contexts which drive the particularities of national citizenship regimes, sometimes on a comparative and/or

---

[8] For contrasting examples, see Fripp (2016) and Annoni and Forlati (2013).

[9] European Convention on Nationality (ETS No 166), signed in Strasbourg on 6 November 1997, entry into force 2000 (for the full text, see www.coe.int/en/web/conventions/full-list/-/conventions/treaty/166).

[10] Important examples include Kesby (2012), Spiro (2011) and Henrard (2018).

transnational basis.[11] Typically, these will mention constitutional issues only as required for the specific case study or studies rather than taking a broader perspective on the constitutional question *per se*. Citizenship, as Char Roone Miller (2001) notes, is generally 'tailored' to its specific national circumstances. Referencing Miller, the point is nicely elaborated by Marcus Llanque:

> There is no "natural" or abstract concept of citizenship which can determine the grounds and limits of a citizen's role without having regard to its place in the institutional setting of a constitution. In a way, political reality shows that all citizenship is "tailored". That is, it is modelled after the necessities of a given political system and it changes in accordance with these necessities. (Llanque 2010, 167)

In sum, there exists little work that attempts to thematize the implications of adopting a constitutional framework to examine the scope or content of citizenship as an idea or practice or to critique the meaning of 'constitution' or 'constitutional law' in this context. This is where this book – at least as regards its first aim – will step in. While the book fills a gap in the literature, it should be noted that the framing of the discussion is indebted to the work of a number of scholars who have wrestled with the relationship between citizenship and constitutions (see, for example, Cohen 1999; Bellamy 2001). As regards the second aim of looking at the wider implications of how citizenship and constitutional law relate to each other, there is already literature that provides significant and useful points of reference for the enquiry, especially in the field of constitutional theory.[12] A notable example is Michel Rosenfeld's (2009) book *The Identity of the Constitutional Subject*, which uses citizenship as an important exemplar of thinking pluralistically about issues of 'constitutional identity' in such a way as to reconcile possible conflicts between the particular (state or individual) and the universal (transnational sphere or community) (see Walker 2010). For example, he argues that 'Both the imagined community that defines the nation and the one that projects an identity on the constitutional order are anchored in the citizen'

---

[11] For a constitutional framing of a national case study, see, in particular, Elisa Arcioni's work on Australia: 2014, 2015, 2018; and with Rayner Thwaites, 2020. Examples of comparative work include Shachar (2012) and de Groot (2012).

[12] Several of the chapters in Shachar et al (2017) provide good examples of the rich analysis possible where constitutional theory meets citizenship, notably Walker (2017) and Gans (2017).

(Rosenfeld 2009, 211). Margaret Canovan's (2005) *The People* also lays down much of the groundwork necessary for reassessing the tensions arising from the simultaneity of the 'turns' to populism and to globalism. This book builds on the insights of scholars such as these, and brings the debate up to date by highlighting a number of recent pertinent examples and challenges.

Perhaps one reason for some gaps in the literature is that both of these terms – 'citizenship' and 'constitutions' – are notoriously broad, hard to pin down and contested in academic and political discourse. The dominant ideas behind both citizenship and constitutions are creatures of the emergence of the modern state. Both are artefacts of the demand for governance and governability. They share family resemblances. It is tricky enough to write about citizenship or constitutions separately. The task is much more difficult when one tries to juxtapose the two sets of ideas, especially when additional comparative elements need to be worked in, in order to gain a broader transnational view of the field. Terms like 'citizenship' and 'constitution' operate in densely networked ideational spheres, also occupied by interrelated concepts such as nationality and the sovereignty of 'the people'. The scope and meaning of each of these concepts is contested. The remainder of this chapter sets the scene for the rest of the book by offering some capsule definitions and preliminary notes on these terms and concepts, on which we can build in later chapters. Finally, since the concepts we choose and the way we interpret them necessarily shape matters of research design and the types of analytical lenses applied, the chapter concludes with brief notes about the methodological inspirations for the work.

Brief notes on core concepts

Citizenship

It is a standard tenet of international law, in relation to what is generally termed (in that context) 'nationality', that it is for each state – according to its sole discretion – to determine issues of legal membership *within* that state.[13] States may in principle apply whatever rules they think fit. Citizenship laws at national level pursue the task of inclusion and

---

[13] See the Convention on Certain Questions Relating to the Conflict of Nationality Laws (League of Nations Treaty Series, vol 179, The Hague, 1930) and Advisory Opinion of the Permanent Court of International Justice of 7 February 1923 on Nationality Decrees Issued in Tunis and Morocco, Series B No 4 (1923).

exclusion, in the first instance, via rules on acquisition and loss. The 'sortation' aspect of citizenship is quite frequently criticized as arbitrary in character, because the allocation of most individuals to 'their' citizenship occurs on the basis of the happenstance of birth, through attachment to territory (*ius soli*) and/or parentage (*ius sanguinis*) (Shachar 2009; Carens 2013). The entire structure is premised on the persistence, however imperfectly, of what is often called the 'Westphalian' system of (nation) states (Farr 2005). *National citizenship* (of a Member State) also provides the exclusive access point to 'citizenship of the (European) Union', that is, having access to the world's most developed form of supranational citizenship, that of the European Union.[14]

Of course, there are now substantial legal and practical constraints on what states may do in relation to the distribution and terms of citizenship (stemming from domestic constitutional restrictions, from international law and from the laws of other states) (de Groot and Vonk 2018). It is widely assumed among scholars and practitioners alike that the somewhat limited international law 'right to citizenship' exists to mitigate the harms caused by statelessness, although there is less agreement about what the meanings or effects of those provisions might be.[15] Chief among the relevant provisions is the 'right to a nationality' and the right not to be arbitrarily deprived of his [sic] nationality, contained in Article 15 of the Universal Declaration of Human Rights,[16] although that provision does not decree *which* state must confer nationality, is not binding on states, and has an uncertain scope (Owen 2018). This provision, as with various instruments on statelessness[17] and Article 7 of the UN Convention on the Rights of the Child concerned with the right to identity and nationality (Ziemele 2014), is intended to be a guarantee of the basic 'right to have rights' as the bedrock of citizenship, famously articulated by Hannah Arendt (1986, 291). Yet as Rainer Bauböck notes, this is only one of the four goals of international law in relation to citizenship, the others being the resolution of conflicts between states, the setting of minimal standards (beyond the sphere of statelessness alone), and (now largely obsolete) the task of avoiding multiple nationality (Bauböck 2018b).

Despite this body of international law, the fundamental principle of state autonomy still holds true as a starting point. It is states that confer

---

[14] See Article 20(1) of the Treaty on the Functioning of the European Union (TFEU).

[15] For contrasting approaches, see Fripp (2016), Gibney (2013), Owen (2018) and von Rütte (2018).

[16] Universal Declaration of Human Rights, 1948 (www.un.org/en/universal-declaration-human-rights/).

[17] See the 1954 Convention Relating to the Status of Stateless Persons and the 1961 Convention on the Reduction of Statelessness.

citizenship on individuals, as a basic sorting principle, and it is states that are required to recognize the citizenship status conferred by other states, subject to what has been termed the 'genuine link' principle articulated by the International Court of Justice (ICJ) in the *Nottebohm* case. Famously, the ICJ postulated that 'nationality is a legal bond having as its basis a social fact of attachment, a genuine connection of existence, interests and sentiments, together with the existence of reciprocal rights and duties',[18] and argued that this underlying principle was relevant for the purposes of determining whether one state was obliged to recognize the conferring of nationality on a person by another state, and thus to accede to a claim to offer diplomatic protection that could flow from that conferral. With the benefit of hindsight, the *Nottebohm* case can be argued to be problematic from a doctrinal perspective,[19] and scholarly criticism of it has revived in recent years (Spiro 2019). But the idea of a genuine link between the individual and the state has emerged as an enduring and useful reference point for many theories of and conceptual frameworks for citizenship (Bauböck 2018a, 2019a), especially when it comes to developing critiques of hard cases such as discretionary naturalization, including investor citizenship (Džankić 2019a), external citizenship (Pogonyi 2017) and loss of citizenship (Bauböck and Paskalev 2015). One point to watch out for, especially in Part II of the book, is whether there is any evidence of states cleaving to the principle of genuine link, either as a matter of constitutional principle ('our people are those persons who have links with us') or as a matter of doctrine.

The comments made so far have been predominantly from a legalistic and top-down perspective, focused in particular on the formal law and on the scope of membership in a rather static sense. This ignores many central political, social and cultural aspects of the concept of citizenship and does not address the ideals of citizenship, such as equality, sovereignty and self-government. It is also a *state-based* perspective and does not address the 'beyond the state' aspects of citizenship, generated by the close interconnections between different national citizenship regimes brought about by international migration and dual citizenship, or the emergence of 'citizenship-like' statuses at the supranational level, notably citizenship of the EU. Nor does it engage directly with the increasing number of options for a strategic approach for some groups of (generally privileged) individuals in a largely post-exclusive world of citizenship, or the strategic approaches of states, which may even use passport purchase as a way of

---

[18] *Liechtenstein v Guatemala (Nottebohm)* [1955] ICJ 1.

[19] For detailed analysis, see Sloane (2009), Macklin (2017a) and Thwaites (2018).

evading responsibilities for groups of otherwise stateless people within their borders (Džankić 2019b).

Of course, we must take seriously the formal legal concept of citizenship as a membership status and as a bundle of rights. This legal architecture is important not least for what it gives us when we need to audit the practices of citizenship and when we compare the approaches of different states and indeed of those non-state entities (like the EU) that engage with 'membership'. There are, however, other ways of understanding citizenship, in particular when it is used as an analytical category. Many of these are pluralist in character, relying on re-conceptualizations of the norms of citizenship that are socio-legal rather than doctrinal, and that adopt a critical perspective on modern citizenship at the same time as observing its paradoxical elements. Drawing inspiration from authors such as Margaret Somers (1993, 1994, 2008; Somers and Roberts 2008) and Claudia Wiesner and collaborators (Wiesner et al 2018), I argue that citizenship is best seen as relational and in flux. According to Wiesner et al (2018, 1), 'a concept such as citizenship does not have one single meaning, let alone an essential meaning. Rather, it should be regarded as being socially constructed and used in a reflexive way.'

Accordingly, citizenship emerges, both as an idea and in institutional form, as a result of dialogical processes that have no fixed endpoint. Citizenship is contested across time and space (Tully 2008; Cohen 2018). It is not just a status imposed top down by institutional fiat, but also a bundle of rights and responsibilities struggled for by different societal forces, and a window on issues of power and power relations within society (Štiks and Shaw 2014). Above all, citizenship does not have a settled meaning. For example, viewing it as a relation, and as a 'dynamic ... institution of domination *and* empowerment that governs *who* citizens..., subjects... and abjects ... are and *how* these actors are to govern themselves and each other in a given body politic' (Isin 2009, 371; original emphasis), Engin Isin develops the argument that citizenship is not, in fact, synonymous with membership, but distinct from it, as a field in which groups can claim access to citizenship rights through what he and colleagues have termed 'acts of citizenship' (Isin and Nielsen 2008). Indeed, the 'bottom-up' idea of individuals and groups acting strategically in relation to citizenship (especially dual citizenship) has become a recognized approach to citizenship not just conceptually, but also from an empirical perspective (Harpaz and Mateos 2019). We shall return to these ideas when we explore the methodological inspirations for this book at the end of the chapter.

While the practice of liberal democracy within relatively stable but porous borders undoubtedly provides a dominant model for citizenship (although, as a model, it is often only implicitly acknowledged as opposed to being explicitly stated), factors such as human mobility, the survival and security of the polity, the presence of internal cleavages between different majorities and minorities, not to mention relations between states and within and across regional and international organizations all frequently impact on the shape and scope of citizenship regimes at different times and in different places and on the evolution of the concept itself. As we shall see in Chapter 2, it is vital to reflect on the different conditions for building citizenship regimes, which govern the situation in post-colonial states and states in the Global South. There is nowhere in the world where the 'national' or 'state-based' realm still retains the prize of being the exclusive space within which the status and rights of citizenship can be practised or recognized. However, the complex relations between states in the global order will have different impacts on citizenship regimes depending on how any given state 'sits' in relation, for example, to current migration and human mobility trends as well as matters of economic development.

The task of trying to understand patterns and trends across citizenship regimes, laws and policies falls to an emergent interdisciplinary field of comparative citizenship studies (Vink et al 2016; Vink 2017), which relies to a high degree on access to reliable primary sources (citizenship laws, detailed information on how citizenship is regulated and applied at the national level, etc),[20] and makes use of a range of quantitative and qualitative methods of research appropriate to the different questions to be researched.[21] According to Rainer Bauböck (2018b, 501), what gives family resemblance to different citizenship regimes, thus rendering them comparable across state borders, is the dominance of three criteria for determining which individual is a member of which polity: birth, residence and choice. In the sphere of legal scholarship, René de Groot has worked towards framing what could be understood as 'European nationality law', binding together evident trends at national level alongside the developing body of international legal standards. His aim is to build a toolbox for assessing nationality legislation (de Groot 2016). In the social sciences, Rainer Bauböck and Maarten Vink have together (Vink and Bauböck 2013) and in collaboration with others, pioneered comparative

---

[20] GLOBALCIT (2017a, b). The GLOBALCIT website also contains databases of full text citizenship laws and international legal norms, as well as case law, and substantial secondary and reflective material in the form of country reports, regional reports, thematic reports, debates or forums and blogs.

[21] For the quantitative research, the indicators on citizenship law and birthright citizenship developed by the GLOBALCIT team are particularly relevant (see GLOBALCIT, 2016, 2019).

research on the regulation of the acquisition and loss of citizenship initially at the European level and more recently at the global level (Vink et al 2019; Vink et al no date), in particular through the analysis of databases and the development of robust indicators evaluating the different aspects of national citizenship regimes, including electoral rights (Schmid et al 2019). This emerging body of work has probed three key questions that shape the field: 'along which dimensions can citizenship regimes be differentiated; which factors structure variation in citizenship regimes; and how do citizenship regimes impact on social, economic and political outcomes?' (Vink 2017, 221).

In contrast, the tools used in this book involve interpretative and evaluative comparisons, which are more common in legal studies, rather than formal data-driven analyses, which many social scientists develop.[22] Making interpretative comparisons places different demands on the scholar. For example, because of the complexities of citizenship and of citizenship regimes and because of the facet of contestation, many scholars break the field of study down into smaller and more manageable blocks (for example, by distinguishing, as Jean Cohen [1999] does, between the juridical, the political and the identitarian dimensions of citizenship). In fact, a similar approach to breaking down citizenship into component elements will be adopted as a starting point and heuristic device in Part II. But these divisions do not always map clearly onto either the various recognized modes of acquisition and loss of citizenship, which are central to Bauböck and Vink's approach, or their interpretation of the various purposes of citizenship laws such as intergenerational continuity or territorial inclusion (Vink and Bauböck 2013).

Finally, it is important to note that Bauböck's work is rooted in normative political theory, and specifically within a theory of what he terms 'stakeholder citizenship' (Bauböck 2018a). This theory articulates what Bauböck argues are the defensible limits of ethical political community within a world that is characterized both by a system of 'Westphalian' states (in which the sortation aspects of citizenship are central to its purposes and scope) and also strong dynamics of human mobility, elements of state instability, and supranational and international legal authority. The latter factors generate what Bauböck terms 'citizenship constellations' (Bauböck 2010b), in which a plurality of sources of legitimation and authority impact on the citizenship relation. Together these amount to the conditions of 'strong interdependence and migration flows between autonomous polities' (Bauböck 2018a, 47). Bauböck's theory presupposes

---

[22] On some of the challenges across the disciplines for citizenship studies, see Mindus (2014).

an empirical assumption that 'a plurality of bounded political communities is part of the human condition' (Baubӧck 2018a, 40), and holds that

> … citizens are stakeholders in a democratic political community insofar as their autonomy and well-being depend not only on being recognized as a member in a particular polity, but also on that polity being governed democratically. Political legitimacy in a democratic polity is not derived from nationhood or voluntary association but from popular self-government, that is, citizens' participation and representation in democratic institutions that track their collective will and common good. (Baubӧck 2018a, 41)

The details of this and the many other competing ethical theories of citizenship, as the basis for human flourishing in (at least partially) bounded political communities, lie beyond the scope of this book.[23] None the less, any work on citizenship, whether interpretative, analytical or empirical in character, inevitably relies to some extent on normative theory and potentially contributes indirectly to building theories through interpretation and reflection. Such normative theories offer insights, for example, into the ethics of political choices, both relating to the scope of citizenship as a legal status and its transmission across generations and communities, and into the scope of citizenship rights, such as the right to vote. I shall therefore draw liberally on citizenship theories in what follows, as well as on conceptual and theoretical work within constitutional studies.

Citizenship and nationality

It may already be obvious from the usage of terminology in these early pages, that, in common with many other legal scholars, I do not worry unduly about using the terms 'nationality' and 'citizenship' interchangeably.[24] However, if we step beyond the realms of legal doctrine (and the English language), we will discover that there are, in fact, considerable complexities to the relationship between these two

---

[23] See, for example, Owen (2013), Carens (2016) and the varied contributions to Fine and Ypi (2016).

[24] See, for example, Vonk (2015). This statement is not entirely true, as Alison Kesby (2012) draws an analytical distinction between the two for the purposes of her own work.

terms and to the different concepts and meanings they signify. There is also profound variation in precise usage across disciplines, languages and cultures, as well as insights to be drawn from history (Thomas 2002, 325–6; see also Stolcke 1997).

International law scholarship generally uses the term 'nationality' when designating the legal status of individuals and the connection between individuals and states, as recognized across the global system of states. Its usage is embedded in the modernist roots of inter*national* law and in projects of *nation* state building, which are often associated with the period of romanticism and the birth of modern nationalism in the 19th century. According to Rainer Bauböck:

> In René de Groot's description, Westphalian citizenship, which lawyers call "nationality", is "an empty linkage concept" [*ein leerer Koppelungsbegriff*] …, in Rogers Brubaker's words it is an "international filing system, a mechanism for allocating persons to states". (Bauböck 2019a, 1017)[25]

The term 'nationality' often remains in common legal use at the state level for similar reasons. For example, the UK applies a confusing mix of the two terms: since the British Nationality Act 1948 (and now under the British Nationality Act 1981, as subsequently amended), the status conferred on members of the polity is that of 'citizen', where previously they were 'subjects' (of the Crown). Public-facing government guidance refers, for the most part, to 'British citizenship', whether it is acquired by birth, by naturalization or by registration.[26] So those who naturalize go through a 'citizenship ceremony', where the status – with its civic connotations (as well as its pledge of allegiance to the Crown) – is formally conferred (Prahbat 2018). Yet the operational guidance aimed at Home Office decision-makers is termed 'Nationality Guidance', and 'nationality' is a term widely used in those materials. Furthermore, in the English criminal courts there is now a statutory requirement that the defendant state his or her 'nationality'.[27] In the US, however, where citizenship is constitutionally regulated, it is this term that dominates the airwaves, the legislation, the case law and the scholarship. This is

---

[25] The references are to de Groot (1989) and Brubaker (1992, 31).

[26] See the relevant Government Gateway site (www.gov.uk/browse/citizenship/citizenship).

[27] The Criminal Procedure (Amendment No 4) Rules 2017 (2017 No 915 (L 13)).

the republican heritage.[28] Furthermore, in a multinational state such as Canada, with more than 600 First Nation communities, considerable ethnic diversity across the country, and a subnational linguistic 'national community' in Québec, no one would use the two terms interchangeably in a domestic context.

Historically, and in many national contexts, the term 'nationality' is not just a synonym for citizenship; it can mean either more or less (Stolcke 1997). In France, also holding a republican and revolutionary heritage at the heart of its conception of modern citizenship, both the terms *nationalité* and *citoyenneté* are used, but in different contexts. It is *nationalité*, for example, in the *code civil* where (Westphalian) citizenship is regulated. But the constitution refers to *citoyens*. Michel Troper (1998) argues that since the French Revolution a distinction has been drawn between nationality and citizenship in order to reinforce that it is the *citizens*, not the nationals, who are privileged with (and obligated to exercise) political rights.[29] Citizenship has an important connotation of shared rule and civic purpose. A similar perspective is also evident in Latin America, where a historical distinction between nationality and citizenship along those lines evolved through the process whereby 'communities' became 'nations' as part of the separation of Spanish America from Spain (Herzog 2007; Acosta 2018). The distinction is preserved in many of the constitutions from the region, and Luicy Pedroza and Pau Palop-García (2017) explain how it remains legally significant, in particular for the rights and status of emigrants.

Disciplinary perspective may also be important. Some political theorists, such as David Miller (1993), embrace nationality in a way that arguably conflates state and nation in order to recover the acceptability of 'nationality' (and a certain form of liberal nationalism). Meanwhile, sociologists David McCrone and Richard Kiely (2000, 25) (focusing on the UK) are clear that they are analytically separate concepts that 'belong to different spheres of meaning and activity.' 'Nationality', in English, can be used to denote a set of concepts more closely linked to ideas of the nation, of ethnicity and of common cultural affinities via language, territory and history, as well as the connection between the state and the individual as recognized in law. This is what leads to the confusion about the use of the term 'nationality' in criminal proceedings in the UK. British citizens will often state that they are 'English' or 'Scottish' because these are widely understood, along with Wales and Northern Ireland, to

---

[28] One important exception to this concerns the recognition of 'national origin' as a protected characteristic under federal civil rights legislation.

[29] For further historical analysis, see Gosewinkel (2001).

be the 'nations' of the UK.[30] In fact, in that context they are being asked to state whether they are British citizens, or citizens of some other state.

The two terms 'nationality' and 'citizenship' obviously have quite different roots (the *natione* or *natio* and the *civis*), and this is frequently also the case also in other languages, including those without strong Latin or Greek foundations (de Groot 2012, 601). South Slav languages, for example, already have two words (*državljanstvo* and *građanstvo*) for 'citizenship', with the former referring to the link between the citizen and the state, with no ethnic connotations, and the latter holding a stronger civic and political meaning, in that it may also refer to the residents of a city. Completely separate terminology and meaning attach to the words for 'nationality', which are *nacionalnost* or *narodnost* (from *narod*, or 'people'), which have powerful ethnic connotations, but could not ever be used to designate the link between a citizen and a state (Štiks 2015, 11–12).

Indeed, there were 'nationalities' recognized within the Austro-Hungarian empire, and in some cases these have been the forerunners of the citizenships of states that have eventually emerged from that empire (for example, Slovak or Slovenian, albeit via two multinational states which have since disintegrated: Czechoslovakia and Yugoslavia). In other cases, these nationalities remain stateless 'national identities', which cut across the boundaries of modern nation states or correspond to modern 'regions' such as Galicia or Transylvania. Sometimes there are 'lost identities', such as that of 'Yugoslav', which was the basis for citizenship for more than 50 years, but never more than a minority 'identity', as census outcomes demonstrated (Sekulic et al 1994). More recently, in Israel, which is widely understood as an ethnic and not a liberal democracy, the Israeli Supreme Court has resisted the argument made by groups of Israeli citizens that their 'nationality' should be entered in the population register not as 'Jewish' or 'Arab', but as 'Israeli'. There is, said the Supreme Court, a difference between citizenship, which gives the right to vote, for example, and 'nationality'. According to the Court, this latter concept is characterized by the 'feeling of unity that prevails among the members of the national group.... Members of the national group are infused by a sense of interdependence, which also means a sense of common responsibility.'[31] It is a solidaristic concept. These concepts, ideas and practices are obviously ripe for comparative investigation, much

---

[30] 'In the British legal terminology, autochton non-English ethnic communities are recognised as "nations"' (Jakab 2016, 277).

[31] See CA 8573/08 *Ornan v Ministry of Interior* (2 October 2013), Nevo legal database. For a critique, see Brandes (2018a).

of which makes use of established analytical categories such as ethnicity and race rather than the term 'nationality' as such, as well as the polyvalent idea of 'identity'.

In this book, the main focus is on the citizenship relation, understood to encompass a number of different elements of status, rights and belonging, as articulated within the framework of a national constitution or in a 'beyond-the-state' scenario. There is less discussion of other affinities based in ethnicity or culture, although these will be touched on especially when discussing how citizenship relates to national and other identities. To that end, the terms 'citizen' and 'citizenship' will generally be used, except where common usage, especially in legal circles, would be to use 'nationality' (for example, in discussing international law) or where, as in regions such as Latin America, the distinction is still commonly, and strongly, made. Where 'nationality' is being used in the context of its relationship to historic 'nations' or ethnicities, this will be made clear.

Constitutions and constitutional law

In its plainest terms, according to the *Oxford English Dictionary*, a constitution is a 'body of fundamental principles or established precedents according to which a state or other organization is acknowledged to be governed.' It is worth noting that the historic pre-modern usage of the term 'constitution' was not fixated on the idea of a constitution being a paramount or governing law. That usage is traced by most scholars to the American Revolution, building on a political doctrine that had taken root gradually in the English common law in the 17th and 18th centuries (Buratti 2019). According to Rainer Grote:

> The constitution in the modern sense is no longer descriptive, but prescriptive. It is a set of legal norms which is set apart from other legal norms, the ordinary law, by its specific purpose and its specific characteristics. The purpose of the constitutional norms is to regulate the way in which legitimate public authority is constituted and exercised. (Grote 2018)

Nowadays, rules and principles feature heavily in most legal accounts of constitutions and constitutionalism, along with powers and procedures, focused especially on the institutions of government, the separation of powers, the rule of law and the protection of rights (Galligan and Versteeg 2013a, 6). Many constitutions also invoke the more or less mythical concept of 'the people', often as the originator of the constitution or 'constituent power'. Constituent power is one of the core reference points for the claimed legitimacy of a constitution.

Most constitutions are 'documentary' in the sense of being contained, more or less, in a single document, perhaps combined with a body of authoritative interpretations, typically by a constitutional or supreme court. Even in such cases, there often exist further norms beyond the written constitution which fill out the gaps left by the constitution, and that are part of constitutional law. A minority of constitutions are entirely composite in character. Famously, the UK is said to have an 'unwritten constitution', but obviously in such an advanced legal order many of the materials that make up the constitution, such as case law (for example, interpreting constitutional conventions or the increasing range of acknowledged constitutional principles) and those legislative measures widely acknowledged to have some constitutional character are, of course, 'written'. It is clear that our study of citizenship and constitutions/constitutional law needs to encompass all of these different types of constitutional frameworks. Adopting a broad perspective on the different types of constitutional norms and constitutional law that impact on citizenship as status, rights and identity is essential for the purposes of offering an effective overview of the constitutional story of citizenship. Identifying the distinctive domain of 'the constitutional' requires us to consider the purpose and function of norms, rather than just taking a linguistic or conventional approach. Clearly the dividing line between 'constitutional' and 'non-constitutional' public law is just as hard to pin down as the dividing line between 'constitutional' and 'ordinary' politics. The book will err on the side of inclusiveness in its approach to that dividing line.

The process for adopting or amending constitutions will be specific to each country, although certain general principles can be discerned. In Chapter 3 we will discuss the importance of the idea of the 'constituent power' – the notion of a pre-political authority to adopt a new constitution for a state. Conventional wisdom holds that as constitutions are a special type of law in each country, they ought somehow to last longer and be harder to change. As the US Constitution was effective from 1789 (on ratification) and has relatively rarely been amended, in particular in recent decades, this may give a misleading impression of the durability of constitutions. In research published in 2009, Zachary Elkins et al (2009)[32] calculated that since 1787, the average lifespan of any given constitution has been only 17 years, and in 2017, the World Bank (2017, 91) highlighted the intensification and increased

---

[32] See also Ginsburg et al (2009).

frequency of 'constitutional events', especially amendments, since the Second World War.

Beyond the bare bones of what is likely to be found in most, if not all, constitutions, scholars do not always agree about the purposes of constitutions, about their social and political foundations (Galligan and Versteeg 2013b) or about their proper normative dimensions. That is to say, there is debate and contestation over the concept of 'constitutionalism' and over the state of 'constitutional democracies', with the practices of constitutional democracy currently seen as being somewhat in retreat since the moment of triumph after the end of the Cold War and the collapse of the Soviet Union. Today, in an era of populist politics, with increasing numbers of semi-authoritarian and illiberal regimes in many parts of the world, constitutions have not so much been overthrown as diluted or degraded as instruments of democracy, while retaining most of the formal institutional trappings (Graber et al 2018).

While it is clear that there is generally a relatively comfortable pairing between the liberal and republican forms of constitutionalism and democratic principles, it is also the case that we should not ignore how citizenship is dealt with under constitutional frameworks that lack some or all of these trappings. To give a different sort of example, which helps to make the same point, when it comes to the issue of statelessness, which is clearly related to citizenship (or rather, its absence), even states with weak democratic credentials may be committed to engaging with the basic humanitarian norms that push back against statelessness, for example, by offering access to citizenship to refugees or by pursuing more effective birth registration.[33] Of course, this is often because international donors and agencies make so-called development aid conditional on such efforts. Whatever the motivation, the result should be an improvement in the life chances of those affected. As, in some cases, these issues are affected by constitutional norms, the mapping of the citizenship/constitutional law relationship in Part II will include examples from different types of constitutional scenarios stretching well beyond the established and stable democracies.

Part III addresses two major challenges that confront the idea of the constitution and the role of constitutional law, in particular in the context of its relationship to citizenship. In assessing the relationship between citizenship and 'the people' in Chapter 6, via the contested idiom of populism, we will face front on the values embedded in many constitutions: the 'isms' of democratic and liberal constitutionalism,

---

[33] EIN News (2019) 'Angola ratifies human rights treaties', 1 August (www.einnews. com/pr_news/492377697/angola-ratifies-human-rights-treaties/).

embodied in principles such as equality, the rule of law and fundamental rights. In Chapter 7, when considering the practices of citizenship (and citizenship rights) beyond the state, we must necessarily also consider the possibilities and challenges of transnational, supranational and even global constitutionalism (Rosenfeld 2014; Lang and Wiener 2017). What types of non-state polities can legitimately lay claim to be 'constitutionalized' and thus to have a 'constitutional law'? To what extent does this imply that such polities have some sort of 'touch of stateness' (Shaw and Wiener 2000) or can such polities ever truly claim to be constitutionalized in a way that escapes normative 'statism' or methodological nationalism?

The people

At the beginning of this chapter, I noted that citizenship has an internal aspect, reflecting the 'stories of peoplehood' that offer a binding element in most, if not all, polities (Smith 2001). Indeed, it is practically impossible to imagine citizenship – both in the formal legal sense and especially in the wider senses of political membership and community identity – without also considering the relevance of fundamental ideas about 'the people' and attachment to the polity (including the dimensions of loyalty, patriotism and allegiance) that often feature prominently in constitutional texts which lack liberal trappings or pretensions (Thio 2012), as well as in many of the more liberal variants. As Dennis Galligan has pointed out, the idea of sovereignty within a constitution is logically prior to the concept of democracy, which is why explorations of the place of 'the people' in the constitution can also encompass constitutional frameworks that are lacking in democratic credentials (including historical examples) (Galligan 2013a; see also Galligan 2013b). All of these elements are the essential raw material for normative models of 'citizenship as community membership' developed by political theorists; on the side of studies of constitutionalism, many of the same ideas inform the extensive body of theoretical work that probes the notions of 'constituent power' and sovereignty as providing the ultimate legitimacy for polity formation and evolution (see Chapter 3).

Further discussion of the concept of 'the people' will appear in subsequent chapters: in Chapter 2, where we re-consider the relationship between state and nation and then sketch out the concept of the 'constitutional citizen'; throughout Part II, as we consider in detail how citizenship and constitutions interact, but especially in Chapter 3, which is focused on the constitutional ideal of citizenship; in Chapter 6, where we turn our attention specifically to the task of understanding the potential relevance of populism and populist politics for the citizenship/

constitutional law relationship; in Chapter 7 when we consider whether the concept of 'the people' can stretch beyond national borders; and finally when we draw the threads of the argument together in Chapter 8, the concluding chapter. To underpin these later discussions, here we need to outline the basic contours of a slippery and difficult concept.

Different scholarly traditions take contrasting positions on how the concept of 'the people' comes about in any given constitutional context: is it a pre-political culturally defined concept, or does it arise politically in the context, say, of a revolution that dramatically forms or reforms a polity (Tushnet 2017; White and Ypi 2017)? 'The people' could refer to at least six different sets of ideas that have ebbed and flowed historically and politically, in line with the growth and sometimes the demise of concepts of sovereignty, constitutionalism and democracy (Canovan 2005; Galligan 2013b). Each is closely related to almost all of the others.

In the first place, we can think of the people as sovereign, but at the same time often, indeed almost always, in reserve and invisible, or 'sleeping', as Thomas Hobbes would have it (Walker 2019a). That is, the people almost never exercise their sovereignty, except on rare occasions where they are asked to take a truly 'constitutive' step, for example, at a revolutionary moment, in the case of independence referendums or at a moment of consensual constitutional renewal. The people can also be understood as the rulers in a democracy and as a political people, although in its earlier forms this concept of the people generally took a corporate and limited form and was certainly not to be understood as 'all of the people'. Many groups (based on criteria of property, gender and race) were conventionally excluded from the franchise of evolving democracies such as the United States and the United Kingdom (and its colonial dominions) up until the 20th century (Galligan 2013b, 147). For Rogers Smith, what is special about the political people is that these are associations, groups and communities 'that are commonly understood to assert that their members owe them a measure of allegiance against the demands of other associations, communities, and groups' (Smith 2015, 2). They build this sense of allegiance not only by reference to economic and political themes common to that group, but also by reference to constitutive themes of race, gender and religion. Furthermore, just as they are when conceived of as the sovereign, so as the 'rulers' the people are mainly hidden, in this case behind the frontage offered by representative democracy.

Another element closely associated with the concept of the people as rulers is the idea of the 'common people'. This is an idea that comes much closer to a universalistic concept of 'the people' and in that sense the idea of the 'common people' was feared by many power brokers during the early stages of the emergence of democracy. Eventually, of course, the common people were enfranchised, as so-called universal suffrage became the norm in democracies. Nowadays, this idea of the 'common people' (in contradistinction to the elite) is one of the animating forces behind populist political movements, as populists claim to represent the interests of the common people as embodying the 'real' people. The idea of the people is thus weaponized against the 'elite'.

The idea of the people as 'the nation' must also be considered. Here we need to face the question of the boundaries between inside and outside. How do we set those boundaries on an ethically, economically and politically defensible basis, while respecting principles of self-determination (Fine and Ypi 2016)? The immediate 'shadow' of the people as nation is the universalistic idea of 'the people' as humanity, where nations become irrelevant. Yet no state or polity – *pace* Linda Bosniak's (2007) principle of ethical territoriality – in practice stands ready to admit all those who seek to enter.[34] But states do not stand alone. As both Rogers Smith and Rogers Brubaker acknowledge, it is not only states that can have 'stories of peoplehood'. So too can other sorts of groups. According to Brubaker (2017a, 797), the term 'people' can be understood 'as a group that is (relatively) stable, enduring, distinctive, encompassing, self-reproducing, and (at least ideally) self-governing.' Articulating these conditions helps to show how closely related the various concepts of 'people' in fact are. Smith's particular focus, or contribution, is on the 'constitutive themes' (in the US case of race, religion and gender) (rather than political or economic themes of peoplehood) that can come to the fore in stories of peoplehood, and which can have an exclusionary force: 'when the ideas, institutions, and practices expressive of established constitutive themes are threatened' (Smith 2015, 65). These are the moments to watch out for, and Brubaker suggests that at a 'populist moment' we should take particular care to look out for them because of the exclusionary effects they are likely to have. We will return to these themes in Chapters 6 and 8.

Methodological inspirations and approach

This book is a study of citizenship in its various constitutional contexts, viewed from a socio-legal perspective. The methodological starting point is that of comparative constitutional law, in a field where (national) public law and both private and public international law intersect (Jenkins

---

[34] On the human right to immigrate, see Oberman (2016).

et al 2014, 2). The subdiscipline of comparative constitutional law is a relatively new kid on the block, at least in terms of it receiving sustained attention from scholars. For a long time, mainstream comparative law rather disdained the task of comparing constitutional or public laws, on the grounds that they were just too *local* and *particular* in terms of values, cultures and contents (Ginsburg and Dixon 2011, 2). Since the possibilities of transplants, at least between established democracies, have seemed remote, much of the classical rationale for comparative law tended to fall away. The emergence of a distinctive subdiscipline has benefited from the creation of effective interdisciplinary frameworks based on institutionalist accounts of legal and political change, such as historical institutionalism and sociological institutionalism, combined with an explosion of constitution-making activity, especially after 1989, which has provided many a new laboratory for study. These 'institutionalisms' emphasize the relationship between individual agents, such as courts, and wider institutional environments, such as 'the constitution', and have also promoted a space within politics to understand both the role of ideas and the power of law's normative force.

This work is inspired by these developments, and it embraces, in particular, the sociological turn in constitutional studies. As Dennis Galligan and Mila Versteeg (2013a) make clear, it is important to look at the social and political foundations of constitutions. This is hardly new. It can be traced back to Abbé Sieyès' account of the emergence of constituent power and constituted power in the 18th century. According to Galligan, Sieyès' account is that of 'the social scientist describing a constitution as a necessary element of a modern nation, an element whose properties and functions can be analysed and generalized' (Galligan 2013b, 148). But one important claim of those, such as Chris Thornhill (2017) or Günther Teubner (2017), who promote the idea of sociological constitutionalism, is that the core promise of the idea lies in the postulation that it is anachronistic and inappropriate to limit the range of phenomena that are studied from a constitutionalist perspective to states alone. This is crucial, as although this book takes as its starting point a mapping of the interactions between citizenship and state-based constitutions, in the latter chapters of the book close attention will be paid to the transnational, supranational, international and indeed subnational dimensions of citizenship and constitutionalism. It is straightforward to observe that the relationships between citizenship and constitutions are profoundly influenced by transnational legal sources: international law and EU law; the laws and constitutions of other states; non-state sources such as international organizations and non-governmental organizations (NGOs). However, it is less easy to understand or explain these phenomena. Examples will appear from time to time throughout Part II, while the shifting spatialities of citizenship in the context of globalization and substate pressures will be the particular focus of Chapter 7 and one theme picked up in Chapter 8. Alongside receptiveness to ideas of global constitutionalism, the book also draws inspiration from the opening out of comparative constitutional law towards the Global South, which provides a different perspective on relations between states and between state law and international law.[35]

The field of citizenship studies has also experienced something of a sociological turn, as may be evident from the discussion of citizenship as a relational concept earlier in this chapter (see, for example, Bloemraad 2015, 2018). But studying concepts and norms sociologically does not necessarily mean departing from adopting a legal, or socio-legal, approach (Cotterrell 1998). The legal status as well as the rights of citizens can be understood sociologically, as Somers has shown. The two perspectives can be combined. Accordingly, citizenship instantiates 'a set of institutionally embedded social practices' (Somers 1993, 589). Drawing on the work of Polanyi, Somers defines citizenship as an 'instituted process'. What is important is that classical and doctrinal legal approaches need to be revised, because 'citizenship cannot be explained by looking for rights granted "ready-made" by states', but must be struggled for at specific times and in specific places. In a key phrase, Somers has argued that citizenship 'laws are free-floating forms of empowerment and cultural resources, whose practical meaning depends on relationships, not individual autonomy' (Somers 1993, 611).

The advantage of adopting such a sociologically informed approach is that it enables us to take a close look at the fundamentals of the legal status of citizenship while exploring other aspects of citizenship that are not as effectively captured purely by a formal legal approach to membership, such as issues of identity and community. To put it another way, constitutions bring with them not only a rule-of-law perspective on the norms of citizenship, but also certain types of 'baggage' that help us to fill out the notion of citizenship, by providing the context and history that underpin the formal rules. Ideas of citizenship and constitutionalism are commonly underpinned by 'thicker' norms rather than just by formal legal frameworks. This makes it harder to understand how citizenship and constitutionalism interact without taking both a

---

[35] See the blog posts collected at https://voelkerrechtsblog.org/category/symposium/global-south-in-comparative-constitutional-law/, as part of a symposium on the Global South in comparative constitutional law, which resulted in the publication of an edited volume: Dann et al (2020).

contextual approach and a critical approach. The approach is contextual as it takes seriously the political and social context in which law operates; it is critical because it acknowledges that examining case studies of how citizenship and constitutions interact in practice inevitably feeds back into our understanding of these concepts and helps to reconstruct the classical ideas of modern citizenship and modern constitutionalism with which we started.

There is also space to combine top-down and bottom-up approaches. One strong axis of scholarship within citizenship studies has been that which has placed the primary emphasis on what states do, how they do it, why they do it, and how the actions of states can be justified against norms of justice, equality and legitimacy, and so on. Pragmatically, this has also been combined with a heavy focus on access to citizenship for immigrants and other vulnerable groups, such as refugees, as these have frequently been the subject of major political debate in many of the countries where scholarship on citizenship has hitherto most often been produced. More recently, the focus has shifted to recognize also the importance of debating citizenship and citizenship rights for emigrant communities, diasporas and other groups of external 'ethnic kin'. But citizenship is not just something that is 'given' (or denied) by states. It is also struggled for, and citizenship operates as much as a (constantly changing) relation as it does as a status (Somers and Roberts 2008). We can illustrate this point by zooming in to observe how citizenship status and citizenship rights have evolved over time. For example, neither the status nor the rights have been remotely universally allocated in most states at least until the beginning of the 20th century and in some cases much later. In all cases, social movements and changes within political parties are important parts of the story, alongside the individual strategies and claims-making of putative citizens and their allies (Przeworski 2009). We need a sociologically embedded critical method in order to understand these changes in the wider context of the evolution of power relations within and across states.

In sum, citizenship is not a static concept, but one which changes by reference to changing geographical coordinates and also over time, both in relation to what are viewed as the legitimate boundary conditions for polity memberships and in relation to what is seen as the 'best-case' scenario in relation to the quality or nature of polity membership. In this book, the enquiry is primarily interpretative and frequently observational in nature, taking into consideration the contestation of citizenship in respect not just of its practices, but also of its underlying meaning and scope as a membership relation. That is to say, normative perspectives on the scope of membership represent an important backdrop to the analysis, but the relationship is iterative in the sense of contributing also to normative reconstruction. The process of the transformation of citizenship can be observed both in the diffuse, gradual and incremental changes in the formal institutional arrangements that govern various forms of citizenship, and in the contestations, conflicts and debates about definitions of, and rights and obligations of, polity membership (Shaw 2007, 84).

This observational and interpretative approach is inspired by the 'constitutional ethnographies' approach to comparative constitutional law, pioneered by Kim Lane Scheppele (2004). Sociologically informed ethnographies endeavour to give us the lived details of citizenship regimes in constitutional settings, offering new perspectives, for example, on how constitutions naturalize, channel and/or legitimate power (Scheppele 2017). The point is not to highlight the abstract characteristics of different systems or to compare them using formal or quantitative methods of analysis in order to predict or explain processes of change, or similarities and differences. Rather, it is to explore the themes that emerge when two dimensions such as 'citizenship regimes' and 'constitutional laws, practices and ideas' are put into conversation with each other by means of deeply contextualized 'thick' readings and descriptions of many dimensions of the issue. This differs from the task of studying variation between systems or regimes. In addition, in common with the ethos of Scheppele's approach, which eschews methodological nationalism, the book allows the 'global' to emerge alongside the 'national', by acknowledging as an important cross-cutting theme, as well as one dimension to be explored in more detail, the nestedness of national citizenship regimes within an international order of states (Scheppele 2004, 391). Accordingly, in her words, constitutionalism emerges:

> ... as a set of practices in which the transnational ambitions of legal globalization flow over and modify the lived experiences of specific local sites, and as a set of practices in which local sites inescapably alter what can be seen as general meanings. (Scheppele 2004, 394)

It is, therefore, a pluralist approach to citizenship*s* and constitution*s* (with an emphasis on the plural of both words). Such an approach, by responding flexibly to the different types of phenomena that we call 'law', makes it possible to retain a strong focus on ethnographies of citizenship as an exercise of comparative constitutional law. As Katharine Young comments, when considering the enterprise of comparative constitutionalism as an interpretative exercise:

> Law is social, humanist, and unscientific (at least, compared
> with the natural sciences). Law is normative, prescriptive, and
> it demands justification. Law is language, it is interpreted, and
> it is constituted through interpretation. These messy, unruly
> facets of law … suggest a different enterprise for comparison.
> (Young 2016, 1383)

Where, however, this book departs from many of the worked-through
examples of 'constitutional ethnographies', including Scheppele's own
work, is in its approach to examples and case studies. It strays rather
far away from the ethos of anthropology, including legal anthropology,
with its use of rich case studies or vignettes. In view of the breadth of
topics to be covered, along with the endeavour to use material drawn
from beyond the standard scripts of western Europe, North America
and the various settler colonies that are now states of immigration, the
focus is on using the empirical material illustratively, rather than in
order to show depth or to offer comprehensive coverage. Moreover, this
book recognizes that some of the most interesting encounters between
citizenship and constitutional law lie not in the present but in the past.[36]
There are certainly dangers in taking this line, as a synoptic approach can
miss the subtleties of and differences between the different regions of the
world that are studied, as well as the deep context of the national case
studies or historical encounters. If words from constitutions are cited,
then it should be remembered that these are precisely what they are: just
words. Context is indeed everything, and both small changes and the
bigger picture could be missed in such a static approach.[37] But with those
risks also come the advantages of developing an approach that cuts across
the legal, political and sociological divides within scholarship and that
offers a comprehensive stock-taking of relevant themes and discourses
on 'constitutional citizenship' globally. The ambition of this book is to
identify and to articulate a clear understanding of the frequently contested
nature and significance of constitutional citizenship, and its relationship
to contemporary pressures and tensions within and across states in the
modern world.

---

[36] For an excellent example, see Constantin Iordachi's detailed study (2019) of the
insertion of citizenship clauses in the 1866 Constitution of Romania.

[37] This approach is mirrored in Nicola Lacey's (2019) analytical exploration of the
interface of the rule of law and populism, especially in her contextually driven
reflections on the rule of law, which can have very different meanings depending on
time and location.

2

What Is Constitutional Citizenship and How Can We Study It?

Introduction

Throughout Chapter 1, I placed inverted commas around the terms 'constitutional citizen' and 'constitutional citizenship', in order to suggest that they are terms of art requiring further definition and specification in the particular context in which I am using them. Rainer Forst (2014) has argued that citizenship is a 'normatively dependent concept' in the sense that its full meaning only emerges through context and usage and by reference to other principles and concepts, themselves contested. So when we combine citizenship *and* constitutions or constitutional law, we have to be doubly clear about what we are referring to, and keenly aware that we are combining and potentially comparing two sets of concepts that are rooted in specific legal, political, social and cultural contexts and about which it is accordingly difficult to generalize.

At one level, constitutional citizenship is simply the place where constitutions and citizenship meet. We have already noted in Chapter 1 that scholars, and sometimes judges, assert that the citizen is *the* core constitutional subject and that the citizen is central to the concept of the modern constitutional state. Another example of this genre comes from Ernst Hirsch Ballin, who asserts that 'in an era of growing migration and trans-border connectivity, the democratic meaning of citizenship finds its fulfilment within the territoriality of states.' Indeed, he argues that:

> The territorial state provides the constitutional setting for citizenship free from ethnic privileges and prejudices. This means that the state should constitute the democratic home for the people who participate in its social, economic and cultural life. (Ballin 2016, 260)

In this book, I will treat this type of claim about the territorial state with a degree of scepticism. Substantial parts of the book recognize that the *deterritorialized* dimensions of citizenship are just as relevant to understanding the membership relation and even its supposedly constitutional core as are those related to the territorial state. Furthermore, the claim that this constitutional setting can set citizenship 'free from ethnic privileges and prejudices' seems to represent an idealism on which the state's performance in relation to citizenship often fails to deliver. But it represents a reasonable starting point for the discussion in this chapter, which explores constitutional citizenship in more detail. One important task of the chapter is to place the relationship between citizenship and constitutions into a wider historical and political context, noting the tensions that understanding this context will bring into the relationship. The conclusions in this chapter thus reflect both the promise of the 'constitutional approach' and some possible challenges.

The constitution, the state and citizenship

When exploring how states regulate citizenship from the perspective of national law, the national constitution, whether this comprises a single document, or multiple documents and associated principles, clearly offers a logical place to start. As noted in Chapter 1, the constitution can be defined as the 'body of fundamental principles or established precedents according to which a state or other organization is acknowledged to be governed.' What is missing from such a definition, however, is a sense of agency and some sense of power: Who brought this constitution into being? Who is acknowledging the authority and legitimacy of the constitutional framework? Who is governing and who is being governed? Who enjoys rights and/or is subject to duties? Going further, there are additional critical and evaluative questions: Is the constitution citizenship's protector? Does the constitution give substance to citizenship? Does citizenship give substance to the constitution? Constitutions can make citizens, but citizens also make constitutions. This is why we need to look at the intersection of concepts of citizenship, democracy and constituent power, at least as regards the constitutional frameworks of states aspiring to democratic credentials. That is to say, beyond the functional dictionary definition with which we started, we can distinguish constitutional law and constitutional politics from the 'ordinary' versions of those things both by reference to formal indicators, such as a special text or a particular amendment process, and by reference to the connection to fundamental polity-defining conditions such as sovereignty, democracy and self-government, and equality.

Indeed, once we go beyond the idea of citizenship as a simple sorting principle and formal legal status, and recognize that citizenship also encapsulates expressions of both collective and individual political autonomy and community identity, and can even be seen as the distillation of the sovereignty of the state, we can discern that the relationship between citizenship and constitutional law and indeed constitutionalism as an ideology is likely to be a complex and iterative one. Moreover, as previously discussed, citizenship is a contested concept and status, and this affects how it is dealt with in a constitutional context.

Just as there are no two identical constitutions, so there are no two identical ways in which constitutions deal with the issue of citizenship. This plurality undermines any easy contention that it is a simple task to discern patterns in relation to constitutional citizenship. There is no straightforward way of summarizing how constitutions deal with the issue of citizenship, as Kim Rubenstein and Niamh Lenagh-Maguire (2011) have previously shown in their work. Instead of searching for non-existent commonalities across time and space, Rubenstein and Lenagh-Maguire endeavour to identify how different systems have dealt with similar challenges, as the basis for formulating the core themes that can inform comparative work. The challenges they pick out are those of defining citizenship, regulating birthright citizenship (by *ius soli* or *ius sanguinis*), dealing with dual nationality and the rights (or lack of them) of dual nationals, identifying and regulating special categories of non-citizen, and dealing with the interface of citizenship and rights. All of these themes or challenges will receive attention in this book, along with one question that Rubenstein and Lenagh-Maguire do not directly address: Why is there relatively little direct constitutional regulation of such an important issue as citizenship, and what are the consequences of such omission in terms of who decides fundamental questions about the scope of the citizenry? If these matters are not in the constitution, are legislatures best placed to decide?

A small number of constitutions are centred on the concept of citizenship. The Constitution of Brazil in Article 1 makes citizenship one of five foundational principles of the Federative Republic, alongside sovereignty, human dignity, social values of work and free initiative and political pluralism.[1] Even so, the Constitution does not tell us what it means by citizenship, or what, if anything, makes Brazilian citizenship special. Many more constitutions simply refer to citizenship without giving more details. The word 'citizenship' appears in 151 constitutions, and 'nationality' in 140. Even more refer to 'citizen' or 'citizens' – nearly 190. The large majority of these references lack substantive or definitional content. Citizens are simply invoked as the baseline actors within the constitutional system, or as the objects of constitutional protection by the state. Some constitutions do regulate at least some of the conditions of citizenship, with a small number offering considerable detail.[2] Yet other countries, such as Australia, do not address citizenship at all in the constitution – at least not directly. But, as we shall see in subsequent discussions, this does not mean that there is no 'constitutional aura' or shadow to the law of citizenship in that country (Pillai 2014; Arcioni 2018). In a small group of countries, it seems to be hard to see any 'constitutional' content to citizenship at all.[3] Alternatively (or additionally), the main constitutional focus in some countries may be on the amorphous concept of 'the people' or 'the nation', who may, or may not, be coterminous with the 'citizenry'. Quite a number of countries refer to aliens (37) or non-citizens (7). Australia, for example, highlights 'the alien', citizenship's 'other', and not the citizen him or herself (Rubenstein 2017; Thwaites 2017). Some constitutions raise protection against statelessness into a constitutional principle, reflecting commitments under international law.[4]

In some regions there are clear affinities across the constitutions of a geographically co-located group of countries. For example, in Latin America, citizenship is regulated by the constitution more consistently

---

[1] See Brazil 1988 (rev. 2010) (www.constituteproject.org/constitution/ Brazil_2017?lang=en). See also Tunisia 2014 (www.constituteproject.org/constitution/ Tunisia_2014?lang=en), discussed in Chapter 3, where Article 2 of the Constitution provides: 'Tunisia is a civil state based on citizenship, the will of the people, and the supremacy of law'.

[2] Good examples of countries (across three continents) where the constitutional provisions on citizenship constitute almost a complete code are Nigeria 1999 (rev. 2011) (www.constituteproject.org/constitution/Nigeria_2011?lang=en), Malaysia 1957 (rev. 2007) (www.constituteproject.org/constitution/Malaysia_2007?lang=en) and Uruguay 1966 (rev. 2004) (www.constituteproject.org/constitution/Uruguay_2004?lang=en).

[3] Sweden is arguably such a case, although both 'citizens' and 'citizenship' appear in the text of the constitution. See 'In conclusion: the promise and limits of the constitutional approach' below for details of the argument.

[4] See, for example, Section 5, Finland 1999 (rev. 2011) (www.constituteproject.org/ constitution/Finland_2011?lang=en).

than in any other region (Acosta 2016, 2018). One more recent trend, which Diego Acosta (2018) has identified, is openness to foreigners. Combined with the heritage of (constitutional) *ius soli* common to the western hemisphere, this, in turn, underpins a relatively open concept of citizenship across the region in the 21st century.[5] Those constitutions also commonly distinguish between 'nationality' and 'citizenship' in the manner that is specific to the region, as mentioned previously. For example, the Constitution of Colombia[6] – one of the few in Latin America that does *not* make provision for birthright *ius soli* citizenship to be conferred on all children born in the territory regardless of parentage – makes the distinction between nationality, as the status all should have, and citizenship, which is a political status under the Constitution, which can be exercised by people only after they have reached the age of 18. Yet it is slightly perplexing that, elsewhere in the Constitution, children are expressly given the right to their name and their citizenship (Article 44), presumably long before they can exercise it. They are not, however, given a constitutional right to nationality, in the Westphalian sense of the word (Escobar 2015a).[7]

Where there do exist constitutional definitions of the scope and conditions of citizenship, such definitions may be very hard to amend. This would likely be the case in the US, if a constitutional amendment to remove or limit birthright *ius soli* citizenship from the 14th Amendment were brought forward, even though, as we shall see later in Chapter 4, a minority opinion argues that Congress can itself already legislate to limit the scope of birthright *ius soli*. Yet when Ireland needed a referendum in 2004 to change the scope of its *ius soli* provisions in order to restrict access to citizenship for children born in the territory only to those at least one of whose parents was either a citizen or entitled to be a citizen, the government of the day had no difficulty garnering the necessary majority for the proposition it put to a referendum vote (Shaw 2007, 259–62). In fact, reflecting the short lifespan of constitutions and the frequency of constitutional amendments,[8] it would be difficult to sustain a general claim that enshrining citizenship in constitutions renders the legal regulation of

---

[5] For the political significance of this, in an age of opposition to birthright *ius soli* citizenship, see Lasso (2019). Fitzgerald and Cook-Martín (2014) point out that Latin American countries removed explicitly racist restrictions in immigration policies before the North American countries.

[6] See Colombia 1991 (rev. 2015) (www.constituteproject.org/constitution/Colombia_2015?lang=en).

[7] See, however, an important supplement to that point in Chapter 4, in relation to Colombia's approach to the citizenship of the children of Venezuelan refugees.

[8] See Elkins et al (2009), Ginsburg et al (2009) and World Bank (2017).

citizenship exceptionally difficult to change. In that sense, the US may be an outlier rather than a standard setter.

In many cases, formal constitutional provisions on citizenship are limited to conferring statutory authority on the legislature to regulate the scope and character of citizenship or citizenship rights. A common style adopted in many constitutions takes this form: 'Citizenship of [State X] is hereby established. Rules of acquisition and loss are regulated by law.' In fact, from the 19th century onwards, legislatures began regularly to write codes of 'ordinary' law, governing matters of citizenship (Brubaker 1992, 35 et seq; Dörr 2006). This form of delegation generally hands considerable discretion to the ordinary legislator to determine the scope of the citizenry. However, sometimes the procedure for regulating those conditions requires the adoption of what some countries call 'organic laws', necessitating a special procedure or majority in parliament.[9] An analogous arrangement is found in Austria, where certain provisions of the citizenship law are entrenched against easy amendment as 'constitutional provisions' that have been passed by a two-thirds majority of the National Rat.[10]

The absence of detailed provisions on citizenship in constitutions combined with the practice of delegation to legislatures means that there are significant questions around the separation of powers and institutional balance in relation to both the 'content' of citizenship and the question of process: that is, who *ought* to be able to settle the scope of the citizenry and *what* should they decide? Is it appropriate that fundamental changes to citizenship law should not be subject to the super-majorities common to the formal constitutional amendment process? And ought legislatures to be able – in effect – to determine their own electorate by changing the terms of citizenship? On the other hand, courts, especially constitutional courts, may be empowered to strike down legislative changes on the grounds that they breach constitutional principles such as equality. Indeed, supervening constitutional principles have regularly been used to determine the proper scope and exercise of legislative power in relation to citizenship. The case of Canada since the adoption of the Charter of Rights and Freedoms in

---

[9] The micro-state of Andorra offers an example, as the regulation of citizenship is by 'qualified law', which requires 'final favourable vote of the absolute majority of the members of the General Council: Article 57(3), Andorra 1993 (www.constituteproject. org/constitution/Andorra_1993?lang=en). See also Tunisia (note 2 above), where Article 65 includes citizenship in the list of fields to be regulated by organic law, requiring the absolute majority of the members of the parliament (Article 64).

[10] Article 44, Austria 1920 (reinst. 1945, rev. 2013) (www.constituteproject.org/ constitution/Austria_2013?lang=en). On the application to citizenship, see Stern and Valchars (2013).

1982 offers a good example (Richez and Manfredi 2015). Throughout the book, we will return to the complex relationship between majoritarian and non-majoritarian institutions, and between the political constitution and judicial oversight as regards the scope of citizenship.

Federal constitutions often incorporate a split in relation to competences between the federal and state levels. For example, in the US citizens are 'citizens' of the state in which they reside, as well as federal citizens. This is a derived citizenship and the legal implications of it are limited. Bifurcated dual-level citizenship was the position in the Socialist Federal Republic of Yugoslavia (SFRY) before its dissolution, and, in this case, there were significant legal consequences after dissolution. Most of the new states have built their fresh citizenship regimes on the prior 'republican' citizenship, rather than by reference to the previous common citizenship of SFRY (Shaw 2011). This has significantly restricted the life chances of some groups of people who found themselves in a different state to the one in which they were born, given the violent dissolution of SFRY and the subsequent difficult birth and transition for those states (Štiks 2015, Chapter 9).

Constitutions may place restrictions on what a federal legislature can do in relation to the scope of citizenship, leaving other matters to be regulated by the constituent states or even at local level (as in Switzerland, where many aspects of naturalization are dealt with at the municipal level[11]). Alternatively, the constitution may strictly limit the capacity of constituent states or devolved legislatures (such as those in the autonomous communities of Spain or the 'nations' of the UK) to legislate in matters related to citizenship and immigration. In some cases, however, welfare and/or fiscal authority that has been devolved can have a significant impact on the content or terms of 'regional' citizenship (Stjepanović 2019). However, authority to alter the fundamental terms of the citizenship settlement, especially in relation to matters such as passports and the external dimension of citizenship, is rarely ascribed to states within federations. The 'hard' case of Bosnia and Herzegovina (BiH), where the central state remains unconsolidated and is substantially contested at substate level, is worth citing in this context. While 'entity citizenship' at the substate level is a legally and politically significant status, all citizens of BiH carry the same identity documents (Sarajlić 2012, 2013).

At the ideational level, we may also find complex and multivalent concepts of 'the people' in many 'multinational' states, bearing in mind factors such as linguistic differences as well cultural and institutional

---

[11] See Achermann et al (2013).

specificities in countries such as Canada and Belgium, as well as Spain and the UK (Banting and Kymlicka 2017). These can also impact on concepts of citizenship at 'ground' level. Federalism does not, however, invariably lead to a complex concept of the 'national' people. In both Germany and Austria, the federal constitutional courts have rejected attempts by the authorities of the *Länder* to introduce the right to vote in local elections by non-nationals with the right to reside, on the grounds that this infringes the constitutionally enshrined uniform concept of the people, defined as the citizens alone.[12] Only citizens may vote, as only they are part of the constitutional people, and the only exceptions for local elections can come from EU law, and these are given special attention within the constitutions of both countries (Shaw 2007, Chapter 9).[13] There are many states where there is constitutional resistance to the idea that there is anything other than a single concept of the *national* people which, in turn, underpins the idea of a single and indivisible republican citizenship (Weil 2008).[14]

One of the key questions, when seeking to understand any given citizenship regime, concerns the role of institutions, many of which are, of course, embedded in a constitutional context, a context that often embodies the principle of the separation of powers. Reference has already been made to the legislature and the judiciary. In the domain of citizenship, as with immigration, executives also have a crucial role to play in policing the boundaries of membership, for example, through decisions on discretionary naturalization or deportation processes, decisions on access to the asylum system or, although these occur less frequently, measures taken to revoke citizenship on grounds of fraud or other conduct of the citizen. The public/private divide is also important. In some countries, executives make use of private businesses, for example, in areas like language testing for naturalization or in due diligence and security aspects for investor citizenship, raising a different set of questions about how accountability to both the broader public and to the specific 'subjects' of those interventions can work effectively.

If one of the core elements of constitutionalism is the rule of law, then the 'double punishments' that exist in many systems for non-citizens (risk of deportation for those who commit crimes, denial of long-term residence or citizenship for tax errors or problems of 'bad character' even

---

[12] Judgments of the German Federal Constitutional Court: BVerfGE 63, 37 (Schleswig-Holstein); BVerfGE 63, 60 (Hamburg), 31 October 1990; judgment of the Austrian Constitutional Court of 12 December 1997, B3113/96, B3760/96.

[13] See 'Persons and citizens as holders of rights' in Chapter 5, this book.

[14] See the judgment of the French *Conseil constitutionnel*, Decision 91-290 DC of 9 May 1991, Act on the statute of the territorial unit of Corsica (www.conseil-constitutionnel. fr/sites/default/files/as/root/bank_mm/anglais/a91290dc.pdf).

as a child) as well as for naturalized citizens (who are sometimes more vulnerable to loss of citizenship) are issues that should be addressed as challenging that notion. It is clear that we must cast the net widely across the many administrative expressions of constitutional principles in order to capture all of the manifold ways in which constitutional shadows can fall on citizenship (or, conversely, to reveal the different ways in which constitutional principles could be used to protect vulnerable groups or to uphold the rule of law or fundamental rights principles within the framework of citizenship law).

Unsurprisingly, therefore, there is a particularly important role for judicial institutions, not least in the oversight of executive decision-making, whether taken directly by the administration or 'delegated' to private entities. Courts, especially constitutional courts, are also frequently called on to decide whether constitutional principles regarding citizenship are broad meta-norms that operate as interpretative principles for other more specific norms, or whether they themselves constitute justiciable rules, as is the case with the 14th Amendment in the US.[15] In some cases, a reference to a 'constitutional principle' of citizenship, as in the UK, which lacks a 'written constitution', is clearly a reference to some other type of meta principle within the structure of the legal system and the state.[16] The status of such a principle – in comparison to much of what we find in written constitutions – is uncertain, reminding us again that the boundaries of a constitution are often not neat and formal. It is not only in the UK where one might find the constitutional principles of citizenship scattered across a wide range of documents, including common law and case law. In Canada, the Charter of Rights, with its equality guarantee, has an impact on citizenship (Winter 2015). The *Conseil constitutionnel*, meanwhile, recognizes a range of principles, including some that are implicit in the laws of the French Republic, as part of the so-called *bloc de constitutionnalité*.[17] Including principles such as freedom of association, these norms are pertinent to the interpretation of citizenship and (especially) citizenship rights. Furthermore, courts in many countries have, from time to time, been called on to resolve tensions between international human rights obligations prioritizing the protection of all as against the domestic prioritization of the interests of the 'constitutional people'.

---

[15] *Afroyim v Rusk* 387 US 253 (1967).

[16] *G1 v Secretary of State for the Home Department* [2012] EWCA Civ 867; [2013] QB 1008.

[17] See Paris et al (2019); for the initiation of the concept, see *Conseil constitutionnel*, Decision 71-44 DC, 16 July 1971, *Liberté d'association*, Rec 29.

In this section, we have briefly surveyed the wide variety of approaches taken in constitutional frameworks to regulating citizenship. Despite the puzzle noted earlier that there is relatively little *direct* constitutional regulation of citizenship, none the less we can already see a number of different angles on the phenomenon of constitutional citizenship that need further exploration. These become visible whenever citizenship discourse flows into the field of constitutional law or when constitutional discourse underpins the narrative of citizenship. But even if the net is cast widely to encompass a broad corpus of constitutional law, no claim is made in this book that looking at constitutional citizenship gathers together all that law has to say about citizenship and citizenship rights. The constitutional perspective, for example, misses much that can be said about the 'street-level' aspects of the regulation of citizenship.[18] Rather the core claim of this book can be stated in the following terms: *the constitutional citizen is a central figure for understanding many dimensions of and tensions within modern citizenship as well for understanding modern constitution-based polities.* To help us figure out how central the constitutional citizen actually is, we must now turn to look at the history and context of the idea and the practices of constitutional citizenship.

Exploring constitutional citizenship in its wider context

Citizenship and constitutionalism in historical context

The idea of the sovereign citizen of the liberal state emerged alongside the idea of the constitutional state in which the separation of powers and the rule of law are paramount in relation to the operation of the national institutions of governance. Both have been widely understood as ideas stemming from the European enlightenment, during the period when the idea of the nation state was starting to emerge after the Treaties of Westphalia and Utrecht, and before the first ideological high point of that idea in the 19th century. The central political power (up to that point, the absolute monarch) was placed under the authority of common institutions at broadly the same point in history as the human subject emerged as a distinctive and sovereign political agent. This agent, now 'the citizen', owes more than a personal relationship of allegiance to the sovereign

---

[18] For example, Kristol and Dahinden (2020) focus their study of naturalization practices (in relation to the difference that marriage makes) specifically on street-level bureaucrats.

(that is, as 'subject'). On the contrary, she is embedded in a network of reciprocal vertical and horizontal relationships (Seubert 2014, 548). The first crucial moments of change for the emergence of sovereign citizens were the revolutions in North America and France.

Dieter Gosewinkel has discussed these issues in detail:

> [These revolutions] opposed hierarchies in the traditional legal and political order – colonial as well as social orders – and replaced them by a new understanding of membership: it was based on the principle of fundamental legal equality among members of a political community. Members of these communities were called "citizens" or "citoyens". This idea became a basic principle of the new American and French constitutions: from now on the status of "citizen" or "citoyen" came to be deeply embedded in the framework of modern constitutionalism itself. Citizenship became not only a fundamental status of membership but also a legitimisation for claiming individual rights. As a constitutional principle, citizenship was no longer restricted to the local or regional level but came to be firmly linked to the state. The nationalisation of European states, which – in the course of the nineteenth century – centred more and more on the principle of nation and nation-building as their basis and main objective, thus deeply transformed citizenship into a national institution. (Gosewinkel 2009, 499)

This is not to say that it is impossible to trace citizenship back further than the French or American Revolutions or the Peace of Westphalia. Indeed, most comprehensive histories of citizenship tend to start in Greek and/or Roman times[19] and also to identify other important developments in the city-states of the Middle Ages. But the distinctive concept of modern liberal and democratic citizenship in the so-called 'Westphalian state tradition' (Falk 2000) is a more recent innovation, albeit one that draws quite substantially on its origins in city-scale membership models both in antiquity and in medieval times (Prak 2018). The modern model relies heavily on a distinctive shift towards both universalist and individualist thinking that owes much to innovations that emerged within the European enlightenment. In that respect, it embodies a tension between the universal and the particular. In terms of its universalism, it also relies in practice heavily on the technologies of the modern bureaucratic state that enable

---

[19] See, for example, Pocock (1992), Riesenberg (1992) and Balot (2017).

the regulation of larger communities of citizens, as well as the empowering of the individual. Moving forward from revolutionary times, Gosewinkel (2017, 17) goes on to explain how, historically, citizenship as a 'state relation' became the 'determining category of political membership in the twentieth century', displacing other forms of political membership such as religion, political parties and class.

A related point emerges from Chris Thornhill's sociological approach. He argues that as the state recognizes citizens, and as citizens acquire more rights, and so on, more law is produced in order to regulate their situation. However, he goes on to argue that any universalism in relation to citizenship may be more theoretical than real, and the challenge of citizens' struggle for recognition is central to this:

> In most societies, the figure of the citizen encountered great resistance, and the rise of citizenship ran up against deep structural checks, which the exercise of national citizenship rights was unable to overcome, so that the process of national integration inherent in citizenship remained inconclusive. (Thornhill 2018, S78)

In this context, Thornhill is not referring to the well-known historical exclusion of citizens on grounds of gender or social class, but rather to other cleavages such as centre–periphery relations. Thornhill's historical reading leads him to identify a 'deep paradox at the centre of modern constitutionalism':

> … namely, that the process of nation and state formation, constitutive for modern society, was carried forward, at the level of constitutional formalism, by the figure of the citizen, claiming rights of equality and promoting political-systemic inclusion and national integration. Typically, however, the constitutional citizen fractured in face of the social realities in which it was expected to perform its integrational functions, and it was unable to establish an order of government that acted as a nationally inclusive entity. In each instance, the fragmentation of the citizen led to a failure of democracy, and it meant that democracy developed on a selective pattern, allowing only incomplete societal inclusion. (Thornhill 2018, S83)

Such insights have led Thornhill to call for the reconsideration of such citizenship classics as T.H. Marshall's (1992 [1950]) account of the progressive allocation of civil rights, political rights and social rights between the 18th and 20th centuries as a process of national consolidation as being an overly teleological way of thinking about how citizenship actually develops. They also lie at the heart of the tensions that are explored in Part III of this book, which focuses on issues of populism and the changing spatialities of citizenship.

Richard Bellamy's neo-republican approach to political constitutionalism adds an important supplement to this perspective on citizens' struggles to be recognized and to achieve equality. His starting point is a reinterpretation of what constitutions are for, which departs from the 'liberal' ideal in which the protection of constitutional rights is the dominant animating force:

> Instead of constitutions being seen as establishing a just foundation and framework for politics, they have to be conceived as institutional mechanisms for preserving the civic freedom of citizens to negotiate different views of rights and justice and reach collective agreements that avoid mutual domination. (Bellamy 2001, 16)

Indeed, politics in general is 'a constitutive process through which citizens struggle to promote their interests by ensuring that the character of the polity is such that it recognizes their evolving ideals and concerns' (2001, 15). This differs sharply from the standard justification for constitutional rights as simply reinforcing an existing citizenship status. Instead, citizenship itself is seen as 'constitutive'. He thus argues that 'citizenship practice is a continuously reflexive process, with citizens reinterpreting the basis of their collective life in new ways that correspond to their evolving needs and ideals' (2001, 38).

It is already evident from these initial notes that a smooth narrative focused on enlightenment-based change and the parallel emergence of modern citizenship and liberal constitutionalism may well elide other important historical and contextual factors that point in the direction of tensions between citizenship and constitutional law and that show up in analyses which focus on the contested nature of citizenship and struggles for citizenship. The following subsections tease out some of these issues in more detail.

The colonial and post-colonial legacy

The classic story about the role of the enlightenment in taming political power tends to erase, or at least limit the prominence of, the external domination (through colonialism) of non-European territories by European states (Bhambra 2017, 2018). Many post-Westphalian analyses of the state simply ignore the external dimension of sovereignty, the implications of this for subjugated and colonialized peoples, and the decimation of their historic arrangements in matters of governance and sovereignty, and the emergence of colonial elites. At best, such peoples were usually only conditionally recognized as (subjugated) 'peoples' of the wider empires or as groups subject to colonial laws at a distance (Isin 2015, 274). As Lea Ypi argues, the categorical 'wrong' of colonialism was that it instantiated an unequal status between the individual members of the colonizing and colonized polities and involved 'the creation and upholding of a political association that denies its members equal and reciprocal terms of cooperation' (2013, 158). In the 18th and 19th centuries, France, Spain and Portugal created special laws for their colonies, excluding the colonies from the new rights that were being granted under the national constitutions (Fradera 2018). Later, in France, the state chose decolonization over acceding to demands from its African subjects for full citizenship and economic equality (Pitts 2010, 220). Decolonization processes in the case of the UK were profoundly painful in terms of splintering statuses under UK law, stripping away rights[20] and creating multiple tiers of 'citizenship' with limited rights,[21] all in the interests of immigration control. The effects of this were felt more than 50 years later with the so-called Windrush scandal, which has seen many people who are now elderly and who moved to the UK from Caribbean countries many decades ago (often as children) have their rights to remain in the UK contested and stripped away (White 2019).[22] According to Omar Khan (2019, 172),

> ... the Windrush injustice that emerged in early 2018 was less a case of migration of Caribbean people, and more a case of the British unwinding of its Empire, and the reorganisation of rights across the post-colonial British state and the newly independent states – nation states – in the Caribbean, Africa and Asia.

---

[20] Dummett and Nicol (1990).

[21] Fransman (2009).

[22] *The Week* (2019) 'Who are the Windrush Generation and how has the scandal unfolded', 6 March (www.theweek.co.uk/92944/who-are-the-windrush-generation-and-why-are-they-facing-deportation). For further discussion, see Chapter 6.

Accordingly, Gurminder Bhambra's (2018) contention that many European states were – prior to decolonization – effectively imperial states, not nation states, should be read into the many attempts to organize citizenship by reference to different conceptions of the nation state, such as the 'civic/ethnic' divide discussed below. Given this ignored history of colonialism, combined with a tendency to simplify processes of decolonialization, the global politics of race, and especially of whiteness, tends to be given insufficient prominence in the context of those discussions of citizenship that claim to fall within the liberal democratic constitutionalist tradition (Sadiq 2017).

This book will endeavour to avoid this pitfall in its approach to interrogating the citizenship/constitution relation by acknowledging the impact of imperialism and colonial violence on citizenship internally and externally, as part of a critical and relational approach to studying citizenship. Such an approach will bring the concept of struggle to the centre of our attention, in line with the relational approach to citizenship outlined in Chapter 1, and acknowledges the relations of subordination associated with the colonization process. It highlights the complex history of 'postcolonial' citizenship, both in the formerly subaltern/now independent and formerly imperial/now postcolonial polities. Neil Walker summarizes the main challenges neatly:

> These postcolonial citizenships, either the novel product of independence or transformed from their previous subaltern status, typically confront a tension between the collective self-vindication involved in the assertion of the kind of exclusive and nationally monolithic model of citizenship of whose most corrupted form they were historical victims, and a search for a form of political community which does not replicate the Western paradigm. The citizenship politics of imperial and postcolonial territories are further complicated by the existence of settled diasporas in either location, often accompanied by complex patterns of dual citizenship, as well as by continuing migratory flows. (Walker 2017, 557–8)

Relatedly, given both the heritage of colonialism and current trends of globalization, it is important to bear in mind how the meanings and possible effects of citizenship in non-western contexts continue to be distinctive right up to the present day. This is implicit in Gosewinkel's analysis, as he makes it clear that his approach is focused only on the European political space, albeit both east and west (in a context where much work concentrates only on the west[23]). This book steps beyond these European boundaries. The case for doing so is obvious. All states must be impacted by the need within the international system for certain recognizable criteria organizing how states ascribe 'nationality' in the international law sense to members, even ones that are almost totally closed to outsiders such as North Korea. Yet our gaze has historically rarely strayed beyond western Europe, North America and the 'white states' that were the settler colonies of the United Kingdom.

Citizenship beyond the 'western' world

In the emergent field of non-western citizenship studies, citizenship is often defined relationally. Working inductively and from the bottom up, Erin Aeran Chung paints a picture of a model of citizenship as a 'constantly changing, interactive, and local process that is contingent on formal paperwork, informal institutions, and everyday practices' (Chung 2017, 432). Such practices may not always be consistent and transparent, of course, and there may be conflicts between what is stated in the constitution and how things work 'on the ground'. Citizenship as a legal status may be universally enveloped in a cloak of law, but we need to be wary about what that actually means in practice. Throughout this book, we will see examples that point in the direction of taking a precautionary approach to possible distinctions between theory and practice.

The task of understanding the history of citizenship outside 'the west' is only just beginning.[24] Indeed the ideal of citizenship as democratic, universal and inclusive is not necessarily a useful lens for observing citizenship in all places and at all times, from both a practical and a conceptual perspective. In fact, as Charles T. Lee explains:

> … the concept of citizenship arises from and is predominantly interpreted through the Western lineage and constellation of democratic political thought [that is, liberal, civic republican, communitarian, deliberative, and radical democratic], and … its material form remains deeply entrenched in Westernized political institutional structure. (Lee 2014, 76)

---

[23] See, however, Bauböck et al (2009).

[24] See the contributions to a special issue of *Citizenship Studies* on citizenship in Asian History, introduced by Bijl and van Klinken (2019).

Since the terms 'west' and 'non-west' are themselves leaky and mutually permeable, it is hardly surprising to see constant spillover and spillback of non-democratic, particularistic and exclusivist ideas across multiple and interconnected citizenship regimes. Not only is the concept of citizenship receiving critical attention in respect of the foundational ideas that lie within it, but citizenship studies as a field is also changing in ways that have often disturbed taken-for-granted assumptions about the conceptual and even moral dominance of 'liberal' citizenship regimes. For example, David Fitzgerald and David Cook-Martín (2014) show that it was the supposedly more 'liberal' states of North America that imposed for longer and with greater impact race-based immigration and citizenship exclusions and not the supposedly 'less advanced' South America.

Thankfully, in order to be able to spread the empirical net more widely, we now have both primary (GLOBALCIT 2017a, b) and secondary material available that makes it possible to study closely the citizenship regimes of almost the entire world, but in particular Latin America,[25] Africa,[26] the Arab world,[27] India[28] and many other parts of Asia.[29] Part of what lies behind the globalization of citizenship studies, however, is not just the post-colonial struggles referred to above, but also the 'neoliberal' trend observed by Barry Hindess (2002). Where once citizenship was seen as a bureaucratic project of 'liberal states' (Brubaker 1992, 48–9), now it is rolled out globally and promoted not least in order to make populations more governable and to open new markets for exploitation. Citizenship, and associated practices such as birth registration and identification documentation, are performance indicators for states, not just for reasons of promoting human rights, but also as part of the project of 'development' (Hunter 2019).[30]

One of the ways in which citizens, or those-who-would-be-citizens, have contested the exclusionary force of constitutions, both historically and still today, has been through what Engin Isin has termed 'acts of citizenship' (Isin 2008). Citizens are not just empty vessels into which citizenship – as status and practice – is poured. They have agency in relation to the choices they make. They struggle. They face resistance. The idea of 'acts of citizenship' refers to cases where institutionalized citizenship practices are disrupted politically (Isin and Nielsen 2008). These may be democratic acts within a non-democratic context.

---

[25] Fitzgerald and Cook-Martín (2014), Vonk (2015) and Acosta (2016, 2018).

[26] Manby (2018).

[27] Parolin (2009) and Albarazi (2017).

[28] Roy (2016), Jayal (2013, 2016, 2019b) and Chaudhuri and König (2018).

[29] Vonk (2018b). Extensive use will also be made of the GLOBALCIT country reports (http://globalcit.eu/country-profiles/).

[30] See also Chapter 5.

'Performative citizenship', as Isin (2017) has termed it more recently, can involve political and social struggles not only by 'citizens' in the formal sense, but also by non-citizens, and it can also involve the enacting, and consequential transformation of, citizenship in non- or semi-democratic settings. Studying the huge demonstrations in Hong Kong in 2019 against an extradition law threatening the special status of Hong Kong within the broader Chinese system builds a complex and ongoing picture of performative citizenship. Part of the object of this is to articulate the case for the recognition of a new and distinct identity and political community of people: that of the 'Hongkonger'. This status is so far only partially recognized within the international states system as the treaty-guaranteed principle of 'one country, two systems'.[31]

Binaries of citizenship

This book attempts to step away from the search for neat models and binaries, which has often marked the domain of citizenship studies, such as Brubaker's classic but widely debunked (including by himself) distinction between a civic model (giving preference to territory and residence) in France and an ethnic model (giving preference to descent and attachment) in Germany (Brubaker 1992). This idea of a civic/ ethnic divide is buttressed by a supposedly sharp distinction between the ideas of *ius soli* and *ius sanguinis* as the predominant principles for ascribing citizenship at birth: birth in the territory versus birth as the child of an existing citizen. In Brubaker's original model, these principles were strongly linked to differing concepts of the nation, with a contrast between those that are based around key civic institutions, which provide a framework for the integration of newcomers, such as schools or the army, and those where the nation has a strong ethnic and nationalist

---

[31] At least one UK parliamentarian has reacted to the events by calling for Hong Kong residents to be given UK citizenship as reassurance, as this should have been done in 1997: see P. Walker (2019) 'UK should give British nationality to Hong Kong citizens, Tugendhat says', *The Guardian*, 13 August (www.theguardian.com/ politics/2019/aug/13/uk-british-nationality-hong-kong-citizens-tom-tugendhat). It was revealed in July 2018 that the UK pressured Portugal not to give citizenship to residents of Macau in the run-up to return of Macau to Chinese sovereignty, on the grounds that this would set a precedent that the UK did not want to live up to: see J. Lam (2018) 'Britain's "disgraceful" pre-handover efforts to deny nationality to Hongkongers revealed in declassified cabinet files', *South China Morning Post*, 24 July (www.scmp.com/news/hong-kong/politics/article/2156385/britains-disgraceful-pre-handover-efforts-deny-nationality).

component. The distinction could be summarized as one between 'demos' and 'ethnos'. Although the ethnic/civic distinction in terms of citizenship regimes remains a useful if broad heuristic, in reality, as Brubaker (1998) himself now acknowledges, it is clear that 'understanding citizenship regimes requires a context-sensitive approach' (Vink 2017, 229).

This is the subtly different story told by historians such as Gammerl and Gosewinkel. For example, Benno Gammerl (2009) undermines the idea of a simplistic east/west divide by taking a careful look at differentiation in citizenship matters *within* two very different empires – the British and Hapsburg empires in the 19th and early 20th century. Without offering all of the empirical evidence fully to demonstrate the point, Gammerl does enough to suggest instead a time-based argument about ruptures and sea changes in (European) politics related to globalization as the basis for such differences in approach. Gosewinkel (2008) develops his argument to show that there is no sharp east/west divide to be seen by reference to the use of the principles of *ius soli* (France) or *ius sanguinis* (Germany). On the contrary, both countries were initially strongly influenced by the Roman law principle of descent for reasons of administrative convenience rather than bloodlines or belonging. Gosewinkel acknowledges the emergence of nationalizing ideas that contested the 'German-ness' of certain citizens (for example, Poles, Danes and Jews) by reference to narrow ethnic or religious criteria, but points out that these found no place in law until the arrival of Nazi citizenship laws in the 1930s. Until then, as Gosewinkel (2008, 98) puts it, 'the legal principles functioned in a more instrumental way, in response to changing economic and demographic policy goals.' In sum, rather than there being some deep-seated pre-political difference that somehow explains changes in citizenship laws and policies, contextual factors and processes of change need to be given full weight within the presentation of citizenship regimes.

The underpinning principles of citizenship regimes do indeed change in response to contingencies of time and location. That is to say, the regimes have evolved, but so have the underlying principles. Take, for example, the idea of *ius soli*, which emerged as the governing principle of subjecthood to the Crown under English common law during feudalism in medieval times (Price 1997; Kim 2000).[32] This predates the modern notion of a constitution, but none the less it was constitutive of state 'membership' at the time. Over the centuries, it morphed from a notion of nested subjecthood under feudal ideas and practices of personal allegiance into a more modern, but none the less rather limited concept of subjecthood and allegiance to the monarch in an institutional sense,

---

[32] *Calvin's Case*, 77 Eng Rep 377, 382 (KB 1608).

as the idea of a constitutional monarchy gradually emerged in England and later Britain.[33] While the practices of *ius soli* were carried across the Atlantic ocean, in particular to the colonies of North America (and later became the dominant norm throughout the western hemisphere because it proved well suited to settler colonialism and immigration nations), it was eventually abandoned in the UK as a result of the British Nationality Act 1981.[34] No constitutional change was needed, only legislation in the form of the British Nationality Act 1981. And although *ius soli* first arrived in US law in common law form, its character was changed decisively as a result of the introduction of the 14th Amendment to the Constitution in order to deal with the legacy of slavery and to give citizenship a distinctive constitutional form (Neuman 2015).

The concept of *ius soli* subjecthood underwent a complex transformatory process as it was taken out across the British Empire, in particular after the loss of the North American colonies at the end of the 18th century, into those parts of the Empire that were not settler-colonies, in many parts of South Asia, Africa and the Caribbean. The idea that subjecthood to the sovereign was a unifying element for all of the peoples of the Empire was undermined by an emerging sense that the freedom of movement to which it at least theoretically gave rise across a large part of the earth needed to be controlled, especially as regards immigration to the UK itself (Gorman 2007). A strong racial dimension was then read into the overall framework of nationality and immigration law in the UK, and nationality law was inescapably linked with immigration law from 1962 onwards (Dummett and Nicol 1990). The concepts of British subjecthood and citizenship of the United Kingdom and Colonies introduced formally by the British Nationality Act 1948,[35] as the Empire morphed painfully into the Commonwealth, were substantially undermined as meaningful statuses by the various legislative measures limiting immigration from the (non-white) Commonwealth, before effectively being abolished by the British Nationality Act 1981 (Dummett 2006; Fransman 2009). However, in the context of the UK's unwritten constitution, it is none the less arguable that these evolving principles of the citizenship regime have had a constitutional status, even if ordinary legislation was all that Parliament needed in order to change them, highlighting the paradoxical and unentrenched character of 'constitutional citizenship' in the UK. That the UK's colonial administrators probably viewed *ius soli* as a constitutional

---

[33] *Calvin's Case*, 77 Eng Rep 377, 382 (KB 1608).

[34] Dummett and Nicol (1990), Dummett (2006) and Fransman (2009).

[35] It was only in the British Nationality Act 1948 that the longstanding common law principle of *ius soli* was finally codified, only to be abolished less than 40 years later.

principle can be supported by reference to the inclusion of the principle in the first post-independence constitutions of the former colonies in Africa in the post-Second World War years, before it was subsequently generally abated by constitutional amendment and legislation in favour of a general preference for a baseline of *ius sanguinis* for birthright citizenship (Manby 2018, 76).

The main point to glean from these narratives is that it is important not to place formal and restrictive borders around the scope of recognized constitutional norms but rather to examine piece by piece how they change over time, in response to exogenous as well as endogenous forces. In other words, the challenges to neat binaries and simple historical ellipses come from all angles.

Ongoing challenges to national models

Coming forward to the present day, it is interesting to see how, in the face of challenges of globalization in the neoliberal world, the various models of national citizenship still remain remarkably resilient, adjusting to allow space for new models of affinity and legal belonging including some that are residence-based (the rise of naturalization) and others that are more 'remote' from a territorial basis for citizenship (such as investor citizenship), without fading away (Hindess 2002). Indeed, in many countries, citizenship has gained attention as a vessel into which states can pour meaning, in the sense of defining who we are (and who we are not). States have responded to immigration in many cases by introducing, usually by legislation rather than constitutional change, language and civic tests as well as tests of probity and self-sufficiency. These moves have been termed the de-ethnicization of citizenship (Joppke 2003), although that would be an inappropriate designation if such tests were systematically designed to exclude certain groups. These changes also amount to an increased 'disciplining' of citizenship, based on state expectations, often of a cultural character, which arguably run counter to the classic aspirations of the liberal state (Orgad 2014). States have also responded to emigration, sometimes by enshrining the position of the diaspora in the national constitution,[36] making provision for the transmission of citizenship across generations, for diaspora voting rights, and for the preservation of cultural

---

[36] For example, Article 19, Armenia 1995 (rev. 2015) (www.constituteproject.org/constitution/Armenia_2015?lang=en) and Article 8(3), Albania 1998 (rev. 2016) (www.constituteproject.org/constitution/Albania_2016?lang=en).

and economic attachments. Christian Joppke has described this as a re-ethnicization of citizenship (Joppke 2003).

The 'citizenship turn', in scholarship and state practice, also begs the question of what status and rights are ascribed to those who are not citizens, both by states and under the international system. Those who lack the status of citizen of the host state may be wholly or partially recognized as 'denizens' (that is, long-term residents), but they may lack substantial legal protection if their presence on the territory does not have a legal basis. Some may lack the citizenship – legally and/or factually – of any state, and so are stateless, and may need to look for recognition of their 'right to a nationality' under international conventions that are widely, but not universally, adhered to by states. Migration is a complex phenomenon: some people are 'forced migrants' and 'displaced persons' (internally and externally) and they, too, may need to look for protection under international law. But once again, state enforcement of the relevant international protections is patchy. In many fields of scholarship, substantial attention has already been given to the statuses of non-citizens, including those who are refugees. It is even possible to argue that 'citizenship' – as an object of study – is evolving to include issues such as non-citizenship, treated not just as a negative, or as an absence of citizenship, but also as, in some cases, a choice made by certain groups to reject a hegemonic power, even if it means accepting the vulnerable status of non-citizen (Bloom 2017, 2018).[37]

Finally, while the 'state' in its Westphalian sense may not be in terminal decline, it does not operate alone in the global system. Gëzim Krasniqi (2019) has shown, by studying performative citizenship practices within 'liminal polities' across the world, that it is misleading just to divide the world into 'states', and thus to limit the study of citizenship to those states, plus other acknowledged 'levels' (subnational polities, supranational polities such as the EU). In reality, many millions of people reside in such unrecognized or semi-recognized polities with constitutional or quasi-constitutional regimes, yet limited sovereignty and often ineffective citizenship regimes. Or they may be part of the diasporas of these entities. Good examples are Kosovo, Northern Cyprus and Taiwan, although each of these cases presents a very different type of 'sovereignty claim', with consequences for citizenship. This, then, is another type of 'status' and set of 'rights' to add to the existing panoply of citizen, semi-citizen and non-citizen, where the strategies of the 'citizens' and of the polities that confer 'citizenship' are important objects of study (Lori 2017).

---

[37] On the 'refusal practices' of Tibetans, see McGranahan (2018).

In sum, the dynamics of globalization demand that we must keep reassessing the meaning of citizenship 'beyond the state' in the modern world. There are dynamics in relation to transnational citizenship (for example, immigration and multinational families: Kristol and Dahinden 2020) and multilevel citizenship (for example, of the EU), which curtail the sovereign capacities of states to set the boundaries of the citizenry and to determine authoritatively the scope of civic, social and political rights. In Europe, for example, states need to have regard to the practices of other states, to developments at the EU level, such as the free movement of persons and EU citizenship and to the case law of the European Court of Human Rights, so far as it affects citizenship. Ideas about citizenship and about constitutionalism have often spread in parallel beyond the state. To put it another way, citizenship and constitutional regimes at the national level are both horizontally and vertically interconnected, and the national, state level no longer – if it ever did – holds a monopoly over the ideas and practices of citizenship or of constitutionalism. In fact, many authors argue that the main focus of scholarship should now be on unpicking the myth that the various dimensions of the citizenship (legal, political, identitarian, etc) need to be aggregated into a uniform bundle at the level of the national state (see, for example, Cohen 1999, 256). This is why the shifting spatialities of citizenship receive close attention in Chapters 7 and 8.

In conclusion: the promise and limits of the constitutional approach

In this chapter, we have started to unpack the idea of constitutional citizenship, showing how it can be used to encapsulate (both as an idea and as practice) those aspects of the membership relation that go to the very heart of a polity and some of the conditions for its existence. That is to say, it has focused on those matters relating to citizenship that are not simple choices of ordinary politics or ordinary law, and which, precisely because they evolve over time, offer a set of messages about the essence of the polity and the principles and norms on which it is founded. The 'unpacking process' is, therefore, part observation and part interpretation. In the process of highlighting some examples of how citizenship and constitutions have interacted, we have also reflected back on the contested concepts of modern citizenship and constitutionalism, contributing in the process to the normative reconstruction of those concepts, initially in the context of the modern territorial state. This is most clearly shown in those sections of the chapter that observed that this relationship, while close, is not necessarily comfortable, highlighting that much of what we take for granted is based on a partial and westernized reading of citizenship (and indeed of constitutionalism and sovereignty). We will take this process much further in Part II when we break the classical conception of citizenship down into its component parts for the purposes of excavating the tensions between in the citizenship/constitution relationship.

Before moving on, we should turn briefly to two direct challenges to the presumption that the citizenship/constitution relation is central to understanding polities. The first challenge stems from the argument, which is perhaps most closely associated with Christian Joppke, that there has been a profound and unstoppable instrumental turn in relation to the practices and policies of citizenship (Joppke 2019). While states have always been instrumentalist in their approach to allocating (or denying) citizenship, the more recent novelty concerns the widespread diffusion of instrumental practices among certain groups of mainly privileged individuals.[38] All of these observations may suggest that the 'value' of citizenship is increasingly seen not as a facet of 'public value' in terms of the interconnections with the essential facets of polity-making at a collective level, but as a facet of 'private value' in the context of a global and individualized marketplace for citizenship in which money and mobility are being traded (Džankić 2019a). Citizenship is now so 'light' as to have been radically transformed as a concept. Conversely, citizenship is also potentially to be resisted and reviled as it spells out the control that states maintain over populations in the name of the (arguably random) allocation of passports, birth certificates and identity cards (Kochenov 2019a).

Joppke suggests that this stems from a more significant influence on modern citizenship of the Roman legalistic conception of citizenship compared to the Athenian republican conception. In Joppke's work this is linked to an emphasis on the core of citizenship being a liberal conception of rights, with little focus on its democratic or cultural elements. Joppke's approach thus presupposes that it is possible to separate the different elements of citizenship, including its internal- and external-facing dimensions. It could be argued that the instrumental turn documented by Joppke, and supported by a number of other scholars such as Peter Spiro (2018), who focuses on the demise of the state as the reference point for citizenship, challenges the very basis of the argument about constitutional citizenship in this book. It suggests that the task of documenting and analysing the relationship between citizenship and constitutions is pointless,

---

[38] Harpaz (2015, 2019) and Džankić (2019a).

since this task seems to presuppose a thicker relationship between state and citizen than the instrumentalization thesis considers to exist. But Rainer Bauböck (2019a), in a paper responding directly to Joppke's argument, makes the point that the current predominantly 'Westphalian' set-up of states allocating membership within an international system is, in fact, not going to collapse any time soon. This is so, despite the rise of some elements of 'light citizenship', such as investor citizenship, or the access to citizenship opened by states seeking to claim additional (external) citizens. Moreover, 'instrumental' conduct does not necessarily undermine either the significance of citizenship or the role of the state. Identity issues may be just as central to the motivations of those who seek the citizenship of a 'kin state' (for example, members of the Hungarian diaspora acquiring Hungarian citizenship, or Bosnian Croats in BiH acquiring Croatian citizenship) as are factors such as acquiring EU citizenship and improved mobility options (Pogonyi 2019). Bauböck argues that 'What is striking [in the cases he is discussing] is that instrumental and identity values of citizenship seem to be closely linked rather than one depreciating the other' (2019a, 1016).

This book recognizes the power of the 'instrumentalization' thesis. I argue that the *national* relation of state and citizen is only a starting point, necessary for explaining some of the ways in which this relation is constructed in legal and constitutional terms. I do not, however, essentialize the state or its power over citizenship. Quite the contrary. As Part III will show, it is still necessary to look at the tensions between 'touches of stateness' (Shaw and Wiener 2000), as exemplified in this book by an enquiry into the tensions between citizenship and populism (see Chapter 6), and the shifting spatialities of citizenship, which ask us to look closely at the impact of globalization and other 'beyond the state' dynamics on citizenship (see Chapter 7). Nor do I essentialize citizenship. Focusing on citizenship does not preclude a deep awareness of citizenship's constant shadow, namely cases of voluntary and involuntary non-citizenships. Some migrants may be in a position to choose between multiple citizenships or between one citizenship and one or more relatively stable statuses of permanent residence in a host state. Many others are in abject situations of insecurity, struggling even to access one meaningful citizenship or residence status, with significant implications for their wellbeing and life chances. The shadowy presence of the non-citizen lurks throughout the book, without being the central focus of analysis.

The second challenge argues that the constitutionalist reading of citizenship does not work in every context, even in northern and western Europe with its relatively stable democracies and liberal constitutions. That is to say, there exist citizenship regimes that are decidedly 'non-constitutional' in character.[39] Christian Fernández (2019) uses the case of Sweden to develop the argument that a 'liberal' citizenship regime does not necessarily equate with one that is 'constitutional' in character.[40] Assessed by reference to standard indices, Sweden has a 'liberal' and open citizenship regime, in respect of naturalization of immigrants, with a short residency period and no integration tests (Lokrantz Bernitz 2012). Unsurprisingly, with a high immigration rate, it also has a high naturalization rate (that is, a high proportion of those who qualify opt to take citizenship by naturalization).[41]

Fernández argues that this is not the result of either a successful multicultural integration strategy or a liberal convergence of European states, but rather, a product of 'the relative dissociation of a fairly administrative and pragmatic conception of citizenship from existing conceptions of nationhood and belonging' (Fernández, 2019, 3). This is an example of what Fernández terms 'ideationally thin' citizenship, which contrasts with the conventional assumption, which has indeed been given prominence so far in this book, that citizenship articulates closely with officially and unofficially expressed ideas of nationhood and national interest, which are frequently to be found in the national constitution. Instead, he points to the 'privatization' of the nation and voluntarism in relation to integration and belonging as distinctive of a 'light' citizenship regime, which separates official membership from sentiment. Yet, as Fernández himself concludes, since the idea of 'Swedishness' as the most important basis for national identity still persists in many areas of national life, including the welfare state and migration policy (Barker 2013, 2017a), notwithstanding its non-appearance in formal membership rules or ceremonies, this can raise more problems for the immigrant seeking to integrate, because of the absence of secure reference points for belonging that she can access without difficulty. The absence of constitutional citizenship does not necessarily imply the absence of exclusionary national sentiment. But is the opposite true? It remains to be seen what implications can be derived from the presence of constitutional citizenship. It is to this detailed analysis that we now turn in Part II.

---

[39] This may be thought to reflect the more low-key approach to constitutionalism generally taken in the Nordic countries, despite recent trends towards judicial review (Hirschl 2011). Nordic constitutions typically also lack 'narratives' in terms of the use of preambles to identify core constitutional values or historical background (Krunke and Thorarensen 2018).

[40] See also Jensen et al (2017).

[41] It is worth noting, however, that waiting times for citizenship applications have increased significantly in recent years: see C. Edwards (2019) 'Sweden sees drastic rise in waiting time for citizenship applications', *The Local Sweden*, 29 July (www.thelocal. se/20190729/waiting-times-for-swedish-citizenship-applications-two-years).

PART II

Constitutional Citizenship Unpacked

In a classic contribution to understanding citizenship, Verena Stolcke (1997, 61) argued that:

> Of the three constitutive elements of the modern state, a territory, a government, a people, circumscribing the "people" proved to be the most controversial issue.... A territory without a people, a government without a clearly bounded community to be governed, makes no sense. Hence, bounding the citizenry, that is determining the conditions for becoming a member of a state, acquired a logic of its own as a fundamental constitutive political dilemma in the formative period of the modern territorial nation-states.

In this part of the book, across three chapters, we will explore how both the practical 'nuts and bolts' of the constitutional framework and the ideas of constitutionalism can operate to structure or fill out this controversial issue relating to the people of the state. We will show how these issues play out by exploring three interrelated sets of questions concerned with (a) constitutional ideals and identities; (b) the definition of who are and who are not the citizens; and (c) the challenge of identifying citizenship in terms of (constitutional) rights and duties. These are above all *what* questions, which enable the study of citizenship as a set of practices: from this thematic approach, what can we discern about the relationship between citizenship and constitutional law? The aim is, through the juxtaposition of conceptual reflection and practical illustration, to pull out a preliminary set of answers to the questions posed in Chapter 1: What does it mean to buttress claims to the legitimacy and authority of national concepts of citizenship (a) by reference to a *constitutional concept* of the citizens or of 'the people' and (b) through the regulation of citizenship (directly or indirectly) via *constitutional law*?

A passing familiarity with many of the standard works on citizenship in the late 20th and early 21st century will reveal that there are strong parallels between the three-way division adopted in this part of the book and many efforts by scholars to encapsulate the sphere of citizenship. The distinction that Jean Cohen (1999) draws, between the juridical, the political and the identitarian elements of citizenship, was highlighted in Chapter 1. There are many other examples of closely aligned citizenship 'triptychs'. Christian Joppke (2007) suggests breaking citizenship down along the lines of status, rights and identity. Antje Wiener (1997) argues that citizenship comprises elements of rights, access and belonging. (To demonstrate the ubiquity of the triadic approach, here are some other examples: Rainer Bauböck, 2001: *membership, rights* and *practices*; Richard Bellamy, 2004: *rights, belonging* and *participation*; and Seyla Benhabib, 1999: *collective identity, political membership* and *social rights and claims*.) Linda Bosniak (2006), meanwhile, postulates that there are five separate but interrelated dimensions of membership, namely status, rights, political engagement, responsibilities and identity/solidarity/belonging. The precise position of the 'cuts', and indeed the number of segments thereby created, is overall less important than the framework or lenses applied for the study of the component elements of citizenship. In this part of the book, it is the idea of *constitutional citizenship in a national context* which is placed at the centre of our attention and which is used, in the following chapters, in order to delimit the field of study and structure the approach taken. Inevitably, there is overlap between the chapters, since any such three-way division can operate merely as a heuristic in order to render the body of material more intelligible. It cannot impose strict dividing lines. Some topics or examples discussed could easily appear in any of the three chapters.

The focus is observational and interpretative, supplemented by reflections on the diverse literatures that have developed which illuminate our understanding of citizenship and constitutions from a conceptual perspective. The enquiry focuses on documenting the iterative flows of citizenship and constitutional discourse, highlighting how each constitutes the other, especially in ideational terms. Citizenship and constitutions exist in a two-way relationship, where each defines the other. Neither can be fully understood independently of the other.

3

Picking out the People: Ideals and Identities in the Citizenship/ Constitution Relation

Introduction

The idea of constitutional citizenship demonstrates how a concept of membership can 'sit' within state polities, all of which possess some form of written or unwritten, documentary or dispersed, constitution, constitutional law and constitutional principles. Since constitutions often articulate the distinctive 'ideals' of the state, this seems to be a good starting point for a mapping of how citizenship and constitutions/ constitutional law interact. To do this, we need to prise open the idea of constitutional citizenship, using associated concepts within constitutional and political theory, such as the people, the 'demos', constituent power, popular sovereignty, allegiance and loyalty to the state, constitutional identity, equality and dignity. That is the task of this chapter.

Woven through the notes that follow are many examples exploring what constitutional citizenship looks like in the specific circumstances of different constitutional frameworks. The conceptual discussions and exemplary case studies are closely linked in so far as the examples help us to understand how the concepts are evolving. Material is drawn from beyond the canon of liberal and democratic constitutionalism. The proliferation of studies of populist constitutionalism,[1] of authoritarian constitutionalism,[2]

---

[1] Blokker et al (2019).

[2] Ginsburg and Simpser (2013) and Alviar García and Frankenberg (2019).

and of constitutions and constitutionalism in illiberal polities[3] demands a response in terms of thinking about the role and character of constitutional citizenship in such contexts. In illiberal, or semi-liberal polities, the 'state is expressly not neutral, privileging a substantive vision of the good, informed by ethnicity, religion or communal morality' (Thio 2012, 136).[4] We will also discuss a number of examples of illiberal constitutionalism in Chapter 6 from the perspective of populism.

There are certainly challenges and risks involved in opening up the field of enquiry in this way. Looking at constitutions and constitutional law in isolation can give a distorted picture of reality. For instance, the Soviet-era constitutions of the states behind the Iron Curtain were full of references to citizens, democracy and various freedoms, but the reality, because they were one-party states, was quite different (Herzog 2012). Even while transition is underway, a constitution can claim to be 'democratic' but not live up to the claim. This was the case with the Constitution of the Federal Republic of Yugoslavia (FRY) (the territorially reduced and short-lived [1992–2003] successor to the Socialist Federal Republic of Yugoslavia [SFRY]), which contained multiple references to democracy, freedoms and the rule of law. Despite this, the domestic institutions of FRY remained in practice indifferent to all such principles. The picture for authoritarian regimes today can be mixed, with partial or periodic adherence to some aspects of the rule of law. For example, in Zimbabwe the Constitutional Court has given rulings that challenge the executive and that uphold constitutional principles in relation to matters of citizenship (Manby 2018, 149–64). The reality of 'citizenship' in Zimbabwe, however, will be quite different for the majority of people, as they will be unable to access the highest levels of the judiciary in order to use litigation to their advantage. As adherents to substantive[5] or contextualized[6] visions of the rule of law would argue, it is not just the fact that there is some sort of rule of law which matters. On the contrary, the key questions concern the types of rules in play and the manner in which they are embedded in the broader societal context. To build a full picture, moreover, we need to consider the response of legislatures and executives to the demands that the rule of law imposes (Lacey 2019).

---

[3] Thio (2012) and Dowdle and Wilkinson (2017).

[4] For examples focused on 'theocratic constitutionalism', see Backer (2006).

[5] Baer (2018).

[6] Krygier (2017).

Constituent power, popular sovereignty and citizenship

One of the most important components of constitutional theory, which has clear implications for citizenship via its invocation of 'the people', is the notion of constituent power (Loughlin 2017). This is the proposition which provides both the legal and legitimacy underpinnings for the creation of a new constitutional settlement. According to Joel Colón-Ríos (2014, 132), 'the theory of constituent power, simply put, holds that in every society there must be a legally unlimited constitution maker – someone who can create constitutions at will.'

The idea of a power to make constitutions, which is distinct from the power that is thereby constituted, emerged, alongside popular sovereignty, at around the same time as the notion of the citizen as a distinct political actor. This historical background was briefly sketched in Chapter 2. In that sense the 'constituent power' can be seen as another of the creatures of an 'enlightenment narrative' that saw the emergence of the early 'liberal' constitutions after revolutions in France and the US (Grimm 2012, 120). Each of these traces their legitimacy to some notion of a people that claimed its own power to establish institutions which, in turn, would provide the rules under which the community would live. The new US Constitution was the first to proclaim itself to be the product of 'We the People' – a much-imitated trope (Galligan 2013a, 707). It was intended to emphasize that the locus of sovereignty had shifted to the people – the expression of the power of the nation over the king.

This part of the narrative is vulnerable, therefore, to the same critiques as were presented in Chapter 2, namely that these enlightenment ideals never embodied anything like the principles of equality that we would regard as fundamental to democracy and citizenship in the 21st century. Thus, we can cite the rejection of citizenship even for freed African Americans (not to speak of slaves) in the ante-bellum US and the denial of suffrage to women and to most men lacking property in France or the US in the early years. In addition, these constitutions turned a blind eye to the colonial and imperial contexts of the emergence of such liberal ideas. The point is made starkly by one of the (problematic) classics of American constitutional law, the 1857 *Dred Scott* case.[7] Writing the majority opinion of the Supreme Court, Chief Justice Roger Taney explicitly linked together 'the people', the 'citizens', sovereignty and constituent membership:

---

[7] *Dred Scott v Sandford* 60 US (19 How) 393 (1857).

> The words "people of the United States" and "citizens" are synonymous terms, and mean the same thing. They both describe the political body who, according to our republican institutions, form the sovereignty, and who hold the power and conduct the Government through their representatives. They are what we familiarly call the "sovereign people", and every citizen is one of this people, and a constituent member of this sovereignty.

Yet these same words formed the baseline against which the Court concluded that Americans of African descent were not, and could not be, members of the people and citizens of the United States.

Constitutional scholars tussle with the problem of whether to treat the idea of constituent power as something consigned to some mythical past, or at least for the most part remaining in the shadows. On that view, it emerges only at revolutionary moments or moments of constitutional upheaval for the purposes of constitutional innovation or renewal. Alternatively, should we think about constituent power as a narrative that underpins the ongoing legitimation of political institutions under conditions of democratic constitutionalism, even though those institutions themselves might lack a formal and identifiable foundation point, which has been democratically acknowledged or consented to? This second point is related to another theory suggesting that constituent power is better thought of as a *capacity* – to replace the status quo, including in a manner which is unlawful at the time – rather than as an *entity* (Doyle 2019).[8] A more radical approach constructs civil disobedience itself as part of the constituent power, in so far as it can politicize elements of state power, such as borders, which are typically taken for granted (Celikates 2019). Unsurprisingly, given the differences across states, most synoptic work on constituent power is conceptual rather than comparative in nature.[9]

Students of citizenship are interested in broadly similar questions, but approach them from the perspective of the proper conditions for democratic self-government and the identity of the *demos* or political people. This leads inevitably to engagement with one of political theory's most intractable problems, namely the so-called 'democratic boundary problem'. This is the proposition that 'the democratic legitimacy of decisions affecting the boundaries of a "demos" (ie those citizens who

---

[8] See also Wandan (2015) on whether democratic constitutional outcomes presuppose democratic origins and, on the complex cases of Japan and South Korea after the Second World war, see Hahm and Kim (2010).
[9] For an exception, see Kay (2011).

are eligible to participate in democratic self-government) presupposes that the demos by whom or on whose behalf a decision is taken is already composed in a way that makes its boundaries legitimate' (Baubök 2017, 60–1). The boundary problem is clearly not confined to moments of constitutional formation or renewal, but it certainly applies most acutely in relation to the definition of 'constituent power', in so far as we might think about that power as *embodied* in the *demos* and indeed the citizenry, and *vice versa*. But equally, the *demos* is also embodied in the constituent power. The problem seems circular. Its more specific application is, however, in relation to the right to vote:

> The act of determining the group of people entitled to vote (the electorate) certainly seems logically prior to the holding of an election, but the fact of determination seems … to presuppose some pre-political authority which claims to determine the boundaries of the polity and thus to distribute political power. The conclusion must be, however, that the definition itself has taken us no closer to understanding who the "electorate" actually is. On the contrary, we need a pre-existing theory of the polity and in particular of the boundaries of the polity to lend meaning to the concept of the "electorate". (Shaw 2007, 60)

Of course, the answer to that question is contested among political theorists, and many argue that there are democratic procedures that can themselves confer democratic legitimacy in the context of determining the scope of the *demos* when looking transnationally beyond or across the boundaries of the state.[10] The different answers given to the 'boundary question' directly affect the scope and ideal of citizenship.

When it comes to implementing solutions to the boundary question, we also run into the acute tension that can emerge between constitutional principle and parliamentary democracy. This becomes clear in a UK case concerned with whether protestors living in a camp outside an airbase housing US nuclear weapons should be allowed to register to vote where they were 'living':

> Voting rights lie at the root of parliamentary democracy. Indeed many would regard them as a basic human right. Nevertheless they are not like the air we breathe. They do not

---

[10] For different approaches see, for example, Beckman (2019) and the contributors to Baubök et al (2019).

just happen. They have to be conferred, or at least defined and the categories of citizen who enjoy them have also to be defined. Thus no one would expect a new-born baby to have voting rights or that citizens could vote in all constituencies or in that of their unfettered choice.[11]

Returning to the level of constitution making, another area of concern as regards the interaction between citizenship and constituent power is the case of referendums that affect constitutional systems. Examples include referendums on secession of part of an existing state, as well as referendums on amendments to or replacement of an existing constitution.[12] Dejan Stjepanović and Stephen Tierney (2019, 266) draw a distinction between 'contained constitutional referendums', which are referendums that take place and draw effects entirely within the framework of the existing constitution, and 'constitutive referendums', which are 'instances of direct democracy deployed to create either new states or new constitutions (or both)'. The second group of referendums poses a legitimacy conundrum, within which the task of determining the scope of the *demos* and of the citizenry undoubtedly has a part to play:

> The importance of constitutive referendums for constitutional theory is not only in the significant role they play in helping to author a new legal order, but in how they relate in fact to a normative break that can be very hard to explain. If a referendum derives from one legal order, but has the power to supplant that order with a new order, where does such a referendum derive the legitimacy to do so, given the extent to which modern constitutionalism is so beholden to the very concept of constitutional supremacy? (Stjepanović and Tierney 2019, 266)

In other words, constitutive referendums raise precisely those legal and legitimacy issues that are central to understanding the nature of constituent power. They do so in a way that raises a number of core questions about the conduct, scope and character of such referendums, including in particular, the question of how they relate to concepts of national and regional citizenship (Bauböck 2019b). These are important for the

---

[11] Sir John Donaldson, MR in *Hipperson and Others v Electoral Registration Officer for the District of Newbury* [1985] 1 QB 1060; [1985] 2 All ER 456 (CA).

[12] Referendums are not universally held by scholars to be democratically required for the inception of a new constitution: see Beckman (2018).

purposes of determining the franchise as well as for settling contested issues of procedure. What links theory to practice is the legitimating factor of 'the people', which fills a sovereignty gap, even if it does so only by invoking a myth or idea:

> As a polity-framing/constitution-framing referendum, the constitutive referendum allows for the manifestation of a people's direct democratic will, and hence of their capacity to act as the legitimising source of constitutional law in foundational constitutional acts. (Stjepanović and Tierney 2019, 267)

What is likely to be powerful about a constitutive referendum is that it will have polity- or nation-building characteristics. Indeed, in Europe since 1989, such referendums have been widely used to give legitimacy to the creation of new states and to processes of constitutional renewal as part of post-communist transition, in places such as Estonia, Slovenia and Montenegro (for the creation of new states) and Poland, Lithuania and Estonia (again) (for the process of post-communist constitutional renewal). Estonia, for example, held two referendums with different franchises during the transition to independence (Day and Shaw 2003). More recently, in western Europe, there have been two referendums – in Scotland, on the basis of enabling legislation passed by the Westminster Parliament and in Catalonia, on the basis of a legal framework established in defiance of the clear terms of the Spanish Constitution – aimed at the putative secession of a region from an existing state, building on movements for increased self-determination.

When a constitutive referendum is held on a question of putative secession, it may be difficult to define, in a legitimate way, the franchise for that referendum, given that in most cases there is unlikely to be a prior existing legally circumscribed 'regional citizenship' (Ziegler et al 2014, 9–11; Shaw 2017a). Even where there has been such a prior regional citizenship, as there was in the case of the disintegration of the former Yugoslavia where republican citizenship was the default basis for citizenship in the new countries after 1992, this has not always solved the problems satisfactorily (Štiks 2015). The question of defining the franchise using concepts of formal citizenship, as well as residence, has posed a challenge not just for constitutional and citizenship scholars, but also at the practical level for international institutions such as the Venice Commission (the European Commission for Democracy through Law), which has, from time to time, been asked for its opinion by contracting states of the Council of Europe on the conduct of regional secession referendums. It has provided guidelines on constitutional referendums, but has managed to avoid elaborating on the tricky question of the proper scope of the franchise.[13] There seems to be no consensus on how to answer that question.[14] Stjepanović and Tierney (2019) call for a case-by-case resolution of the issue. Meanwhile, Jean-Thomas Arrighi (2019) suggests that the political calculations of elites, who are typically driving such processes, may point in favour of a more inclusive approach to the franchise on the grounds that this may reassure those who are voting about the nature of the choice they are making. That may work for Scotland and Catalonia. But the case of the former Yugoslavia points in the opposite direction; for the most part, political elites manipulated a narrower franchise, as with the independence referendum in Montenegro in 2006, where a special franchise law was needed to restrict the numbers of potential external voters.

One final question concerns whether the UK's referendum of June 2016 on whether to leave the EU was such a 'constitutive referendum', akin to an exercise of constituent power. Or was it a referendum that left the UK's constitutional *status quo* merely amended but not effectively replaced? Rainer Bauböck (2019b) argues that there should be a unilateral right to secede from regional unions such as the EU, which seems to presuppose an argument that such referendums do not affect the core of the state in question, unlike a secession referendum *within* a state. A related point concerns the conduct of such referendums. Sandra Kröger (2019; see also Weale 2017) subjects the EU referendum, and especially its franchise, to searching scrutiny against democratic standards, finding the referendum to be lacking in terms of input legitimacy from a number of perspectives. The problem with the franchise, as she and others have argued, concerned the exclusion of resident EU citizens, along with many UK citizens who had been resident outside the UK for more than 15 years, many of whom had been relying on their UK-derived EU citizenship as the basis for their residence in another Member State (Shaw 2017b). These were the groups most directly affected by the outcome of the referendum in terms of the impact on their legal status, making an argument that their exclusion should – if it were deemed necessary – have received a specific and thorough justification in the legislation. Instead, it happened by default, through the application of pre-existing rules already in place for general elections.

---

[13] *Guidelines for Constitutional Referendums at National Level* (2001) European Commission for Democracy Through Law, CDL-INF (2001) 10.
[14] See the diverse contributions to Ziegler et al (2014).

Constitutional identity and citizenship

Scholars acknowledge that constitutional identity is a difficult-to-define concept. It may well be, as José Luis Martí (2013) has argued, that the issue has become hard to understand because scholars fail to distinguish between two concepts: the 'identity of the constitution' and the 'identity of the people'. This reflects Rosenfeld's identification of the citizen as 'the constituent unit of the constitutional subject in all its multiple *identities*' (2009 211; emphasis added).

Gary Jacobsohn presents 'constitutional identity' as a dialogic and mutable concept:

> A constitution acquires an identity through experience; this identity exists neither as a discrete object of invention, nor as a heavily encrusted essence embedded in a society's culture, requiring only to be discovered. Rather, identity emerges dialogically and represents a mix of political aspirations and commitments that are expressive of a nation's past, as well as the determination of those within the society who seek in some ways to transcend that past. It is changeable but resistant to its own destruction, and it may manifest itself differently in different settings. (Jacobsohn 2011, 129–30)

Sometimes, as Jacobsohn goes on to suggest, different elements of constitutional identity may not only be in flux, but also in actual or potential disharmony with each other. The challenge of reconciling the twin characteristics of Israel as a Jewish and democratic state – of reconciling ethnos and demos – offers a good illustration of this point. This has significant implications for understandings of citizenship.

Israel's core state ideology of Zionism, which provides the basis for a co-ethnic preference for Jews in relation to immigration, stands in tension with modern citizenship's basic tenet of equality, not to mention certain democratic principles regarding self-rule. The Law of Return in effect regulates access to citizenship by Jewish returnees, so that the 1952 Law on Citizenship is largely limited in its application to Israel's non-Jewish immigrants and minorities (Harpaz and Herzog 2018). The underlying desire to preserve demographic balance has led, for example, to stark differences in family reunification rights for Jewish and non-Jewish Israelis (Masri 2013). Moreover, as Israel's patchwork constitution, comprised of Basic Laws enacted by the Knesset, has developed, further deep schisms have emerged (Masri 2017). The latest of these concerns the effects of the controversial Basic Law: Israel as the Nation-State of the Jewish People, finally passed in the summer of 2018, long after it was originally proposed.[15] The proponents of the text as adopted argue that the Law simply reiterates the point that Israel was founded to be the Jewish nation state. In that sense, it operates as a mission statement for Israel, containing details about specific manifestations of the state such as the flag, the anthem, and the connection to the Jewish diaspora (Koppel and Kontorovich 2018). Opposition centres on issues of equality, both in the context of individual rights and also in the context of the status of minorities within Israel (Brandes 2018b), along with references to other universal values and democracy. The Basic Law omits the complex, paradoxical and (arguably) balancing phrase: 'Israel as a Jewish and a democratic state.'[16]

Opposition has come not only from activists and scholars, but also from Israel's Arab citizen minority and, perhaps more significantly, from the Christian Druze minority who, in many respects, serve the state loyally, for example, in the army. Even the country's President, Reuvin Rivlin, has expressed opposition, castigating the Law as part of a trend of polarization of societies (in Israel and beyond) into 'them and us'.[17] In fact, criticisms of the Nation-State Law are quite widespread among liberal Zionists, as the extended coverage on the website of The Israel Democracy Institute highlights.[18] The lack of a widespread societal consensus on the details of the Law, which was passed by a narrow majority in the Knesset, has been widely noted (Harel 2018). One of the main aims of those proposing the law was, in fact, to reinforce the distinctiveness of Israel, and to resist what some saw as too much of a westernization and secularization of its legal system. It was interesting to see, therefore, the first usage of the Law before an Israeli court. A judge well known for his conservatism used it to justify imposing punitive damages on the Palestinian organization Hamas for the severe post-traumatic stress suffered by a Jewish Israeli person wounded in a terror attack in Tel Aviv in 1998. This was in addition to

---

[15] For details of the context of the Law, including a translation of its text, see Navot (2018).

[16] This phrase entered in the Israeli constitutional lexicon in the 1980s in the Basic Law: The Knesset and was given prominence in the important Basic Law: Human Dignity and Freedom, which lays down in Article 1 that 'The purpose of this Basic Law is to protect human dignity and liberty, in order to establish in a Basic Law the values of the State of Israel as a Jewish and democratic state.'

[17] T. Staff (2018) 'Israel's president: Nation-state law is "bad for Israel and bad for the Jews"', *The Times of Israel*, 6 September (www.timesofisrael.com/president-nation-state-law-bad-for-israel-and-bad-for-the-jews).

[18] The Israel Democracy Institute (2018).

the compensatory damages that the person was granted (Brandes, 2018b; Kremnitzer 2018).

Anti-Zionist critics, meanwhile, counter that the Nation-State Law should not surprise the liberal Zionists as it represents a logical extension of the direction of travel of the state and highlights the impossibility, ultimately, of triangulating democracy, equality and ethnic preference, as Israel has always sought to do.[19] An appeal against the Law to the Israeli Supreme Court brought by an organization representing the interests of Israel's Arab citizens has yet to be heard,[20] and it may be too soon to be sure what the effects of the Law will be (Fuchs 2019).

In similar terms to Jacobsohn, Rosenfeld argues that constitutional identity 'emerges in the context of a dynamic process that must constantly weave together self-identity's two facets, sameness and selfhood' (Rosenfeld 2012, 758). As a pluralist, Rosenfeld suggests that constitutional identity is 'the most basic means by which we seek to secure individual and communal pluralism' (Walker 2010, 679). For him, it is not an exclusionary concept. Rosenfeld sketches some ways in which this relates to citizenship:

> [C]onstitutional identity as it emerges through the prism of citizenship also projects an unresolved tension-filled state of affairs. Citizenship seems caught between its functional pole oriented towards the universal and its identitarian pole deeply entrenched in the particular. The constitutional subject as embodied in the citizen appears therefore split between an inclusionary self aspiring to the universal and an exclusionary self clinging to a singular community as against all others. (2009, 243)

Seyla Benhabib makes a related point, although couched in terms of the social contract:

> The tension between the universalistic scope of the principles that legitimize the social contract of the modern nation, and the claim of this nation to define itself as a closed community, plays itself out in the history of the reforms and revolutions of the last two centuries. (1999, 735)

---

[19] For a discussion, see Ben-Youssef and Tamari (2018) and Jabareen and Bishara (2019).
[20] HCJ 5866/18, *The High Follow-up Committee for Arab Citizens in Israel, et al v The Knesset* (www.adalah.org/uploads/uploads/Jewish_Nation_State_Law_Petition_English_Final_October_2018.pdf).

This suggests that constitutional identity is focused as much on the *process* of determining the 'we' as it is on the *outcome* of that process. This is what gives rise to its 'constructed', 'restless' character (Polzin 2017). It also suggests that elements of constitutional identity that are central to conceptions of citizenship may result from exogenous forces and factors, and, moreover, require political and sociological investigation.

However, other scholars have focused on the task of identifying the unchanging elements of any constitutional set-up, and argue that constitutional identity effectively captures the assumed essence of the state, rather than the tensions within it (Troper 2010). This seems to be largely a court-driven phenomenon. To some extent, in the European context, this approach has been strongly influenced by the existence of a multilevel constitutional framework in which national apex (supreme or constitutional) courts have been concerned about the encroachment on their prerogatives as a result of EU law and of the interpretations provided by the CJEU. Accordingly, these national courts have laid down markers to define the limits of EU law *vis-à-vis* national law by highlighting the essence of the national constitutional framework.[21] In that context, the national courts have been disarmed by the invocation, by the CJEU, of the so-called 'common constitutional traditions' of the Member States. This could be taken to suggest that there are, in fact, no stark dissonances between those different national constitutional traditions. But this would be a hard point to prove empirically, unless one limits the discussion to high-level concepts such as 'separation of powers' or 'rule of law'. Inevitably, therefore, those apex courts have bitten back, asserting their own spheres of interest and competence, often focused on the unity of the 'national people'. In the case of Germany, this involves harking back to a much longer tradition of upholding ideas of 'constitutional identity' (Polzin 2016). In the current conjuncture, to which we shall return in Chapter 6 when we focus on populism, constitutionalism and citizenship, it is an important and contested question as to whether this identity will be interpreted, by powerful political and legal actors, in civic or in ethnocultural terms (Kovács 2017).

These comments draw us back to the critique, made in Chapter 2, of the ethno-cultural/civic divide as the basis for distinguishing between citizenship regimes and different ideas of constitutional citizenship. While such ideas are often an important part of how constitutional citizenship plays out in specific national or temporal contexts,[22] we should not

---

[21] For analysis, see Fabbrini and Sajó (2019) and van der Schyff and Callies (2019).

[22] See the different 'constitutional visions of the nation' presented in Jakab (2016, Chapter 10).

allow the appealing yet potentially misleading idea of a binary divide to become emblematic or explanatory in relation to understanding matters of constitutional identity. As I explained in Chapter 2, the better view is to take full account of all contextual factors and processes of change when assessing and interpreting citizenship regimes, and constitutional citizenship in particular. This would necessarily include the way that non-dominant actors within a polity contest the scope of citizenship. The contextual approach is also the best way of articulating the interface between constitutional identity and constitutional citizenship in the context of states that do not conform to what remains, in scholarly terms, the western liberal democratic norm for thinking about constitutions. These include the communitarian constitutions of some states of South East Asia that impose communal duties on citizens, for example to promote religious harmony (Thio 2019).

The ethnic/civic divide likewise works poorly in a post-colonial context, where we can see many examples of an 'anti-colonial nationalism', which unites the whole population and which fuels the initial transformation from 'imperial subject' to citizen, evolving in tension with emergent majoritarian nationalisms focused on religious, linguistic or ethnic divides (Sadiq 2017, 184–7). Over time, these have influenced in significant ways the figure of the constitutional citizen, not least in large, diverse democracies such as India (Jayal 2013, Rodrigues 2008). Equally, and this may be a provocative contention, there may be something of the 'post-colonial' in the situation in which the post-communist states of central, eastern and south eastern Europe have found themselves since 1989 (Fowkes and Hailbronner 2019). Since a widespread turn to populism and even authoritarianism can be discerned, including in several states that are now EU Member States, and since this turn has often played out in constitutional amendments and constitutional interpretations, the question needs to be asked whether there is a liberal 'norm' against which these should be judged. If there is, is it an appropriate yardstick for states still in transition?

These reflections all reinforce the point that 'constitutional identity', and its articulation with constitutional citizenship, can never simply be a question of describing any given constitutional set-up straight from the text.[23] On the contrary, it is something that can only be made sense of in the light of context, history and the various theories that illuminate

---

[23] This is also the implication of the line of scholarship that treats constitutions as a specialist form of 'memory law', that is to say, a 'political construction rooted in the process of selecting, creating and marketing a certain conception of the past' (Miklóssy and Nyyssönen 2018, 323).

the tensions between ideas of community and universality developed by scholars such as Rosenfeld and Benhabib.

The complex relationship between text and context is nicely illustrated if we focus briefly on the case of Australia. Australia's Constitution does not directly regulate citizenship, as highlighted in Chapter 2. It does, however, mention the citizen's 'other', the alien, as one subject where the federal parliament has power to legislate. Section 44(i) of the Australian Constitution also discusses 'foreign powers' and 'allegiance, obedience or adherence' thereto as the basis for prohibiting dual citizens from standing for election and being elected as members of the federal parliament.[24] (We will discuss this issue further in Chapter 4, when exploring the constitutional dimension of dual citizenship.) The wording of 'allegiance' to a foreign power might be thought of as being a hangover from the time when the Australian Constitution was adopted, at the beginning of the 20th century. At that time, Australia was still a dominion within the British Empire and there was no status of Australian citizen, but merely that of 'British subject'. This latter point highlights why there is no head of power in the Australian Constitution to regulate citizenship as it would have been inappropriate at the time. Over time, despite the emergence of Australian citizenship as an autonomous legal status after independence, that sense of subjecthood has been read back into the judicial interpretation of Section 44(1).[25] This has reinforced a somewhat anachronistic notion that the mischief of dual citizenship (for parliamentarians at least) is the impossibility of dual allegiance and the inference, from the text of the Constitution, that the person who owes allegiance elsewhere somehow measures this as outweighing, or certainly substantially undermining, her allegiance to Australia.

Allegiance – or lack of it – has also played a role in the increasingly fraught debates about deprivation of citizenship in Australia under the Australian Citizenship Amendment (Allegiance to Australia) Act 2015, offering an important example of the statutory regulation of citizenship being conducted under the shadow of a purportedly central element of the Australian polity. In practice, as Helen Irving (2019) shows, the concept is slippery and elusive, and fails to offer a secure constitutional foundation for the radical practice of citizenship deprivation.

One further important dimension of allegiance concerns its relationship with ideas of community. What type of theory of citizenship can provide a satisfactory account of the level and type of allegiance that citizens must

---

[24] See Australia 1901 (rev. 1985) (www.constituteproject.org/constitution/Australia_ 1985?lang=en).

[25] *Re Canavan* [2017] 91 ALJR 1209.

show to 'their' institutions in order to maintain effective community cohesion, without incurring the accusation of being closed to outsiders (Gustavsson 2019)? Reflections on this question can produce some paradoxical outcomes. For the liberal states of western Europe and North America in an age of global migration, questions of boundaries have become most salient around the dynamics of immigration and integration and the possible reciprocal adjustments that need to be made between different communities.[26] A 'thin' theory of community cohesion might be equated with a commitment to constitutional institutions – a form of 'constitutional patriotism' (Müller 2007) – which can scarcely be said to be placing an insurmountable demand on the newcomer in terms of her adjustment to her new circumstances. Oaths of allegiance to a constitution may raise some issues,[27] but they are less demanding than, say, more nebulous cultural requirements embedded in civic integration tests or similar requirements, which, in practice, often represent a means of ensuring the hegemony of the dominant majoritarian culture (Mouritsen et al 2019). The situation is quite different in some of the states of central and eastern Europe. Levels of recent immigration are typically much lower, but unresolved insecurities about cultural and ethnic diversity from the recent or more distant past may remain. In this context, the challenges posed by migration have been raised to the level of an existential threat to 'constitutional identity', with all the uncertainty – given the constructed nature of that identity – about what that might mean in practice for the newcomer or member of a non-majoritarian group (Körtvélyesi and Majtényi 2017). After a brief discussion later in this chapter of the case of Hungary, we will explore this issue in more detail in Chapter 6.

Equality, dignity and related constitutional principles in conversation with citizenship

Citizenship has long been mythologized as a central dimension of the most desirable condition for humanity, namely that which permits the 'fullest realization of human capacities' (Hindess 2004, 308). Yet the reality is quite different. Citizenship's struggles with equality and dignity, on which this section will focus most closely, are just one of several troubling dimensions of citizenship. Or, to put it in the vivid words of Linda Kerber:

---

[26] For a review of the main issues, articulating the range of questions raised in a special issue to which this is the introduction, see Bast and Orgad (2017).

[27] For a liberal argument against loyalty oaths, see Orgad (2014).

> ... the dream of an unranked citizenship has always been in tension with the waking knowledge of a citizenship to which people came by different routes, bounded by gender, race, and class identities. (Kerber 1997, 846)

The relationship between citizenship, constitutions and equality was noted by Aristotle, who famously stated that 'in most constitutional states the citizens rule and are ruled by turns, for the idea of a constitutional state implies that the natures of the citizens are equal, and do not differ at all.'[28] Of course, equally famously, Aristotle only considered a very narrow class of people to be 'citizens', using tests of 'like' and 'unlike' in order to identify precisely who was to be in the most favoured class capable of self-government, thus excluding slaves and women. So clearly Aristotle's concept of equality would differ from that which is commonly applied in liberal democracies in the 21st century, but equally the point highlights an enduring issue: does the core of the problem lie in the scope of the concept of citizenship, or in the unequal allocation of rights? A more recent version of the equality mantra comes from T.H. Marshall (1992, 18): 'Citizenship is a status bestowed on those who are full members of a community. All who possess the status are equal with respect to the rights and duties with which the status is endowed.' So we are back with the same problem. How do we ensure such 'fullness'? What tools exist to guarantee full membership for all? T.H. Marshall's perhaps overoptimistic prospectus of a stepwise evolution through civil rights, political rights to social rights, with a core focus on equality, even if it could be regarded as applicable beyond the case of England on which he was focusing when he wrote his famous essay, has encountered significant challenges more or less since the moment it was published early in the postwar era.

More recently, from the economic recession of the 1970s engendered by the oil crisis to the continued political choice for austerity in many countries during the long economic tail of the financial crisis of the late 2000s, via the transition of the former socialist countries after 1989 to neoliberal welfare state systems (Polese et al 2014), welfare states across the world have faced relentless challenges and pressures for adjustment to new conditions.[29] Equality, we can already discern, was never going to have a simple relationship to citizenship, despite the prevalence of general guarantees of equality, which appear in nearly every single constitution

---

[28] *The Politics*, Book 1, 12.

[29] For discussion, see Farnsworth and Irving (2012), Greve (2012) and Kennett and Lendvai-Bainton (2017).

in the world (186 of the 193 in-force constitutions collected by the Constitute project). For example, 167 of those constitutions have some form of gender equality clause, even though, in respect of many aspects of citizenship-as-membership, women still face entrenched discrimination and higher levels of socioeconomic hardship right across the world. Constitutionalized gender equality does not match the reality (MacKinnon 2012; World Bank 2017). Equality guarantees in constitutions, while more prevalent than detailed provisions on citizenship, take such a huge variety of different forms that it is hard to draw any general conclusions about the place of equality in constitutional law (Baer 2012).

The modern ideal of citizenship demands a form of equality defined by reference to universal personhood. It starts, in that sense, as a 'thin' and 'formal' concept. But the reality of citizenship in practice is often one of differentiation, especially in relation to issues of status and rights (van Waas and Jaghai 2018). Drawing on Elizabeth Cohen's insight that we should think of citizenship as a 'gradient category',[30] thus treating instances of what she terms 'semi-citizenship' as a normal part of the panoply of citizenship-related statuses but with variable access to rights, it is not hard to think of examples that challenge the ideal of equality. Those whose access to rights as citizens may be incomplete include children, those with disabilities or mental illnesses (Pincock 2018), people in poverty and/or excluded from the labour market, indigenous or (ethnic, linguistic or religious) minority communities, prisoners (McGinnis 2018), LGBTQ+ people, along with women. Migrants may find it hard to accede to the formal status of citizen. In any culturally diverse society, in any society even, it may be hard to say what 'equal' actually means, given the cross-cutting elements of legal, socioeconomic, political and cultural definitions of equality, the fundamental distinction between formal and substantive equality, and the cross-cutting and intersectional nature of most equality claims (Crenshaw 1989, 1991). The case of the US citizenship of Puerto Ricans provides a good example of this phenomenon. Puerto Ricans do not enjoy birthright US citizenship under the Constitution, but citizenship established by statute, and the manner in which this works its way through the US political and legal system means that Puerto Ricans experience a citizenship that is partial, differentiated and imbricated by a complex politics of race.[31]

Differentiation may be a vehicle for inequality, but, as Iris Marion Young (1989) has shown, it may also be essential for the purposes of giving all groups and individuals voice under circumstances where some

---

[30] See Cohen (2009), especially Chapter 3.
[31] For discussion see Perez (2008) and Valle (2019).

may lack the capacity otherwise to participate in the general will that is assumed to be part of the paradoxical universality of citizenship. These are the many structural dimensions of inequality, as opposed to mere instances of individual or group prejudice. Indeed, as Chris Thornhill shows, there is more to 'equality' than simply formal claims on the part of citizens. It goes to the very foundations of the polity. Thornhill argues that:

> The constitutional construct of the citizen contains the implication that the state obtains legitimacy by recognizing all citizens as equal rights holders, such that laws are only likely to be seen as legitimate if they are applied equally to all persons and if they provide protection for shared rights. (2018, S74)

Equality also has political dimensions, in the sense that it is not something that is only 'given' to citizens, but also something over which they deliberate and indeed disagree (Bellamy 2001). Some states acknowledge and engage with the issue of differentiated citizenship in ways that seek the accommodation of difference. Will Kymlicka and Wayne Norman provide a helpful resumé of the types of claims raised by different cultural or other groups, that might challenge the equality norm. They highlight eight items, listed here:

> Exemptions from laws that penalize or burden cultural practices; ... assistance to do things the majority (or otherwise privileged group) can do unassisted; ... self-government for national minorities and indigenous communities; ... external rules restricting non-members' liberty in order to protect members' culture, internal rules for members' conduct that are enforced by ostracism and excommunication; ... incorporation and enforcement of traditional or religious legal codes within the dominant legal system; ... special representation of groups or their members within government institutions; ... [and] symbolic recognition of the worth, status, or existence of various groups within the larger state community. (Kymlicka and Norman 2000, 25–30)

We can anticipate that measures responding to such claims – which amount to important cases of recognition of difference – might impact on all of the dimensions of citizenship, whether as status, bundle of rights or identity. Acknowledging that 'differentiated citizenship is not a contradiction in terms, nor even particularly uncommon', Kymlicka and Norman have an important question:

[W]hen do differentiated rights involve some real disadvantage or stigmatization (and not just difference) in citizenship status – eg some inequality in respect, or in life chances, or in influence over government policy? That is, when does differentiated status start to create first-and second-class citizens? (Kymlicka and Norman 2000, 32)

That is to say, the question is *when*, and I might add *how*, does equality come into play, and *how* does it affect constitutional citizenship (either of the affected group or of the 'majority')? But equality does not sit alone. Other constitutional provisions can also interact with equality claims, including those relating to human dignity, autonomy, solidarity and cultural diversity.

For our purposes, it is helpful to focus on dignity and to consider its relationship with citizenship. Ideas about dignity not only as the foundation of much thinking about the human condition but also as a key element of political organization long predate the explosion of constitutional references to dignity after the Second World War. More than 150 constitutions worldwide in fact now refer to (human) dignity as a foundational concept or a right or freedom to be protected by law. But in studying dignity and citizenship, Jeremy Waldron (2013, 333) goes much further back than the Second World War and reasons, following Immanuel Kant, that 'citizenship is a certain sort of dignity', in that it is, at least in part, a status concept. Waldron shows that citizenship as a status, as a 'dignity', shares much in common with 'human dignity'. In particular, this lies in the capacity of this idea, this prize, to be cherished universally, even though each and every one of us in a community has it, or ought to have it. The act of sharing does not reduce the value of either citizenship or dignity in our eyes. Together, what Waldron describes as 'the normal or normative incidents of citizenship' 'add up to a status in each polity that is special, equal, and pervasive' (Waldron 2013, 334). It is the pervasiveness of citizenship that allows us to tie it to constitutions, the latter being the similarly pervasive foundation stones of polity formation and maintenance in our (still, at least partially) Westphalian world (Glenn 2013).

In this regard, the 'dignity of the citizen' operates as one way in which we, as humans, can assist in the realisation of 'human dignity'. There are cracks in the edifice, as we shall see in subsequent chapters, especially as regards loss of citizenship, the lack of citizenship for many groups of migrants, and statelessness. The infliction of loss of dignity is one eloquent way of capturing the consequences of some state policies on the attribution and loss of citizenship (as we shall see in Chapter 4). The idea of citizenship as a dignity may not effectively capture all of the collective as well as the individual work that the concept of polity membership is doing, when we consider the constitutive role of citizens in public deliberations and the role of such deliberations in settling disagreements about what constitutes the good life. Even so, the aspiration is clear, both as regards the idea of the dignity of the citizen as part of a self-ruling community and the link between citizenship and (universal) human dignity, leaving the conclusion that it is useful, when thinking about the constitutional norms that underpin citizenship, to include dignity as well as equality.

The interplay of equality, dignity, and religious and cultural differentiation provides a good example of the complex issues at play here. In the case of bans on women wearing burqas, or similar face-coverings such as niqābs, in certain situations, we can see how ostensibly neutral measures can burden the exercise of citizenship and challenge norms of equality and freedom (of religion and in relation to private life). While facially neutral, such laws have the effect of restricting the occupation of public space in particular by women from one specific religious group, namely Islam. France is the country that has received most attention in respect of the taking of measures relating to burqas and niqābs (building on earlier measures relating to the wearing of the hijab, or headscarf, for example in public schools). France has ostensibly adopted these measures in pursuit of the fundamental republican principle of laïcité, or the secularized state in which religion and public affairs are kept separate. Its other published motivation is to defend a notion of 'living together' in public space. France's laws, including one banning the wearing of full-face coverings in public, have survived judicial scrutiny both at the national level and, perhaps more surprisingly, in the European Court of Human Rights (Mechoulan 2018).[32] The latter Court concluded, by a majority, that such a national measure, although it falls within the scope of Article 9 ECHR (protecting freedom of religion), can be justified by reference to the principle of vivre ensemble (living together),[33] accepting the French government argument that facial visibility is necessary for the purposes of proper socialization within an open and democratic society. In contrast, the United Nations Human Rights Committee (a quasi-judicial body) found that the ban did violate the human rights to religious freedom of two women who were fined for wearing the niqāb, on the grounds that a general criminal ban on wearing the niqāb

---

[32] SAS v France [2014] ECHR 695.

[33] On the concept of living together, see Patrignani (2018).

outside the home failed to find the appropriate balance between public and private interests.[34]

Even before the ban on full-face veils was adopted, the wearing of the niqāb had previously been used as the basis for refusing citizenship on the grounds of insufficient assimilation in French society.[35] Citizenship has also been refused to a Moroccan man who forced his wife to wear the niqāb[36] and to a woman who refused, on religious grounds, to shake hands with a male official at a citizenship ceremony.[37] The latter ruling was upheld by the *Conseil d'État*.[38] By way of contrast, in Canada the federal courts set aside a policy to refuse naturalization to women wearing niqābs at their citizenship ceremonies, introduced in 2011 (Macklin 2017b). This was a different approach to that adopted in France, as it did not treat the wearing of a full-face veil as evidence of lack of assimilation, but instead attached importance to being unveiled and visible to the public at the citizenship ceremony itself. While arguments based on breach of freedom of religion, as protected by the Canadian Charter of Rights and Freedoms, were prepared and put before the courts, the federal courts in fact set aside the policy on the administrative law grounds that the minister who adopted the measures was exceeding his powers.[39] The Charter argument based on freedom of religion was never considered during the legal challenge, so it is not clear precisely what the relationship between the citizenship ceremony and freedom of religion might be in such a context. Meanwhile, when considering the impact of measures taken against the wearing of full-face veils, it is worth noting that in Canada, France and Belgium and in other countries where they have been introduced or considered, measures relating to the full-face veil will only apply to very small numbers of women

---

[34] OHCHR (Office of the High Commissioner for Human Rights) (2018) 'France: Banning the niqab violated two Muslim women's freedom of religion – UN experts', 23 October (www.ohchr.org/EN/NewsEvents/Pages/DisplayNews.aspx?NewsID=23750&LangID=E).

[35] For background, see Vakulenko (2009) and Hajjat (2010a, b).

[36] L. Davies (2010) 'France denies citizenship to Moroccan man who forces wife to wear full veil', *The Guardian*, 2 February (www.theguardian.com/world/2010/feb/02/france-values-republic-veil-women).

[37] A. Breeden (2018) 'No handshake, no citizenship, French Court tells Algerian woman', *The New York Times*, 22 April.

[38] ECLI:FR:CECHR:2018:412462.20180411.

[39] *Ishaq v Canada* (Minister of Citizenship and Immigration) 2015 FC 156; *Ishaq v Canada* (Minister of Citizenship and Immigration) 2015 FCA 194.

(Brems 2014; Macklin 2017a).[40] And unlike some previous moral panics over the wearing of religiously based head coverings, such as the Sikh turban, there is an intersectional gender element involved on top of the religious and often racial overtones. On those grounds alone, it is hard to see why these measures should survive a rigorous proportionality assessment, when their impact on individuals is measured against their wider societal impact.

It is possible to see conflicts around the wearing of certain types of religious dress as being products of the high levels of anti-Muslim sentiment present within many states at the present time, especially, but not only, in Europe (Dauvergne 2019; Law et al 2019). In this context, the question of what types of clothing are worn by tiny numbers of Muslim women becomes a proxy for a widespread fear of Muslims as racialized and threatening 'others' (Edwards 2016; Burchardt and Griera 2019). But as Ronan McCrea (2013) has pointed out, bans on full-face veils are often defended on grounds of protecting the interests of the liberal and secular state, as well as on grounds of egalitarianism. However, this must be an egalitarianism of a very paternalistic type, involving levels of coercion that go well beyond the ordinary force of law, if it is to be grounded in the conclusion that the wearing of a full-face veil or other form of clothing (for example, the so-called 'burqini' on the beach) is presumptively bad for the 'equality' of a woman who freely chooses to wear it (Howard 2012). It is interesting to note the contrasting reaction of the Spanish Supreme Court, which, unlike its judicial neighbours in France, pointed out that banning the full-face veil would be likely to undermine 'living together', because its effect would be either to coerce women who chose to wear the veil to remain within the private space, or to force them to compromise on deeply held religious commitments.[41]

As Amélie Barras has argued, in relating the debate about Islam in France back to the issue of citizenship, Muslims in France are captured by various discourses of *laïcité* and security (after the terrorist attacks of 2015) which, taken together,

> ... project an image of French Muslims defined almost
> exclusively in terms of a fixed and rigid religious identity,
> which is constructed as incompatible with "the Republic, our

---

[40] A. Yuhas and C. Moses (2019) 'Dutch officials decline to enforce new partial ban on burqas', *The New York Times*, 1 August. Only an estimated 150–400 of the Netherlands population of 17 million wear full face-covering veils.

[41] As discussed and quoted in Michaels (2018, 231).

values, equality between men and women".[42] This discursive apparatus forecloses any possibility of capturing the complexity of being and commitments of French Muslims, as well as the variability of religious practices. (Barras 2017, 928)

The same, she argues, could be said about the discourse of 'living together'.[43] This point links the discussion on the full-face veil back to the discussion of constitutional identity above, and the challenge for minority groups facing hegemonic majoritarian cultures projecting what amounts to a *Leitkultur*.[44] In this case, it is a public culture that continues to treat Islam as an invasive 'other'. Barras concludes that a renewal of French (constitutional) citizenship can only be achieved through recognition and respect for difference, rather than a coercive push for more sameness.

Complex examples of multiple and potentially conflicting equality objectives enshrined in constitutional texts are often to be found in the post-colonial and/or transitional contexts.[45] Two contrasting examples come from India[46] and South Africa.[47] Both of these countries have long struggled with reconciling unity and diversity. Substantive as well as formal guarantees of equality are included in both constitutions, although the approaches taken in the texts and in subsequent judicial interpretations are strikingly different.[48]

For South Africa, with a history of restricted citizenship during the apartheid era, it has become a cardinal principle of the concept of constitutional citizenship not only that it should be 'equal' (Klaaren 2010)

---

[42] A quotation from then Prime Minister Manuel Valls: see L. Joffrin, G. Biseau, L. Alemagna and L. Bretton (2016) 'Manuel Valls, "Depuis plus de trente ans, on me demande si je suis de gauche"', *Libération*, 13 April (www.liberation.fr/france/2016/04/12/manuel-valls-depuis-plus-de-trente-ans-on-me-demande-si-je-suis-degauche_1445774).

[43] See Trispiotis (2016).

[44] Literally 'leading' or 'guiding' culture. While increasingly used in Germany, the concept remains controversial: see Scholz (2017).

[45] For further discussion on whether and how it is possible for postcolonial citizenship to be 'equal', see Coetzee (2019).

[46] See India 1949 (rev. 2016) (www.constituteproject.org/constitution/India_2016?lang=en).

[47] See South Africa 1996 (rev. 2012) (www.constituteproject.org/constitution/South_Africa_2012?lang=en).

[48] For contrasts in the ways in which South Africa and India deal with gender equality, compare MacKinnon (2006) and Kapur (2016) with Cold-Ravnkilde (2019).

but also that it should reflect the equal dignity of all humans.[49] Apartheid effectively alienated non-whites from the enjoyment of most citizenship rights, including the right to vote and the right to choose where they reside. South Africa provides an example where constitutional change has helped to liberate a country from a narrow, exclusivist and racist project of citizenship. The post-apartheid South African Constitution accordingly emphasizes in § 3 that there is a *common* South African citizenship in which rights and obligations are held *equally* (Hobden 2018, 2). § 20 also expressly excludes deprivation of citizenship, although the legislation none the less provides for a number of ways in which South African citizenship can be lost. The strength of the guarantee has yet to be judicially tested to the full.

In India, issues of equality cut across questions of gender, religious, caste and socioeconomic difference. Among the strongest (and most passionately defended) provisions of the Constitution are those establishing 'reservations', including for 'Scheduled Tribes', 'Scheduled Castes' and 'Other Backward Classes' (Sitapati 2016). Over time, dissonances have emerged between the welfarist and equality goals of the Constitution, with measures taken to mark out those who benefit from those provisions in ways that risk perpetuating histories of stigma:

> To the extent that welfare provisioning is not universal, it is detached from the equality of citizenship that obtains in the case of, say, the civil and political rights of citizenship. Those who are entitled to welfare by virtue of their poverty or lower incomes are also formally citizens, entitled to civil and political rights. However, they have to belong to especially denominated categories in order to enjoy the additional provisioning of welfare, which is contingent upon their belonging to groups designated as especially deserving. On the one hand, by making them visible and legible to the state, this strategy furthers the goal of inclusion and lends substance to their notionally equal civic status. On the other hand, it also stigmatises them as well as the welfare services to which they are entitled. (Jayal 2019b, 45)

Both these constitutions offer illustrations of how processes of constitution-making and subsequent polity-building can be adapted to facilitate the struggle to work against historic disadvantages or inequalities across many

---

[49] The dignity point comes across particularly clearly in the discussion of prisoner voting in post-apartheid South Africa in Chapter 5, 'Voting and the imposition of citizenship and residence qualifications'.

vectors of privilege and disadvantage, and highlight the challenges of matching together social citizenship and political participation.[50]

But do constitutions really matter?

Is there a gap between rhetoric and reality when it comes to constitutional citizenship? Dennis Galligan (2013a) argues that there is, and uses an analysis of how 65 constitutions, all more or less democratic in character, deal with issues of 'the people' and 'sovereignty' in order to make the point. He points out that many of these references are 'we the people'-type preambular and exhortatory statements. In addition, 'the people' may also put in an occasional appearance in those provisions related to processes of constitutional approval and amendment, and in those concerned with the election of representatives (Galligan 2013b). Galligan concludes that not only are there very significant differences in approach between different countries, which are hard to systematize or thematize, but that there is also a substantial gap between the symbolism and the empirical materials that he has charted. He asserts that 'Modern constitutions use the concept of the people liberally, without explanation, and without definition' (Galligan 2013a, 705).

From Galligan's perspective, the idea that the constitution belongs to 'the people' might be said to be a convenient fiction that can barely be sustained as fact on the basis of a detailed assessment of the content of constitutions or an interpretation of what they signify. There is, in reality, little to be found in constitutional texts that goes beyond the superficial invocation in a legal and constitutional context of the types of ideas developed by political theorists as ideal types or cited by judges fond of the odd constitutional flourish. This situation amounts, in Galligan's view, to a sovereignty deficit. He concludes that, 'if sovereignty is the concept through which the people express self-government and hence democracy, then constitutions fall far short of being clear and firm affirmations of government for the people, by the people, of the people' (Galligan 2013a, 730).

Not all scholars agree with Galligan's assessment. Adeno Addis (2018) takes a less restrictive view of the heft of declaratory statements of peoplehood often to be found in national constitutional preambles, suggesting that we should view these statements as 'autobiographies', drawing on the historical synopses, references to divine authority or

---

[50] See also a similar argument made in respect of Brazil, which is another large and diverse country: Hunter and Sugiyama (2014).

invocations of sources of law (for example, international law) that they often offer. His argument is that these types of statements should open rather than close conversations about constitutional identity, as he cleaves to a normative and perhaps aspirational position in which stories of peoplehood are ongoing and never completed. Certainly, they are often contested, as can be seen from the conflict over the Preamble to the 1997 Polish Constitution.[51] The Preamble that was adopted is something of a compromise, inevitably pleasing no one. It refers to 'We, the Polish Nation', but then invokes 'all citizens of the Republic', suggesting a more demotic approach. It refers to both 'those who believe in God as the source of truth, justice, good and beauty', as well as 'those not sharing such faith but respecting those universal values as arising from other sources.' This position reflected a balance felt necessary at the time, and needs to be seen in the context of the insight drawn by Anna Śledzińska-Simon (2015) that after its establishment, the Polish Constitutional Tribunal was 'militant' in evoking a sense of national constitutional identity in 'the preservation of national identity in areas related to the nation's history, culture, or religion.'

These personal 'biographies' can certainly change, and are subject to manipulation by political forces. This is certainly true in Poland (Sadurski 2019). Furthermore, small changes can already make a considerable difference to core narratives or to constitutional identity, and thus affect citizenship in both its internal and external aspects. Hungary is a case in point. It was the only central and eastern European state not to adopt a new constitution after the end of the Cold War in 1989. In fact, the adoption of a formal constitution for Hungary was delayed until 2011 (although it has since been amended several times, most recently in 2018).[52] It was a highly politicized and controversial process when it happened, as the text sought to address not only negative dimensions of the communist era, but also Hungary's perceived unjust treatment in relation to boundaries under the Treaty of Trianon after the First World War. The process has deep historical roots (Miklóssy and Nyyssönen 2018). The name of the state was changed from the *Republic of* Hungary to 'Hungary', and the Preamble to what is termed the 'Fundamental Law' now refers to 'the Hungarian Nation', reinforcing links with diaspora/external Hungarians

---

[51] For analysis of the Preamble to the Constitution of Poland, see Poland 1997 (rev. 2009) (www.constituteproject.org/constitution/Poland_2009?lang=en); see also Zubrzycki (2001), Hałas (2005) and Popławska (2011).

[52] The most recent version of the Hungarian Constitution is not available via the Constitute project. See instead The Fundamental Law of Hungary (www.kormany. hu/download/f/3e/61000/TheFundamentalLawofHungary_20180629_FIN.pdf).

(and their descendants) in neighbouring states, who have been given increased access to Hungarian citizenship on a 'restitutionary' ethnic basis in recent years, as well as the right to participate in national elections as external voters (Pogonyi 2017). Thus Hungary, so defined, is not a nation of its citizens but the nation of a 'people' (Körtvélyesi 2012). This change to the definition of constitutional identity is only one example of what has since become a substantial constitutional change to the balance of power in Hungary. These changes have facilitated the evolution of an authoritarian populism in Hungarian politics, dominated by the ruling *Fidesz* party. We will return to the impact of changes in Hungary when discussing *ius sanguinis* in Chapter 4, and then look in more detail at these questions, through the prism of opposition to (non-European) migration, in Chapter 6, under the rubric of citizenship and populism.

Away from the preamble, we can also find statements in the body of constitutions about the foundations of citizenship. While we might have expected these to have helped in the task of showing that citizenship is more than, for example, just a club membership, in practice invocations of citizenship as the basis of any given constitution seem to add more in terms of symbolism than they do in terms of 'heft' (Macklin 2007). This is indeed what Galligan's analysis of 'the people' seems to suggest will be the case. A good example can be found in the recent and generally progressive Tunisian Constitution of 2014 introduced after the revolution in 2011. It boldly declares in Article 2 that 'Tunisia is a civil state based on citizenship, the will of the people, and the supremacy of law',[53] but offers little detail to flesh this out in terms of citizenship as a status, with the exception of a guarantee against deprivation of nationality in Article 25. One must look to the ordinary law and other sources for further direction on citizenship, and this has changed little if at all since the 2014 Constitution (Parolin 2009; Albarazi 2017), raising the question of what the impact of the new constitution might actually be.[54] However, the Constitution does go on to make extensive reference to citizens' rights and duties, including social rights and political participation rights, reinforcing once more the point made above that invocations of equality can often offer more in the way of substance than mere constitutional invocations of citizenship, and indeed that these concepts can help to fill out the substance of citizenship (Santini 2018, Chapter 1).

---

[53] Article 2, Tunisia 2014 (www.constituteproject.org/constitution/Tunisia_2014?lang=en).

[54] *Code de la nationalité Tunisienne*, 2011 (bringing together much earlier laws) (downloaded from globalcit.eu).

Some constitutional dispositions on citizenship, however, undoubtedly do have a value belong the merely symbolic. The 14th Amendment to the US Constitution provides an excellent example. It was expressly introduced to cement the citizenship of African Americans after the end of slavery, in the face of the problematic Supreme Court judgment in *Dred Scott*.[55] As such, it stands out as a special case. We will return to the US definition of citizenship in the following chapter, as it refers specifically to one mode of acquisition, namely birthright *ius soli*. Having one mode of acquisition constitutionally entrenched in this manner raises many interesting legal and political questions.

Rubenstein and Lenagh-Maguire (2011, 148) venture the hypothesis that definitions of citizenship are more likely to be included in constitutions after traumatic events. There is some evidence to support that proposition, with examples including not only the US Constitution after slavery, but also the South African Constitution after the trauma of apartheid. In some cases, such as France, citizenship was originally included in the constitution straight after the Revolution, but was already 'moved' to the ordinary law on the adoption of the *code civil* in 1804. Historical trauma is also one reason why many post-communist countries have limited the possibility of loss of citizenship except where it is given up voluntarily by a citizen, in the light of historic experience. Article 34(2) of the Polish Constitution probihits the loss of Polish citizenship except by renunciation. Article 116(2) of the German Basic Law (*Grundgesetz*) provides for the restoration of citizenship to 'former German citizens, who between 30 January 1933 and 8 May 1945 were deprived of their citizenship on political, racial, or religious grounds, and their descendants'. Citizenship is to be restored 'on application'.[56]

Similarly, for historical reasons, Article 9(2)(1) of the Irish Constitution proclaims birth 'on the island of Ireland' to give an entitlement and

---

[55] See note 2 above.

[56] The implementation of this constitutional provision has become more controversial in recent times. Since the Brexit referendum in June 2016, the increase in the number of applications from the UK, especially from the descendants of Jews who escaped Nazi Germany, has highlighted some of the exclusions from the scope of Article 116 GG, which are not apparent on the face of the text, such as inequalities between descendants of men and women who were exiled and lost their citizenship, and differences based on precisely when the persecuted person lost his or her citizenship. For more details, see Whitehouse (2019) and the website of the Article 116 Exclusions Group (www. article116exclusionsgroup.org/). The German Government has resorted to special measures relating to discretionary naturalisation in order to ameliorate some of the gaps (see https://uk.diplo.de/uk-en/02/citizenship/renaturalisation), but this has not satisfied the critics who call on Germany to live up to the spirit of the Constitution.

birthright to be part of the 'Irish nation'. This was universally interpreted as instituting a *ius soli* provision at the level of the Constitution. Consequently, Ireland required a referendum to amend that provision in order to permit the *Dáil* to legislate to restrict *ius soli* entitlements only to the children of citizens or persons with lawful and long-term residence (Shaw 2007).[57] Ireland's constitutional provisions that extend its citizenship territory throughout the island, including those parts of the island over which it does not exercise governmental authority, that is, Northern Ireland, find a counterpart in UK law, in the sense that the UK accepts that those born in Northern Ireland are entitled to identify as British, Irish or both as their 'birthright'. There is no formal constitutional or even statutory provision on this as such in UK law, but it forms an important part of the Good Friday Agreement or Belfast Agreement.[58]

To put the implications of this in context, some words about the UK legal framework are needed. Since the UK does not have a written constitution, it can be rather difficult to discern what the constitutional fundamentals of citizenship might be, in large measure because of the piecemeal manner in which it is regulated. At the end of the 2010s, a review commission was charged by then Prime Minister Gordon Brown with investigating what might lie at the heart of citizenship in the UK.[59] The commission's report struggled to identify precisely what this 'common bond' might be composed of, and expressed concern that in many respects UK citizenship seems to be diluted as a concept by, for example, the historical anomaly of the voting rights that are given to Irish citizens and Commonwealth citizens in the UK (Shaw 2009). This ambiguity lies behind the difficulties inherent in identifying the boundaries of citizenship, especially in Northern Ireland.

---

[57] It should be noted that there continues to be opposition to this change within Ireland, and the opposition Labour Party recently proposed to introduce legislation to allow the *Dáil* to legislate for a more generous approach to the children of migrants: see B. Howlin (2018) 'Labour to bring forward legislation to amend citizenship law', Statement, Labour, 20 October (www.labour.ie/news/2018/10/20/labour-to-bring-forward-legislation-to-amend-citiz). The proposal was supported in the Upper House, the Seanad: see M. O'Halloran (2018) 'Seanad backs giving citizenship rights to all Irish-born children', *Irish Times*, 21 November (www.irishtimes.com/news/politics/oireachtas/seanad-backs-giving-citizenship-rights-to-all-irish-born-children-1.3706181).

[58] Northern Ireland Office (1998) *The Belfast Agreement* (www.gov.uk/government/publications/the-belfast-agreement).

[59] Lord Goldsmith QC (2008) *Citizenship: Our Common Bond* (https://webarchive.nationalarchives.gov.uk/20090607152140/http://www.justice.gov.uk/reviews/citizenship.htm).

The precise status and nature of the UK's recognition of complex identities in Northern Ireland has recently come before the UK's immigration tribunals. The question raised was whether those born in Northern Ireland who have only ever, for themselves, recognized and taken Irish citizenship can still be treated, under UK and EU law, as British *and* Irish. Alternatively, in order to be recognized as *only* Irish, do they have to first 'renounce' a UK citizenship that they do not acknowledge, but that appears to be vested on them by operation of law?

The argument was raised in the *DeSouza* case that involved the application for a residence card under EU law (as implemented into UK law) by the US citizen husband of an Irish citizen born and resident in Northern Ireland. The DeSouzas argued that EU family reunion rules rather than the much tougher (and income-dependent) UK rules should apply. The UK argued that it was entitled, after confirmation of this position by the CJEU in the *McCarthy* case,[60] to treat someone who had both UK and another citizenship (in this case Irish), who had never exercised their right to free movement, as not covered by the relevant EU rules and therefore subject only to UK immigration law. After they succeeded in the First Tier Tribunal (whose determination was not published), the decision in favour of the DeSouzas was overturned in the Upper Tribunal.[61] The DeSouzas could only take advantage of EU law if Emma DeSouza first renounced UK citizenship (paying a fee for the privilege). From being 'simply' a case about family reunion, the whole issue has now developed into a constitutional test of the Good Friday Agreement (GFA),[62] and it also raises issues that may have even more substantial implications, now that the UK has left the EU pursuant to its June 2016 referendum decision. The interpretation of the GFA affects the status of many hundreds of thousands of people and the post-referendum process has involved a significant worsening of relations between Ireland and the UK (Teague 2019).

The Upper Tribunal's approach to nationality law is quite conventional and formalist (McKinney 2019). It rejected the argument made by DeSouza that pursuant to the GFA, and notwithstanding the absence of any relevant words on the matter in the primary UK implementing

---

[60] Case C-434/09 *McCarthy v Secretary of State for the Home Department*, ECLI:EU:C:2011:277.

[61] *SSHD v Jake Parker DeSouza*, Appeal Number: EA/06667/2016, 14 October 2019. For an accessible explainer of the case, see S. Carswell (2019) 'Explainer: What is the Emma DeSouza case about?', *The Irish Times*, 15 October (www.irishtimes.com/news/ireland/irish-news/explainer-what-is-the-emma-desouza-case-about-1.4051238).

[62] For background, see Donnan (2019) and House of Commons Library (2019a, 19–20).

legislation,[63] the provisions of the British Nationality Act 1981 on the conferral of citizenship should be read as if they contained the words 'and if they consented to identify as such' as a supplement to the provisions conferring citizenship in different circumstances. Citizenship and immigration law specialists such as Simon Cox have welcomed this finding, because the alternative seems to suggest that people in Northern Ireland are effectively born stateless until they assent to identify as Irish, British or both.[64] This confuses the concepts of identity and citizenship and sets a dangerous precedent that an authoritarian government could exploit in order to deny the citizenship of those who are not deemed to be identifying themselves as (sufficiently) British. In an era of increased citizenship stripping, which we will examine in more detail in Chapter 4, introducing such a subjective element into nationality law represents the top of a slippery slope. A formal arrangement that would preclude persons in the situation of Emma DeSouza being regarded as UK citizens *by operation of law* could only be introduced by express statutory language, not the deliberately broad words of an international treaty such as the GFA. Viewed from that perspective, there is no easy fix in terms of detailed measures.[65] As things stand, holding the content of the Northern Ireland Act 1998 as central to the effects of the GFA inevitably leads to the conclusion that DeSouza should indeed be considered British until she has formally renounced the status, because the Northern Ireland Act contains no measures regulating citizenship. Yet for those whose focus is on interpreting the deliberately ambiguous constitutional settlement governing Northern Ireland since the GFA rather than the formalism of British citizenship law, the Tribunal's approach represents a failure to acknowledge 'the constructive ambiguity inbuilt into the GFA as a peace accord', not an ordinary international treaty.[66]

Meanwhile, the DeSouzas have received substantial political support for their position in the context of the increasingly fraught politics of Ireland/Northern Ireland under the shadow of Brexit, and the case may be appealed into the higher courts where a constitutionally grounded argument could receive a warmer hearing than it has in the immigration

---

[63] Northern Ireland Act 1998.

[64] See two Twitter threads by Simon Cox before (https://twitter.com/SimonFRCox/status/1172143186837409797) and after (https://twitter.com/SimonFRCox/status/1183744749796286465) the Upper Tribunal decision.

[65] S. Creighton (2019) 'It's going to be difficult to establish a solution to the problem that the DeSouza case creates', *The Journal*, 14 October (www.thejournal.ie/readme/emma-desouza-citizenship-identity-northern-ireland-case-4850986-Oct2019).

[66] See the critical Twitter thread by the Performing Identities project (https://twitter.com/performidentity/status/1183736498727870464).

tribunals. Somewhat surprisingly (and perhaps as a result of Irish Government pressure), as part of the package of measures agreed with the Irish Government and the main political parties in Northern Ireland in order to restart devolved government in Belfast, the UK Government appears to have conceded the DeSouza case in a new set of 'commitments' around family migration:

> 13. The Government has reviewed the consistency of its family migration arrangements, taking into account the letter and spirit of the Belfast Agreement and recognising that the policy should not create incentives for renunciation of British citizenship by those citizens who may wish to retain it.
>
> 14. The Government will change the rules governing how the people of Northern Ireland bring their family members to the UK. This change will mean that eligible family members of the people of Northern Ireland will be able to apply for UK immigration status on broadly the same terms as the family members of Irish citizens in the UK.
>
> 15. This immigration status will be available to the family members of all the people of Northern Ireland, no matter whether they hold British or Irish citizenship or both, no matter how they identify.[67]

However, the more favourable arrangements for Irish citizens in the UK may only last so long as EU law remains in force. After Brexit and the end of the transitional period, this statement may not offer a durable fix. Furthermore, these commitments – although apparently clearly expressed – require detailed implementing legislation. In sum, the future of citizenship in Northern Ireland remains uncertain.

Staying with the importance of 'traumatic events', it is perhaps not surprising that in many new states – of which there were numerous examples in Europe after the end of the Cold War and the break-up of three multinational federations (the Soviet Union, Czechoslovakia and Socialist Federal Republic of Yugoslavia [SFRY]) – citizenship is

---

[67] *New Deal, New Approach*, January 2020 (https://assets.publishing.service.gov.uk/government/uploads/system/uploads/attachment_data/file/856998/2020-01-08_a_new_decade__a_new_approach.pdf). For brief commentary, see Irish Legal News (2020) 'Proposals to reform family reunification rules welcomed by rights campaigner Emma DeSouza', 10 January (www.irishlegal.com/article/proposals-to-reform-family-reunification-rules-welcomed-by-rights-campaigner-emma-desouza).

often a contested issue as the new constitutional settlement emerges (Shevel 2009). This is especially the case as fragile new or renewed states often turn to constitutional nationalism, defined by Robert Hayden as 'a constitutional and legal structure that privileges the members of one ethnically defined nation over other residents in a particular state' (Hayden 1992, 655). We have already seen one example in the 2011 Constitution of Hungary, discussed earlier in this section. As Rogers Brubaker (2011) has observed, the states of central and eastern Europe, as well as those that have emerged from the former Soviet Union in Asia, have often behaved as 'nationalizing states', in response to the challenges that they have faced. There have been a number of examples of this at play during the fraught history of citizenship (both in constitutions and ordinary legislation) in the new states of south east Europe, which have emerged from the former SFRY. Both the Republic of North Macedonia (with an initial post-independence constitutional formula that excluded its Albanian minority) and Croatia (which rejected its original socialist constitution that had recognized Serbs as a titular minority) have now moved away from the narrowest formulations of 'the people', as a result of the 'Europeanization' of the 'polity foundations' of those states (Štiks 2015; Shaw and Štiks 2012). However, this is not to say that matters of citizenship are necessarily regulated in detail in the constitutions of new states. This has certainly not been the case in the new states of south east Europe. Most constitutions pass the task to ordinary laws. Only in the case of Bosnia and Herzegovina, with its externally negotiated and imposed Dayton constitutional settlement are matters of citizenship dealt with in any detail in the Constitution.[68]

But trauma is not the only reason why some groups of constitutions contain definitions of citizenship. Historical factors can operate in other ways. Thirty out of 35 countries in the western hemisphere have unlimited *ius soli* (Culliton-González 2012; Vonk 2015), and the vast majority of these states include it in their constitutions, especially those in South America (Acosta 2016). The reason why *ius soli* is a *policy* of choice relates to the historical status of those countries as countries of immigration and/or settler colonial states and to the fact that *ius soli* was used in Spain until 1889 (de Groot and Vonk 2018, 320). Its appearance, legally speaking, in many *constitutions* owes much to the 1812 Spanish or 'Cádiz' Constitution (Acosta 2018), which contained what has been called a 'constitutional overture' (Acosta 2016, 3) along the following lines: 'the Spanish nation

---

[68] Article 7, Bosnia and Herzegovina 1995 (rev. 2009) (www.constituteproject.org/constitution/Bosnia_Herzegovina_2009?lang=en). For analysis, see Sarajlić (2012, 2013).

was the reunion of all Spaniards from both hemispheres. The nation was free and independent, and sovereignty resided in it.' This was imitated in the first constitutions of many of the newly established republics in Latin America in the following years as they became independent from Spain, and in many cases similar texts remain there today. It is a twist of the republican sovereignty overture, in the sense that it is understood to be the best way of making 'citizens out of colonial subjects' and to forge 'national communities from colonial societies marked by stark social divisions'.[69]

Turning finally to look briefly at Africa, the powerful and problematic heritage of colonialism and imperialism has not given rise to a consistent or coherent approach in this very diverse continent to the constitutionalization of citizenship, in particular at the levels of constituent power, constitutional identity or norms of equality, as discussed in this chapter. Bronwen Manby (2019a) notes a recent resurgence of interest in looking at what the idea of 'the state' means in Africa, including questions about membership that remain primarily the domain of national citizenship. 'The state' in this modern sense is, of course, the result of a series of successive 'overlays' in most parts of Africa, with the post-colonial state arriving on top of pre-colonial polities and tribal or group identities followed by colonial states and empires that paid little if any attention, in terms of issues of borders and citizenship, to what had come before. Manby (2019a) notes that, 'In most of the Commonwealth countries, new constitutions agreed as part of the transitional package with Britain included detailed provisions on the acquisition of citizenship at independence and thereafter.' One substantial exception to the pattern is provided by Liberia, which was never colonized by a western power, although it was originally established with a view to providing a destination for emigrants (that is, freed slaves) from North America. In its first Constitution of 1847 a clause was included restricting citizenship to those of African descent, and this provision has been preserved in the latest Constitution of 1986 in Article 27(b): 'In order to preserve, foster and maintain the positive Liberian culture, values and character, only persons who are Negroes or of Negro descent shall qualify by birth or by naturalization to be citizens of Liberia'.[70] However, this clause, and the prohibition on dual citizenship is not uncontested in Liberia (Pailey 2018). Elsewhere in Africa, the manipulation of citizenship law for political purposes and fears about the impact of citizenship on politics (that is, through demography) has led to the introduction of a number of

---

[69] See Appelbaum et al (2003, 4), cited in Acosta (2016, 3) and Lasso (2019).

[70] See Liberia 1986 (www.constituteproject.org/constitution/Liberia_1986?lang=en). For analysis, see Manby (2018, 58–9).

ethnically based restrictions, including some of a constitutional character.[71] Meanwhile, only six constitutions provide for the right to nationality for everyone, including children.[72]

Brief conclusions

In sum, we can see that many constitutions offer multiple and often contradictory and contested engagements with concepts of citizenship and peoplehood. It is hard to draw singular conclusions from the material, beyond suggesting the need for close contextualized and historically sensitive readings of each constitutional set-up, making use of the conceptual frameworks surveyed in the earlier sections of the chapter. This is an important chapter in so far as it lays the groundwork for understanding what types of conceptual frameworks shape the treatment of citizenship at the level of ideas, symbols and norms, even though there is no single unifying narrative that binds together the idea of 'constitutional citizenship' across space and time. It can be argued that as soon as we get below the surface of the citizenship/constitution interface, we quickly see that states are prepared to treat the nature of citizenship as simultaneously both constitutionally significant and yet ethically fungible. In fact, in many of the examples discussed in this chapter, dignity and equality for those facing the exclusionary effects of the measures surveyed are in short supply. We need to keep these ideas in mind as we move, in the next chapter, to the close study of the constitution/citizenship interface at the level of acquisition and loss of citizenship.

---

[71] See Chapter III, Nigeria 1999 (rev. 2011) (www.constituteproject.org/constitution/Nigeria_2011?lang=en). For further discussion, see Chapter 4, 'Naturalization'.

[72] Angola, South Africa, Ethiopia, Rwanda, Malawi and Guinea Bissau: see ACHPR (2015, 23).

4

The Acquisition and Loss of Citizenship in a Constitutional Context

Introduction

In this chapter, we go under the bonnet of constitutional citizenship by examining how constitutions shape or affect the processes of acquisition or loss of citizenship. The conceptual connection between questions of acquisition and loss and those core issues of constitutional and citizenship theory, which structured the discussion in Chapter 3, is very hard to pin down. Patrick Weil issued a warning about this, arguing that there is often a 'complete opposition between the mechanism used to attribute nationality to a person and the one used to constitute the nation' (2008, 185). This suggests taking a precautionary approach to any attempts to read those ideas and concepts across into this chapter. It also reflects the observation that citizenship should be principally seen as 'an artifact [sic], a creature of government' (Orgad 2018, 792).

The chapter proceeds thematically. First, we address some examples where constitutional provisions have had an impact on the main modes of acquisition of citizenship (*ius soli* and *ius sanguinis* birthright citizenship, along with naturalization), before looking at the topic of dual citizenship. We then look at constitutional provisions on loss of citizenship, before shifting the focus onto a broader discussion of how constitutional principles and norms can impact on acquisition and loss even in the absence of constitutional provisions directly regulating citizenship. By this point in the chapter we can finally begin to see some links between the materials discussed here and the presentation of foundational constitutional principles, including equality and dignity, in Chapter 3. The chapter concludes with a short comment bringing together material focused on campaigns to enhance aspects of the 'right to a nationality' via constitutional amendments (and thus to eliminate statelessness), drawing on issues discussed in previous sections. This concluding section also highlights, by way of comparison, another field of campaigning, in the area of gender equality. In some cases, the two sets of campaigns merge together, as in the case of efforts to ensure that mothers and fathers are in the same position to pass their citizenship to their children (whether born within or outside the national territory).[1]

As previously observed, only a minority of countries explicitly regulate one or more modes of acquisition or loss in their constitutions. Most leave these matters to be regulated instead (or in addition, and/or in detail) in legislation and administrative rules. In some countries, conflicts exist between the legislation and the constitution (Vonk 2018a, 28), or there are difficulties in interpretation stemming from trying to combine the two (Jerónimo 2018, 413). In Zimbabwe, inconsistencies between the 2013 Constitution and the existing law and practice (still unamended at the date of writing), especially in the matter of dual citizenship, have spilled over into several constitutional court judgments ruling in favour of complainants arguing for the 'recovery' or recognition of their Zimbabwean citizenship, when they had been refused registration by the Registrar General.[2]

This book started with the shorthand, and perhaps misleading, proposition that states 'choose' citizens. In fact, since the vast majority of people acquire citizenship by birth, this is hardly a case of 'choosing' (either by states or by individuals), certainly not at the granular level. The arbitrariness of the allocation of birthright citizenship has received widespread attention from scholars; Ayelet Shachar (2009), for example, suggests that the allocation of public goods by virtue of the vagaries of birthright citizenship is an important element of global inequality, which could be at least partially corrected by measures such as taxation. She calls it the 'birthright lottery'. In practice, rather than citizenship being substantially about 'choice', states set up the boundaries of membership, with citizenship laws regulating the classic modes of acquisition and

---

[1] For a description of the different approaches to what they call *ius filiationes*, to reflect the legal tie of parentage, see de Groot and Vonk (2018, 326–8).

[2] For details, see Manby (2019b). The leading case is *Mawere v Registrar General & Others* (CCZ 27/13) [2015] ZWCC 04 (25 June 2013). For further discussion, see 'Dual citizenship' below.

loss,[3] and individuals fit, or do not fit, into these categories. Shachar consequently developed the argument, based on a global justice perspective, for another pathway alongside birthright *ius soli* or *ius sanguinis* citizenship, namely *ius nexi*, which recognizes the 'closeness' of a person to a polity, most likely on the basis of domicile or residence.[4] It draws on the more limited international law principle of the 'genuine link', expressed not as a condition but as a potential mode of acquisition that states could choose to adopt. It is intended to express recognition of engagement with or rootedness in the polity, not a disposition of mind or commitment as such. As a normative argument, it is similar to the claim of residence-based citizenship for immigrants (Rubio-Marín 1998). However, we will see, as we go through the various elements of the acquisition and loss of citizenship, that states rarely make use of this principle, at least not at the level of constitutional principle. Only in the area of naturalization can we see some elements of *ius nexi*, but in that context the dominant approaches often channel moral ideas about 'earned citizenship' and 'citizenship as a privilege, not a right'.[5] This also has implications for the stability and security of this status, in the face of revived denaturalization practices (see 'Loss of citizenship' below).

The new wave of comparative citizenship studies pioneered by authors such as Maarten Vink (2017) has helped us to understand better how the main modes of acquisition at birth, namely *ius soli* (territory) and *ius sanguinis* (parentage), are rarely simple alternatives.[6] More often they operate in a complementary manner and stand in tension with each other and with post-birth acquisition modes, such as naturalization (whether of an 'ordinary' or 'preferential' type) and special regimes whereby states recognize exceptional contributions, including in pecuniary form or through activities such as sport (Vink and Bauböck 2013; Vink et al no date). Citizenship acquisition should also be assessed in the light of the conditions under which citizenship can be lost, voluntarily or

---

[3] See GLOBALCIT (2017a, b) and Waldrauch (2006b, c).

[4] For detailed exploration, see Shachar (2011); see also Owen (2018).

[5] For example, for the UK: 'Tony Blair Speech on Migration', *The Guardian*, 27 April 2004 (www.theguardian.com/politics/2004/apr/27/immigrationpolicy.speeches); 'Minister says citizenship "is a privilege not a right"', *ITV News*, 30 January 2014 (www.itv.com/news/update/2014-01-30/minister-says-citizenship-is-a-privilege-not-a-right/). For Australia: 'Learn about being an Australian citizen', Australian Government, Department of Home Affairs webpages, last updated 15 March 2019 (https://immi.homeaffairs.gov.au/citizenship-subsite/Pages/Learn-about-being-an-Australian.aspx). For a discussion of the UK case, see Puzzo (2016).

[6] On the preliminary steps to create a methodology for identifying and classifying the different modes of acquisition and loss, see also Waldrauch (2006a).

involuntarily. Other relevant factors include the extent to which states permit, or encourage, 'external' citizenship where a person acquires, or maintains, citizenship by descent but with little or no connection to the territory of that state or its institutions, and the extent of toleration of dual citizenship for different categories (immigrants, emigrants, children of mixed citizenship marriages, and so on). However, such comparative studies of citizenship regimes typically do not control for the specific impact of the constitutional law and constitutional principles on the law of citizenship, whether directly through the regulation of one or more modes of acquisition or loss or through the prohibition or restriction of dual citizenship, or indirectly via the impact of norms such as the equality principle, especially in relation to gender. In such studies, all law is generally treated as having the same normative quality, which ignores both formal issues such as the hierarchy of sources of law (giving higher rank to constitutional sources) and also the symbolic and ideational issues that underpin constitutions.

We cannot here give a full picture of how the main modes of acquisition and loss of citizenship work in practice,[7] articulate the main trends in modern citizenship law,[8] or group citizenship regimes according to common features or distinctions.[9] Much of the material relevant to answering those large and important questions is to be found in legal and policy sources that are not constitutional in nature, and addressing those questions in full lies beyond the scope of this book. In addition, some examples drawn on here lie at least partly in the past. But bringing in the constitutional question permits us to provide the deep context for issues that are often thought to be merely 'technical'. When viewed in the light of benchmarks of dignity, equality and other constitutional principles, the material covered in this chapter takes on a different timbre, as will become apparent when we discuss the impact of constitutional norms on citizenship laws. The struggles to move or to retain the existing boundaries of the citizenry are often contested, reflecting issues of constituent power and constitutional identity, even in cases where it is not immediately evident that constitutional values or principles are placed in question. The task of this chapter is to put these issues in the foreground, and not to leave them as assumed background.

---

[7] For fuller exposition, see de Groot (2012, 2016) as well as Waldrauch (2006b, c).

[8] As summarized by Shachar (2012, 1010–16).

[9] Vink and Bauböck (2013).

Ius soli

Ius soli birthright acquisition means that citizenship of a country is given to all those born in the state, in principle regardless of the status of their parents. In recent years, (more or less) unconditional *ius soli* has substantially been in retreat. It is now used as the primary principle of the ascription of birthright citizenship only in a small minority of countries, most of them in the western hemisphere (de Groot and Vonk 2018). Outside the western hemisphere, Lesotho is the only country to provide for unconditional *ius soli* in its Constitution.[10] The case of Azerbaijan, which continues to have a *ius soli* provision in its constitution, is somewhat contested, although it is clear that as of 2014 *ius soli* was removed from its domestic citizenship law. According to Maxim Tabachnik (2019), unconditional *ius soli* was used in Azerbaijan (and in the somewhat analogous case of Moldova that retains *ius soli* in its legislation) as part of a territorially based national identity strategy to combat ethnic separatist movements on its territory, supported by Russia.

Large numbers of countries have abolished unconditional *ius soli* in recent years, including by changing their constitutions. While many African constitutions contained *ius soli* at the point of independence, picking up on the then applicable common law heritage from the UK, *ius soli* has now more or less disappeared as a constitutional principle on the African continent in favour of *ius sanguinis*.[11] De Groot and Vonk (2018) identify a number of countries that appear to apply *ius soli* but do not in practice, for example, because it is subject to conditions related to ethnicity and/or indigeneity (for example, Nigeria and Uganda). More countries – up to 30 worldwide – have forms of conditional *ius soli*, in the sense of granting citizenship at birth to children, one or both of whose parents is lawfully resident or domiciled in the country without being citizens, sometimes automatically by operation of law, and sometimes on registration by the parents. For example, France, which had unconditional *ius soli* in its revolutionary constitution at the end of the 18th century, has, since 1993, provided only for a limited form of *ius soli* for the second generation in its legislation. From the age of 16, a child born in France to non-citizen parents may declare for French citizenship. A small group of countries apply double *ius soli*, where children acquire citizenship if they are born to parents who were themselves born in the country, regardless of status. This acts as an amnesty provision across

---

[10] Article 38(1), Lesotho 1993 (rev. 2011) (see www.constituteproject.org/constitution/Lesotho_2011?lang=en).

[11] For details, see Manby (2018, 84–4, Table 5.1).

several generations. Substantial numbers of countries also provide for *ius soli* for foundlings or in other circumstances where a child would otherwise be stateless (because of parents who are stateless or of unknown nationality), including in constitutional provisions (for example, Angola, Mozambique and East Timor). These types of positions are broadly supported by political theorists on migration justice grounds (Benhabib 2004; Carens 2016). Many of the provisions on *ius soli* are not contained in the relevant national constitutions but in legislation, as in France, which since the 19th century has included its nationality regulations in the *code civil*. However, the recent publication of verbatim transcripts of *Conseil constitutionnel* deliberations,[12] during a case in which the constitutionality of the 1993 amendments was discussed, shows that some members of the *Conseil* seemed to be of the opinion that the underlying principle of *ius soli* was indeed a constitutional norm in France. That is to say, if the law had sought to abolish it altogether, this might have been unconstitutional (Lepoutre 2019).

The most prominent example of constitutional *ius soli* citizenship is the 14th Amendment to the US Constitution, which gives constitutional form to birthright *ius soli* citizenship and, what is more, establishes what has been judged by many scholars to be the constitutional *sovereignty* of the citizen. It lays down that, 'All persons born or naturalized in the United States, and subject to the jurisdiction thereof, are citizens of the United States and of the State wherein they reside.' As is well known, this provision was inserted in the US Constitution – which in its original form referred to, but did not define, citizenship – to reverse the *Dred Scott* judgment of the Supreme Court which ruled that African Americans could not be citizens of the US.[13] The reference to 'born in the United States' has been interpreted as implementing a race-blind constitutional *ius soli* rule, such that it covered the child of Chinese immigrants who themselves could not, at that time, naturalize as US citizens because of the exclusionary naturalization laws enacted by Congress.[14]

The dominant interpretation of the 14th Amendment by scholars and political commentators applies a narrow approach to the phrase 'subject to the jurisdiction thereof'. Indian tribes were certainly originally excluded by this formulation,[15] and members of Indian tribes living on reservations were finally granted statutory *ius soli* citizenship only in 1924.

---

[12] Deliberations for 20 July 1993 (www.conseil-constitutionnel.fr/sites/default/files/2019-01/pv_1993-07-20.pdf).

[13] *Dred Scott v Sandford* 60 US (19 How) 393 (1857).

[14] *United States v Wong Kim Ark* 169 US 649 (1898).

[15] *Elk v Wilkins* 112 US 94 (1884).

The children of diplomats and of members of armies waging war on US territory are also excluded and will not acquire US citizenship.[16] This narrow interpretation holds as much for those who take an originalist position on constitutional interpretation, bearing in mind that at the time the concept of 'illegal immigration', as it is used today, was unknown (Ho 2006), as it does for those who prefer their constitutional interpretations to be more dynamic and to reflect changing times (Martin 1985; Bosniak 2006, Chapter 4). A minority opinion argues that the concept of 'subject to the jurisdiction' should properly exclude one group from birthright *ius soli* citizenship, and that is the children whose parents are residing in the US without permission. Part of that argument depends on the principle that there should be a consent basis to citizenship, and those who are present on the territory of the US without permission cannot be brought within the circle of consent. Peter Schuck and Rogers Smith (1985), who pioneered this view, also argued that Congress would be justified in legislating to make it clear that the children of unlawfully present parents would not be birthright citizens.[17] However, successive attempts to pass laws in Congress to restrict birthright *ius soli* citizenship have failed. This is partly because there is a deep-seated commitment across much of US public life to the principles that the unconditional *ius soli* rule instantiates and partly because there is a widespread understanding that the Supreme Court would rule against any Congressional attempts to limit the scope or effects of the 14th Amendment, judging by its historical jurisprudence on the matter.

Many of these arguments were reheated in late 2018, when President Donald Trump raised the spectre of passing an executive order to limit birthright citizenship for 'illegal immigrants'. At the time, the issue did not remain in the public eye for long, since it was essentially being used as an electoral ploy for the midterm elections to the Congress, but it was raised by Trump once again in August 2019. Challenging the scope of birthright citizenship has been one of a number of ways in which Trump

---

[16] A recent example of the 'diplomacy' exception is provided by the case of Hoda Muthana, who was born in New Jersey to a father who had recently left the diplomatic service of Yemen, but whose departure had not yet been notified to the relevant authorities. Muthana was radicalized and travelled to Syria at the age of 20 (on a US passport) to support ISIS. Her repatriation to the US has been refused on the grounds that a mistake was made at the time of her birth and she is not, in fact, a citizen, a point supported by a US federal judge in November 2019: see M. Kennedy (2019) 'Judge rules that US-born woman who joined ISIS is not a US citizen', *NPR*, 15 November (www.npr.org/2019/11/15/779788549/judge-rules-that-u-s-born-woman-who-joined-isis-is-not-a-u-s-citizen?t=1574933914153).

[17] For a review of the debate, see Aleinikoff (2000, 125–8).

has intervened in the sphere of immigration and citizenship in order to seek electoral gain and to create insecurities for undocumented US residents (Béland 2019).[18] The chances of constitutional success of the attack on birthright citizenship are very low indeed, but their political salience is high. At the same time, the defence of the 14th Amendment and birthright citizenship is something that unites 'conservatives' and 'liberals' (as regards constitutional interpretation) in opposition to Trump.[19] We will discuss the populist politics of citizenship and immigration in the US in more detail in Chapter 6.

The case of the 14th Amendment provides a specific, and perhaps unusual, example of a constitutional standard for citizenship, which would be exceptionally hard to amend, not least because of links to other political and constitutional principles.[20] It is arguable that, as a result, opposition within the US to the current position on citizenship acquisition has been deflected away from constitutional debate and from legislative proposals, given the lack of prospect of success. Instead, efforts have been directed towards administrative and evidentiary questions as a means to restrict the scope of the constitutional provision. In the US, the registration of births is regulated at state rather federal level, and in recent years it has become exceedingly difficult for undocumented parents to obtain birth certificates for their US citizen children in a number of states along the Mexican border. The state of Texas has been at the forefront of these efforts by administrators.[21]

Having a constitutional guarantee of *ius soli* citizenship was, however, not a bar to change in Ireland. In 2004, in order to restrict *ius soli* to the children of citizens or those entitled to citizenship, a measure was introduced by a referendum distinguishing between membership of the Irish nation (by birth on the island) and entitlement 'by law' to be a citizen.[22] For the latter, responsibility was passed to the legislature. This reflects a trend in Ireland whereby constitutional referendums have increasingly passed responsibility for 'social affairs' (for example, divorce, abortion, gay marriage) to the legislature. Another example of changes to a constitutional notion of citizenship can be found in India. These changes have occurred even though citizenship was a dominating theme

---

[18] For analysis, see also Open Society Justice Initiative (2019).

[19] For a salient example of this, see Conway and Katyal (2018).

[20] On the frequency of constitutional amendment and renewal, see Elkins et al (2009), Ginsburg et al (2009) and World Bank (2017).

[21] For a discussion, see Liu (2017), Lichtenberger (2018), Petrozziello (2019a) and Open Society Justice Initiative (2019).

[22] Article 2, Ireland 1937 (rev. 2015) (www.constituteproject.org/constitution/Ireland_2015?lang=en).

in the debates of the Constitutional Assembly in the late 1940s (Rodrigues 2008). The changes have had the effect, arguably, of rolling back the original conception by giving more scope for legislative choice to give voice to a range of different factors:

> The framers of India's constitution adopted a modernist, secular notion of citizenship by seeking to incorporate a broadly *ius soli* conception of citizenship in the Constitution. Over time, this has been modified to incorporate various elements of a *ius sanguinis* model of citizenship, with the insertion of notions of descent, common religious identity and common "national" values into the discourse of citizenship. (Ashesh and Thiruvengadam 2018, 173)

So far, the consequences of these changes have had limited exclusionary effects, although Rodrigues (2008, 174) has argued that it has already given rise to a more ethnic conception of citizenship. However, this may change decisively in the future, as shown by a Citizenship Amendment Act, which was passed by the Indian Parliament at the end of 2019 and which came into force in January 2020, amid widespread protests across India. This Act challenges in fundamental ways the legal equality of Muslims in India. These issues will be discussed in more detail in Chapter 6.

Changes to *ius soli* in the Dominican Republic have been the basis for prolonged contestation of the citizenship status of many of those who are resident in that state. The Dominican Republic is one of the few countries in the Western Hemisphere that does not have unconditional *ius soli* (Sagas 2017). Many of the difficulties have stemmed from the uncomfortable cohabitation of the Dominican Republic and Haiti on the island of Hispaniola in the Caribbean, combined with complex relationships with former colonial powers and dominant powers in the region. This resulted in the Dominican Republic having *ab initio*, from the date of independence, a stronger emphasis on *ius sanguinis* than on *ius soli*, compared to most of its neighbours. This was in order to create a system that reflected the continuity of the historic population. The *ius soli* provision in the Constitution was accompanied by an exception excluding those born to parents 'in transit' in the Dominican Republic at the time of the birth. For many decades there has been substantial labour migration – much of it undocumented – from Haiti to the Dominican Republic, in response to labour shortages within the latter economy, and political turbulence and poverty in the former. The divisions are also racialized: Haitian migrants in the Dominican Republic are seen as being 'blacker' as well as poorer. In practice, Haitian migrants in the Dominican Republic often had difficulties registering their children, because they were unable to prove – if they were undocumented – that they were not 'in transit', even if they had been resident for many decades (Wooding 2018).

The legal position was 'clarified' with an amendment to the Constitution in 2010 which explicitly excluded the children of those residing 'illegally' from benefiting from the *ius soli* provision.[23] But for Haitian migrants worse was to come, as a judgment of the Dominican Republic Constitutional Tribunal (DRCT) of 2013, which has been very widely criticized,[24] effectively cancelled retrospectively the citizenship of all of the children of Haitian irregular migrants born in the Dominican Republic between 1929 and 2010. The DRCT's (unproven) assumption was that they had Haitian citizenship, so there was nothing to worry about. In fact, the judgment resulted in a massive statelessness problem, including among many people who had no ties to Haiti and who had only ever lived in the Dominican Republic. Moreover, the approach taken within the Dominican Republic, even before the DRCT's intervention and the constitutional amendment, has been sharply criticized within the supranational judicial and human rights bodies of the Americas as a result of activists taking cases through the inter-American human rights system. After the first judgment in *Yean and Bosico*,[25] a further judgment of the Inter-American Human Rights Court (IAHRCt) reviewing subsequent legislative and constitutional developments in the Dominican Republic again emphasized the incompatibility of the position in the Dominican Republic with the inter-American human rights system.[26] This provoked a domestic reaction on the part of the DRCT which subsequently purported to cast doubt on the IAHRCt's jurisdiction within the Dominican Republic on constitutional grounds (Huneeus and Urueña 2017). The strength of these international interventions may go part of the way towards explaining why the Dominican Republic government did belatedly devise a regularization programme that has made some impact on the widespread statelessness problem that has arisen.

[23] Article 18(3), Dominican Republic 2015 (www.constituteproject.org/constitution/Dominican_Republic_2015?lang=en).

[24] *Deguis* (TC-168-13). For a critique, see Glen (2007) and Kosinski (2009).

[25] *Case of the Yean and Bosico Girls v Dominican Republic*, 8 September 2005 (full judgment available at www.corteidh.or.cr/docs/casos/articulos/seriec_130_%20ing.pdf). For more details on the case of the Dominican Republic, see also Inter-American Commission on Human Rights (2015) *Situation of Human Rights in the Dominican Republic* (www.oas.org/en/iachr/reports/pdfs/DominicanRepublic-2015.pdf).

[26] *Expelled Dominicans and Haitians v Dominican Republic* 28 August 2014 (https://iachr.lls.edu/cases/case-expelled-dominicans-and-haitians-v-dominican-republic and full judgment at http://corteidh.or.cr/docs/casos/articulos/seriec_282_ing.pdf).

The ongoing problem for Haitian migrants within the Dominican Republic has been less the constitutional provisions themselves than the embedded discrimination against this group of people within culture and society. This prejudicial attitude seems to have extended as far as the DRCT when it decided to give a narrow and exclusionary reading of the constitutional provisions. The point was emphasized by an anthropologist, Samuel Martínez, who acted as an expert witness before the IAHRCt in the 2005 case of *Yean and Bosico Girls v Dominican Republic*. He argued that:

> Dominico-Haitians are not only struggling for legal citizenship but also for cultural citizenship, so that a broader recognition is given to their belonging in the Dominican Republic such that they may legitimately be part of the country. Cultural citizenship is a broad term which legal scholars and social researchers have created to describe the aforesaid unwritten presuppositions about those who, in race-ethnic-class terms, belong totally to the nation which defines their fundamental identity. The exclusion from cultural citizenship may have negative social, economic and psychological consequences for people who are internally colonized or disadvantaged ethnic-racial minorities who see themselves relegated to the permanent condition of second class citizen or whose citizenship may be totally denied. (quoted in Wooding 2008, 372)

Furthermore, as Allison Petrozziello (2019b) has argued, looking at the matrilineal transmission of statelessness in a context of pervasive direct and indirect gender discrimination, much more needs to be done to look at the 'beyond' the legal (or perhaps better, 'soft law') causes of statelessness in cases where many of the challenges cluster in the evidentiary area of birth certification. Indeed law, and especially constitutional law, is unlikely to be the only answer to human rights violations such as those that have occurred in the Dominican Republic. But given both the regional human rights system to which aggrieved persons and the organizations that represent them have had recourse and the desire by the Dominican Republic to be seen to be complying with rule of law standards evident in some of its more recent actions, law clearly has had and will continue to have a role in drawing attention to, and in some cases ameliorating the situation.

The position in the Dominican Republic, which is driven by historic tensions between the two states, can be contrasted with the approach taken in Colombia, which is another of the small number of western hemisphere states not to have unconditional *ius soli*. In August 2019, faced with an enormous influx of refugees, Colombia granted citizenship to babies born in the territory of Colombia to Venezuelan refugee mothers, who would otherwise be stateless. The measures apply from August 2015 (since when approximately 25,000 likely stateless babies have been born) until August 2021. They take the form of an executive decree and a later law (Castro 2020), which do not affect the constitutional position in that country.[27] Colombia's actions were welcomed by UN agencies dealing with refugees and children,[28] although there have been fears that this was only a temporary and partial fix for a larger problem, until a ground-breaking decision of the Colombian Constitutional Court in January 2020. The Court decided that the state authorities could not refuse to register the births of the babies of Venezuelan refugees as Colombian citizens, if they would otherwise be stateless, as this would be contrary to the Constitution (Castro 2020).[29]

Ius sanguinis

The second mode of acquisition of citizenship at birth is *ius sanguinis*, or citizenship by descent. *Ius sanguinis* is now the dominant mode of acquisition of citizenship at birth worldwide, although it can be subject to a variety of different conditions, especially in respect of children born outside the country. It is also a common site for gender discrimination against women in a number of countries, especially in the Middle East and North African regions,[30] and sometimes against men, who cannot pass their citizenship outside the country unless they are married. A substantial number of constitutions refer to the concept of *ius sanguinis*,

---

[27] D. Baddour (2019) 'Colombia grants citizenship to 24,000 children born to Venezuelan mothers', *The Washington Post*, 5 August (www.washingtonpost.com/ world/the_americas/colombia-grants-citizenship-to-24000-babies-born-to-venezuelan-mothers/2019/08/05/390f6042-a8b3-11e9-8733-48c87235f396_story. html).

[28] UNHCR (2019) 'Colombia acts to ensure children born to Venezuelan parents are not left stateless', 6 August (www.unhcr.org/uk/news/briefing/2019/8/5d4937754/ colombia-acts-ensure-children-born-venezuelan-parents-stateless.html).

[29] M. Janetsky (2019) "No country to call home: Some babies born in Colombia to Venezuelan parents lack birthright citizenship', *USA Today*, 12 August (https:// eu.usatoday.com/story/news/world/2019/08/11/birthright-citizenship-babies-venezuela-migrants-colombia/1887388001/). See Judgment T-006/20 of 17 January 2020 (www.corteconstitucional.gov.co/Relatoria/2020/T-006-20.htm).

[30] For details, see de Groot and Vonk (2018, 326–8).

in so far as they state that citizenship is acquired as a result of birth, if at least one of the child's parents is a citizen.[31] A good case is Togo, where as-of-right *ius sanguinis* through birth in or out of the territory is the *only* part of citizenship law regulated at constitutional level. This conveys an important message about the nature of the polity and how the concept of intergenerational continuity is perceived.[32] *Ius sanguinis* can be a political tool for building relations with the diaspora, as in the case of Bolivia, which recently introduced automatic *ius sanguinis* in its Constitution for children of citizens born abroad.[33] This is an example of a 'mechanism to produce population' (Caggiano 2018, 268). The measure was part of a broader package including measures to permit dual nationality, to assist those Bolivians outside the national territory to obtain citizenship documentation and to vote abroad. For a *ius soli* state largely historically focused on immigration, but belatedly accepting its status as a sending country both within Latin America and beyond, this was an important change.

In Greece, where citizenship is regulated by law, not by constitution,[34] it would seem that the principle of *ius sanguinis* may none the less be constitutionally embedded as a superordinate principle of citizenship acquisition. The legal basis for this claim of declaratory constitutionalization is the reference to the protection of the 'nation' under Article 1 of the Greek Constitution. The issue arose in the context of a challenge to the constitutionality of a 2010 liberalizing reform of Greek citizenship law adopted by Parliament (Mavrommatis 2018). The challenge was largely successful both before the Fourth Chamber of the Council of State and subsequently before the Council's Plenary, although the latter was noticeably less trenchant in its insistence on the constitutional character of *ius sanguinis* than the former. None the less, the Plenary rejected reforms that would have *inter alia* seen *ius soli* citizenship granted at birth to children of immigrant parents who had resided in Greece for five years at

---

[31] For example, the 1987 Constitution of the Republic of the Philippines (www.officialgazette.gov.ph/constitutions/1987-constitution/).

[32] Article 32, Togo 1992 (rev. 2007) (www.constituteproject.org/constitution/Togo_2007?lang=en).

[33] Article 141, Bolivia (Plurinational State of) 2009 (www.constituteproject.org/constitution/Bolivia_2009?lang=en). Previously, Bolivian nationality for children born abroad to Bolivian parents only arose when the parents registered the birth in the consulate. Some chose not to do so, for example, in Spain, where the risk that the child might otherwise be stateless would result in the child obtaining Spanish citizenship (Caggiano 2018, 273).

[34] Article 4(3), Greece 1975 (rev. 2008) (www.constituteproject.org/constitution/Greece_2008?lang=en).

the date of the birth. It concluded instead that any form of membership of the Greek nation that was not by descent could only proceed on the basis of an individualized assessment of integration. Accordingly, general conditions such as five years of residence or, on the part of children born in the territory, six years of education were not sufficient to guarantee integration in the nation without further individualized assessment. *Ius soli* (even of such a conditional character) would, in short, risk watering down 'the nation', which the Council of State argued had a cross-temporal character based on ethnic belonging.

For critics, the Council of State has overstepped the mark in claiming a right to define who is the nation, by not leaving these matters primarily to the legislature. Critics suggested that the Council should only step in if the legislature clearly contravened a constitutional principle (for example, by passing a rule that stated that 'Greek citizenship is only available to white men') (Christopoulos 2017, 489). Those critics have suggested that other matters, such as the level of inclusivity to extend towards long-term resident immigrants and their families, should be issues for democratic deliberation rather than constitutional *fiat*. In the view of Dia Anagnostou (2016), the very fact that the issue became a political football between left and right interests within the Greek political system suggests that Parliament would be the best place for these questions to be resolved because of the problems such judicial activism in the 'name of the nation' will generate. In later amendments, which have not been challenged, Greece has enacted double *ius soli* to cover children born to parents themselves born in the country (de Groot and Vonk 2018, 333).

One group that does not make any use of *ius soli* provisions in their citizenship regulations, and for whom descent and bloodline belonging could be said to be a core principle for continued existence, are Indigenous Peoples, especially in settler states.[35] In the modern world, membership of indigenous or tribal communities will, in most cases, sit alongside (but not necessarily comfortably with) formal membership of the settler state, with the former increasingly legally and constitutionally recognized by the latter. However, in former times, indigenous communities were often excluded from state citizenship (Volpp 2015). Tendayi Bloom (2017) argues that states have an obligation to offer citizenship to indigenous groups or otherwise colonized peoples, but her work also shows how

---

[35] For detailed analysis, see Gover (2017) and Adams (2016). For further discussion of the citizenship implications of indigeneity in Australia, see the brief presentation of the *Love* and *Thoms* cases below in 'The impact of constitutional norms on citizenship acquisition and loss'.

such groups may 'resist' the imposition of an unwanted citizenship as a strategy of chosen 'non-citizenship'.

In settler states, the legal position can be complex, as Kirsty Gover explains:

> There is a growing divergence, for instance, between the long-standing category of legal indigeneity (allocated by settler governments) and the status of tribal citizenship (decided by tribal governments, within certain constraints imposed by settler law). Neither category aligns with the other, nor is either co-extensive with settler-state citizenship. Many legally indigenous persons are not members of recognized tribes, and some indigenous people, including tribal citizens, are not citizens of the state that encompasses their tribal territories. Likewise, some tribal citizens are not legally indigenous, and a growing number of people with indigenous ancestry are neither legally indigenous nor citizens of a tribal nation. (Gover 2017, 454)

The claim to base access to legal indigeneity and tribal citizenship on descent alone is rooted not just in a claim to (endangered) cultural or minority ethnic status, but also in claims to authority and property, often constitutionally recognized both within the settler state and in the autonomous constitutions of the tribal communities. Gover acknowledges suspicions among scholars of citizenship as a liberal discourse about *ius sanguinis* as a birthright citizenship rule. However, despite that concern, citizenship law should recognize that:

> Shared biological descent is a paradigmatic marker of tribal nationhood in settler law precisely because it is thought to be a more "objective" measure of continuity and succession than contextual and mutable identity markers such as "political integrity" or "cultural distinctiveness". (Gover 2017, 457)

Several Latin American constitutions take steps to ensure that Indigenous Peoples are formally recognized as part of the 'nation'. Article 3 of the 2009 Constitution of Bolivia states that 'The Bolivian nation is formed by all Bolivians, the native indigenous nations and peoples, and the intercultural and Afro-Bolivian communities that, together, constitute the Bolivian people'.[36] Colombia's Constitution explicitly refers to the (state)

---

[36] See Bolivia (Plurinational state of) 2009 (www.constituteproject.org/constitution/Bolivia_2009?lang=en).

citizenship of Indigenous Peoples straddling state borders, to ensure that they have the backstop of state citizenship.[37] Ecuador is widely recognized as having Latin America's strongest indigenous movement, promoting enhanced constitutional recognition.[38]

Indigenous citizenship has been a contested issue in Costa Rica for many decades, and it offers an interesting example of interplay between indigenous rights, citizenship law, bureaucratic requirements, the impact of international law and the increasing role of constitutional courts and judicial oversight in Latin America.[39] In 2019, to mark the International Day of the World's Indigenous Peoples, Costa Rica adopted a law recognizing the 'nationality' of cross-border Indigenous Peoples.[40] This is the culmination of a legal process that dates back to a 1993 judgment of the Constitutional Court on a challenge brought by a number of cross-border groups of Indigenous Peoples regarding access to citizenship.[41] Because of their traditional lifestyles, largely separated from the formal structures of the Costa Rican state, members of the community found it hard to comply with registration requirements imposed on them, which resulted in them being treated as foreigners, eligible only for citizenship by naturalization. This affected their standing as members of the nation as conceived by the Costa Rican Constitution. The Constitutional Court decision assessed the statutory measures taken to ensure inclusion of the Indigenous Peoples not by reference to constitutional standards, but by reference to the International Labour Organization (ILO) Convention 169 of 1989 concerning Indigenous and Tribal Peoples in Independent Countries,[42] to which Costa Rica is a party. The constitutional gateway for this approach is Article 7 of the Costa Rican Constitution, which gives international law an authority superior to national law.[43]

---

[37] Article 96(2)(c), Colombia 1991 (rev. 2015) (www.constituteproject.org/constitution/Colombia_2015?lang=en).

[38] For detailed analysis of Latin American indigenous movements and the implications for citizenship, see Yashar (2005).

[39] Helmke and Ríos-Figueroa (2011).

[40] *AFP/Tico Times* (2019) 'New Costa Rican law recognizes nationality for indigenous populations', 10 August (https://ticotimes.net/2019/08/10/new-costa-rican-law-recognizes-nationality-for-indigenous-populations).

[41] The 1993 judgment (1786-93) can be found in Chacón (2001), with the key passages at 189–91. See also Quesada (2015, 11).

[42] The text is available at 'Indigenous and Tribal Peoples Convention, 1989', C169 (www.refworld.org/docid/3ddb6d514.html).

[43] See Costa Rica 1949 (rev. 2015) (www.constituteproject.org/constitution/Costa_Rica_2015?lang=en).

Two points made by the Court are of particular interest and reinforce an impression that it is rather activist in the area of indigenous affairs (Wilson 2011). The first is that membership of such groups should be decided by those groups themselves according to their own criteria, rather than by (state) legislative authority, echoing the point made by Gover (2017). Second, the Court found that the members of the indigenous communities should – in view of their pre-Colombian history – be recognized as Costa Ricans by birth, and not naturalized foreigners, disapplying the national legislation in question to achieve this outcome. Formal legislative measures should have ensued after 1993, and this point was recognized in successive comments made in the review processes carried out by the ILO in conjunction with the Costa Rican authorities.[44] The 2019 legislation would appear to be the culmination of this work.

Ius sanguinis does, none the less, raise some problematic issues in other circumstances. One aspect that has come under particularly close scrutiny concerns the acquisition of citizenship *outside* the territory of the state, especially across multiple generations.[45] *Ius sanguinis* is sometimes criticized as being an intrinsically problematic mode of citizenship acquisition, since it seems to give preference to ethnic belonging (Dumbrava 2015). This, however, is to misunderstand the historical record, according to historians such as Dieter Gosewinkel (2017) and Jannis Panagiotidis (2018). Panagiotidis (2018, 93) warns against conflating 'ius sanguinis as descent from a citizen' and 'co-ethnic inclusion', which often relates to non–citizens. It is not *ius sanguinis* as such which raises issues, but rather 'the respective contexts in which it is embedded.' That is to say, the effects of *ius sanguinis* are not intrinsic, but rather the product of what constitution makers (and interpreters) and legislators make of that mode of citizenship acquisition.

It is widely acknowledged that *ius sanguinis* is part of the technologies of the modern state. Once the modern state started to 'see' its citizens,[46] it followed naturally that it would be interested in using acknowledged parentage as a way of ensuring generational continuity of population. What such a historical explanation cannot take into account, however, is the interaction between extensive *ius sanguinis* rules and the types of special or additional rights that flow when access is not just to *national*

---

[44] Requests by the ILO authorities to the Costa Rican government and comments relating to Convention 169 are available by searching the ILO Normlex database (see www.ilo.org/normlex).

[45] See, for example, Italy (Tintori, 2016). For a general discussion, see Dumbrava (2014a, 2018).

[46] Scott (1998).

citizenship but also to *EU* citizenship by virtue of national citizenship, with the various mobility and political rights to which the latter gives rise. Yossi Harpaz (2019) describes this contingency, which depends on access to *ius sanguinis* across generations as well as tolerance of dual citizenship, as one of the forms of 'compensatory citizenship'. It is a strategy for global upward mobility. It is one of the aspects of the 'lightness' of citizenship, when it is viewed from the individual strategic perspective. Casting the net widely for external citizens also arguably distorts the constitutional basis of EU citizenship itself (Shaw 2019a).

One important gateway for creating more expansive external citizenship policies stems from how the concept of 'the people' (who may be inside or outside the borders) is constructed as a notion within the national constitution. The perception of a large external constituency can arise as a result of either people or borders moving. In both cases this can create a diaspora or group of so-called 'ethnic kin'.

Many of the national constitutional provisions do not assume that the target groups, whether inside or outside the territory, have or should have citizenship. Article 2 of the Irish Constitution refers to the Irish nation's 'special affinity with people of Irish ancestry living abroad who share its cultural identity and heritage'.[47] Ireland continues to be marked, as a state, by its history of emigration, much of it forced by economic under-development and famine, even though it has become a state of immigration in recent years. The post-Soviet state of Armenia recognizes relations with its diaspora in Article 19 of its constitution: 'The Republic of Armenia shall carry out a policy aimed at developing comprehensive ties and preserving Armenianness with the Armenian Diaspora, and shall facilitate repatriation.'[48]

Alternatively, the Constitution may provide that special facilities will be made available. Article 5 of the Constitution of Slovenia provides that 'Slovenes not holding Slovene citizenship may enjoy special rights and privileges in Slovenia.' Slovenia is a new state established in 1991. Elsewhere in the former Yugoslavia, Article 10 of the Croatian Constitution lays down that 'parts of the Croatian nation in other states shall be guaranteed special concern and protection by the Republic of

---

[47] Irish citizenship law provides for second-generation *ius sanguinis* transmission of citizenship, thus giving rise to an intense interest in Irish-born grandparents in the UK after the 2016 Brexit vote. On Irish ancestry and Irish citizenship, see Burke Wood and Gilmartin (2018).

[48] See Armenia 1995 (rev. 2015) (www.constituteproject.org/constitution/Armenia_2015).

Croatia'.[49] It is important to read this provision in the light of the long story of asserted Croatian sovereignty, dating back to early medieval times, which is presented in the Preamble to the Constitution. This suggests a *prima facie* extensive notion of the 'nation' is embedded in constitutional discourse. Article 52(5) of the Polish Constitution states that 'Anyone whose Polish origin has been confirmed in accordance with statute may settle permanently in Poland', although this provision makes any real benefit dependent on subsequent legislation.[50] Poland has introduced the so-called *Karta polaka*, or Polish Ethnicity Card, partly as a response to unresolved national debates around the reinstatement of Polish citizenship, given border and human mobilities over the last century or so[51] and partly as a legacy of Poland's own colonial history.[52] It is a form of semi-citizenship, offering only limited rights.[53]

We have already discussed the connections that can be drawn between citizenship and belonging in relation to exclusionary visions of a country's constitutional identity, such as the impact of the shift in the constitutional identity of Hungary on citizenship matters. Article D of the 2011 Fundamental Law concerns the unity of the 'Hungarian nation', including those members living beyond the boundaries of Hungary, following earlier boundary changes. This has been an entry point for the development of ethnically based diaspora laws and policies, including arguably over-inclusive external citizenship policies. These have resulted in around one million people who are residing outside Hungary acquiring citizenship between 2011 and 2017 on a co-ethnic basis.[54] The majority of these new citizens come from countries outside the EU, especially Serbia and Ukraine, although there are also large groups of external citizens in Romania, which is a fellow EU Member State. In addition, measures have been introduced to grant voting rights to non-resident citizens and these have generally strengthened the hand of the governing party *Fidesz*, for which these groups predominantly vote (Majtényi et al 2018).[55] The final outcome involves a combination of a particular set of constitutional

[49] See Croatia 1991 (rev. 2013) (www.constituteproject.org/constitution/Croatia_2013?lang=en).

[50] See Poland 1997 (rev. 2009) (www.constituteproject.org/constitution/Poland_2009?lang=en).

[51] Górny and Pudzianowska (2013).

[52] Ładykowski (2018).

[53] For a discussion, see Kicinger and Koryś (2011, 355) and Sendhardt (2017).

[54] See Tóth (2018); for a more general discussion of the Hungarian case, see Pogonyi (2017, 2019).

[55] For criticism of the Hungarian parliamentary elections in April 2018, see the OSCE observers' report (www.osce.org/odihr/elections/hungary/385959).

circumstances with the use by a governing party of ethnic preferences in order to cement its electoral and societal position through legislation.

Myra Waterbury (2014) discusses the wider phenomenon of non-resident ethnic citizenship in post-communist Europe and highlights the links that can be drawn between such projects and right-wing governments. She also points out that the changes in Hungary came much later than in other countries, such as Croatia and Romania, where citizenship for ethnic kin was embedded in the immediate post-transition legal settlement.[56] In a sense, then, what is important about Hungary is that it was a shift compared to an earlier period, when a constitutional discourse giving primacy to European integration largely prevailed, even though issues of citizenship and identity had already become salient (Batory 2010). In addition, given the significance of the constitutional gateway created in 2011, it can be understood as part of a process of 'constitutional acceleration' (or 'the increased propensity of different actors to engage in (formal) reform of the constitutional order'[57]) described by scholars such as Paul Blokker.[58] We will discuss this process more extensively in Chapter 6 in the context of populist constitutionalist interventions in the sphere of citizenship.

Problems with the relationship between ethnicity and citizenship are certainly not confined to Europe. *Ius sanguinis* is now the dominant mode of birthright citizenship on the continent of Africa. Bronwen Manby has shown how, over several decades, this shift has been accompanied by a number of controversies involving the application of racially defined preferences plus other ethnically based restrictions, which have produced populations of stateless or marginalized people.[59] She pinpoints hotspots including Sierra Leone (measures taken to restrict access to citizenship by the Lebanese minority)[60] and Kenya (resistance dating back to independence to incorporating a number of different ethnic groups including, but not only, South Asians).[61] Many of the restrictions now appear in citizenship legislation rather than in constitutions and the explicit reference to 'persons who are Negroes or of Negro descent' in Article 27(B) of the Constitution of Liberia remains a standout example of constitutional regulation.

---

[56] See also Dumbrava (2014b) and Žilović (2012).

[57] See Blokker (2017, 1).

[58] Blokker draws in his work on Prandini (2013).

[59] The details can be found in Manby (2018, Chapter 7).

[60] For more details, see 'The impact of constitutional principles on citizenship acquisition and loss' below. See also Beydoun (2013), Malki (2017) and Hale and M'Cormack-Hale (2018).

[61] For further details, see Ng'weno and Aloo (2019).

Naturalization

As the idea of individuals as subjects of the crown transformed into the modern idea of citizenship, so this called into question the natural law doctrine of perpetual allegiance, which was embedded in the common law.[62] It was hard to argue that the sovereign citizen could be a person who remained perpetually the subject of whichever crown she happened to be born under, with no possibility of change regardless of where she lived or what life choices she made. Hitherto, under a feudalist approach, switching allegiance to a new prince could have been seen as treason or at the very least as an act of disloyalty. This hardly suited the emerging colonies of the so-called 'new world', or the interests of those who migrated to those colonies. The former wanted permanent and loyal populations; the latter required the option of shifting allegiance to the new state of residence and protection against impressment to serve in the armed forces of the original state, and being forced to fight even against the new state. Yet a settled pattern of formal naturalization was slow to emerge because, as Peter Spiro puts it, 'During the nineteenth century many European states refused to recognize the validity of naturalization before other sovereigns, leading to serious diplomatic disputes and, in at least one case, armed conflict' (the War of 1812) (2011, 700). Naturalization in the UK was only possible by Act of Parliament until 1844, when an administrative form of naturalization was introduced by statute. The possibility of renunciation of British subject status was finally introduced by the Naturalisation Act 1870.

The importance of naturalization today cannot be overstated given the prevalence of human mobility (much of it permanent or semi-permanent) and the continued significance of states within the international system. It is significant that this is an area where the European Convention on Nationality endeavours to set a standard: immigrants should not have to wait more than ten years before being able to naturalize (Article 6(3)). While the possibility of naturalization is referred to in many of those constitutions that deal with citizenship, the process of naturalization is rarely dealt with in any depth, as it is perhaps more suitable for detailed regulation by statute or in the context of administrative procedures.[63] This is because naturalization tends to be hedged around by complex

---

[62] *Calvin's Case*, 77 Eng Rep 377, 382 (KB 1608). For a discussion, see Koessler (1946), Price (1997) and Cohen (2010).

[63] Exceptions include Article 12, The Gambia 1996 (rev. 2004) (www.constituteproject. org/constitution/Gambia_2004?lang=en) and Article 19, Malaysia 1957 (rev. 2007) (www.constituteproject.org/constitution/Malaysia_2007?lang=en).

conditions (for example, length of residence, probity and self-sufficiency tests, integration and language tests, in some cases renunciation of prior citizenship, as well as requirements to take an oath or attend a ceremony). With such conditions, it may, of course, reflect the constitutional identity of that state. Liav Orgad captures how the law of naturalization functions as a gatekeeper:

> ... it is designed to include the desirable people and exclude the undesirable ones. In so doing, naturalization provides a unique platform to reflect on three fundamental issues: [1] defining the "We" – who "we" are, and what kind of nation "we" want to be; [2] setting criteria for identifying the desired "They" – who is, in the state's view, a "good citizen," and the current understanding of what it means to become a citizen; and [3] finding the substance and form to which "they" should subscribe in order to join the "We". (Orgad 2017, 337)

While political theorists have discussed the reasonable conditions attached by states to the acquisition of citizenship, and scholars such as Peter Spiro (2011) have argued that international law increasingly circumscribes the discretion of states in relation to matters such as naturalization, in practice, no constitution comes close to postulating a 'right' to naturalization, even in countries such as the 'settler colonies', where it was historically a settled assumption that new arrivals would do so. There is often a discretion vested in the executive in the receiving state that makes it hard to challenge the refusal of naturalization, despite the principle of review being also included in the European Convention on Nationality (Article 12).

It is not uncommon for constitutions to set up regional preferences, or to acknowledge the opportunity for people who fulfil certain objective criteria to become citizens more easily. This is sometimes by naturalization and sometimes by registration (according to a fixed and typically less discretionary procedure).[64] Thus Article 96(2) of the Constitution of Colombia makes it easier for people born in Latin America or the Caribbean to become Colombian nationals 'by adoption'. In contrast Article 92 of the Constitution of St Kitts and Nevis allows for registration as a citizen by a person married to a citizen and by a person

---

[64] This is the distinction drawn in GLOBALCIT (2017a).

who is a Commonwealth citizen with 14 years of ordinary residence in the country.[65]

Some constitutions enact ethnic preferences. Article 25(2) of the Bulgarian Constitution provides that 'A citizen of Bulgarian origin shall acquire Bulgarian citizenship through a facilitated procedure'.[66] These 'facilitated procedures' often do away with the requirement of residence, as well as being based on shaky foundations when it comes to proving a criterion such as 'national origin', which may be based simply on self-declaration or inadequately documented personal histories. This procedure benefits above all those from the Republic of North Macedonia. The Bulgarian case, and its typical beneficiaries, represents a further example of strategic 'trading up' to EU citizenship on the part of citizens of states whose prospects for EU membership are remote. Such cases are very similar in approach to the some of the *ius sanguinis* cases for citizenship acquisition discussed in the previous section, and raise the same concerns about the over-inclusiveness of such ethnic preferences.

Other important forms of preferential naturalization include citizenship by investment schemes – the so-called *ius pecuniae* – but none of these cases are explicitly regulated in the respective national constitutions (Džankić 2019a). This is perhaps a telling omission, as critics of such schemes might suggest that investor citizens, as the ultimate citizens of convenience, are not really 'constitutional citizens' in the sense envisaged in this book (Shachar 2017). They represent the ultimate 'marketization' of the services of the state (that is, to provide passports and perhaps diplomatic protection, although in the latter case it is worth reverting to the *Nottebohm* case which established that a state was not obliged to recognize the conferring of nationality on a person with whom the receiving state had no 'genuine link'). The exception to the constitutional omission comes from those states that also provide for 'catch-all' special merits and 'state interests' provisions that can be used as surrogates for investor citizenship. An example is Article 12(2) of the Constitution of Georgia which provides, 'The President of Georgia may grant Georgian citizenship to an alien who has made a contribution of exceptional merit to Georgia. The President of Georgia may also grant Georgian citizenship

---

[65] See Saint Kitts and Nevis 1983 (www.constituteproject.org/constitution/St_Kitts_and_Nevis_1983?lang=en).

[66] See Bulgaria 1991 (rev. 2015) (www.constituteproject.org/constitution/Bulgaria_2015?lang=en).

to an alien based on state interests.'[67] These provisions represent the only exceptions to the ban Georgia otherwise maintains on dual citizenship.

It is, finally, quite common for constitutions to make a distinction between birthright and naturalized citizens, and generally to the disbenefit of naturalized citizens. Examples can be found in a number of Latin American constitutions (Acosta 2016, 14), although it is notable that Latin America also provides the best examples of countries that assimilate non-citizens into their voting publics, in advance of naturalization (Chile, Equador and Uruguay: see Acosta 2018: 161–2). In Egypt and Ecuador naturalized citizens may lose their citizenship if they reside outside the country for a certain period of years. In Romania, citizenship 'cannot be taken away from anyone who acquired it at birth'[68] while Malaysia makes extensive provision for deprivation of citizenship obtained by naturalization if the person 'has shown himself by act or speech to be disloyal or disaffected towards the Federation'.[69] The distinction between naturalized and 'birthright' citizens is perhaps most significant in relation to access to (high) public office, and such provisions regularly appear in constitutions. The Egyptian Constitution[70] and the Constitution of the Tunisian Republic[71] require that those holding certain offices need to be the children of citizens, and similar provisions are widely in use throughout Africa and Asia. However, perhaps the most famous constitutional restriction on holding high office is the requirement that

---

[67] See Georgia 1995 (rev. 2013) (www.constituteproject.org/constitution/ Georgia_2013?lang=en/). In similar terms, Article 10(6) of the Austrian Citizenship Law is a so-called 'constitutional provision', and it allows for naturalizations in return for 'extraordinary achievements in the interests of the Republic' (which permit dual citizenship even though this is generally prohibited in Austria) and has been used to confer citizenship on investors (Džankić 2019a, 2).

[68] Article 5(2), Romania 1991 (rev. 2003) (www.constituteproject.org/constitution/ Romania_2003?lang=en).

[69] Article 25, Malaysia 1957 (rev. 2007) (www.constituteproject.org/constitution/ Malaysia_2007?lang=en); see also Low (2017).

[70] Article 141, Egypt 2014 (www.constituteproject.org/constitution/Egypt_2014? lang=en).

[71] Article 74, Tunisia 2014 (www.constituteproject.org/constitution/Tunisia_ 2014?lang=en).

the President of the US must be a 'natural-born citizen', thus excluding naturalized citizens.[72]

Dual citizenship

If citizenship can still be understood as a bastion of national sovereignty, then nothing challenges that proposition more obviously than the possibility of dual or multiple citizenship. This is the simple, and historically paradoxical, idea that an individual can simultaneously be a citizen of two countries. It is easy to suppose that opposition to dual citizenship must lie in some cardinal principle of indivisible sovereignty (as given expression through concepts such as allegiance and loyalty), but the reality for much of the period of time when this was widely regarded as an issue (from the emergence of modern citizenship until the end of the Second World War) was that it was the much more prosaic challenges of organizing how diplomatic protection ought to work in such circumstances that dominated discussion.[73]

At the same time, no area of citizenship law and practice has altered so greatly in as short a time as that relating to dual citizenship, as states have grown much more tolerant of dual citizenship however it arises (Spiro 2017). The main factors 'causing' dual citizenship are 'mixed' marriages and partnerships, international mobility (often combined with the intersection of *ius sanguinis* and *ius soli* acquisition rules), and changing international borders, especially after secession. States have progressively abolished the legal provisions that ensured that women automatically lost their own citizenship on marriage to a foreigner and acquired his citizenship instead (Irving 2016), removed the obligation for children acquiring two citizenships by birthright to opt at the age of majority for just one, stopped requiring the renunciation of prior citizenship on naturalization, and ceased the practice of 'expatriating' citizens automatically when they acquire the citizenship of another state. According to Peter Spiro (2011), if there could be said to be one emerging norm of an 'international law of citizenship' it is that which

---

[72] Article II, Section 1, United States of America 1789 (rev. 1992) (www.constitute project.org/constitution/United_States_of_America_1992?lang=en). The Philippines also has a similar restriction on those eligible for election as President, but in *Poe-Llamanzares v COMELEC* GR No 221697, 8 March 2016, the Supreme Court held that a foundling is not a naturalized citizen but a 'natural-born' citizen. For discussion, see La Vina et al (2017).

[73] See Jennings and Watts (2008). On changing practices in diplomatic protection, see Denza (2018).

postulates and encourages greater toleration of dual citizenship. We are surely now beyond the point where dual citizenship can be regarded as an 'evil', yet even as late as 1974, the German Federal Constitutional Court was stating that 'it is accurate to say that dual or multiple nationality is regarded, both domestically and internationally, as an *evil* that should be avoided or eliminated in the interests of States as well as the interests of affected citizens'.[74]

This all suggests that dual citizenship has decisively overcome its fraught history, which has regularly seen diplomatic tensions between states and restrictions on the autonomy of people affected. States abandoned their attachment to perpetual allegiance, and thus allowed naturalization and expatriation, long before they started shrugging their shoulders and accepting dual citizenship in large numbers. By the end of the 20th century, international law had shifted away from supporting states to find ways of instituting and maintaining the single nationality principle towards encouraging states to have regard to the interests of persons affected as well as their own interests. The transition is well captured in the different approaches of two regional multilateral instruments. We have moved from the era of the 1963 European Convention on the Reduction of Cases of Multiple Nationality and Military Obligations in Cases of Multiple Nationality (the clue is in the title) to that of the European Convention on Nationality of 1997, which requires states parties to permit the dual citizenship of children (Article 14), and where the whole tenor reveals a move towards greater toleration of dual citizenship within the framework of generally reflecting state autonomy in the matter. The shift in state practice is visible not only in Europe, but also on other continents such as Latin America[75] and Africa.[76] Up to three-quarters of countries now do not require a person acquiring citizenship by naturalization based on residence to renounce the citizenship of the country of origin, up from around one-third only 50 years ago.[77] There are still outliers (for example, Austria and the Netherlands in Europe),[78] plus a persistent trend resisting dual citizenship in Asia.[79]

---

[74] German Federal Constitutional Court, BVerfGE 37, 217, 21 May 1974; emphasis added; quoted and translated in Spiro (2008).

[75] Acosta (2018, 155).

[76] Manby (2018, 109). For recent discussion, see 'Dual citizenship in Africa', *Deutsche Welle*, 29 January 2019 (www.dw.com/en/dual-citizenship-in-africa-benefits-outweigh-disadvantages/a-47276279).

[77] Vink et al (2015, 2019).

[78] On dual citizenship in the EU, see Gallagher-Teske and Giesing (2017).

[79] Vonk (2018b).

Attention is now moving to finding explanations for why states abandon certain practices, such as expatriation (Vink et al 2019), or, from an analytical perspective, to calling for distinctions to be drawn between the different 'types' of dual citizenship (Wautelet 2018). Indeed, far from being resisted, dual citizenship is now regarded by many states as being part of the armoury of strategies they have for 'power politics' (Nyyssönen and Metsälä 2019). So, according to Yossi Harpaz and Pablo Mateos, 'For states, dual citizenship policies are used to include absent ethnic kin and emigrant diasporas, revive territorial claims, and even justify the denationalization of undesirable persons' (2019, 853). We can once more cite the co-ethnic inclusion policies pursued by Hungary as raising another important and potentially constitutional question related to modes of acquisition and loss. Shortly after Hungary changed its citizenship law in 2010 to remove a residence requirement (thus allowing the wider 'diaspora' to naturalize on the basis of an ethnic preference), Slovakia – home to a substantial Hungarian minority – changed its own citizenship law to make voluntary acquisition of the citizenship of another country into a ground for loss of citizenship.[80] Slovakia thus (re)entered into a minority of countries moving away from allowing dual citizenship in the case of voluntary acquisition of another citizenship.

Dual citizenship rules in constitutions can become part of wider conversations about diaspora policies and the design of appropriate policies.[81] The point here is not the normative 'claim' to dual citizenship, whether for migrants, the children of migrants or the children of dual-national families but rather the broader state interests in international migration. For example, in India, single citizenship is constitutionally mandated.[82] This is related to India's concerns – at the point of the establishment of the state – about the relationship between its citizenship regime and that of Pakistan, not least since from the start India did not accept the basis for partition (Rodrigues 2008). To overcome this, successive Indian governments have developed a form of quasi-citizenship for emigrants, to allow them to maintain a sense of belonging and to protect the state's connections especially with a wealthy business diaspora elite (Xavier 2011). It allows beneficiaries to reside and work in the state without a time limit and without the need for a visa. It is, however, marked in another way by India's increasing concern to posit strict limits to its citizenship regime, in so far as no person whose parents or

---

[80] For a discussion, see Bauböck (2010a) and Kusa (2010).
[81] Collyer (2013, 2014) and Vink et al (2019).
[82] Article 9, India 1949 (rev. 2016) (www.constituteproject.org/constitution/India_2016?lang=en).

grandparents have held the citizenship of Pakistan or Bangladesh may hold the status. In 2019, the status was peremptorily withdrawn from the British writer Aatish Taseer, who had written an article critical of India's President Narendra Modi. While ostensibly this was on the grounds that he had 'concealed' the fact that his father was a citizen of Pakistan, in reality he had never made any secret of this fact, although he had absolutely no contact with his father until much later in his life and his mother was his sole guardian.[83] From time to time, dual citizenship 'proper' is discussed in the Indian Parliament, but change would require a constitutional amendment.[84]

In Lithuania, we can see a dialogue between the Constitutional Court and other organs of the state – in this case the legislature – around the interpretation of an ostensibly rigid constitutional text. The issue concerns the extent to which dual citizenship is recognized, since Article 12 of the Constitution makes it clear that dual citizenship should be an exception, rather than a widespread occurrence.[85] We can chart an extended dialogue between the Constitutional Court – which insists that the Constitution is strict and can only be changed with a referendum[86] – and the *Seimas* (Parliament), which is particularly interested in the potential dual citizenship of the many people who left Lithuania between 1940 and 1990, during the period when Lithuania was forcibly incorporated into the Soviet Union, and that of their descendants. There are also another set of interests relating to the citizenship of those Lithuanians who have left since independence in 1990 in search of employment opportunities, especially elsewhere in the EU, and that of their children. The legal situation is both complicated and in flux, as the *Seimas* continues to test the possible outer limits of Article 12 of the Constitution in order to bring Lithuania towards the mainstream of European countries' positions

---

[83] J. Slater (2019) 'Modi critic stripped of citizenship status in step denounced as "vindictive"', *The Washington Post*, 8 November (www.washingtonpost. com/world/modi-critic-stripped-of-citizenship-status-in-step-denounced-as-vindictive/2019/11/08/164cec40-01f1-11ea-8341-cc3dce52e7de_story.html).

[84] 'India to consider dual citizenship as "Global Indians" dominate international business', *Eastern Eye*, 13 August 2019 (www.easterneye.biz/india-to-consider-dual-citizenship-as-global-indians-dominate-international-business/).

[85] See Lithuania 1992 (rev. 2006) (www.constituteproject.org/constitution/Lithuania_2006?lang=en).

[86] Judgment of October 2017 (summary: www.lrkt.lt/en/news/court-news/the-extension-of-the-possibility-of-holding-multiple-citizenship-is-allowed-only-by-amending-the-constitution-in-a-referendum/971/).

on dual citizenship.[87] In May 2019, a referendum overwhelmingly backed dual citizenship with 43 countries which satisfied 'the criteria of European and transatlantic integration' (that is, excluding Russia and other associated countries deemed to be a threat to Lithuania). However, further legal steps need to be taken before Article 12 of the Constitution is formally amended.[88]

Like Lithuania, the Philippines has been and remains a country of significant emigration. It does not, however, have quite such a recent history of 'imperial' domination, having been an independent country since 1946. The Filipino Constitution includes a provision that addresses not 'dual citizenship' but the 'dual allegiance of citizens', which is 'inimical to the national interest and shall be dealt with by law'.[89] However, the reference to legislative measures has opened a gap on the basis of which the legislature has been able to construct a dual citizenship law allowing *emigrants* from the Philippines to naturalize in the destination country. Because they are understood to take such a step without 'the love' that they feel for the Philippines, this is deemed not to endanger their allegiance to the home country. This sleight of hand has been supported by the Constitutional Court, which has drawn a distinction between dual citizenship and dual allegiance (Aguilar Jr 2018). In other words, the constitutional provision has not posed an insuperable problem for the Philippines in triangulating between the different, and sometimes competing, interests of the state in keeping its diaspora close while making it possible for emigrants to be as effective as possible in their host countries. Of course, it treats immigrants and emigrants in different ways.

Dual citizenship is not always simply a boon for those who hold it, as it can also imply restrictions on what a person may do. In similar terms to the restrictions on naturalized citizens holding high office, so there are some constitutional restrictions on dual citizens. A paradigm example is the ban on dual citizens holding elected office (at federal level) in Australia, which needs to be understood against the backdrop of Australia's limited constitutional regulation of citizenship. The Constitution of Australia emerged out of the gradual process of independence, the loosening of relationships with the British Empire and the UK, and the federalization process within the country. This is one reason why the Constitution refers,

---

[87] For developments up to 2015, see Ruškytė (2015). Further information on Lithuania is also available via the GLOBALCIT website (blogs and news items) (see http://globalcit.eu/?s=lithuania).

[88] GLOBALCIT News (2019) 'Lithuanians support dual citizenship with 43 countries', 14 May (http://globalcit.eu/lithuanians-support-dual-citizenship-with-43-countries).

[89] Article IV, Section 5, Philippines 1987 (www.constituteproject.org/constitution/Philippines_1987?lang=en).

at various points, to the 'people of the Commonwealth' (of Australia), and emphasizes that the important feature of this 'people' is that it is democratic (Arcioni 2018). The Constitution predates the creation of Australian citizenship as a freestanding status under national law (and as such the Constitution refers to 'subjects of the Queen'), and in fact the formal legal status of 'Australians' until 1948 and the passage of the first citizenship legislation was that of 'British subjects'. The Constitution does not define or directly regulate citizenship, but it provides a power for the federal Parliament to regulate the status of aliens and mandates that elected representatives in the federal Parliament should owe no allegiance to a foreign power. Indeed, at several points it references allegiance, which has become an important marker of Australian citizenship in modern times, as discussed in Chapter 3 (Irving 2019).

Between 1948 and 1987, Australians had the dual status of British subjects *and* Australian citizens. Despite this duality, the new state initially had a rather restrictive approach to dual citizenship, as the space for a distinctive Australian citizenship was carved out in the postwar period. Later developments have seen an increased toleration of dual citizenship, both for Australians acquiring another citizenship, who no longer lost their Australian citizenship (after 2002), and also for 'new Australians', who no longer had to renounce a previous nationality (after 1949).[90] Even so, the long colonial legacy plus the pre- and post-independence immigration policies focused on maintaining a 'white Australia' are still visible in Australian citizenship and its approach to citizenship (Arcioni 2015).

Recent controversies relating to the application of the constitutional prohibition on elected representatives at federal level holding dual citizenship in Section 44(i) of the Constitution,[91] in particular by reference to the notion that such persons necessarily have split allegiance, have culminated with the fates of numerous politicians being decided by the High Court and many other parliamentarians becoming embroiled in the controversy. These cases have demonstrated that the process of 'modernizing' the conditions governing Australian citizenship has encountered limits when it comes to the interface between democratic inclusion and the requirement of *exclusive* allegiance to Australia written

---

[90] For the history of Australian citizenship, see Rubenstein (2017), especially Chapters 2 and 3.

[91] See Australia 1901 (rev. 1985) (www.constituteproject.org/constitution/Australia_1985?lang=en).

into the Constitution.[92] The High Court judgments in *Re Canavan*[93] and *Re Gallagher*[94] confirm the stringent requirements of section 44(i) of the Australian Constitution, applying a strict test whereby it was not necessary for a person to know about their second citizenship status for them to fall foul of the constitutional restriction. Only cases where renunciation is literally impossible or where it would be conditioned on the performance of tasks involving 'risks to person or property' or the completion of active military service before renunciation will not breach the constitutional restriction.

Yet this strict approach places Australia outside the mainstream of liberal democracies in relation to the application of bars on parliamentarians holding dual citizenship (and indeed, less strict arrangements are applicable in relation to some Australian state legislatures). For many observers, this represents an excessive restriction (de Groot 2017). In a country such as Australia, where a high proportion, probably more than half, of all citizens, have parents or grandparents who have been born outside the country,[95] it may indeed be hard to say what citizenships may have been 'accidentally' or unknowingly conferred by descent, or where – because of legislative measures adopted in another country – citizenship has been re-conferred on a descendant on an automatic basis. Where citizenship is not known about, it cannot so easily be renounced. Moreover, this restriction is constitutionally enshrined and not amenable to straightforward change by legislation. An opportunity was missed in 1997, when a parliamentary committee recommended changing the Constitution to put the disqualification provisions into legislation, which would then be amenable to change, only keeping a constitutional requirement that representatives be Australian citizens.

Once the issue became salient once more, the dual citizenship restriction became a tool among political parties seeking to gain advantages inside and outside Parliament. It has reduced the perceived legitimacy of elected parliamentary representatives among voters and it threatens to create a precautionary approach in which large swathes of Australia's multicultural population are effectively excluded from federal election (Orr 2018).[96] Yet up to 2018, every single disqualified parliamentarian who re-stood in a by-election was re-elected by their electorate, highlighting a lack

---

[92] For discussion, see Arcioni and Irving (2017) and Orr (2017).

[93] [2017] 91 ALJR 1209.

[94] [2018] 92 ALJR 502.

[95] See data at Australian Bureau of Statistics (2017) 'Census reveals a fast changing, culturally diverse nation', Media Release (www.abs.gov.au/ausstats/abs@.nsf/lookup/Media%20Release3).

[96] For critical comment and a call for constitutional amendment, see McIntyre (2017).

of concern among the Australian public about dual citizenship (Bloch and Rubenstein 2018). Indeed, Noa Bloch and Kim Rubenstein (2018) argue that there was a missed opportunity in the context of the High Court judgment to recognize explicitly that the constitutional provision was written for a time when hostility to dual citizenship was very high.

In fact, ironically, many judgments on citizenship and alienage in the Australian constitutional context have recognized one important historical change. At one point in time, a British subject could not be an alien, but nowadays such a person most certainly can be. Consequently, it would seem that there has been only a selective 'reading in' of the relevant historical context, with a failure by the High Court to recognize that its approach to dual citizenship does not match broader public perceptions. Unfortunately, if change has to come through an amendment to the Australian Constitution (there have been only eight since its inception), success is by no means guaranteed. The removal of the strict ban on dual-citizen federal representatives lacks the political salience and intellectual 'colour' of the other main constitutional issue actively under consideration, namely the recognition as part of 'the people' of Australia of the Aboriginal and Torres Strait Islander peoples (Arcioni 2015; Rubenstein 2018).

Besides Australia, other examples of such constitutional restrictions include Azerbaijan (a ban on dual-citizen presidents) and Pakistan (a ban on dual-citizen parliamentarians and presidents). All of these provisions hark back to the idea of the impossibility of dual allegiance. This continues to be a notion that enjoys some support in state practice, if one looks at national constitutions, even though, in many other spheres, states have lifted their opposition to dual citizenship, sometimes under external pressures. In the *Tanase* case involving parliamentary elections in Moldova,[97] the European Court of Human Rights held that a dual citizenship restriction on standing for election was intended to have political effects rather than to protect the sovereignty of the state. It was thus contrary to Article 3 of Protocol 1 of the ECHR (free and fair elections). This law was introduced after the restrictions on holding dual citizenship in the constitution of Moldova had been removed in 2002. This liberalization led to large numbers of Moldovan citizens accessing Romanian citizenship because of the very broad *ius sanguinis* rules on citizenship acquisition in Romania (of the type discussed above).

Despite the prevalence of these bars on holding or standing for office, it is more or less inconceivable that a bar on voting by dual citizens per se could be introduced or work in practice, except in the specific cases of a

---

[97] *Tanase v Moldova*, Application No 7/08, ECtHR, 27 April 2010.

bar on voting twice (either as a dual citizen, or as an EU citizen resident in another Member State) in European Parliament elections (Shaw 2007, 105), or where one of the two countries does not permit external voting by non-resident citizens. There have been initiatives to amend the Dutch Constitution to remove voting rights from dual citizens put forward by the far-right politician Geert Wilders.[98] These have been rebuffed by the need for a two-thirds majority and the lack of a political consensus. None the less, these types of proposal play well, electorally speaking, because of the relative unpopularity of dual citizenship in Dutch society, at least for immigrants (Vink et al 2019).

Loss of citizenship

There are many different modes of loss, some of which are voluntary and some of which are involuntary.[99] In this section, the focus is mainly on teasing out the constitutional implications of involuntary loss of citizenship.

Many scholars have remarked that modern citizenship is a less conditional status for individuals when compared to concepts of subjecthood, as elaborated under the common law in England, or even to modern legal concepts of citizenship as developed and applied in the 19th and early 20th centuries (Weil 2017a). Denationalization was common even in what we would now describe as the 'western democracies', in the 19th century and the early part of the 20th century, partly as a result of wars and other conflicts (creating categories of enemy aliens and making naturalized citizens from enemy states inherently 'suspect') and partly because of a focus on the singularity of citizenship (Gibney 2013, 2017). This latter focus led to resistance to dual citizenship (so that acquisition of one citizenship generally required the renouncing or loss of the previous citizenship) and a widespread insistence on the idea of a single nationality for a family (which in turn led to many women in transnational marriages losing their citizenship) (Irving 2016). Expatriation has a rich, complex

---

[98] 'PVV plan to strip dual nationals of voting rights unlikely to succeed', Dutch News, 18 February 2019 (www.dutchnews.nl/news/2019/02/geert-wilders-pvv-plan-to-strip-dual-nationals-voting-rights-unlikely-succeed/); 'Dutch far-right leader Wilders drafts bill to ban dual citizens from voting, candidacy', *Daily Sabah*, 16 February 2019 (www.dailysabah.com/europe/2019/02/16/dutch-far-right-leader-wilders-drafts-bill-to-ban-dual-citizens-from-voting-candidacy).

[99] For data on loss of citizenship, see GLOBALCIT (2017b), and for a discussion of the range of cases, see Bauböck and Paskelev (2015).

and often problematic history[100] and it is not only privileged migrants who suffer adverse consequences.[101] However, across the board, much less attention has been paid to those who leave than to those who arrive (Green 2009).

From a normative perspective, there is little doubt that the right to a nationality could also be said to encompass the right to change one's nationality and the right to naturalize (Owen 2018). But international law is not always as clear as it might be. However, we can find norms in international law related to the right to leave one's own country.[102] These buttress references in constitutions worldwide to the right to a passport and freedom to travel. The link between loss of citizenship, freedom to leave and return and access to documentation is nicely made by Article 5 of the Constitution of El Salvador:

> No Salvadoran shall be expatriated, nor his entry into the Republic prohibited, nor a passport or other documents of identification for his return be denied. Neither shall the right to leave the territory of the Republic be prohibited, except by resolution or sentence of a competent authority, dictated in accordance with the laws.[103]

However, Ben Herzog (2012) wisely reminds us that we should beware of surface impressions, whether now or in the past. A comparison of the pre- and post-1989 situations reveals some remarkable similarities between the formal positions of the Soviet and post-Soviet states. In other words, it is important to go beyond the formal law to recognize the cases where, in reality, to leave has meant to have your citizenship cancelled.[104] Cancellation by virtue of residence abroad *without permission* can still happen as, for example, in Laos (Vonk 2018a, 25).

Following significant misuse of denationalization capacities in the interwar years by a number of totalitarian regimes, a commitment to the right to a nationality and the prohibition on the arbitrary deprivation of nationality was included in the Universal Declaration of Human Rights and Conventions dealing with statelessness were negotiated and opened for

---

[100] On one part of that history, see Troy (2019).

[101] See, for example, Kunz (2016) and Low (2016).

[102] Council of Europe Commissioner for Human Rights (2013) *The Right to Leave a Country*, Issue Paper (https://rm.coe.int/the-right-to-leave-a-country-issue-paper-published-by-the-council-of-e/16806da510).

[103] See El Salvador 1983 (rev. 2014) (www.constituteproject.org/constitution/El_Salvador_2014?lang=en).

[104] For discussion, see Gitelman (1982) and Alexopoulos (2006).

signature. This seems to have heralded a new dawn in which citizenship gained recognition as a stable, even a 'sovereign', status (Weil 2017b). On that account, citizenship comes to be seen less as a privilege, and more as a right. Invoking US case law, such as *Afroyim v Rusk*,[105] in which the Supreme Court declared that denaturalization for any reason other than fraud or mistake violated the Constitution, Ayelet Shachar has referred to the 'constitutional right to remain a citizen' (2012, 1012). Hannah Arendt's words on the 'right to have rights' resonated widely in the period after the Second World War, and they were picked up in remarkably similar terms by Chief Justice Warren in the case of *Trop v Dulles*,[106] which assessed the constitutionality – against the 8th Amendment standard of 'cruel and unusual punishment' – of legislative measures that included loss of citizenship among the roster of available punishments for certain offences.[107] Furthermore, international human rights law has added another layer of protection so that the right to enter and remain 'in one's own country' can also cover non-citizens with close family ties and other 'private life' interests in the state.[108]

Yet continued and, in many countries, revived practices of denationalization seem to challenge that view, although Elke Cloots does pick out the 'national constitutional constraints' to be found in the US and German systems as explaining why in these two systems there is less likely to be citizenship stripping for convicted or suspected terrorists than is happening in many comparable countries.[109] The case of Germany is moot, as the discussion below shows, and there has in fact been a noticeable revival of denaturalization in the US,[110] along with passport revocation as 'proxy denaturalization' (Kassem 2014). The constitutionality of some of the measures taken has yet to be tested, but there are, indeed, few states that adopt the position of 'constitutional sovereignty' of the citizen, which has hitherto held sway in the US, in large measure as a necessary corollary to the 14th Amendment and its correction of the historical denial of citizenship to slaves. For Patrick Weil (2012), this is an

---

[105] 387 US 253 (1967).

[106] 356 US 86 (1958).

[107] For discussion, see Weil (2012) and Waldron (2013).

[108] *Stewart v Canada*, Merits, Communication No 538/1993, UN Doc CCPR/ C/58/D/538/1993, (1996) 4 IHRR 418, United Nations Human Rights Committee; *Beldjoudi and Beldjoudi née Teychene v France*, Judgment, Merits and Just Satisfaction, App No 12083/86, Case No 55/1990/246/317, A/234-A 14 EHRR 801, 26 March 1992, European Court of Human Rights [ECHR].

[109] See Cloots (2017, 60); see also Smith (2010).

[110] Frost (2019), Open Society Justice Initiative (2019) and Robertson and Manta (2019).

important dimension of the republican tradition that enables the rollback of racially tainted historical narratives and resists pressure to water down the resulting outcomes, which currently protect the sovereignty of the citizen. These ideas clearly connect back to the reflections in Chapter 3 on matters of sovereignty and constitutional identity.

As Bauböck and Paskalev (2015) point out, in mapping the terrain of loss of citizenship from the perspective of normative theory and models of citizenship (rather than from a human rights perspective), there remain many other state practices beyond the realm of public security and public safety under which the majority of states justify the involuntary removal of citizenship essentially on the grounds that the basis for conferring citizenship has been removed. There are many cases where revocation of citizenship is provided for in national law, including cases where those losing citizenship have no other nationality to fall back on. These include cases of fraudulent acquisition by naturalization (Fargues 2019), which is cited as a ground for citizenship deprivation in a number of national constitutions.[111]

Many countries within and beyond Europe have undoubtedly faced serious questions about how to deal with the potential return of those who have gone to Syria to fight with the so-called Islamic State (IS) (and also what to do about their children who have acquired citizenship by descent or who risk statelessness). Citizenship stripping has become a chosen tool, one that risks characterizing whole groups of Muslims and refugees as suspect (Abbas 2019). This sees the return of citizenship deprivation, this time as a tool of state security policy (Zedner 2016). The reprise of citizenship stripping in the 21st century has a different optic to the earlier phases of denationalization. Many have compared it more to medieval practices of banishment than to 19th and 20th-century denationalization. Parallels can also be drawn with ancient Greece (Gray 2011). Its legal nature has also changed, as this time around it is generally applied as an administrative sanction subject to limited judicial review, rather than as an element of formal punishment imposed within criminal process (Coca-Vila 2019). Audrey Macklin (2014) goes so far as to characterize citizenship deprivation as a form of civil death, analogizing to the other punishment used by states when they wish, permanently, to

---

[111] For example, Article 40(1)(b), Zambia 1991 (rev. 2016) (www.constituteproject. org/constitution/Zambia_2016?lang=en). For further reflection on the ethics of loss of citizenship see Honohan (2019).

be rid of someone: the death penalty.[112] It certainly challenges the human right to a nationality, in its current manifestation, and seems to fall, on the whole, more heavily on those who – despite holding national citizenship – are seen, for some reason such as having dual citizenship or belonging to an ethnic or religious minority, as too foreign wholly to belong to the polity (construed in this case in the sense of the nation).[113]

The introduction of dual citizenship provisions has had the paradoxical effect for some states of opening the door to citizenship stripping. In Norway and Denmark, when dual citizenship was introduced as an option for new citizens, who will no longer be subject to a renunciation requirement, this was precisely in order to make it easier to revoke the citizenship of naturalized citizens considered to be threats, without making them stateless. Had they been at risk of statelessness, this would have been a defence against citizenship deprivation (Midtbøen 2019). Australia is one another state that has introduced new citizenship-stripping provisions as a response to the 'war on terror', including ones aimed at native-born citizens who have a second nationality (Irving 2019).

Not all countries have not gone so far. For example, France has seen the discussion of such provisions in Parliament without formal adoption (Fargues 2017); Austria has instituted new provisions but barely used them; and Canada has legislated for citizenship stripping only for the law to be abolished by a subsequent government, after the idea of citizenship being conditional for some but not for others became one area of political contestation during the election campaign (Winter and Previsic 2019).

The UK has been the undoubted leader in putting citizenship stripping into practice, and it has adopted the practice of stripping the UK citizenship of those suspected of terrorist offences or certain types of terrorist or jihadist involvement when they are outside the UK.[114] This means that they can be refused re-entry under immigration law as they are now non-nationals and must contest any measures taken against them from outside the territory.[115] This also raises diplomatic issues, as the UK

---

[112] It is the logical consequence of the UK's policies that a person could face the death penalty as a result of citizenship stripping: see *R (Islam) v Secretary of State for the Home Department* [2019] EWHC 2169 (Admin).

[113] See Mantu (2018) and Gibney (2019).

[114] Figures are only available up to 2017. According to the Home Office, while only 14 people were deprived of British citizenship on the basis that to do so was 'conducive to the public good' (the widest ground) in 2016, in 2017 the equivalent figure was 104: Home Office (2018) 'Factsheet: Disruptive & investigatory powers transparency data', 23 July (https://homeofficemedia.blog.gov.uk/2018/07/23/factsheet-disruptive-investigatory-powers-transparency-data).

[115] For detailed discussion, see Fripp (2015, 383–412) and Yeo (2019).

has on several occasions taken a position on whether the subject of the deprivation order has access to another citizenship (on the facts or in law), which does not necessarily accord with the view of the other state. It also raises broader questions of security, justice and fairness towards dual nationals.[116] This approach certainly encourages other states to take a proactive approach to citizenship stripping, based on a motivation not to be the last state that acts.[117]

The case of Germany offers a neat link between cases of fraud in the acquisition process and the new practices of citizenship deprivation. Germany has a somewhat confusing constitutional provision on loss of citizenship.[118] Given Germany's history, it is not surprising that the *Grundgesetz* or Basic Law seems to set its face against denationalization in the sense of the state *withdrawing* citizenship (Article 16 of the *Grundgesetz*).[119] Yet the same provision goes on to suggest that it is possible that a person might *lose* citizenship, opening the door to cases involving fraud or deceit in the process of naturalization. In 2019, this logic was taken a step further with the introduction of an amendment to the citizenship legislation to provide for the *loss* of citizenship if a person has been actively fighting for a terrorist militia abroad, provided that the person does not become stateless due to this deprivation (Farahat 2019). This adopts and takes further the fiction, which has been constructed on the basis of the text of the *Grundgesetz*, that certain acts of a person can lead to him or her losing citizenship, such as the previously-provided-for case of voluntarily enlisting with the armed forces or a comparable armed organization of a foreign state whose citizenship he or she possesses (Steinbeis 2019).

Given Germany's restrictive rules on dual citizenship, however, and the non-retroactivity of the rules in respect of the existing case of foreign fighters and IS in Syria, the applicability of these new provisions within the framework of the *Grundgesetz* may lie some way in the future. However, the immediate challenge – both for Germany and other countries such as the UK that have been proactive in stripping IS fighters of citizenship – is not so far off, given the determination of Turkey to return to 'their' countries the escaped IS fighters it captured during its 2019 military

---

[116] See Sardelić (2019a) and S. Khan (2019).

[117] Hewitt (2019) and Macklin (2019).

[118] For discussion, see Kirsch (2011), Hailbronner and Farahat (2015) and Steinbeis (2019).

[119] See Germany 1949 (rev. 2014) (www.constituteproject.org/constitution/German_Federal_Republic_2014?lang=en).

offensive in Northern Syria, even if they had been supposedly stripped of citizenship.[120]

The final point here concerns the interaction between national provisions on loss of citizenship and the constitutional framework of the EU and its provisions on EU citizenship (Shaw 2019a). One further mode of loss of citizenship not previously discussed is loss of citizenship by operation of law owing to absence from the territory of the country, in particular for naturalized citizens.[121] This mode of loss is in place in the Netherlands (in citizenship legislation, not the Constitution), and applies even to birthright citizens. There are several important provisos: that there must be habitual residence in another country involving an uninterrupted period of absence from the Netherlands and from the EU; the person in question must have the citizenship of the state of residence or other citizenship (so there is no risk of statelessness); and the lapsing of the citizenship can be halted by the person applying for a Dutch passport every 10 years. The significance of the loss of Dutch citizenship in such a case is that the person will also lose EU citizenship and thus access to the various benefits that this supranational status provides, including in particular the right to reside and to work in any Member State.

In the 2010 *Rottmann* case,[122] which involved the German legal provisions on fraud or deceit in applications for naturalization, the CJEU repeated in its judgment the grandiose statement it has made many times in its case law since 2001, namely that 'citizenship of the Union is intended to be the fundamental status of the nationals of the Member States'.[123] This statement can be taken – as will be elaborated further in Chapter 7 – as the EU/CJEU equivalent to those statements of judicial rhetoric from national courts that articulate the link between the citizen, the constitution and the state, as discussed in Chapters 1 and 2. Like those statements, it lacks analytical precision but suggests instead a rhetorical commitment to the significance of EU citizenship. The CJEU went on in *Rottmann* to find that although competence in matters of nationality law remains with the Member States, none the less, in situations which are covered by EU law, states have the obligation to apply their national rules in a manner that has due regard to EU law.

---

[120] 'Turkey vows to return IS suspects to Europe', *DW News*, 2 November 2019 (https://p.dw.com/p/3SN5A).

[121] For details on the relatively large number of examples from Asia, see Vonk (2018a, 25). One of the few national constitutions to spell out this matter of relative detail is that of El Salvador, in Article 94(1), El Salvador 1983 (rev. 2014) (www.constituteproject.org/constitution/El_Salvador_2014?lang=en).

[122] Case C-135/08 *Rottmann v Freistaat Bayern*, ECLI:EU:C:2010:104.

[123] Case C-184/99 *Grzelczyk*, ECLI:EU:C:2001:458, para 31.

Having articulated the constitutional significance of EU citizenship for Member State nationals, it was not hard for the CJEU to conclude that such a case of loss of citizenship 'by reason of its nature and consequences' falls within the scope of EU law. Here the nationality of Germany was withdrawn because of fraud, but the person in question did not automatically regain his previous Austrian citizenship, which he had lost by operation of law (on becoming German). Mr Rottmann was thus left both stateless and lacking EU citizenship, at least in the short term. The CJEU further concluded that each case of loss of national citizenship entailing loss of EU citizenship would need individual consideration, under a proportionality test to control arbitrary national action, with the possibility of recourse to a national court by way of an appeal against an adverse decision. The CJEU thus entered the sphere of national citizenship law, but restricted its incursion in so far as it indicated that it did not see anything intrinsically problematic in the German provisions. According to the European Commission,

> Having due regard to EU law means taking into account all rules forming part of the Union legal order and includes having due regard to norms and customs under international law as such norms and customs form part of EU law.[124]

The CJEU's next incursion into the field of loss of citizenship came in the 2019 *Tjebbes* case, concerned with the Dutch rules on loss of citizenship sketched above.[125] In *Tjebbes*, the CJEU repeated its *Rottmann* findings, and concluded that in principle the Dutch provisions, including so far as they affected children, could be acceptable in principle, notwithstanding their falling within the scope of EU law, so long as there was scope for an individual examination of circumstances and compliance with the proportionality principle. In a balanced assessment of the judgment, Caia Vlieks (2019) concluded that the case reinforced the Court's willingness to take its incursions into national citizenship law so far, but not too far, but expressed disappointment that the judgment undermined the case, made by some academics, for saying that EU citizenship could be emerging not just as the 'fundamental status' of nationals of the Member States but also as an incipient autonomous and freestanding status in law. We will return to this point in Chapter 7, regarding in particular issues relating to

---

[124] Commission Report, Investor Citizenship and Residence Schemes in the European Union, COM/2019/12 final, 23 January 2019.

[125] Case 221/17 *Tjebbes and Others v Minister van Buitenlandse Zaken*, ECLI:EU:C:2019:189.

Brexit, the UK and the other 27 Member States. The wider implications of the *Rottmann* and *Tjebbes* line of case law concern the as-yet untapped potential for the CJEU's requirements of individualized assessment and a proportionality test as an EU level constitutional test of national provisions on citizenship deprivation in the types of terrorism cases discussed above, or in some other future scenario, for example if one of the more authoritarian governments in the Member States were to try and strip their political critics of citizenship in order to stifle dissent.[126] The potential applicability of EU law was raised, and flatly rejected, in several of the most problematic UK citizenship deprivation cases, such as *G1*[127] and *Pham*,[128] and so far the issue has not been raised with the CJEU via any of the national legal systems within which citizenship deprivation on national security grounds is practised.[129] In sum, these constitutional questions – both at the national and the EU level – remain unresolved.

The impact of constitutional norms on citizenship acquisition and loss

Away from the direct constitutional regulation of modes of acquisition, another important area in which we can see an interaction between constitutions and constitutional law, on the one hand, and citizenship, on the other, is where *other* constitutional norms can influence or affect citizenship. We have already highlighted, in earlier sections of this chapter, a number of unwritten constitutional norms in our studies of acquisition and loss, such as the cases of *ius soli* in France and *ius sanguinis* in Greece. Scholars and activists sometimes refer to broad general principles in order to articulate claims for reforms to citizenship laws. For example, Mariette Brennan and Miriam Cohen (2018) argue that Canada's strict one-generation *ius sanguinis* rules for transmission of citizenship by descent

---

[126] The example of the stripping of Indian Overseas Citizenship from a critic of the government (discussed at note 83 above) highlights that these are the sorts of legal manoeuvres in the minds of authoritarian regimes.

[127] *G1 v Secretary of State for the Home Department* [2012] EWCA Civ 867; [2013] QB 1008.

[128] *Secretary of State for the Home Department v Pham (formerly known as B2)* [2015] UKSC 19. In *Pham*, the majority of the judges indicated that they were applying a strict 'constitutional' standard of proportionality review to the decision taken by the Secretary of State, and doubted whether this would be any different than the 'European' standard: see Fripp (2016, 306).

[129] The approach to *Rottmann* as part the feedback loop to the CJEU is analysed by Horsley (2018, 241).

to children born outside the territory breach international law. They also question their compatibility with the rule of law, by which Canada is governed, on the grounds that the law fails to treat different groups of citizens equally. This has yet to be tested in court. Michael Sullivan (2018) has argued that Canada ought to embed a right to nationality into its Charter of Rights in order effectively to protect Canadian citizens against the risks of statelessness.

There have been numerous examples of success in invoking general principles in order to contest restrictions in citizenship law in the past. These include a 2008 ruling that denying citizenship to children born out of wedlock to a Japanese father and a foreign mother was discriminatory and unconstitutional, contrary to Article 14 of the Japanese Constitution (Chung and Kim 2012, 199). One important, and not exactly successful, historic example concerns Sierra Leone, where an early constitutional amendment to the country's fresh 1961 post-independence Constitution was introduced retrospectively to deny access to citizenship on the part of members of the country's Lebanese minority, using racial categories under which only those of 'negro descent' could be citizens. A case brought before the Sierra Leone courts had mixed success. At first instance, the Chief Justice held that this measure was contrary to the principle of non-discrimination built into the independence constitution.[130] This was reversed on appeal. But a further appeal to the Privy Council in London, then the court of last resort for Sierra Leone, was successful, once again on the basis of the principle of non-discrimination.[131] But in the event, the judgment was never implemented in Sierra Leone. The plaintiff himself was apparently 'bought off' by the offer of an ambassadorship (Malki 2017, 354), and the relevant discriminatory provisions have been retained. Meanwhile, they have been moved out of the Constitution into the (ordinary) citizenship law.

Even though Sierra Leone has been through much upheaval over the decades, including constitutional renewal on several occasions, the discriminatory provisions survive and seem to be protected by the Sierra Leonian Constitution. It remains difficult for those without 'negro ancestry', as defined in the citizenship laws, to access birthright citizenship. Yet among the political objectives in Article 6 of the Constitution of Sierra Leone is the following: 'the State shall … *discourage* discrimination on the grounds of place of origin, circumstance of birth, sex, religion, status,

---

[130] *John Joseph Akar v Attorney-General* (1968) 12(2) Journal of African Law, 89–109.
[131] *John Joseph Akar v Attorney-General of Sierra Leone* (1969) 13(2) Journal of African Law, 103–16.

ethnic or linguistic association or ties' (emphasis added).[132] However, while Article 27 of the Constitution prohibits discriminatory laws, explicit exceptions are made for laws in respect of those who are not citizens of Sierra Leone and those who acquire citizenship of Sierra Leone by registration or by naturalization, or by resolution of Parliament. It is clear that all these exclusions and restrictions must be understood by reference to the politics of citizenship and identity in Sierra Leone, not just those of post-colonial times, but also those dating back before independence from imperial Britain when a number of minority groups, including the Lebanese, arrived in the regions that were to become the country of Sierra Leone.[133] The politics of racial classifications have been historically significant and remain so today.

The most significant arena where constitutional norms have impacted on the acquisition and loss of citizenship relates to gender equality (Knop 2001). Many states have been faced with the challenge of correcting the blight that was introduced into the core of citizenship law through the widespread enforced denationalization of women, in the pursuit of the ideal of single-family nationality alongside the principle of the avoidance of dual nationality (Irving 2016). While denationalization was not generally effected by means of constitutional law provisions, its correction has often taken on a constitutional character, either with the help of activist courts wielding constitutional provisions or through constitutional change.

For example, after the Second World War, the Italian Constitution, which included a general norm of gender equality including in matters of political citizenship, was in conflict with its citizenship law, under which women's nationality should follow that of their husbands and under which they could not transfer their (original) nationality to their children. It took a number of Constitutional Court rulings before the citizenship law was changed in the 1970s and 1980s to introduce those two essential principles.[134] A similar story is evident in Canada, with the vital role being played by interpretations of the Charter of Rights and Freedoms in the *Benner* case,[135] as well as in Botswana, where judges in the 1992 *Unity Dow*

---

[132] See Sierra Leone 1991 (reinst. 1996, rev. 2013) (www.constituteproject.org/constitution/Sierra_Leone_2013?lang=en).

[133] For detailed background, see Beydoun (2013) and Malki (2017).

[134] For details, see Zincone and Basili (2010, 9–10).

[135] *Benner v Canada (Secretary of State)* (1997) 1 SCR 358. Further federal court cases on distinctions drawn in Canadian law between descent from male and female citizens that have been struck down by reference to Section 15 of the Charter include *Taylor v Canada (Minister of Citizenship and Immigration)* 2006 FC 1053 and *Augier v Canada (Minister of Citizenship and Immigration)* (2004) FC 613.

case had to explore the conflict between the 1984 citizenship legislation and the country's Constitution, in relation to the in-country transmission of citizenship by a married mother (with a non-citizen husband).[136]

The story in the US is more complex, especially as regards the position of unmarried parents, with unmarried fathers typically not in a position – or not as easily – to transmit their citizenship to their children who are born outside the US, compared to unmarried mothers. On quite a number of occasions, measures treating US citizen fathers and mothers differently in relation to births outside the territory of the US have survived scrutiny by the Supreme Court, and the most recent Supreme Court intervention in the *Morales-Santana* case[137] has proved a double-edged sword. The Court found that the provision in question violated the Constitution's equal protection clause. However, in terms of a remedy, the Court mandated a levelling down of the standard (for the future only, not for the past), effectively ensuring more restrictions on access to US citizenship for all unmarried parents.[138] As these cases are concerned with *ius sanguinis* citizenship, not *ius soli*, these issues are regulated statutorily (with often quite complex rules; see Calvo, 2016), rather than in the 14th Amendment.[139] Such legislative norms are, as has been seen, still subject to constitutional principles such as equal protection and due process.

Gender inequality in the area of citizenship acquisition continues to be a profound problem in several parts of the world. It is important to note that intergenerational statelessness problems are exacerbated by the retention or installation of restrictions on women's ability to pass citizenship to their children. Nepal offers an interesting – and problematic – case study where gender, statelessness and evidentiary difficulties relating to 'proving' citizenship are all intertwined. Subin Mulmi and Sara Shneiderman (2017) chart in detail the intersection between legislative and constitutional change that still leaves substantial numbers of people, especially children of unmarried mothers or children of Nepali mothers and foreign fathers,

---

[136] *Unity Dow v Attorney General (Botswana)*, (1992) 36 *Journal of African Law*, 91–2. See also the 8th Amendment to the Constitution Act in Lesotho (http://citizenshiprightsafrica.org/lesotho-8th-amendment-to-the-constitution-act-2018/). For more information, see Manby (2018, 98).

[137] *Sessions v Morales-Santana* 137 S Ct 1678 (2017).

[138] For a discussion, see Saucedo and Cuison-Villazor (2019).

[139] See also Collins (2014) making an argument that this area of US citizenship law is strongly permeated by the politics of race.

unable to prove citizenship, even though the official discourse denies a problem of statelessness.[140]

The absence of clear constitutional principles can also cast a shadow over understandings of citizenship (Rubenstein 2020). The treatment of certain groups in Australia, including Indigenous Peoples, highlights this. After the independence of the formerly Australian-administered territory of Papua New Guinea, the Australian High Court held that although Papuans had previously been statutory Australian citizens, in practice they had a constitutionally inferior form of Australian citizenship that did not confer on them membership of the 'constitutional people'. According to the High Court, it was thus permissible to deny them entry to Australia. A whole category of Australian citizens was thereby effectively expatriated by a reading of the Constitution in conjunction with measures taken under international and municipal law (that is, the independence of Papua New Guinea and the creation of its own citizenship regime) (Rubenstein with Field 2017).[141] Australia's constitutional distinction between citizens and aliens (with the latter having no privileges) has produced some astonishing consequences. The majority of the High Court in *Al-Kateb v Godwin*[142] interpreted immigration legislation to the effect that it was not unlawful for the state indefinitely to detain stateless people who had no lawful cause to be in Australia (for example, after an asylum claim had been refused), even where there was no reasonable prospect of removal (that is, no other state would take them and they could not return to where they had come from). Such detention could, logically, last the entirety of a person's lifetime, with no constitutional restriction on this problematic and damaging treatment of aliens (Irving 2008).

The most recent example of the shadow of the constitution on citizenship again concerned the issue of indigeneity. In February 2020, the High Court decided the cases of *Love* and *Thoms*, concerned with whether persons of Aboriginal descent, who were not citizens of Australia, could be deported as 'aliens' under Australian law because of their history of criminal convictions.[143] The premise of the scenario in which the persons in question found themselves concerned the energetic visa cancellation

---

[140] Nepal's 2015 Constitution left citizenship gaps not only in relation to issues of gender, but also with discrimination against Madhesi and indigenous populations: see Bhatta and Morch (2019).

[141] See *Ex Parte Ame* (2005) 222 CLR 439.

[142] (2004) 219 CLR 562.

[143] Case B43/2018 *Love v Commonwealth*; Case B68/2018 *Thoms v Commonwealth* [2020] HCA 3 (http://eresources.hcourt.gov.au/showCase/2020/HCA/3). Full details and documentation for the case are available from the High Court (www.hcourt.gov.au/cases/case_b43-2018). For details of the judgment, see Arcioni and Thwaites (2020).

and deportation policies of current and recent governments, applicable to those residents without Australian citizenship who are convicted of criminal offences of sufficient severity (Foster 2009). Press reports[144] on the case noted that one of the men was a native title holder, highlighting that the issues raised by these cases should also be linked to the question of how indigenous communities use *ius sanguinis* descent principles to define membership, as discussed earlier in this chapter. The immediate threat to deport at least one of the men was lifted, after widespread concern was expressed about the government's action,[145] but the High Court action continued, in order to clarify important issues about Australia's responsibilities, as a country, towards its indigenous communities (Murphy 2018). In 2019, the matter was certified as a constitutional issue. The argument developed on behalf of the applicants can be summarized as follows:

> For descendants of Australia's first peoples, a decibel part of the Australian community, to be "aliens" for the purpose of Australia's Constitution, is antithetical to their indigneity and to the social, democratic and political values which underpin and are protected by the Constitution.[146]

The crux of the argument mounted by the applicants in the case was that Aboriginal Australians occupy an interstitial 'third space' in the Australian constitutional scheme of membership. As Indigenous Australians they cannot be 'aliens', not least because of the attachment to the land of their ancestors, which long predates colonisation. Yet it is acknowledged that these applicants are not citizens (because of anomalies in the citizenship by descent legislation applicable at the time of birth and matters of

---

[144] 'High Court hears of bid to deport Aboriginal 'aliens'', *The Australian*, 8 May 2019 (www.theaustralian.com.au/nation/high-court-hears-of-bid-to-deport-aboriginal-aliens/news-story/6029be35541359bb7a2aad0b04202641). See also P. Karp and H. Davidson (2019) 'Citizenship test: Government argues Indigenous connection to land "important" but no bar to deportation', *The Guardian*, 5 December (www.theguardian.com/law/2019/dec/05/indigenous-citizenship-test-lawyers-argue-up-to-a-third-of-australians-at-risk-of-deportation).

[145] H. Davidson (2019) 'High court to rule on whether Indigenous people can be deported from Australia', *The Guardian*, 8 May (www.theguardian.com/law/2019/may/08/high-court-to-rule-on-whether-indigenous-people-can-be-deported-from-australia).

[146] The document from which this quotation is drawn (Written Submissions of the Plaintiff, dated 2 April 2019) is part of the materials made available online (see note 143 above).

happenstance relating to the actions of their parents). They argued that they are 'non-alien non-citizens', and as such they cannot be subject to deportation measures adopted under the relevant head of power in the Australian Constitution.

It was hard to predict in advance which way the case would be decided. This was the first time that indigeneity has played such a decisive role in relation to the formal contours of membership in Australia (Arcioni and Thwaites 2020), and the constitutional and other materials that the High Court had before it in order to settle this issue were somewhat sparse in nature. However, the leading case of *Mabo*[147] established a tripartite test of belonging based on descent, identity and community recognition that the High Court in *Love* and *Thoms* adopted. Before noting the terms of the decision, which was reached by a bare 4–3 majority of the judges of the High Court, it is important to highlight that the High Court has hitherto typically demonstrated a high level of deference to the prerogatives of the legislature in matters of citizenship definition, as the latter is the delegated representative of the democratic 'people of the Commonwealth' recognized in the Constitution. In that context, the absence of formal constitutional recognition of Indigenous Peoples in Australia has continued to be a troubling element. The majority who found in favour of Love and Thoms offered different reasons in their separate judgments, but all agreed that the correct test of indigeneity should look at matters of descent, identity and recognition. Beyond that, the majority all agreed that those recognized as Indigenous Australians could not be touched by the head of power given by the Constitution to Parliament to regulate the status of aliens. The detailed implications of the decision, including the judgments of the minority, who offered some possible avenues for Parliament to draft its way around the problem now posed, will not be fully understood for many years to come (Arcioni and Thwaites 2020; O'Sullivan 2020; Rubenstein 2020; Twomey 2020).

The international dimension: statelessness, the right to a nationality and campaigns for change

If citizenship can be understood as the constitutional corollary of the international states' system requirement for a national sortation system for populations, then statelessness could perhaps best be viewed as the consequence of the absence of an effective, consistent and universally applicable approach to allocating people to states (Bauböck 2018b).

---

[147] *Mabo v Queensland* [1992] HCA 23; (1992) 175 CLR 1.

It goes without saying that no state makes creating statelessness into a constitutional objective, although it can readily become the core by-product of constitutional exclusivity, as in the case of Sierra Leone, or of a changing constitution in conjunction with changing citizenship laws, as in the case of the Rohingya in Myanmar.[148] Historically, international policy-makers have long harboured the hope that both dual citizenship and statelessness could be eliminated if there were to be a sufficient harmonization of national citizenship laws along common principles. This has proved a vain hope, although scholars have not been shy about offering resources and suggesting 'toolboxes' to help at least with the task of eliminating statelessness and generally installing 'liberal' and consistent norms into the sphere of nationality law.[149]

The right to a nationality or right to citizenship, as recognized in the Universal Declaration of Human Rights, is given attention in constitutions both expressly (for example, Article 28(D)(4) of the Constitution of Indonesia[150]) and in terms of substantive provisions, for example, restricting the loss of citizenship to cases where a person has another citizenship.[151] Some constitutions specifically protect vulnerable groups such as refugees. This is also true of the position of children. Several countries link citizenship, the right to a nationality and the right to a name for children (for example, Malawi, South Africa and Colombia). Quite a number of countries have put specific measures to prevent statelessness into their constitutions (for example, by giving *ius soli* citizenship to otherwise stateless children), especially in regions of the world that are post-conflict (for example, Angola, Mozambique and East Timor) or post-transition (almost all of the countries of east central, eastern and south eastern Europe). Of course, not everything needed to ensure an effective right to a nationality will necessarily be in any given constitution. A useful handbook issued by the African Commission on Human and Peoples' Rights (ACHPR) on *The Right to a Nationality in Africa* draws on a much wider range of legal sources in order to explain the position in that continent and to offer resources for campaigns to support basic norms (ACHPR 2015).

Statelessness is not an issue that can be understood by reference only to constitutions or even formal legal sources, but it also requires close attention to be paid to administrative and evidentiary questions.[152] There are many

---

[148] For discussion, see Parashar and Alam (2019).

[149] For examples, see de Groot (2016) and de Groot and Vonk (2016).

[150] See Indonesia 1945 (reinst. 1959, rev. 2002) (www.constituteproject.org/constitution/Indonesia_2002?lang=en).

[151] Article 37, Cape Verde 1980 (rev. 1992) (www.constituteproject.org/constitution/Cape_Verde_1992).

[152] See Lawrence and Stevens (2017) and Hunter (2019).

who belong to the state who, hitherto, have literally not been 'seen' (Scott 1998). Campaigns for universal birth registration can make an enormous difference in this respect, without the need for legal change,[153] and the task of establishing statelessness determination processes to protect stateless persons[154] is one of the most important actions within the framework of the UNHCR's campaign to end statelessness within 10 years from 2014.[155] Through these campaigns, attempts to end statelessness have become inextricably linked to the international and, some might say, neoliberal development agenda, with donors assisting states above all to 'see' their own citizens and eventually to produce new markets, for example for technology companies selling the gadgets and the internet access that become essential once the registration process is taken online. This has happened in India in respect of many aspects of the management of welfare benefits.[156] It can still leave large groups out in the cold, who are excluded by constitutional restrictions that predetermine the way in which the state 'sees' its citizens, as is the case with Myanmar and the Rohingya, and as may be occurring in India, as will be explained later in Chapter 6. Moreover, as Lindsay Kingston has shown, statelessness still has less international visibility than might be expected, not least because it is a difficult task to frame it effectively in visual terms as a human rights challenge (Kingston 2019). We shall return to the topic of statelessness in Chapter 7.

As shown above, in relation to the use of constitutional norms to challenge restrictive or discriminatory national citizenship laws, the issue of gender is of enormous importance in the context of constitutional change. In Kenya, the inclusion of new provisions on gender equality in relation to citizenship in the Constitution, as part of a wider 2010 reform, came about as a result of pressure internally from women's and children's rights movements, even though not all of the changes to citizenship that the human rights groups had pressed for were introduced.[157] More generally, Bronwen Manby has commented that 'gender equality in nationality law followed the global trend, and was above all the prize of the women's movement across Africa, drawing inspiration from the UN

---

[153] See Hunter and Brill (2016) and Hunter and Sugiyama (2018).

[154] See UNHCR (2014) *Establishing Statelessness Determination Procedures to Protect Stateless Persons*, Good Practices Paper, Action 6 (www.refworld.org/pdfid/57836cff4.pdf).

[155] For details of this work, see UNHCR, #ibelong (www.unhcr.org/ibelong/). There are also multiple efforts at regional level, for example on indexing statelessness procedures in Europe (https://index.statelessness.eu/).

[156] For a discussion of the so-called Aadhaar scheme, see Jayal (2019b) and Chaudhuri and König (2018).

[157] Manby (2018, 188–9).

Convention on the Elimination of all forms of Discrimination against Women (CEDAW)' (Manby 2018, 188–9). However, as she notes for Africa, and as is evident elsewhere from the continued work of the Global Campaign for Equal Nationality Rights,[158] there are still many countries around the world that discriminate in their nationality laws on the basis of sex (in law or in practice) and/or that deny women the right to pass on their citizenship to their children. Curiously, many of these discriminatory measures are themselves a hangover from colonialism; they were rules embedded into the structures of the states before independence, or at the moment they became independent, which take many decades to remove, given the patriarchal structures of societies and the exclusion of women from power (Manby 2018, 98). While an organization such as the Global Campaign for Equal Nationality Rights does not limit its concerns only to issues of constitutional change, constitutional change has established itself as a central part of the toolkit of gender equality, at least in the eyes of influential actors such as UN Women (2017), and this also rolls across to the field of citizenship.

Aside from the related issues of statelessness and gender, it is not clear that questions of citizenship have attained a high salience in the context of either international development work or international human rights promotion. Attempts have been made to mainstream citizenship issues within the framework of working towards sustainable development.[159] It may be, of course, that CEDAW has simply proved to be a more effective base instrument to engineer change than any of the protective measures in the area of citizenship, or a regional standard such as the European Convention on Nationality. It is certainly the case that constitutions globally hold a more consistent baseline in relation to the inclusion of equality as a principle than they do in relation to citizenship.[160] But it may equally be that campaigns which emphasize gender equality (including in matters of citizenship) as part of larger constitutional overhauls or 'constitutional engineering',[161] however long they take and whatever obstacles they face, are simply less challenging to the embedded constitutional identity of a polity than campaigns to overhaul citizenship laws to make them more inclusive across all dimensions including ethnicity. This may explain the imbalance that can be discerned at present.

---

[158] See The Global Campaign for Equal Nationality Rights (www.equalnationalityrights. org/).

[159] This is explained in Bloom et al (2019).

[160] See 'Equality, dignity and related constitutional principles in conversation with citizenship' in Chapter 3.

[161] This phrasing is used by Waylen (2006) and Pailey (2019).

5

Filling out Citizenship: Citizenship Rights, Constitutional Rights and Human Rights

Introduction: constitutional rights and citizenship

This final chapter of Part II turns to the topic of the rights associated with citizenship.[1] Here we will need to confront the ambiguous role of the state and of state institutions in relation to citizenship. Significant questions can be raised over whether it is appropriate to equate citizenship rights with constitutional rights, and what conclusions can be drawn from the differing treatment – across the globe – of the various types of constitutional rights, from the civil and the political to the economic

---

[1] An obvious omission from this book concerns duties and the responsibilities associated with citizenship. This omission – for lack of space – is all the more egregious because quite a large number of constitutions address the issue of duties, including 87 that reference the duty to pay taxes (obviously not just a 'citizens' duty'), 120 that refer to the duty to serve in the military, and fully 124 that refer to the duty to obey the law. As with rights, the appearance of a 'duty' in the constitution is not conclusive as to what this actually means for citizenship, for example is it enforceable, who does it apply to, etc? However, it is certainly arguable that an account of citizenship and constitutions is incomplete without an assessment of the arguments that relate duties to ideas about individuals as rights bearers or which posit that certain responsibilities have an essential role to play in the maintenance of societal cohesion. For a review of some of these arguments, see Bellamy (2015); on the case of EU citizenship, see Komarek (2018). Both are responding to Kochenov (2014).

and the social.[2] The story of the evolution of citizenship rights highlights the differing ways in which state institutions have been co-opted into processes of struggle and resistance in relation to the enhancement and spread of citizenship rights, sometimes promoting the interests of citizens and citizen groups, and sometimes pushing back. Even though the *leitmotiv* of modern citizenship is supposed to be equality, it has still been the case that struggles for citizenship rights that are simply asking for equality can endure over many decades before achieving a positive outcome. A good example is the struggle for female suffrage (Ramirez et al 1997), where women 'citizens' could be excluded from full citizenship rights precisely because the law did not, in effect, recognize them as full citizens. It is hard, in that sense, to draw a line distinguishing between claims for citizenship and claims for rights. What is more generally true is that for citizens' rights to be legally enforceable, as opposed to merely aspirational, the institutions of the modern constitutional state – judicial, legislative and executive – will inevitably have a role to play.

Against the backdrop of the uneven and sometimes sparse treatment of citizenship across the world's constitutions, it is interesting to note the ubiquity of rights in those same documents. They appear in literally every constitution in the world, including those inspired by Islamic principles that rely to a much greater extent on the language of duties and community rather than that of rights. Moreover, 38 current constitutions explicitly refer to the 'rights of citizens'. More generally, the rights provisions of many constitutions are frequently drafted by reference to rights enjoyment by citizens, and with a view to those institutions required to protect those rights (courts, executive, special offices such as Ombudsman, and so on). The range of different rights covered varies enormously, but almost every constitution (186) incorporates a general guarantee of equality (O'Regan and Friedman 2011). As we have seen in previous chapters, equality, in its different guises, is central to the concept of citizenship and to maintenance of the constitutional claim to legitimacy, despite being frequently disdained in practice. Here, it would seem, is one promising source of answers to the question of what makes citizenship opposable to other statuses: it is one of the key sources of rights. However, what renders the topic of this chapter both broad and complex is that the story of citizenship rights in a constitutional context raises some profound questions about the issues of 'constitutional rights' and 'human rights'.

Formal constitutional rights for citizens crystallized as part of the first modern constitutions in the 18th and 19th centuries. There is a clear

---

[2] On constitutional rights, see Gardbaum (2011).

historical link between the emergence of rights and citizenship status. According to Gosewinkel,

> The nationalising state of the nineteenth century used to codify and refine its legal rules on nationality the better to identify its members and control claims for rights and social assistance addressed to the state. (2009, 500)

That is to say, as the state expanded its roles, it needed a clearer sense of who fell within and who fell outside the coverage of its protective cloak, in order to know who was entitled to rights or subject to duties. Constitutional rights have gone from strength to strength in the centuries that have followed. Different groups of rights have appeared in new constitutions at various points in history, reflecting the bargains that underpin those constitutional settlements. For newer democracies, especially since the end of the Cold War, the inclusion of socioeconomic rights into constitutions has often been a major area of struggle between different interests. But since rights are issues over which citizens will legitimately disagree, scholars such as Richard Bellamy (2001) have argued that the primary role of constitutions in relation to rights should be to create discursive spaces for such disagreement, not to give priority to enforcement by non-majoritarian institutions such as courts. This argument usefully articulates two contrasting perspectives on the nature of 'constitutional citizenship': should we understand the citizenry to be constituted because the constitution says so, and because it confers rights to that effect on them such as equality, or because they operate as free and equal citizens, deliberating and disagreeing, within a discursive space established by the constitution?

Constitutions and the standard palette of citizenship rights

Scholars and political commentators often have a hard time articulating what rights in modern states are, in fact, restricted to citizens alone. To put it another way, they have trouble isolating the essence of the *internal* as opposed to the *international* right to citizenship (Lenard 2018a). This is one domain where the line between citizen and alien has become blurred. This may be why some scholarship has focused instead on the 'hallmarks' of citizenship rather than on the rights (Gardner 1997). The standard palette of rights specifically related to citizenship includes those associated with presence on the territory (the right to leave and to return to one's country), those associated with protection of and by the state (diplomatic protection, military service, restrictions on extradition), those associated with democracy and the role of the body of citizens as 'the people' (the right to vote and stand for election, and to hold high office), and those that involve some sort of share in the collective resources of the country (social and economic rights). Probably the unconditional right to return is one of the few rights given exclusively to citizens, although patterns and processes of denationalization[3] and deportation[4] have rendered even that story much more complex in recent years. Some countries, such as Canada, recognize the 'right to a passport'[5] as part of the right of return, but others, such as the UK and US, regard passports as discretionary privileges that can be revoked.[6]

Furthermore, democracies in the Global North frequently extend many of the rights noted above to those who have been lawfully resident on the territory for a certain period of time, albeit sometimes subject to additional conditions. This point is especially true of social and economic rights, although many countries reserve most welfare protection for citizens alone. While the very 'fullest' membership may normally be reserved for citizens – for example, only a very small minority of countries allow any people other than citizens to vote or seek election in *national* elections[7] – it is consistent with viewing citizenship as a 'gradient status'[8] that states will accord at least some of the political rights associated with citizenship to lawfully resident non-citizens, not least in order to promote their integration as immigrants. This is the case, for example, with the right to vote in local elections.[9] In that context, the EU, which prohibits discrimination against nationals of other EU Member States in any area covered by the EU Treaties and encompasses a relatively wide range of political rights, provides a standout example of the extension of most 'citizenship rights' to what are sometimes called 'second country nationals' (to distinguish their situation both from nationals or citizens of the host state and so-called 'third country nationals' from non-EU states).[10]

---

[3] Gibney (2017, 2019).

[4] Lori (2017).

[5] *Abdelrazik v Canada (Minister of Foreign Affairs)*, 2009 FC 580, [2010] 1 FCR 267. For a brief discussion of the right to a passport as a dimension of loss of citizenship, see 'Loss of citizenship' in Chapter 4.

[6] See House of Commons Library (2017, 12–15) and Weil (2014).

[7] Shaw (2017c).

[8] Cohen (2009).

[9] Arrighi and Bauböck (2017).

[10] Shaw (2007).

More generally, provisions in the texts of constitutions that guarantee that non-citizens who are lawfully residing should enjoy the normal protections of the rule of law under the constitution are quite common across the world. Other types of constitutional rights, such as rights to bodily integrity, civil rights and due process rights (that is, those rights that protect against arbitrary behaviour on the part of the state) are also often accorded to 'everyone' – that is, to anyone falling within the jurisdiction of the constitution, whether lawfully resident or not (and, indeed, on occasions outside the territory of the state). However, this is not universally true. Aside from the obvious restrictions within immigration law, some countries, whether by constitution or ordinary law, reserve the right to own land or real property to citizens alone, restrict all political activities by foreigners, including the joining of political parties or the exercise of political expression, and even restrict access to the courts by non-citizens. In the latter case, such restrictions may often coincide with the presence of weak state institutions and high levels of corruption also impeding access to justice.[11] There is also considerable variation in the extent to which privacy and associated information rights (freedom of expression, freedom of information, access to information held by the state, data protection etc), which are increasingly important in the digital age, are granted to citizens, residents or anyone in the territory of any given state.[12] It is insufficient, moreover, to discuss the role of rights in the constitution of citizenship without reference to the role of international law. International human rights and humanitarian laws are particularly important for the protection of those within states who are not citizens (or who are citizens but are denied effective recognition as such), especially those who are stateless or are otherwise in need of protection, for example, refugees and asylum-seekers (Kesby 2012), although precisely how will vary from country to country.

Since the adoption of the Charter of Rights and Freedoms in 1982, Canada offers a good illustration of the interplay of citizenship, citizens' rights and constitutional rights. Neither the Canadian Constitution as such, nor the Charter (which is constitutionally entrenched but separate from the Constitution), defines citizenship, and the term 'citizenship'

---

[11] For some evidence of this, see Law and Versteeg (2013) and Chilton and Versteeg (2018).

[12] Compare Article 28, Venezuela (Bolivarian Republic of) 1999 (rev. 2009) (www.constituteproject.org/constitution/Venezuela_2009?lang=en), 'Anyone has the right of access to the information and data concerning him or her or his or her goods which are contained in official or private records' with Article 41, Uganda 1995 (rev. 2017) (www.constituteproject.org/constitution/Uganda_2017?lang=en), 'Every citizen has a right of access to information in the possession of the State'.

does not appear in any constitutional documents (Winter 2015). But citizens' rights have been more clearly articulated since the inception of the Charter, as it distinguishes between those rights that are given to citizens (in essence, rights to enter and leave, democratic rights and, in a particularity of Canadian federalism and multiculturalism, minority education rights) and those that are given to everyone.

One of those rights for 'everyone', the equality guarantee in Section 15 of the Charter, does effectively open up the possibility that the Charter can have a wider impact on citizenship and citizenship rights. We mentioned already in Chapter 4 how the Charter has been used in order to strike down rules that differentiated as regards citizenship by descent between male and female citizens. More pertinently to this chapter, the first case before the Supreme Court on Section 15 concerned the possibility of using citizenship itself as a protected ground. In *Andrews*,[13] the Court held that it was not permissible for access to the legal profession to be restricted on grounds of citizenship to Canadians alone. This was important as citizenship is not an enumerated ground for equality in Section 15, but even so, the Supreme Court stated that discrimination on grounds of citizenship was covered by the Charter, and the restrictive measure was not justified.

Despite this opening, subsequent case law, notably the case of *Lavoie*,[14] has shown the limits of this approach. In *Lavoie*, while most of the judges accepted the principle that distinguishing between citizens and non-citizens in relation to access to employment in the public service in principle fell within the scope of Section 15, the majority none the less concluded that the measures in question were saved by Section 1 which allows for 'reasonable limits [to Charter rights] prescribed by law as can be demonstrably justified in a free and democratic society'. In particular, one interest that the majority of judges accepted needed promoting was the value of citizenship: why would any non-citizen choose to naturalize if it carried no advantages at all? This illustrates nicely one of the main constitutional law points to be made about rights under national constitutions, which is that their protective scope is generally subject to various balancing limits and tests such as proportionality, which are applied by the courts. Of course, this is precisely why rights sceptics such as Bellamy (2001) worry about the role of courts, because it arguably gives them a great deal of discretion in relation to such matters. On the other hand, Catherine Dauvergne (2013) has argued, on the basis of a comprehensive review of the case law, that the overall impact of

---

[13] *Andrews v Law Society of British Columbia* [1989] 1 SCR 143.

[14] *Lavoie v Canada* [2002] SCC 23; [2002] 1 SCR 769.

the Supreme Court's case law applying the Charter protections in cases involving non-citizens has been disappointing, perhaps because the Court accords too much deference to matters of governmental discretion in relation to immigration and security when it comes to the balancing of rights to equality on grounds of citizenship against other interests.

This descriptive approach will not, however, take us very far. For example, the point made right at the beginning of this book about the dominance of local particularities in relation to the citizenship/constitution interface (Rubenstein and Lenagh-Maguire 2011) becomes even more stark when it comes to assessing how any given constitution deals with the constitutional rights associated with citizenship. It becomes very hard indeed even to identify and articulate some common themes if we start with the myriad variety of texts before us. Equally we must remain wary of those texts; as noted previously, the rhetoric of constitutions does not always match the reality in practice, and this is certainly the case in relation to long catalogues of hard-to-enforce and aspirational social and economic rights that appear in many constitutions across the globe. Many countries simply lack effective enforcement mechanisms, or the rule of law is insufficiently embedded within the political order. Furthermore, what we miss in concentrating only on the constitutional texts is both the history of citizenship rights struggles (how we got to where we are) and the contestedness of citizenship rights at the present time. Yet at the same time we must not lose sight of the constitutional dimension and the question of how we can assess the role that constitutions do or might in the future play in the identification, communication and/or enforcement of 'citizenship rights', in so far as these exist as a distinct category. This preoccupation shapes the questions that this chapter seeks to ask and to answer.

The discussion in the rest of this chapter builds on what has gone before in previous chapters, where we have already touched on several important aspects of the rights/citizenship interface. As we have seen, citizenship itself can be seen as a right (to have rights), and we have worked through some of the constitutional issues that underpin this insight in the earlier chapters. In Chapter 3, we took a look at how dignity and equality, concepts which play a prominent role in most rights/liberties catalogues, affect the scope and quality of citizenship as a constitutional ideal. Throughout we have acknowledged the contested and reflexive character of citizenship, such that we must recognize that one of the most important functions of constitutions has been to open and close the discursive space in which citizens have worked together to realize what Bellamy calls 'their evolving needs and ideals' (2001, 38). We return to this point below, when we press harder on the question as to whether citizens' rights, protected within a constitutional framework, can assist in finding an answer to the questions of what makes citizenship special and why constitutions might matter (or not). The section on 'The franchise' looks in a little more detail at a case study of how one citizenship right works in practice: the right to vote. The final section serves as a conclusion not just to this chapter but also to this part of the book. All of these discussions are prefaced by some reflections on the ubiquity and contestedness of rights.

The ubiquity and contestedness of rights

The ubiquity of rights in constitutions can be traced back to two roots. One has already been averted to, namely the innovation of rights provisions within the two revolutionary constitutions (the US and France) from which so many countries have drawn constitutional inspiration in the following centuries. The other stems from the emergence of a global human rights regime after the Second World War, comprising in particular the Universal Declaration of Human Rights, the 1966 International Covenants on Civil and Political Rights and Economic, Social and Cultural Rights, and various regional human rights instruments including the European Convention on Human Rights and Fundamental Freedoms (ECHR), the inter-American Human Rights System and the youngest of the three regional judicial or quasi-judicial human rights systems, that for Africa.

Institutionally speaking, the global human rights regime, which has been described as an 'amalgamation of law, permanent institutions, courts, global campaigns and funding' (Hopgood 2014, 68), dominates the rights sphere. As a regime, it incorporates not just the specific global or regional level measures and institutions, but also the state-level frameworks for rights and infrastructures. Human rights offer an excellent example of multilevel governance, with multiple sites of authority dispersed across both vertical and horizontal planes.

But the ubiquity of rights should not be taken to convey the impression that rights are now uncontroversial incidents of modern life; quite the contrary, in fact. The whole topic of 'rights' is highly contested today. In the contemporary world, every claim, be it political, social, economic or private, is almost without exception founded on or justified by 'rights'. We see ourselves by definition as rights-bearing individuals. They have, as Samuel Moyn has put it, a hold on our utopian imagination (2014, 57). In an earlier paper with Igor Štiks, we argued that:

> Since the rhetoric of rights is all around us, we end up with
> a blurring of the very definition of what rights are, not to

mention a blurring of the boundaries between different bundles of rights, their sources and the various institutional practices through which they are "enjoyed" or asserted. More specifically, "human rights talk" dominates our discourse to the extent that it seems almost impossible to talk about any types of rights without relating them somehow to human rights, which are in themselves a vast category differently interpreted around the globe. Against that background, it is very tricky to define the concept of *citizenship rights*. Are these to be seen only as the rights *of citizens*, or more broadly as the rights related to *citizenship* as a status? And if so, how do they differ from the universalistic category of *human* rights, or as some might have it, *fundamental* rights? (Štiks and Shaw 2014, 73–4)

Concerns about rights protection and especially the future of the global human rights regime are commonplace. Issues are raised about the complexity and enforceability of many rights, especially regarding the more recent proliferation of social and economic rights; about the alleged imposition of liberal ideas contrary to the specificities of local circumstances; and about a backlash against rights, driven by the challenge of demonstrating that liberal rights, especially those protecting the interests of LGBTQ+ people, and religious sensibilities can be concordant and not clashing (Hopgood et al 2017). Just because human rights have been a ruling idea in our age, and an accepted way to deliver a moral vision of the world, this does not automatically secure their future status (O'Neill 2005).

As a project of globalism, human rights have come under attack from numerous directions (O'Byrne 2019). In the UK, adherence to the ECHR has come under challenge from the Conservative Party that has dominated government since 2010. One of the primary motivations for the initiative to recover rights from Europe was a deep-seated objection within the party to the body of case law developed by the European Court of Human Rights (ECtHR) on prisoner voting under the ECHR.[15] Other concerns relating to what opponents think to be an over-intrusive human rights regime have extended to areas of immigration and counter-terrorism law. In 2019, the US Secretary of State Mike Pompeo (2019) established a Commission, led by a conservative Catholic jurist, Mary-Ann Glendon, with a remit to look at re-embracing the core of 'unalienable rights',

---

[15] See the line of case law from *Hirst v United Kingdom (No 2)* (2005) ECHR 681 onwards.

a term drawn from the American Declaration of Independence and referring to 'life, liberty, and the pursuit of happiness'.

Just as British conservative politicians do not reject rights out of hand when they propose to repeal the Human Rights Act 1998, but pursue them instead under the heading of a brand new 'British Bill of Rights', which will cut the UK off from the mainstream of European regional human rights protection,[16] so an American politician of the right has explicitly embraced rights as part of his strategy, so long as the starting point is a restrictive conception. In Pompeo's (2019) words: '[America's founders] designed the Constitution to protect individual dignity and freedom. A moral foreign policy should be grounded in this conception of human rights.' While happy to praise a narrow conception of rights, as pushing the spread of liberal ideas, the thrust of his argument is focused on rejecting the wider body of rights that are now widely recognized, and the claims-making activities of certain groups. These are what he calls the 'ad hoc rights granted by governments', which are not apt to be recognized as universal. By basing the work of his Commission on recovering an historic and perhaps archaic term and set of practices, this once more emphasizes the localization of the rights appropriate to what he sees as American circumstances. It is one way of pushing the global to the periphery, and of giving priority to the local. With the reference to this historic standard, focused on 'natural' rights and property rights, it may once again be the case that the rights of vulnerable minorities will be brought into question by a panel which pulls together members from the religious conservative right and the far (secular) right (Moyn 2019). Those who migrate across borders and LGBTQ+ people are obvious targets. It seems clear that the intention in creating such a Commission is to signal that their claims making will be hampered in the future (Carden 2019).

While these types of attacks on rights do not normally take direct aim at the main rights of citizenship as summarized in the opening section, they do raise the question as to whether certain groups, especially cultural, ethnic or sexual minorities, may be vulnerable to losing some aspects of the full enjoyment of their status as citizens, as full members of society. They engage the large question of whether the stepwise evolution of rights and membership articulated by T.H. Marshall (1992 [1950]), from

---

[16] See Harvey (2018) and Gearty (2019). The UK's withdrawal from the EU Treaties and its proposed withdrawal from the ECHR are two separate issues, and the former has now largely pushed the latter from public discourse. Brexit has its own human rights dimension, with the enactment of measures to ensure, even with withdrawal of an orderly nature under an Article 50 TFEU agreement, the EU's Charter of Fundamental Rights will not be among the elements of EU law retained at least for the transition period: see Markakis (2018) and Barnard (2019).

civil, to political, to social rights, which enjoys wide currency both among commentators and practitioners, can be put into reverse, either under adverse economic or security conditions or in circumstances where political and legal liberalism and even constitutionalism comes under threat from a robust majoritarianism, invoking the populist call of democratic consent. This takes us back to the constitutional underpinnings of the citizenship idea (and ideal), which we explored in Chapter 3, and asks the additional question of how these can impact on the scope and nature of rights-holding in the contemporary constitution. It is only when we are equipped with this understanding that we can judge the extent to which those people whose rights and claims have previously been asserted can resist the restriction of those rights in hostile circumstances.

Persons and citizens as holders of rights

Ayelet Shachar highlights the inappropriateness of holding fast to:

> ... the standard or static vision of citizenship, according to which "all the members of the political community [are] bounded by the borders of the state – and only they – were to have equal rights and duties and an equal stake in decisions regarding matters of the state".[17] This unified and state-centered understanding of citizenship has always been more of a myth than a reality, but it is arguably harder to sustain in an increasingly interconnected world that has given rise to new and more dynamic forms of multilevel governance and attachment that are proliferating, both above and below the nation state level. (Shachar 2012, 1016)

Since the end of the Cold War, or perhaps already before, there has been a resurgence of interest in citizenship.[18] This has extended to renewed interest not only in the nuts and bolts of national or state citizenship, as discussed throughout this part of the book, but also in other political and sociological aspects of citizenship within and beyond the Marshallian paradigm. So rather than being seen as 'just' a vehicle for rights, citizenship has also been valorized as a space for claims-making by different groups, with a shift from a focus on aspects of redistribution (to facilitate full

---

[17] Shachar is quoting here from Horváth and Rubio-Marín (2010, 72–3).

[18] Early examples of the genre, mapping the field, are Kymlicka and Norman (1994) and van Steenbergen (1994).

membership) towards a concept of recognition.[19] To some, this move has involved excessive concept stretching, taking citizenship away from its analytic core. Christian Joppke criticizes what he terms 'hyphenated citizenships', that is, concepts such as sexual citizenship or ecological citizenship. He argues that 'such "citizenship" is less a distinct and clearly demarcated object of study than a conceptual metaphor for a bewildering variety of rights-based claims in contemporary societies, particularly if raised by marginal groups' (Joppke 2003, 429). What Joppke seems to underestimate is the extent to which such claims-making has, historically, often been the making of citizenship (Chacón 2018). What was once marginal may now be mainstream, and vice versa, so it is tricky and self-defeating to make snap judgments about what counts and what does not. Leti Volpp points out that 'feminist, sexual and queer approaches to citizenship have foregrounded human questions of dependency and reproduction that had long been neglected in citizenship discourse' (2017, 154). A similar point will be made about constitutional discourse later in this section. The point is how to recognize and contest 'second-class citizenship'. Introducing a special issue devoted to these questions, Avigail Eisenberg and Patti Lenard remind us of just how second-class citizenship for certain groups can arise, returning to the classic work of Iris Marion Young (1989) on differentiated citizenship. In their words, Young argued that:

> ... differences in class and cultural identity could be predicted to intersect with public policies, with the effect of denying access for some people to certain key benefits of citizenship and thereby creating a de facto class of the second-class citizenship. Her goal was to expose these exclusions as a direct result of the pursuit of universal citizenship and to propose group-differentiated citizenship as a remedy. (Eisenberg and Lenard 2018, 1)

Around the same time, the idea of citizenship faced another challenge as the argument gained traction among some scholars that it was becoming 'postnational'. This argument hung on the proposition that there had, in substantial measure, been a de-linking of questions of rights and (to a more limited extent) access and belonging, from the exclusive purview of a single nation state.[20] Postnational citizenship has been the subject of heavy criticism, not least for its apparent tendency to downplay the

---

[19] The classic reference is Fraser (1995); see also Štiks and Shaw (2014, 81).

[20] Two classics of this genre are Soysal (1994) and Jacobson (1997).

importance of the state, not just in relation to rights, but also to the issue of citizenship status.[21] Notwithstanding such criticism, it is still correct to say that, from a political, legal and sociological perspective, there is now a complex and fragmented governance of citizenship in which the state plays one important part, but not the only part.[22] This concern animates our discussion in Chapter 7 of the shifting spatialities of citizenship. Indeed, it is helpful that Yasemin Soysal points out that 'postnational citizenship is not a legal status – it is an analytically heuristic device to explain the reconfiguration of citizenship in the post–World War II period' (2012c, 50). Much the same point can be made about the 'shifting spatialities of citizenship' frame used in Chapter 7 of this book to look at the 'beyond the state' pressures on the classic tropes of citizenship. Moreover, as I have argued previously, 'empirically it still remains important to specify the precise changes and evolving institutional practices which constitute or construct forms of membership which are not attached solely to traditional state-level forms of polity organisation' (Shaw 2007, 35). To that end, it matters less whether we describe citizenship beyond the state as 'transnational' (Fox 2005) or 'postnational'. What matters is the careful specification of whatever it is we study.

What needs to go alongside our close reading of these forms of membership (and the contexts in which they exist) is more awareness of the constitutional significance of choices regarding the scope of rights, who can hold them and how they came to be valorized. Another way of putting this point is to ask whether there is more to the apparently scattergun choices of constitutions about the scope of rights and about whether certain rights are given only to citizens, or to larger categories of person, than simply haphazard selections of constitutional actors in different countries and at different points of history. For example, can it be argued that one way of completing that particular circle is to refer back to the complex concept of dignity, as presented in Chapter 3? As I argued there, 'the 'dignity of the citizen' operates as one way in which we, as humans, can help realize 'human dignity'.

Certainly, the persons/citizens distinction is an important one. The idea of a distinction between the ethical universalism of personhood and the situatedness of citizenship is discussed in detail in relation to US constitutional law and history by Linda Bosniak (2010). Normatively, Bosniak finds it preferable that the US Constitution should be (largely) predicated on the concept of constitutional rights for persons rather than the narrower category of citizens' rights, as it renders the space

---

[21] For a critique, see Hansen (2009) and Koopmans (2012).
[22] See Soysal (2012a, b).

between citizen and alien much smaller, generally for the benefit of the latter in terms of access to rights.[23] She acknowledges, however, that the edges of the two concepts are frequently contested, with consequential impacts on the justiciable scope of rights. Moving away from a US focus, Naila Kabeer proposes a neat way of tying the two concepts together by arguing that 'citizenship is a way of defining personhood, which links rights and agency' (2006, 91). She finds that the history of citizenship (and presumably also the scholarship associated with it) has been highly exclusionary, and points out there are two major omissions from the 'Marshallian paradigm', namely immigration and colonialism. But she calls for a concept of 'inclusive citizenship' effectively encompassing both the personhood and citizenship dimensions of rights-holding:

> The concept of "inclusive" citizenship is taken to refer both to people's ability to claim their legally recognised rights on an equal basis as well as to the extent to which that law deals with them in a way that guarantees their equality. (Kabeer 2006, 91)

From that perspective, personhood and citizenship sit alongside each other, and do not stand in opposition. So far, so good. But we still need to get behind this concept of equality, which keeps reappearing.

Ruth Rubio-Marín (2015) has pointed out (at least in relation to gender) that it will make little difference whether constitutions refer to 'persons' or 'citizens' if the analysis dodges the realization that constitutions are not gender-blind or race-blind (or, more generally, 'difference-blind') statements of values or principles. Thus, as Rubio-Marín shows, traditional constitutional conceptions of women have been little disturbed by claims for female suffrage or 'equal treatment'. These can be incorporated without really shocking the body constitutional in its traditional forms. For there to be a transformative effect above and beyond formal equality, she argues, the public/private divide needs to be broken down, and issues such as care and responsibility must be brought within the framework of the constitution. Only in this way can 'egalitarian citizenship' be built in a manner that goes beyond the traditionally gendered character of liberal constitutions. Such a step has occurred, in a rather isolated example, in Article 69(1) of the 2008 Constitution of Ecuador, which gives equal weight to the responsibilities of mothers and fathers.[24]

---

[23] For further discussion of related issues, see also Aleinikoff (2002) and Cole (2007).

[24] See Ecuador 2008 (rev. 2015) (www.constituteproject.org/constitution/Ecuador_2015?lang=en).

Anna Södersten makes an interesting comment on this clause, noting that:

> ... in the case of Ecuador, caretaking is framed as a duty and not a right. Child-rearing becomes a responsibility of the citizens toward the polity. It is a duty, just like military service in some countries. And it becomes a manifestation of citizenship. (Södersten 2017, 1182)

Similar points could, of course, be made about other assumptions which are embedded within constitutions and constitutional history and which challenge the narrative of liberal neutrality, including issues of race, indigeneity, ethnicity, language and sexual preference. Hence the significance attached to the constitutional recognition of communal rights and indigenous law in Bolivia, Colombia and Ecuador, as 'critical in expanding state legitimacy through a sense of shared citizenship'.[25]

But we should still beware of investing too much hope in constitutional rights. Even a critical approach to constitutions will only take us so far. Södersten warns us (and this specifically in the case of gender and care, but the point equally applies in other contexts) that there are limits to what can be achieved by constitutions, and that most often, in order to effect real change beyond the symbolic, we need to turn to (ordinary) politics, in order to attain a consensus around the redirection of societal resources or the recognition of other forms of difference. This resonates with Bellamy's (2001) reflexive approach to citizenship in which rights are the basis for deliberation, not primarily for judicial enforcement. In that respect, the example of the US, with its strong judicial review approach involving the Supreme Court, which has had manifold consequences in areas of the 'private sphere' such as abortion regulation and same-sex marriage, probably does not offer much of a useful 'message' to other constitutional and political systems.

Moreover, and this is a point that will be pursued in more detail in the next chapter, there are significant dangers in an age of populism, xenophobia and anti-immigrant sentiment that rights that were once thought almost to be set in stone are now starting to unravel, and neither citizens' deliberation nor judicial enforcement seem to help. Notably there is a renewed precarity for immigrants, with the 'border' moved away from the physical edge of the community and re-sited at its heart, and involving many different forms of immigration policing.[26] This is not

---

[25] From the World Bank (2017, 90), referencing Yashar (2005).
[26] See Ellermann (2019).

just the case with the UK and its 'hostile environment' for immigrants (supposedly only for 'illegal' immigrants, but actually impacting on all migrants and others who cannot prove their 'insiderness'),[27] but in many other states too.[28] Data collected by the World Prisons Brief[29] show that in many countries, including larger ones where the data are statistically significant, non-nationals form an astonishingly high percentage of the prison population (for example, Switzerland: 71.5 per cent; Austria: 54.7 per cent), as much for offences against immigration law that are now treated as criminal infractions as for other criminal conduct.[30]

Fear of outsiders can take a variety of different shapes. In the Nordic countries, this has taken the form of walling off the welfare state. Pressures on the welfare state were used in Sweden as the express motivation for closing borders to refugees in 2015 (Barker 2017b). Denmark has highly restrictive family reunion requirements for migrants from outside the EU, forcing many young Danes of immigrant background to move to Sweden in order to take advantage of EU law.[31] Other countries have created new forms of temporariness for migrants, such as Canada and Australia, and some countries, such as the United Arab Emirates, resolutely refuse to bring the outside to the inside, and maintain statuses involving 'permanent temporariness' (Lori 2019). At the same time, the traditional border itself has not been forgotten, and it is increasingly securitized in different ways, including through the building of walls, fences, detention camps and other elements of the technology of deportation and exclusion in different parts of the world.

If there ever were a golden age when the rights of migrants were in a steady process of enlargement, it is now certainly over. Discrimination and differentiation are back[32] with a vengeance, along with the prizing of national citizenship as a legal status, and this time with a clear impact not just on the outsiders, the immigrants, but also on certain categories of insiders, such as naturalized citizens or the children of immigrants, who may be seen by policy-makers as still just too 'foreign' to be 'authentic citizens'. The point matters especially in relation to loss of citizenship, as Matthew Gibney (2019) shows in detail, but it also applies to the degradation of rights of those unable to prove they are, in fact, insiders or citizens, such as those who have been the victims of the Windrush

---

[27] See Zedner (2019).

[28] See Berg and Fiddian-Qasmiyeh (2018) and Suárez-Krabbe and Lindberg (2019).

[29] World Prison Brief online database (www.prisonstudies.org/).

[30] For discussion, see Barker (2017b).

[31] On these processes of displacement, see Rytter (2011) and Schmidt (2013).

[32] Dauvergne (2007).

scandal, who successively lost access to jobs, bank accounts, driving licences, rented accommodation, welfare benefits and healthcare, and who, in some cases, were deported to places they had left as children or had never known, as a result of the UK's 'hostile environment' policies.[33] As part of similar processes of exclusion, other people have found their legal status changing through no decision or fault of their own, as with those EU27 and UK citizens affected by the vote to leave the EU in the UK's June 2016 referendum.[34] But it is not just those who are themselves outsiders or quasi-outsiders who are affected, but anyone who has some contact with them. Any person contracting a cross-border marriage may find themselves under suspicion of having entered into a so-called 'sham marriage' and experience a significant interference with their rights to family life and privacy.[35]

In sum, it is clear that 'full citizenship' is not a stable end state, but rather a continuously reinstituted process, involving struggles and contestations, as scholars such as Margaret Somers (2008) have shown us. Many of the measures and policies noted above are likely to be contested judicially, using legal resources from national constitutions and national legislation or from international law. In addition, civil society mobilization, even civil disobedience, as well as deliberation in the political and legislative spheres are all part of the range of activities that can rightfully be said to involve the construction or performance of citizenship in these contexts.[36] At the same time, such restrictive measures, whether to be found in immigration law, in criminal law or elsewhere in the legal order, will be defended on majoritarian grounds, on security and public order grounds, or on the grounds that they are simply measures pushing 'integration', which can be defended as an apparently self-evident public good. Equality and freedom for the minority may bend to the will of the majority.

The franchise: the internal and external limits of the constitutional people

The right to vote is a paradigmatic dimension of modern democracy. It is 'the individual fulfilment of a right that allows for the collective self-fulfilment of a self-governing community' (Shaw 2017c, 291). By looking at the right to vote, we can address the internal and external

---

[33] See Gentleman (2018, 2019), Webber (2018) and Favell (2019).
[34] D'Angelo and Kofman (2018).
[35] For details, see Moret et al (2019).
[36] Isin and Nielsen (2008).

limits of the 'constitutional people', and consider the question of how best the rights of citizens can be protected against encroachment by states. We see the internal limits when we look at how much discretion legislatures may have to limit the right to vote of certain groups of people (for example, prisoners or those lacking certain capacities). These types of cases force us to consider directly the question of whether all citizens are truly legally equal under certain constitutional systems. In terms of the external dimensions of the people, we will examine the constitutional limits of extensions to the franchise for non-citizens or non-resident citizens. To what extent are the boundaries of the suffrage constitutionally mandated, and what do these tell us about the nature of constitutional citizenship? These two examples neatly foreshadow some of the discussions that will ensue in Part III of the book, as the right to vote lies precisely at the point where citizenship as a legal status meets citizenship as membership of a political community.[37] The issue of political participation is coming increasingly under scrutiny in an age simultaneously marked by national populism and global mobility and the fragmentation of citizenship governance.

How universal is 'universal suffrage'?

We have mentioned already, on a number of occasions, how the historical struggle for universal suffrage can be seen as an incident of the wider struggle for full membership rights within a democracy. The history of the franchise is one of contestation and social struggles, paralleling the history of struggles by certain groups to be seen as full citizens. Persons without property or who were illiterate, women and people of colour including Indigenous Peoples, were all routinely denied the vote during the 19th and well into the 20th centuries, precisely because they were not seen as 'full' citizens and thus denied capacity in the same way that children, for example, are still generally denied the right to vote. If these groups were not full citizens, it was simply 'natural' that they should not have full civil, political and indeed, social, rights. The outcomes of these struggles can be seen in legislation and sometimes in judgments of courts, as in the famous 'Persons' case in Canada in the 1920s, which established that women were qualified 'persons' to sit in the Senate.[38]

---

[37] See Balibar (2012) and Kesby (2012).

[38] *Edwards v Canada (AG)* [1930] AC 124. For more details on the right to vote and its relationship to the voting process and to elections, see Shaw (2017c).

Nowadays, elections are held in nearly every country in the world (and indeed are mentioned in almost every constitution), although in rather a lot of countries the process of election provides merely the veneer rather than the reality of democracy.[39] The Office for Democratic Institutions and Human Rights within the Organization for Security and Cooperation in Europe (OSCE) runs election observation missions in OSCE member countries, and election monitoring against international standards (of universality, fairness, transparency, and so on) is regularly undertaken by many international organizations. International law recognizes the importance of the right to vote in the form of universal and equal suffrage guarantees in texts such as Article 21 of the Universal Declaration of Human Rights, Article 25 of the International Covenant on Civil and Political Rights and Article 3 of Protocol 1 of the ECHR. The ECtHR has successfully reworked the relatively unpromising reference to 'free elections at reasonable intervals by secret ballot, under conditions which will ensure the free expression of the opinion of the people in the choice of the legislature' into an enforceable individual right to vote for a legislature (although it does not extend to referendums or local elections).[40] The ECtHR's case law also reads into the right to vote the usual margin of appreciation, such that European states may include limitations that are 'necessary in a democratic society' (a phrase that is included in many of the ECHR's provisions). No state fails to impose age limits on the right to vote, and states generally impose citizenship and residence requirements. Quite a number still impose competency requirements, although this is another area where the ECtHR has stepped in to oppose blanket bans, alongside prisoner voting.[41]

The right to vote appears – or is assumed – in many national constitutions. For example, many people think that there is a constitutional 'right to vote' in the US. In fact, the right to vote does not explicitly appear in the US Constitution, but numerous constitutional amendments have restricted the limitations that can be placed on the right to vote, for example, on account of race, sex or failure to pay a poll tax. The states, which otherwise manage the voting process, cannot impose an age limit above 18. Critics of the US position have argued that the absence of such an express right makes it harder to contest the various 'burdens' that many states place on the practice of voting, such as voter ID laws, changes or restrictions in the timing or location of voting, or

[39] Diamond (2002).
[40] For discussion, see Green (2018).
[41] *Alajos Kiss v Hungary*, no 38832/06, 20 May 2010. See Pincock (2018).

the management of voter registers.[42] In the absence of the immediate prospect of a constitutional amendment to correct this omission, and after a Supreme Court ruling which allowed states to purge voters from registers if they have failed to vote, despite the apparently plain language of the National Voter Registration Act 1993,[43] contestation over alleged voter suppression has become a major partisan dividing line in the US (Shattuck et al 2019).

In the US, the story of restrictions on the right to vote is fully embedded within the broader post-slavery story of gradual black emancipation. While significant constitutional and legislative steps have been taken, including the 15th Amendment and the Voting Rights Act 1965, especially at federal level, at state and local level *de jure* and *de facto* restrictions have proved remarkably enduring and have continued to damage the democratic fabric of the country. As was also the case in many Latin American countries,[44] racially focused restrictions often acquired the surrogate form of a literacy requirement. From the 19th through to the 21st centuries, many of the same concerns have coalesced about the issue of felon disenfranchisement, which is a standard and often permanent consequence of certain criminal convictions in the US. This practice disproportionately impacts African Americans and it may have affected the outcomes of elections, including the 2000 US presidential election (Uggen and Manza 2002).

Constitutional courts have come up with some striking prose in their discussions on the right to vote, drawing an explicit connection between the right to vote and respect for human dignity and equality (Kesby 2012, 72). This is particularly important in the case of prisoner disenfranchisement, as the continued exclusion of convicted prisoners from the suffrage in many countries is based on an explicit departure from the premise that all citizens are equal (Tripković 2019). A certain minimum of delinquency, for some countries, is enough for a departure from the principle of equality to be justified.

So when constitutional courts do take aim at restrictions on prisoner voting rights, they can deliver a powerful message. According to Justice Sachs of the Constitutional Court of South Africa, '[t]he vote of each and every citizen is a badge of dignity and of personhood. Quite literally, it says that everybody counts'.[45] The historical and political context of

---

[42] See Soros (2013).

[43] *Husted v A. Philip Randolph Institute*, 138 S Ct 1833 (2018).

[44] For discussion, see Hernández (2014).

[45] *August and Another v Electoral Commission and Others* (CCT8/99) [1999] ZACC 3; 1999 (3) SA 1; 1999 (4) BCLR 363 (1 April 1999) (www.saflii.org/za/cases/ZACC/1999/3.html).

apartheid gives poignancy to those words. Also under attack has been a blanket ban on prisoner voting in Canada, which fell foul of Section 15 of the Charter of Rights and Freedoms on the grounds that it violated the principles of equality and equal membership.[46] As Alison Kesby notes (quoting from the *Sauvé* judgment), the majority:

> … dismisses as "ancient" and "obsolete" the notion that certain classes of people are not "morally worthy to vote". By disenfranchising prisoners, the government of Canada was making this precise statement. It was asserting that certain people do not "deserve" to be considered members of the community and therefore may be deprived of their basic constitutional rights. Disenfranchisement implies that those denied the vote are "no longer valued as members of the community" but rather are "temporary outcasts from [the] system of rights and democracy". (Kesby 2012, 73)

Both the South African and the Canadian judgments were cited in the leading criminal disenfranchisement judgment of the ECtHR, which addressed the UK's blanket ban on prisoner voting. But *Hirst (No 2)*[47] has just been the first strike in a long-running, and still unresolved, conflict between the UK and the Council of Europe institutions, which has left UK law thus far materially unaltered.[48] Meanwhile, the UK courts have been pushed into a position where there are no more effective remedies they can give under the Human Rights Act 1998 as an initial declaration of incompatibility has been ignored by the legislature.[49] The UK's adherence to the ECHR has been left hanging by a thread, as prisoner voting has been used as the motivation to advance plans for a British Bill of Rights in which the UK would cut itself off from the mainstream of European supranational human rights supervision.[50] In marked contrast to the reluctance of the UK to shift, significant changes have been apparent in a number of parts of the world in relation to prisoner disenfranchisement, highlighting that a substantial shift in the

---

[46] *Sauvé v Attorney-General of Canada* (No 2) [2002] 3 SCR 519.

[47] *Hirst v the United Kingdom (no 2)* [2006] 42 EHRR 41 (http://hudoc.echr.coe.int/eng?i=001-70442).

[48] Except for the tiny change in Scotland (for details up to August 2019, see https://researchbriefings.parliament.uk/ResearchBriefing/Summary/CBP-7461) and, as of February 2020, the Scottish Elections (Franchise and Representation) Act.

[49] For details, see Green (2014).

[50] For details of the contestation between the UK and the ECHR, see Gearty (2019) and Harvey (2018).

internal boundaries of the right to vote is often led by courts rather than legislatures. In Africa, in addition to South Africa, a number of cases have been brought before national courts challenging restrictions both on the right to vote in principle and the restrictions placed in practice on the process of registration (ACJR 2019). Politically and normatively, however, there is no consensus about whether (all or some) prisoners should vote.[51]

Voting and the imposition of citizenship and residence qualifications

Mobility and migration (including immigration *and* emigration) provide important laboratories for political scientists to try to figure out how and why states make certain choices about voting rights, as well as for lawyers and political theorists to observe the real-world traction of the models of the *demos* that they construct, such as the ones discussed in Chapter 3. As with citizenship rights more generally, voting rights provide a laboratory for considering the wider question about whether resident and non-resident (that is, external) citizens should enjoy the same package of rights and duties, and likewise what version of 'equal treatment' properly applies to resident non-citizens.

In a world in which all populations were neatly parcelled within 'nation states', with stable borders and relatively homogeneous populations, it might be possible to imagine that the boundaries of the suffrage could be fixed and free from pressures, and that they could be based on clear limits derived from principles of citizenship and residence that are straightforward to apply and widely approved. This, however, is certainly not the world we have today, and this model has probably never been an accurate representation of reality. Consequently, there are substantial questions about whether voting should be limited to resident citizens or extended to non-resident citizens (external voting) and resident non-citizens (sometimes called 'alien suffrage').[52] The policy contexts for these issues are diaspora engagement (that is, citizenship, voting rights and other policies to engage those not on the territory) and the integration of immigrants (measures to support the voting rights and practices of those who do not have citizenship or who may only recently have acquired it). The two questions are interconnected in significant ways, as are the questions of access to citizenship and access to the franchise. For example, in the US, many Asian Americans were effectively excluded from the franchise for many decades because they were refused access to citizenship

---

[51] For a range of views, see Ramsay (2013), Marshall (2018) and Tripković (2019).
[52] See Shaw (2007) and Caramani and Grotz (2015).

by a combination of legislation such as the Chinese Exclusion Act of 1882 and case law which interpreted access to naturalization as being restricted to 'free white people'. In contrast, those of Asian descent born in the US did benefit from the *ius soli* protection of the 14th Amendment.[53] Furthermore, the right to vote of emigrants has also been slow to develop.

The question of *who* can (at least in theory) vote *where* is still only half the story in these types of cases. Judging the extent of electoral inclusion is a complex and subtle business involving not just legal provisions but also administrative practices.[54] Moreover, scholars have also observed that states may often extend electoral rights to wider constituencies such as non-resident citizens, but take steps to limit unexpected electoral outcomes (Hutcheson and Arrighi 2015). These are large topics, and the following comments merely pick out some questions that directly relate to the interface with national constitutions.

In the 21st century, well over 100 states now permit external voting by non-resident citizens under a wide variety of different conditions (IDEA 2007).[55] This phenomenon emphasizes the loosening of the territorial link between citizen and state. Along with the rise of dual citizenship, the spread of external voting could be said to be the second 'new norm' of citizenship from the later decades of the 20th century onwards. In some constitutions, external voting is well established. Constitutions play a significant role in the regulation of external voting and in providing for an accompaniment that exists in some cases, namely special constituencies in the national parliament to represent the interests of the external voters. For example, Article 48 of the Constitution of Italy[56] provides that legislation will lay down:

> … the requirements and modalities for citizens residing abroad to exercise their right to vote and guarantees that this right is effective. A constituency of Italians abroad shall be established for elections to the Houses of Parliament; the number of seats of such constituency is set forth in a constitutional provision according to criteria established by law.

---

[53] Lopez (2006).

[54] For underpinning data, see Arrighi et al (2019), and for a data-led approach, see Schmidt et al (2019).

[55] For detailed information, see the website of the ACE Electoral Knowledge Network (https://aceproject.org/ace-en/topics/va/explore_topic_new).

[56] See Italy 1947 (rev. 2012) (www.constituteproject.org/constitution/Italy_2012?lang=en).

The provision reflects in many respects the political aspirations of Italy's very large diaspora (Tintori 2016). But having a constitutional provision is not an automatic guarantee of the right to vote. Article 51(4) of the Constitution of Greece provides for external voting, but until 2019 it was never implemented, so members of the Greek diaspora wishing to participate in elections needed to return to Greece in order to register their votes (Christopoulos 2019).

Case studies on different regions have emphasized the extent to which constitutional change has often been a trigger for the introduction of external voting.[57] Pau Palop-García and Luicy Pedroza also note long time lags in their work on Latin America and the Caribbean, showing that Greece is not a one-off case. Where constitutions neither prohibit nor explicitly mandate external voting, those campaigning for diaspora political interests may use political campaigns and lobbying to shift the dial by making a rights-based claim for equality for external voters (as in the case of Malaysia[58]) or turn (as in Canada) to constitutional litigation. Section 3 of the Charter of Rights and Freedoms guarantees the right to vote for Canadian citizens, and in *Frank v Canada (Attorney General)*[59] the claimants successfully argued that the limitation of the right to vote externally to five years after departure from Canada was not a 'reasonable limitation' within the meaning of Section 1 of the Charter. The case is notable for the lack of deference shown by the majority in the court to the choice of the legislature and for their embrace of a position that argued that:

> Canadian voting policy ought to reflect the interconnected world we live in. Laws should recognize that Canadians live abroad while still maintaining close connections with Canada. Non-resident voters are Canada's "best and brightest" who act as "ambassadors of Canadian values". (Burton 2019)

A smaller but still significant number of polities permit resident non-citizens to vote, although for the most part only in local elections. More than 60 countries worldwide allow for some or all resident non-citizens to vote in some or all local or municipal elections, but fewer than 10 countries

---

[57] For Africa, see Hartmann (2015); for Latin America and the Caribbean, see Palop-García and Pedroza (2019).

[58] See Low (2018).

[59] 2019 SCC 1.

allow some or all resident non-citizens to vote in national elections.[60] The best-known case of so-called 'alien suffrage' is undoubtedly the EU, which requires its Member States, since the Maastricht Treaty, to confer the right to vote in local (and European Parliament) elections on resident (that is, mobile) non-national EU citizens (Shaw 2007). This is a unique (thus far) example of international impact on domestic voting rights legislation and of a comprehensive reciprocal framework, with limited but interesting examples of upgrades and adjustments. For example, when Slovenia introduced EU voting rights prior to its accession in 2004, it included the right to vote (but not to stand for election) for third country nationals in its new legislation. The UK also gives the right to vote and to stand for election to EU citizens not only in municipal elections but also in the elections to devolved bodies and legislatures (for example, Scotland and Wales). This adds another layer of complexity to the UK's existing bricolage of voting rights in which Commonwealth and Irish citizens, rather unusually, have the right to vote in all elections.

The UK's position on voting rights for Commonwealth citizens was recognized as a constitutional principle in a case that came before the CJEU, where Spain challenged the UK's extension of the right to vote in European Parliament elections in Gibraltar to resident Commonwealth citizens (Shaw 2007, 185).[61] It would most likely take constitutional amendments for most countries to widen the scope of the franchise to give resident non-citizens the right to vote in national elections. Ireland needed such an amendment for its limited extension of the right to vote in *Dáil* elections to UK citizens in the 1980s. In 2015, a referendum was held in Luxembourg on the question of giving electoral rights in national elections to migrants, but the proposal was rejected by 78 per cent of voters (Finck 2015).

Cristina Rodriguez (2010) argues that it is hard to discern clear patterns driving the decision to grant or to deny voting rights for third country nationals in elections, across groups of states. Her comparison of the US, New Zealand and Ireland – states which all have a history and/ or a present practice of alien suffrage – indicates that there is no fixed relationship between granting electoral rights, the national constitutional structure or evolving perceptions of immigration. In fact, if anything, that history shows that as national constitutional principles achieve greater clarity and solidity, the options for non-citizen voting that existed in some states of immigration have been closed down (the US, Canada and

---

[60] See Bauböck (2005), Honohan and Hutcheson (2015) and Arrighi and Bauböck (2017).

[61] Case C-145/04 *Spain v UK (Gibraltar)*, ECLI:EU:C:2006:543.

Australia are good examples of this). The UK's imperial and colonial history represents a decidedly hard-to-pigeonhole case, and Ireland's constitutional shift was made precisely in order to respond to the UK's inclusivity towards Irish citizens (Shaw 2007, 202–6). New Zealand, with its broad electoral inclusivity towards all permanent residents, enshrined in 1975 legislation, seems to reflect what Kate Macmillan (2017) describes as a shift from being the Commonwealth's 'dutiful daughter' to being a young multicultural nation. Shifts between immigration and emigration can certainly be significant, as Cristina Escobar (2015b) has shown in the case of Latin America, where Chile, Ecuador and Uruguay represent important examples of non-citizen voting (Acosta 2018, 161–2).

Likewise, we can see the impact of constitutional principles on political campaigns. Constitutional blockages have restrained subnational entities from proceeding with more liberal policies towards third country national voters where local political opinion in some *Länder* has differed from the national-level mainstream in Germany and Austria.[62] Ultimately it is difficult to generalize simply on the basis of case studies, and Rodríguez concludes, from a constitutionalist perspective, that 'a society's decision to adopt a particular set of alien suffrage practices reflects its own political culture' (2010, 49).

Conclusion and summing up of Part II

The three chapters that form Part II of the book have surveyed the domain of citizenship across three dimensions. There is no claim to completeness in respect of the material presented here. In no sense does this material represent a valid 'sample' in the social scientific sense of the word. Rather, it is presented illustratively as a means of opening up and mapping the interactions of citizenship and constitutional law, in a manner that is cognisant of the main intellectual trends within the broad interdisciplinary fields of citizenship studies and constitutional studies. As explained in the Introduction to Part II, these three dimensions can be closely mapped onto the classic triptych of identity, status and rights, which is frequently used to capture the core elements of the rich concept of citizenship. Through this mapping, we can, therefore, also begin the process of interpreting the interrelationship between citizenship and constitutions.

---

[62] See Shaw (2007, Chapter 9). For further details, see note 12 of Chapter 2. For a counter-example of regional differentiation in the franchise see the recently enacted Scottish Elections (Franchise and Representation) Act.

'Constitutional citizenship' has been used as a heuristic device. Working with the question 'What does it mean to regulate citizenship within a constitutional framework?', we have seen that states often invest constitutional significance in citizenship, for example, by providing for citizens' constitutional rights. Yet at the same time states regularly treat the status as ethically fungible, so that it can be bestowed on groups whose membership can benefit the interests of the state or taken from others deemed unworthy. Constitutions can add to the heft of citizenship (Macklin 2007), although this sometimes seems to happen in a haphazard way. But the interpretations given here provide reasons going beyond those emerging from empirical sociological research as to why citizenship matters.[63] Overall, we can see that citizenship can be both a paradoxical element within constitutional settlements and also an empty box or cypher that has to be given content by some other legal or political means.

Some key questions that can help to make sense of this material have emerged on several occasions. For example, we have explored to what extent it is possible to use concepts such as 'equality' and 'dignity' as touchstones underpinning constitutional citizenship. We have seen episodic rather than consistent adherence to the principle of the genuine link. It fades in and out of view, depending on what purposes states are pursuing through their citizenship laws, sometimes as an enabler and sometimes as discipline. And we have explored the tensions to which constitutional citizenship can give rise between majoritarian and non-majoritarian institutions. When courts engage directly with the statutory or constitutional regulation of citizenship or citizenship rights, in particular against the apparent will of legislatures, in the name of upholding higher-level rights or principles (whether derived from the constitution or from international law), this may import additional tensions into the constitutional system. In all those senses, the work has been not merely interpretative, but has also acknowledged that we cannot 'interpret' the world without bringing to the fore our ethical and normative choices about what *ought* to be invested in the citizenship concept, especially when it is viewed constitutionally. In that sense, citizenship may be flawed, but equally it may still – in its constitutional guise – be one of the best instruments we have for ensuring equality.

The rest of this section now seeks to draw a link between these ideas and the discussion in Part III of the book. In an article published in 1999, Jean Cohen argued that constitutionalism at the national level struggles to synthesize effectively the three core components of the citizenship principle (the juridical, the political and the identitarian), without running

---

[63] See Bloemraad and Sheares (2017).

the risk of setting arbitrary limits to membership and participation. This is what Cohen calls:

> ... the paradoxical dialectic inherent in modern constitutionalism that drives republican or liberal democratic conceptions of citizenship into the arms of thicker, more communitarian understandings of identity. (1999, 256)

Cohen's reflections are rooted in a conceptual and normative tradition of scholarship, not in the observational, documentary and interpretative tradition of socio-legal studies, which drives this book. She points out the tensions within the modern paradigm of citizenship which reveal themselves when, for example, the equality principle is brought into conversation with the cultural ideas which seem, almost inevitably, to underpin the identitarian dimension of citizenship. But even if those claims for national specificity are entirely civic in nature, there is still an inevitably unsatisfactory outcome because of the continued relevance of boundaries:

> Because the nation–state equates the citizen with the member of the nation it collapses a political/legal category into a category of identity and perverts the egalitarian logic of the constitutional state by rendering those who are not members of the nation implicitly into second-class citizens. (Cohen 1999, 253)

A fortiori in a world of widespread mobility and blurred boundaries *between* states, the idea of democratic and equal citizenship *within* states struggles to find its feet. In keeping with the postnational heuristic, Cohen's answer to the problems she highlights is to focus on going beyond the modern and national paradigm of citizenship. At the end of her article, she explores some dimensions of postmodernism, which challenge standard tropes of liberalism and republicanism without trending towards nationalism. She argues that the only way to overcome this potential degradation of the liberal essence of modern constitutionalism in a normative sense is to disaggregate the component elements of the citizenship principle, and to render the dispersion of political authority and legitimacy across different sites and 'levels'.

The material I have presented in these three chapters – with its focus on the shaping of citizenship by constitutions and constitutional law – is concordant with Cohen's conceptual reflections. Despite the initially unpromising perspective on constitutional citizenship developed in the first chapters, where it seemed that there was more to the rhetorical claim that the citizen is central to the constitutionalized polity than there would be to the substance, this fear has not been borne out. On the contrary, each chapter has only scratched the surface of the multitude of ways in which constitutional law steps in, at regular intervals, to tell the story of citizenship from a constitutionalist perspective. As foreseen earlier, we have seen how constitutional narrative has flowed into the discourse of citizenship and vice versa. The two are productively interlinked across many dimensions.

Throughout these chapters, what has been most apparent is the struggle to reconcile boundaries with equal treatment, collective identity with individual rights, democratic self-government with individual self-realization, and the ideal of a 'universal personhood' with the realities of a particularistic 'citizenship', which for many is nominal at best.[64] Citizenship as ideal continually disappoints, and as Cohen points out, the reasons for this emerge once we start to unpick the concepts themselves.

Cohen's article was written during the post-1989/pre-09/11 'moment', before the non-citizen and the migrant came (once more?) to be seen as threats to the economy, the culture and the security of host states. But it is sufficiently prescient to provide us with an initial blueprint to ask some questions about the age in which we now live. The task now is to consider what significance all the insights gathered in the book thus far might have when recalling that we live, simultaneously, in ages of national populism and of globalism. These are movements that seem to pull in different directions, and to suggest diverse and potentially discordant futures for both the idea of citizenship as a membership status and for the still dominant practice of national citizenship. What significance might they have for constitutional citizenship?

---

[64] See Pfeifer (2020).

PART III

Citizenship under Pressure: National and Global Tensions

This part of the book aims to exploit the current conjuncture in order to explain why it has been important to gain additional insights into the constitutional law/citizenship interface. These insights go beyond the observation, mapping and interpretation that have formed the predominant mode of analysis hitherto. Two particularly significant challenges to citizenship at the level of state or national constitutions stem from the political forces of populism and from trends towards globalization and other 'beyond the state' dynamics. These challenges highlight a variety of different ways in which the state-based model of constitutional citizenship has been put under pressure.

Populism is a style of politics that can operate to close down the discursive space within which citizens can operate as free and equal political agents. It can be said to eat away at those elements of the citizenship/constitutional law interaction that emphasize citizenship as a universal status, as a result of the populists' appropriation of the notion of 'the people'. It ramps up the split between the ideal of equality that citizenship seeks to embody and the reality of a sharp divide between insiders and outsiders. Combined with other ideological stances such as nationalism, populism poses a threat to liberal democratic orders, and this can tear at the fabric of a conception of state-based citizenship premised on the ideal of equality.

Globalization, meanwhile, describes the intensification of interactions or integration between countries, people and other actors such as companies, potentially without regard to the existence or disciplines of state borders and the legal orders within them. Globalization challenges the citizenship/constitutional law interaction, because it puts into question the singularity of that relationship, pointing to multiple membership interactions between people and various legal orders at the national, supranational and international levels that need to be described and conceptualized. This pressure from above on the state is often paired with pressure from below (the substate level), as well as horizontally from other state-level legal orders likewise simultaneously challenged by global forces. In that context, it seems better that our focus should be the broader topic of 'the shifting spatialities of citizenship' rather than just 'the impact of globalization on citizenship'. The fragmentation of governance arrangements is the watchword in this context. One of the most important questions that needs to be asked is whether any loss of autonomy or control at the national level in relation to the scope or quality of polity membership can be effectively compensated by reference to conditions for legitimate political action pertaining within the other legal orders. Or does the scenario of 'citizenship beyond the state' have an irresolvable democracy problem? A related puzzle concerns the role (and legitimacy) of supranational and international courts, and their relationship both to national legislatures and national courts.

Populism and shifting spatialities are not parallel or even countervailing forces in the way that one might suggest 'nationalism' and 'internationalism' could be. They raise very different types of questions. There are distinct and obvious tensions between the two sets of ideas, not least because, as we shall discuss in Chapter 6, populist politics are in some respects a national reaction to what some would argue is the undemocratic liberalism of the international order that we will examine in Chapter 7. One way in which this tension comes across in both chapters lies in the selection of case studies. For example, both of them address some of the citizenship consequences of the UK's Brexit referendum vote in 2016, first as regards the impact of populist politics and second as regards the implications of the leaky or blurred boundaries of the state for the status of citizens.

6

The Populist Challenge to Constitutional Citizenship: The Closing of Discursive Space

Introduction

This chapter presents reflections on how constitutional citizenship is challenged by the practice of populist politics. It includes, among other examples, a short exposition of the remarkable explosion of populist politics in the UK, its move from the fringes to the mainstream and its impact on issues of citizenship, in particular in the context of the referendum on leaving the EU. This discussion is framed by further case studies focused on Canada, the US, Hungary and India.

Following the apparent triumph of liberal and constitutional democracy in the wake of the end of the Cold War and the fall of the Soviet Union, alongside the rise of human rights as both ideological framework and legal practice since the Second World War, some were inclined to suggest that 'history' had somehow ended, because the last ideological alternatives to liberalism and capitalism had been eliminated.[1] Indeed, capitalism does seem to have triumphed (for now), but liberalism is not in such good health 30 years after the end of communism.[2] Nationalism, and associated ideologies, have hardly disappeared, and now seem to live on, embedded within many ostensibly liberal democratic constitutional settlements. Astute commentators noticed this rather quickly.[3] In the second decade of

---

[1] Fukuyama (1992); for latter-day reflections, see Menand (2018).
[2] Chang (2019).
[3] See, for example, Fox and Vermeersch (2010).

the 21st century, many aspects of nationalism have become central topics of political commentary, along with the discourse of 'populism', which seems to have become predominant, not just in authoritarian polities, or in Latin American countries with personalized presidential systems and high levels of socioeconomic inequality,[4] but in more or less every polity, including those with well embedded parliamentary systems and liberal constitutional frameworks incorporating multiple checks and balances.[5] We now live, many people have claimed, in an era of populism, or, as it is sometimes called 'the new populism'. This is also reflected by the extended discussions of populism we can find in the media.[6] However, the controversial topic of populism covers a much wider range of issues than can be discussed in this chapter.[7]

It is 'modish' to describe more or less any sort of invocation of 'the people' within political discourse as being a manifestation of 'populism' (Walker 2019b). However, there is a discernible 'discursive and stylistic repertoire'[8] of populists. This 'style' of politics distinguishes populism from more pluralistic approaches to politics. For these purposes, Nicola Lacey (2019) provides an apt definition, adopted for the purposes of asking her own questions about the relationship between populism and the rule of law that bear some relationship to the questions about populism, constitutionalism and citizenship that I shall ask in this chapter:

> ... populism is a highly moralized approach to politics that pitches a homogeneous "we the people", often conceived in ethnic or national terms, embodied in a leader who speaks for and expresses the will of that undifferentiated collectivity against a presumptively "corrupt" – hence the tendency to conspiracy theories in this genre of political discourse – "elite" (as well as against "outsider" minorities of various kinds).

Commentators tend to agree that populism is not an ideology as such, or if it is, then it is a 'thin-centred' ideology (Mudde and Kaltwasser 2017, 6), which is parasitic for its substance on other fuller political ideologies on the left–right, liberal–authoritarian, solidaristic–individualistic scales.

---

[4] De la Torre (2017a) and Grigera (2017).

[5] For fuller exposition, see Brubaker (2017b).

[6] For an accessible introduction, see *The Guardian* series on 'The New Populism' curated by one of the leading academics in the field, Cas Mudde (www.theguardian.com/world/series/the-new-populism).

[7] For an extended consideration of the issues raised by populism, see, from a huge literature, Kaltwasser et al (2017b) and Mudde and Kaltwasser (2017).

[8] Brubaker (2017b, 360).

Where they disagree is on whether it is populism, as such, which is the problem, or the fact that in the contemporary world it is commonly paired with authoritarian approaches to government that are often inimical to core dimensions of the rule of law and of democratic and liberal constitutionalism.

Populism has existed as an approach to politics for a lot longer than the current 'crisis'. Populism's antecedents lie in Russia and the US in the 19th century, especially in the context of agrarian policy-making, and it has periodically played a role in politics within many different countries, notably in Latin America, but also in places as diverse as Canada, the US and New Zealand. There have been populisms of the left and of the right, perhaps even of the political centre.[9] Advocates of left populism often decry the fear of populism as being actually a fear of radical politics and about the decline of liberalism.[10] Here, however, is not the place to pursue a detailed diagnosis of the backlash from globalization[11] or of the breaking of the postwar consensus around redistributional policies that underpinned what were taken to be the stable liberal democracies in the Global North.[12] Many observers understand these changes to be central to what is sometimes termed a populist 'revolt' against neoliberalism.[13] Nor can we consider what those developments mean for progressive politics now or in the future.[14] Scholars such as Mouffe (2018) argue that populism could offer a fruitful basis for the reinvigoration of democracy itself. Likewise, the cultural factors that some scholars claim lie behind current political movements are beyond the scope of this book,[15] as indeed is a detailed analysis of the political antecedents of the rise of populist politics of a distinctly authoritarian variety, as in central and eastern Europe, Turkey or India. However, two of these cases (Hungary and India) will be briefly discussed in what follows.

There is a well-established literature on populism and democracy.[16] The relationship between the two is complex. For example, Cas Mudde and Cristóbal Rovira Kaltwasser (2018, 1670) argue that 'populism is in

---

[9] Former UK Prime Minister Tony Blair is one politician sometimes said to have displayed populist tendencies from the centre, as the dominant trope of his New Labour government was making policy for the benefit of 'hardworking families'. This fits the definition of a 'pure people' perfectly: see Burtenshaw and Jäger (2018).

[10] See, for example, Howse (2019).

[11] Rodrik (2018).

[12] With a particular focus on the US and the UK, see Moran (2020).

[13] See Brubaker (2017b) and Bugarić (2019).

[14] Fraser (2016); Howse (2019).

[15] Norris and Inglehart (2019).

[16] See, for example, Kaltwasser et al (2017b) and Stockemer (2019).

many ways an illiberal democratic response to undemocratic liberalism',
so far as the latter has become a feature both at the national level and
– most pertinently – at the supranational (think of the EU, especially
the institutions of the eurozone) and the international levels (think of
the financial institutions such as the International Monetary Fund that
involved themselves in crises such as the post-2008 sovereign debt crisis in
countries such as Greece). Such institutions, many argue, have eviscerated
democracy at the national level. Populism generally thrives where systems
of interest intermediation through political parties become destabilized.[17]
The success of populist movements seems to rely on a combination of
appropriate circumstances for the colonization of the body politic by
the populist 'ideal', a wider public sense of being antagonized by and
from an elite and the 'seizing of the moment' on the part of political
entrepreneurs who foster and foment that same antagonism into a sense
of political crisis in which they can step forward as the saviours of the
people (Cohen 2019). Scholars of populism disagree about whether this
is inevitably 'bad for' democratic constitutionalism or for democracy as a
whole, but the majority argue that it is.[18]

With these ideas in mind, this chapter looks at how populism relates
to constitutional citizenship, both as an antecedent dimension of populist
politics and as an outcome. The focus throughout this book has been on
observing the changes in the quality and scope of polity membership,
taking into consideration other dimensions of legal and institutional
change. Cases of populism offer excellent laboratories to study these
changes and to draw conclusions about what is happening. We can look
at how populist ideas have played out in the context of referendums,
both before and after such votes. We can also observe that where populist
parties have come into government, their ideas have often found their way
into constitutional practices in the form of amendments that emphasize an
exclusionary concept of the national people and in some cases challenge
the liberal fundamentals of those constitutions. This point reminds us
once again that we cannot interpret the world, without understanding it
in some sense as a normative imperative. In addition, we will look at how
what Lacey (2019) calls 'legislative populism' carries through into effects
on constitutional citizenship, as politicians become more responsive to
certain types of agenda setting that carry a strong whiff of anti-elitism and
negativity towards outsiders, and they propose corresponding legislative or
executive action. These types of changes do not require populist parties

---

[17] Kaltwasser et al (2017a) and Roberts (2017).

[18] For examples of different approaches, compare Howse (2019) with Lacey (2019)
and Müller (2017).

or movements to come into government, but they do presuppose some sort of impact on the landscape of partisan politics. Mudde and Kaltwasser underscore the importance of researching these changes in these terms:

> … under certain circumstances segments of the establishment can end up promoting populist ideas.… This means that the success of populism is also related to its capacity to both set the political agenda and shape public policy. In other words, when studying populism, we should keep in mind that its impact on democracy is strongly mediated by the role of mainstream political forces and by the extent to which they undergo a process of programmatic adaptation and, sometimes even, transformation. (2018, 1687)

It could, of course, be countered that states (with authoritarian governments in particular, but not only with authoritarian governments) have been manipulating citizenship in what they see as 'the national interest' for as long as it has existed as a constitutional phenomenon. The shameful interwar histories of European fascism, especially but not only the racial laws in Germany that denationalized and dehumanized Jewish people, not to mention the crimes of apartheid in South Africa, are just some of the most salient examples. We could also discuss the Chinese exclusionary laws in the US, or focus on the internment of 'enemy aliens' – including refugee Jews in some cases – in many allied countries in the Second World War. We have mentioned briefly in Chapter 4 the example of a constitutional amendment in newly independent Sierra Leone to denationalize members of that country's Lebanese minority. Every instance of decolonialization has involved a substantial element of 'engineering' of citizenship, often based on problematic 'ethnic' choices, not least because the borders of many states have been imposed by colonial powers without regard to issues of diversity and ethnicity. As long as there have been states, powerful elites have been manipulating citizenship in order to obtain and maintain power. Mazen Masri (2017, 77) puts it in these terms: 'Citizenship as a formal normative category is open to social engineering.' Why, then, study populism in particular? The answer lies in the importance of 'the people'.

Looking for 'the people' in 'constitutional citizenship'

The case for looking at populism in the context of constitutional citizenship derives from the intimate links between the invocation of a 'pure' people, unsullied by a corrupt elite, on the one hand, and the role of the people in democracy (Canovan 2005) and in constitutionalism (Walker 2019b), on the other. Of course, the various sets of ideas should not be conflated. The concept of 'the people' is playing a different role in each case. But dynamics of 'the people' are central to each set of ideas and practices (Espejo 2017).

Democracy may be simply defined as government by the people and for the people. But under conditions of populism, the notion of the people is marked by the insistence that a part of the people can speak for the whole, in a manner that suggests a monolithic and singular interest. The role taken on by this part of the people differs, however, from the interest intermediation function typically taken by political parties in the context of representative and pluralist democracy. The dominant idea is that there exists, for each state, an identifiable 'people' who are to be contrasted with both an unrepresentative 'elite' and groups judged to be 'outsiders'. That is, populism represents both a vertical challenge (by an insurgent 'people' against a dominating elite in order to work towards a 'true democracy') and a horizontal challenge against outsiders (that is, a group that may include those who legally 'belong' in the polity as citizens but who diverge on some key vector, for example, of race or ethnicity). In the latter sense, populism, so far as it is seen as an ideology, often elides with nativism, exclusivist approaches to nationalism and national identity, and even racism, and may also be paired with a government that uses authoritarian techniques to limit democratic discussion or opposition and is inimical to the disciplines of the rule of law.

It is the vertical challenge that most concerns us here. Under populist politics, the sovereign people may be set against 'elite' institutions, certainly courts and even parliaments. Executives often set themselves up as the people's 'friend' and claim directly to be channelling the people's interests and to be offering a deceptively simple sense of delivering 'the will of the people', even though Albert Weale (2018) has persuasively argued that this latter idea is a myth. Intermediate institutions, including legislative assemblies and courts, normally stand between the people and many of the levers of power, but they are often dismissed as remote and out of touch. Referendums can also act, in one sense, as intermediary institutions, although, as Weale has argued, they can also appear as prime moments when 'the people' can wrest control from an unrepresentative elite and steer matters decisively in a different direction. Referendum campaigns and outcomes can flatten out the complexities of political decision-making. In that sense then, referendums are useful institutions that can help us to understand the relationship between the 'democratic people' and the 'people' of the 'political identity' of populism, but they are also instruments that can be politically manipulated. Scholars have been careful to sketch a complex relationship between populism and democracy. To that end, Fabio Wolkenstein (2019a) contends that populism can remain consistent with liberal democracy provided that it remains within certain 'discursive norms' in which the notion of who 'the people' are defined in a way that it is compatible with liberal democratic norms. Bart Bonikowski and Mathijs Rooduijn both argue that in certain circumstances populism can be 'used' within democratic norms, for example, to energize democratic debate on issues that have been ignored by the political mainstream (Bonikowski et al 2019). Kolja Möller (2018) goes so far as to suggest that populism is part of the basic 'contestatory grammar' of democratic politics, and for that reason should not be rejected out of hand.

The connection between constitutionalism and populism is similarly complex, but also relates to the centrality of 'the people'. According to Neil Walker:

> Populism is neither a surface distraction from other deeper trends nor wholly anomalous within our political tradition – an aberrant or extraordinary departure from modern constitutionally embedded politics. Rather it can be seen as a product of and response to a series of stress factors that are intrinsic to the modern constitutional condition.... [P]opulist constitutionalism ... involves a reaction against what its proponents view as the neglect of the *unitary collective particular* in influential strands of modern constitutionalism (2019b, 519; original emphasis)

The grievance of the modern populist, then, is focused on her finding that modern constitutionalism focuses on individualism, universalism and plurality at the expense of collectivism, particularism and a unitary structure (Walker 2019b, 531). That is, the populist objects to any characterization of 'the people' within the traditions of modern constitutionalism, which allows the concept to frame an open discursive space, reflecting competing and diverse tensions of history, geography, culture, society, law and politics. In similar terms, Paul Blokker argues that populism is non-pluralistic, or anti-pluralistic:

> But where the thrust in democratic constitutionalism is the widening and deepening of possibilities of de facto citizen engagement with constitutional politics and norms, in populist constitutionalism the actual engagement of (different groups

of) citizens in society is substituted for by the idea of a united people, represented by the populist leader. (2019, 540)

Of course, it is hard to fix causalities. It remains an open question as to exactly what role populism plays in relation to any given example of constitutional change or shift in the meaning or interpretation of a constitution, when this change is placed in the broader context of other pressures on constitutional democracy, such as nationalism, authoritarianism, the economic downturn and globalization.[19] None the less, the impact of populism on the discursive space in which 'the people', as a concept, is defined and continually redefined under each constitutional settlement is an important site for socio-legal research, and that research can, in turn, draw on work in other disciplines that is focused directly on the language and discursive strategies of political actors.[20]

After a slow start, the research topic of 'populist constitutionalism' has exploded in volume, intensity of scrutiny and geographical coverage in recent years, with notable special issues in the *International Journal of Constitutional Law* and the *German Law Journal*. Luigi Corrias has attempted to read populism as a 'constitutional theory'. He argues that populism can be seen as 'a constitutional theory which combines specific readings of the theories of constituent power, popular sovereignty and constitutional identity' (Corrias 2016, 9).[21] His argument thus matches the constitutional dimension of populism precisely to some of the key elements that we picked out in Chapter 3 as foundation stones for examining the ideational aspects of constitutional citizenship. This conclusion in turn maps rather neatly onto Michael Freeden's articulation of the 'populist core'. Limiting himself to right-of-centre European populisms, Freeden highlights three features:

> ... an insistent monism: that is, an inclination to conceive of society as a singular unitary body ...; an appeal to the origination and integrity of a defining founding moment or natality, even if not articulated as such; and a visceral fear of imported change in law, customs and people. (2017, 4)

---

[19] This is nicely illustrated by the many contributions to Graber et al (2018).

[20] Good examples are offered by Ajanovic et al (2015, 2018).

[21] Compare, however, Thornhill's argument that more needs to be done to develop a (historical)-sociological account of constitutionalism in order to understand better the ways in which it is challenged by populism.

The first two points address questions of constituent power and sovereignty, and suggest a notably anti-pluralist perspective on the part of populist actors, and the latter point clearly links to the issue of constitutional identity. It does so while taking an exclusivist perspective. Furthermore, Freeden points to the significant absence of equality from foundational tenets of the versions of populism he is discussing: 'substantive notions of material equality or equality of respect are hard to find in recent European populist versions' (2017, 4). In earlier chapters, we focused on equality as an important constitutional quality of citizenship, and its absence from the framing of at least those variants of populism to which Freeden refers must be regarded as significant when we come to assess how populist political systems will engage with constitutional framings.

It is important to be aware of where the animus that populists often display against many facets of public law may lead.[22] Julian Scholtes argues that 'populist platforms [are] often at odds with constitutionally entrenched rights' and 'populists also reject the constraints on political power that emanate from those rights', because the formal and substantive constraints of the constitution cannot override the true will of the people (Scholtes 2019, 353). We can therefore expect to see hostility to courts, a populist conception of sovereignty driven by an unmediated link between power and the people (except for the leader, of course…) and a rejection of public law in general as illegitimate. This explains why, in Scholtes' view, populists have often pursued 'aggressive constitutional politics' (2019, 354). Moreover, Scholtes argues that – ultimately – the law cannot save the law from the populists. Only the extra-legal political reasons that inhere in public law can (alongside democratic self-correction) eventually provide the answer if populists attack the constitutional order and alter the basic settlement on which it is founded, thus rendering any argument based on legality itself unsuccessful. Scholtes' closing words are powerful and cautionary:

> Constitutionalists must defend public law in political discourse in order to help secure the prerequisites that constitutional democracy needs to survive, but cannot guarantee by its own force. Public law, in this era of political populism, is a discourse. It is not defended in court, it is defended in the streets. (2019, 361)

---

[22] Borrowing from Loughlin (2017, 156), this can be defined as those measures concerned with the acquisition, generation, institutionalization and exercise of political power.

It may not always come to this, but it is important to bear in mind that this may sometimes be the end result of combating populism.

Populism and citizenship in practice

The bulk of the discussion in this chapter is focused on examples that allow us to see the interface of populism and citizenship from different angles. In the conclusion to Chapter 5, we acknowledged that (at least within the national paradigm) citizenship is always likely to disappoint those who invest in it the hopes that it will deliver equality and inclusion. Cohen (1999) goes so far as to argue that because of the impossibility of squaring the circle of modern citizenship's three elements, there is an inescapable push towards thicker and more exclusivist conceptions of identity. There was ample evidence of this in Part II of the book, although it is also true that the same chapters at times demonstrated that this was not necessarily the whole story when it came to citizenship. The point is reinforced by Sara Wallace Goodman's argument that 'populism is not an aberration; it is a response to a system designed to define national boundaries and sustain pluralism, with limited means to regulate the beliefs of those within those boundaries' (Wallace Goodman 2019, 7). The following sections of this chapter explore in greater detail what happens when the discursive space in which citizenship and constitutions can operate as mutually constitutive core elements of polities is closed down to a greater or lesser degree, because of pressure from particularistic and moralistic demands on the construction of 'the people'. These illustrations highlight the dangers that populism may pose to open, equal and inclusive conceptions of membership, based on substantial deliberation among members of the polity as free political agents and backed up by evident adherence to the core precepts of the rule of law.

Where populism is paired with a host ideology based on nationalism, 'populist moves' on constitutional citizenship are likely to include some or all of the following:

- shifting the formal boundaries of citizenship as a legal status in order to reinforce the idea of 'the people' as postulated by the populist leader (that is, changing citizenship laws, including placing obstacles to citizenship acquisition by individuals or groups seen as 'foreign' to the people; one favoured technique is to cut the supply of potential citizens off at source by denying long-term residence to migrants and promoting only circular and temporary migration);

- scapegoating of those outside the ring of favoured members, importing higher levels of insecurity and new precarities;
- depletion of civil and social rights, including welfare chauvinism,[23] restrictions on minority rights, and restrictions on religious freedoms for some groups;[24]
- in extreme cases citizenship stripping, often accompanied by the manipulation of conceptions of allegiance and loyalty;
- re-creating structural inequalities and hierarchies more commonly associated with colonialism;[25]
- establishing stronger relations between criminal law, immigration law and citizenship law, including a blurring of the boundaries between the different types of law and the introduction or enhancement of double sanctions (e.g. deportation for immigration offences or criminal offences);[26]
- finally, at the structural level, instituting certain changes that directly attack the separation of powers and institutional integrity on which the rule of law itself depends.[27]

It is interesting to juxtapose these points with some counter-examples where populist governments of the left have endeavoured to open up citizenship, beyond the existing 'national' range, as was in the case of Greece with a draft amendment to the citizenship law brought forward by the Syriza government.[28] As discussed in Chapter 4, the block on the proposed legal change came from a narrow *nationalist* reading of the scope of Greek citizenship by a court, based on the idea that a constitutional principle of *ius sanguinis* meant opposing the introduction of elements of a more open *ius soli* conception.

There are also a range of typical changes to constitutional citizenship related to the conditions under which political citizenship is exercised, which are common to any polity where a populist style of politics is dominant regardless of the 'host ideology' within which the populist forces are nested. They may include:

---

[23] See Ketola and Nordensvard (2018a, b).

[24] In this context, see also the discussion of 'burqa bans' in 'Equality, dignity and related constitutional principles in conversation with citizenship' in Chapter 3.

[25] Jones (2016).

[26] For a discussion of 'crimmigration', see Bosworth et al (2018) and Zedner (2019).

[27] Gardbaum (2019).

[28] Font et al (2019, 9).

- appeals to authenticity by leaders to fellow citizens based on demagoguery rather than reason ('post-shame politics', according to Wodak 2019);
- increasing challenges to the authenticity of elections and political communications in the age of digital democracy and new media ('post-truth politics');[29]
- the destabilizing of established patterns of political parties in favour of new 'insurgent' movements;[30]
- a shift towards direct democracy and away from representative democracy, with a preference for using referendums to decide key questions,[31] a move that seems to be supported by citizens who have populist attitudes, suggesting leaders are in tune with their constituencies;[32]
- and resistance to judicial scrutiny, especially that based on constitutional norms.[33]

The examples that follow are necessarily both synoptic and selective across several dimensions. First, the focus on constitutional citizenship does not cover all aspects of the citizenship/populism interface, especially in the political domain. Second, the discussion omits, for reasons of space, one region of the world where the citizenship/populism interface takes a rather different form, for reasons of political history, namely Latin America.[34] However, the examples chosen (Canada, US, UK, Hungary and India) enable us to see a variety of challenges to the institutions of state and government in the name of 'the people'. In 1999, Margaret Canovan offered a definition of populism that somehow suggested that it was an aberration in modern democratic states, as it was 'against' what the society stood for:

> Populism in modern democratic societies is best seen as an appeal to 'the people' against both the established structure of power and the dominant ideas and values of the society. (Canovan 1999, 3)

---

[29] See Brubaker (2017b, 378), Müller (2019) and Nadler (2019).
[30] Mudde and Kaltwasser (2017).
[31] Caramani (2017).
[32] Freyburg et al (2019).
[33] Blauberger and Kelemen (2017).
[34] De la Torre (2017a, b).

The examples developed here demonstrate that under the conditions of the 'new populism', this definition may no longer hold, in that the prevalence and usage of populist discourse may have transformative and irreversible effects.

Canada

It may seem odd to start with the case of Canada which, under the premiership of the Liberal Party's Justin Trudeau, has appeared to be one of the rare beacons of liberal politics in the modern world. Indeed, Trudeau made a virtue of inclusive citizenship during his election campaign in 2015, committing to repeal the citizenship-stripping legislation introduced by the previous Conservative government of Stephen Harper.[35] This was the same government that had also attempted unsuccessfully to make it compulsory that those giving the citizenship oath must have their faces uncovered, as discussed in Chapter 3. Yet despite its omission as a case study in the *Oxford Handbook of Populism*,[36] populism in Canada has had a significant historical and contemporary presence, albeit more often at the provincial than the federal level.[37] Right-wing populism manifested itself most strongly within Canadian federal politics during the Harper governments of 2006-2015, not so much because the Conservative Party of Canada itself morphed into a populist party, but because of the increasing impact of a populist approach in the areas of immigration and citizenship policy.[38] For political reasons, the Conservatives tacked towards a set of populist policy prescriptions, which produced distinctive legislative outcomes. Furthermore, by 2019 the populist People's Party of Canada had made sufficient ground in terms of gathering support to be included in the federal election debates. In the event, Trudeau's Liberal Party held on to form a minority government after the 2019 election (although the Conservative Party won the popular vote but did not get the most seats) and the People's Party suffered an electoral disaster, failing to hold even the one seat it had previously held, polling less than 2 per cent nationally. However, that is unlikely to be the end of populist politics in Canada.

---

[35] 'Justin Trudeau vows to repeal "2-tiered" citizenship law', *CBC News*, 29 August 2015 (www.cbc.ca/news/politics/justin-trudeau-vows-to-repeal-2-tiered-citizenship-law-1.3208571); see also Winter and Previsic (2019).

[36] Kaltwasser et al (2017b).

[37] Laycock (2006).

[38] Carlaw (2017) and Dobrowolsky (2017).

The 'politics of people' is central to Canadian politics as a whole. Canada was founded as a white settler state superimposed on a substantial but now marginalized indigenous community. Long-term patterns of immigration have brought people to Canada from all parts of the world, ensuring significant racial and religious diversity across the entire country.[39] Levels of immigration remain high, with official targets planning for something over 300,000 new permanent residents per year, and a naturalization rate (of eligible candidates) of over 85 per cent – one of the highest among the states of the Organization for Economic Co-operation and Development (OECD).[40] Furthermore, Canada, in common with most western hemisphere countries, has unconditional *ius soli* for citizenship by birth.[41] In addition, it is a federal state with elements of asymmetry, notably to protect the specific interests of language and culture in Québec. Québec enjoys substantial autonomy in relation to its immigration policy and its 'choice' of immigrants. Federally, the official policy is one of multiculturalism, which permits the maintenance within the private sphere of ethnic values and practices, while requiring an adherence in the public sphere to 'Canadian values' at a level that rises and falls according to political pressures.[42]

Positive sentiments outweigh negative ones among the general public in relation to immigration, including current levels of immigration and the impact of immigration on the economy.[43] However, birthright citizenship – enshrined by legislation and not constitution in Canada[44] – has also been a matter of public debate, especially in relation to so-called 'birth tourism', in which women come to Canada specifically for the purpose of giving birth, and then return to their home countries with their babies who have gained Canadian citizenship.[45] A majority of existing citizens believe that children born to parents present in the country on tourist visas should not gain Canadian citizenship. Xenophobia and Islamophobia are also especially prevalent in some parts of the country.[46] Thus, for example, Québec enacted 'strong' secular rules in 2019 (after repeated failed attempts to do so through the 2010s), banning certain public servants

---

[39] Macklin (2017a).

[40] Immigration, Refugees and Citizenship Canada Departmental Plan 2018–2019, December 2018 (www.canada.ca/en/immigration-refugees-citizenship/corporate/publications-manuals/departmental-plan-2018-2019/departmental-plan.html).

[41] Winter (2015).

[42] Sobel (2015).

[43] Neuman (2019).

[44] Sullivan (2018).

[45] Angus Reid Institute (2019).

[46] Lenard (2018b).

from wearing religious symbols at work.[47] These clearly impact most on the religious freedom of Jews, Muslims and Sikhs. Legal challenges to the law have been mounted, but they face considerable hurdles as the law has been carefully drafted effectively to 'oust' the rights and freedoms provisions of the Canadian Charter.[48]

Clearly, therefore, Canada is a space hosting many countervailing forces and trends affecting the inclusivity and exclusivity of constitutional citizenship, and we can see that a range of potentially paradoxical policy positions have been taken across the country at different times. Critics point to certain facets of policy and law-making on crime and immigration during the period of the Harper federal government as having distinct populist overtones. These included not just the attempt to prevent women from taking the citizenship oath while covering their faces (as discussed in Chapter 3), but also a transparent attempt to 'make a statement' by adopting The Zero Tolerance for Barbaric Cultural Practices Act,[49] largely focused on criminalizing certain practices around forced marriage and polygamy that were, in fact, already illegal. The law remains on the statute book as a symbol. The 'tip line' promised by the Conservative government, an opportunity for citizens to inform the authorities about practices among their neighbours that they thought might infringe the law, did not come to pass as the Conservative Party of Canada lost the ensuing election to their Liberal opponents. This was just one dimension of a 'discourse of distrust' (Dobrowolsky 2017, 202) that marked a period of intensive legislative activity around citizenship and immigration. Significant restrictions were placed on family migration, impacting low-income families much more than higher-income families and on the processing of refugee applications. Deportations of foreign national prisoners were stepped up, and the language of immigration became highly disciplinary, suggesting that there was a risk that immigrants, who were increasingly lumped together in a single category marked 'undeserving', were primarily out to take advantage of Canada's

---

[47] 'Québec passes religious symbols secularism bill', *BBC News*, 17 June 2019 (www.bbc.co.uk/news/world-us-canada-48477086).

[48] J. Montpetit (2019) 'Québec's religious symbols law passes 1st legal test as judge refuses injunction', *CBC News*, 18 July(www.cbc.ca/news/canada/montreal/quebec-religious-symbols-law-upheld-superior-court-1.5216576); J. Montpetit (2019) 'As fight over Quebec's religious symbols law shifts to courts, legal experts debate best way to challenge it', *CBC News*, 8 July (www.cbc.ca/news/canada/montreal/as-fight-over-quebec-s-religious-symbols-law-shifts-to-courts-legal-experts-debate-best-way-to-challenge-it-1.5204112).

[49] SC 2015, c29 (see https://laws-lois.justice.gc.ca/eng/annualstatutes/2015_29/page-1.html).

taxpayer-funded welfare and healthcare services. A fraud hotline was also opened. Critics have suggested that one of the aims of the period of intensive legislative activity was the recreation of some sort of settler colonial identity.[50]

Changes in discourse came with the election of Trudeau's government, although there remain concerns that Canada may be drifting towards a much greater receptivity to populist rhetoric and politics,[51] as evidenced by the Québec 'muscular secularism' law in 2019, which itself was accompanied by a rise in verbal assaults and harassment of Muslim women choosing to wear the hijab.[52] Political commentators have suggested that the characteristic mode of European politics, in which the populist far right has achieved hegemony through an opposition to immigration, which in turn has chimed strongly with a set of fears among more sedentary populations that they were the victims of forces of globalization (including immigration), may be transferring to Canada.[53] In the event, the electoral outcomes from the General Election in October 2019 that many expected[54] did not come to pass. But the Québec legislation shows that this shift does have a culturalist dimension to it, just as it does in Europe, with white Christianity posing as defending itself against an 'invading' Islam. It seems, therefore, that the state of constitutional citizenship in Canada at the present time would need to be marked as 'in transition'. Future electoral outcomes, combined with the continued question of how the courts may judge certain legislative initiatives, remain uncertain.

The United States of America

Since 2016, Canadians have sometimes gazed over the border to their south and said, with decreasing levels of justification, 'It couldn't happen to us'. It could be argued that Donald Trump represents the paradigmatic populist leader, someone whose rhetoric around a certain notion of 'the people' has enabled him to build a coalition to be elected as President, while making use of the Republican Party as a 'host body'. Immigration and citizenship issues have been at the forefront of Trump's populist rhetoric, much of which is focused on 'cleansing' the US of

---

[50] Carlaw (2017).
[51] Marcus (2019a).
[52] Marcus (2019b).
[53] Yılmaz (2012).
[54] Graves and Valpy (2018).

'foreign bodies' via 'strong borders', notably 'the Wall'. His rhetoric has ramped up over time, from attacks on 'gang members' in 2017, where law enforcement authorities should 'get them the hell out of here',[55] to verbal attacks in 2019 on four Democratic congresswomen of colour, who should, he said, go back to the 'broken and crime infested places from which they came'.[56] All are US citizens, three of the four were born in the US, and the fourth came to the US as a refugee when a child. He took this one step further at a rally, goading the crowd into chanting 'send her back' after he attacked one of the congresswomen.[57] So what started as a reinforcement of the logic of securing and criminalizing the border has shifted into a broader attack on those whose faces do not fit. Critics have suggested that he articulates a vision of a return to an age of selective citizenship, when citizenship meant being white.[58] Trump has also challenged the political citizenship of other groups, accusing Jewish people who voted for Democratic Party candidates of showing 'great disloyalty'.[59] This echoes a 'toxic back story' in which Jews in Germany during the 1930s were accused of being disloyal before their citizenship was stripped from them (Davis 2019). It is notable that Trump's attacks draw the admiration of populists in other countries; Trump was described by Nigel Farage, now leader of the Brexit Party in the UK and one of the architects of the successful referendum campaign in 2016, rather candidly as 'remarkably good at what he does'.[60]

While many of his attacks on the dimensions of citizenship in the US have been rhetorical, they have also been accompanied by, or associated with, some significant changes in law and policy. Together, the rhetoric and the measures have undoubted effects on the lives of those who are

---

[55] As cited by Bosworth et al (2018, 35). The full text and video of the relevant passage is available at I. Schwartz (2017) 'Trump on illegals: "Get them the hell out of here, bring them back to where they came from"', RealClear Politics, 19 February (www.realclearpolitics.com/video/2017/02/19/trump_on_illegals_get_them_the_hell_out_of_here_bring_them_back_to_where_they_came_from.html).

[56] A. Smith (2019) 'Trump says congresswomen of color should "go back" and fix the places they 'originally came from', NBC News, 15 July (www.nbcnews.com/politics/donald-trump/trump-says-progressive-congresswomen-should-go-back-where-they-came-n1029676).

[57] T. McCarthy (2019) 'Trump rally crowd chants "send her back" after president attacks Ilhan Omar', *The Guardian*, 18 July (www.theguardian.com/us-news/2019/jul/17/trump-rally-send-her-back-ilhan-omar).

[58] Cobb (2019) and Gross and de la Fuente (2019).

[59] 'Trump accuses Jewish Democrat voters of "great disloyalty"', BBC News, 21 August 2019 (www.bbc.co.uk/news/world-us-canada-49417157).

[60] 'Farage cuts back pints to take up yoga', *The Times*, 3 August 2019, p 13.

undocumented immigrants (and their families), raising precarity and insecurity to new and higher levels.[61] Yet it is worth recalling that all of these changes have been framed within the US's system of separation of powers and a constitutional guarantee of birthright citizenship. We have previously discussed, in Chapter 4, that Trump has mooted, on several occasions, issuing an executive order, 'clarifying' the scope of the 14th Amendment as regards the children of undocumented migrants. At the same time, it is unlikely that there will be either a change to the US constitution or a dramatic change in interpretation of the citizenship clause by the Supreme Court. In the same chapter, we also mentioned the re-energized denaturalization campaign in the US and restrictions on birth registration. These are executive moves that may be harder to subject to effective judicial scrutiny, as is the treatment of migrants, including children, at the border with Mexico, many of whom have been subject to concentration camp-like conditions. These incarcerations have often involved the forcible separation of children from parents, which has been criticized by a UN human rights body as undignified and damaging.[62]

Elsewhere, there has been a further struggle between the executive, the judiciary and civil society organizations over the attempt by the US Department of Commerce to include a question in the US census of 2020 about the citizenship status of all census returnees.[63] Such a question has not been asked since 1950. This move received a judicial 'knockback' during the course of 2019, although largely only on procedural grounds. The ruling stated that having the question in the census was not in and of itself unconstitutional.[64] This finding was a blow to civil rights lawyers (Wolf and Cea 2019b). The census – which is constitutionally mandated in the US – would probably return an undercount of immigrants *with* citizenship, if such a question were introduced, because of fears about implicating family members *without* citizenship or legal status (Epps 2019). Such an undercount would profoundly affect issues such as voting rights and 'districting' (that is, the allocation of seats in the House of Representatives on the basis of demographics).

The battle over the census is part of the broader picture relating to the authenticity of elections in the US and especially the right to vote, in the context of what has been characterized – in partisan terms – as 'the war

---

[61] See Nienhusser and Oshio (2019) and Open Society Justice Initiative (2019).

[62] J. Dalton (2019) 'Trump's migrant camps on US border "undignified and damaging", says UN human rights chief', *The Independent*, 8 July (www.independent.co.uk/news/world/americas/us-border-migrant-camp-mexico-trump-un-human-rights-children-a8994831.html).

[63] For full analysis, see Wolf and Cea (2019a).

[64] *Department of Commerce v New York*, No 18–966, 588 US ___ (2019).

on voting rights' (Shattuck et al 2019). That is to say, the 'war' is being conducted between Republicans (and the institutions they lead), who argue that voter fraud is rife and introduce various measures that make it harder to vote, especially for those who are socioeconomically or racially marginalized within society, and Democrats (and the institutions they lead), who claim that the right to vote has historically been a battleground of racial politics in the US, and that as many steps as possible need to be taken to correct the US's historically low voter participation rates. Although the right to vote is not a constitutional right at federal level in the US, none the less the general framing of the issue is constitutional, in two senses: much of the most important case law comes direct from the Supreme Court, plus the politics of race is deeply imbricated within the fabric of the US Constitution. But given the long history of the legal contestation of voting rights and voter suppression in the US, which stretches way beyond the current populist moment, it is rather hard to draw a direct causal link between current developments and the present dominance of a populist discursive style within the US.

In sum, as with Canada, we are left with a picture of how constitutional citizenship may be in transition. However, we can also see that the constitutional framing of citizenship in the US can still be used to protect the pluralism that Trump's opponents would argue is essential to the US as a complex multi-racial society of immigration. Although there have been attempts by Trump and allies to change the character of the US judiciary, which could impact on citizenship in the future, it would seem that for now the wide range of constitutionally mandated checks and balances that protect the separation of powers in the US remains relatively robust.

The United Kingdom

Those who date the 'arrival' of populism in the UK, in the sense of a substantial impact on parties, elections and governments, to the June 2016 referendum on EU membership have probably not been paying sufficient attention to two key factors. The first is the rise of the UK Independence Party (UKIP) (since its founding in 1993). The second is the 'framing' of much immigration policy within a populist rhetoric from the mid-2000s onwards, and certainly under the Conservative-led coalition government from 2010 onwards. This 'framing' found its way into policy outcomes as an example of the 'legislative populism' discussed by Nicola Lacey (2019), with clear effects in at least three domains: the treatment of foreign national prisoners, the emergence of a criminalized border, and the creation of the so-called 'hostile environment', which brought the border inside the country and made immigration enforcement officers out of every landlord, bank, employer and even healthcare worker. This legislative populism has, in turn, fed back into the citizenship dimensions of Brexit, as populist ideas have moved decisively into the core of UK politics.

The rise of UKIP and the electoral traction it gained from 2000 onwards, especially in European Parliament elections where it benefited from the proportional representation electoral system and a strong Eurosceptic protest vote, was one of the major factors that led to the holding of a referendum on EU membership (Crewe 2020). In turn, the referendum has led to an explosion of populist rhetoric, with significant implications for constitutional citizenship. Since the date of the referendum, the watchword of many of those who campaigned for the vote to leave has been that politicians must heed 'the will of the people', despite the tendentiousness of that statement in political theory terms (Weale 2017, 2018). Furthermore, it is profoundly unlikely that 'delivering Brexit' is actually resolving the tensions, divides and differences that underpinned the vote to leave in 2016 and UK politics since that date (Marsh 2020). It is rather difficult to explain the 'politics' of Brexit in its full glory, given the multiple actors involved and the simultaneous games of three-dimensional chess underway, which set support for or opposition to leaving the EU, with or without a deal, against partisan support across political parties and the search for electoral advantage and power at the ballot box.[65] By way of contrast to that complexity, the impact on individuals in terms of 'citizenship consequences' is rather clear, harsh and simple to explain (Reynolds 2017), despite the uncertainties at the date of writing as to exactly what the long-term consequences of Brexit could be. The wider constitutional effects, although already substantial not least because of the volume of Brexit-related litigation, remained uncertain even after the December 2019 General Election delivered a decisive majority for the government of Boris Johnson, which promised to 'Get Brexit Done', and the UK's consequential exit from the EU on 31 January 2020.

At the UK Conservative Party conference in October 2016, the newly appointed Prime Minister Theresa May famously stated: 'if you believe you're a citizen of the world, you're a citizen of nowhere and you don't know what citizenship is.'[66] It cemented the impression, along with May's references to the country having 'spoken' over Brexit so that 'Brexit means

---

[65] For detailed analysis, see Diamond et al (2018).

[66] See T. May (2016) 'Theresa May's conference speech in full', *The Telegraph*, 5 October (www.telegraph.co.uk/news/2016/10/05/theresa-mays-conference-speech-in-full/).

Brexit'[67], that here was a politician prepared to use populist discourse for her political ends. It can be argued that this sentence was actually aimed at a relatively small number of 'global actors', particularly those responsible for companies that have used tax jurisdiction shopping in order to boost their profits, by evading their taxation responsibilities in the places they do most business. Be that as it may, the dictum has been almost universally taken to express a disdain for those with cosmopolitan inclinations and – worse – anyone whose cross-border life had led them to a situation where they were living in a country of which, legally, they were not a citizen. One of the many different responses of EU27 citizens resident in the UK, facing continued uncertainty about their legal status after the Brexit vote,[68] has seen a substantial rise in the numbers seeking naturalization.[69] In one sense, those naturalizing, albeit under duress, are accepting the veracity of Theresa May's post-Brexit dictum. Under pressure, they are making themselves citizens of *somewhere*: the UK. But at the same time, their sense of 'home' has been profoundly destabilized by populist discourse (Miller 2019).

Brexit, along with the populist movement with which it is closely associated, has placed profound strains on the UK's rather ambiguous constitutional framework and the relationships between legislature, executive and judiciary, while offering the opportunity for populist grandstanding. It has left the situation unclear as to whether the UK's traditional notion of parliamentary sovereignty still holds, or whether the UK is now a country based on popular sovereignty, with the executive holding the ring against a recalcitrant parliament on behalf of a dispossessed people.

The post-Brexit phase has been punctuated by a number of cases before the UK courts testing, among other matters, the breadth of executive discretion versus legislative competences. The first such case to hit the headlines involved an attempt by the applicants to establish that Parliament must legislate before notice was given by the executive to the EU institutions under Article 50 of the Treaty on European Union (TEU)

---

[67] Of the various three world slogans that have dominated the Brexit process (including 'Take Back Control' and 'Get Brexit Done'), 'Brexit means Brexit' gained by far the least traction.

[68] See Reynolds (2017), Cambien (2018), Strumia (2018) and Shaw (2018).

[69] In 2018, there was a 23 per cent increase in EU27 citizens applying for naturalization in the UK, with this group accounting for 30 per cent of all applications: National Statistics, *Summary of Latest Statistics*, 28 February 2019 (www.gov.uk/government/publications/immigration-statistics-year-ending-december-2018/summary-of-latest-statistics).

that the UK intended to withdraw from the EU.[70] The 2016 first instance judgment – delivered by an unusual three-judge bench of senior members of the judiciary – accepted the arguments of the applicants and made a declaration that legislation was needed under the UK's constitutional system before the Article 50 notification could be made. This led to a furious media reaction, led by a *Daily Mail* headline screaming – over pictures of the three judges – 'Enemies of the People'.[71] Things were made worse by a singularly weak defence of the judiciary by the executive in the following days.[72] A similar media reaction praising the government for 'giving effect to the will of the nation' came from another newspaper in the wake of the approval of an Order in Council of the Queen proroguing (that is, suspending) Parliament during September and October 2019.[73] This was ostensibly to allow for the beginning of a new parliamentary session, but the suspicion could not be set aside that it was also to limit opportunities for Parliament to debate stopping the departure of the UK from the EU without a deal on 31 October 2019. It was a step of doubtful constitutional propriety (Craig 2019), which was itself challenged and eventually overturned in the courts, setting a new constitutional standard based on a vigorous, but not uncontroversial, defence of parliamentary

---

[70] *R (Miller) v Secretary of State for Exiting the European Union* (2016) EWHC (Ch) 2768, [2017] UKSC 5.

[71] See, for a headline that has everything, 'Enemies of the people: Fury over "out of touch" judges who have "declared war on democracy" by defying 17.4m Brexit voters and who could trigger constitutional crisis', *Daily Mail*, 3 November 2016 (www.dailymail.co.uk/news/article-3903436/Enemies-people-Fury-touch-judges-defied-17-4m-Brexit-voters-trigger-constitutional-crisis.html) (for a facsimile version of the actual newspaper headline, see https://twitter.com/hendopolis/status/794305335158853634). For a summary of how other newspapers reacted, see C. Phipps (2016) 'British newspapers react to judges' Brexit ruling: "Enemies of the people"', *The Guardian*, 4 November (www.theguardian.com/politics/2016/nov/04/enemies-of-the-people-british-newspapers-react-judges-brexit-ruling). The extent to which the UK has become a divided country was emphasized by a mocking 'Heroes of the People' headline produced by *The Scotsman* on 12 September 2019, celebrating the judgment of the Scottish Court of Session declaring the prorogation of Parliament in September/October 2019 to be unlawful (https://twitter.com/TheScotsman/status/1171883889796767746).

[72] 'Liz Truss defends judiciary after Brexit ruling criticism', *The Guardian*, 5 November 2016 (www.theguardian.com/law/2016/nov/05/barristers-urge-liz-truss-to-condemn-attacks-on-brexit-ruling-judges).

[73] For facsimile versions of the newspaper headlines, see @hendopolis on Twitter (https://twitter.com/hendopolis/status/1166815977989967877).

sovereignty and the accountability of the executive to Parliament by the Supreme Court.[74]

Eventually the stalemate resulted in the calling of an election on 12 December 2019, which – because of the effects of the UK's first-past-the-post electoral system – produced a majority that enabled Prime Minister Boris Johnson to push his Brexit legislation based on the Withdrawal Agreement through Parliament. Johnson controversially termed his new government 'the people's government' in his victory, reinforcing the perception that a new era of populism is gearing up.[75]

The use of populist language has proliferated in the political sphere. The distrust of 'authority figures', best articulated in Vote Leave campaigner Michael Gove's most famous pre-referendum quotation 'People in this country have had enough of experts',[76] has opened the door to a fractured public sphere when it comes to discussions of Brexit. Members of the public appear to prefer the reassurances of certain politicians that 'no deal' will do no substantial harm, rather than the warnings of experts, including government departments.[77] Despite the House of Commons voting massively for the legislation that led to the Article 50 notification at the beginning of 2017,[78] by August 2019, after marked difficulties in negotiating with the EU and then agreeing internally an orderly exit, new Prime Minister Boris Johnson was happy to accuse his parliamentary opponents of being 'collaborators'. His precise phrase, delivered during a so-called 'People's PMQs'[79] held on Facebook, with no journalists

---

[74] *R (on the application of Miller) (Appellant) v The Prime Minister (Respondent)*; *Cherry and Others (Respondents) v Advocate General for Scotland (Appellant) (Scotland)* [2019] UKSC 41. For analysis of the various arguments raised, see Craig (2019).

[75] See 'General Election 2019: Boris Johnson victory speech celebrates Conservative win' (www.youtube.com/watch?v=RGuFuHk3W2Q); see also Shaw (2019c).

[76] Interview with Faisal Islam, *Sky News*, 3 June 2016 (www.youtube.com/watch?v=GGgiGtJk7MA). See also the evidently low opinion of economists' analyses expressed by Leader of the House Jacob Rees-Mogg in October 2019: *Hansard* (http://bit.ly/35Yat6r and http://bit.ly/2pEXXbi).

[77] J. Gray (2019) 'We asked people who want a No-Deal Brexit why they think it's a good idea', *Huffington Post*, 8 August (www.huffingtonpost.co.uk/entry/no-deal-brexit-supporters-why_uk_5d498b20e4b0d291ed070188). None the less, public trust of experts in the UK seems to be quite high; see Dommett and Pearce (2019).

[78] On the second reading of the European Union (Notification of Withdrawal) Act 2017 the vote was 498 in favour to 114 against, with only one Conservative MP voting against, 47 Labour MPs, and the majority of the other votes against triggering Article 50 TEU coming from the Scottish National Party (SNP). The outcome was a mainly a function of party discipline, with neither the Conservative Party nor the Labour Party wanting to be seen as 'against' Brexit, and fear of the reaction of the press.

[79] Prime Minister's Questions.

involved and only pre-vetted questions allowed, was: 'There's a terrible kind of collaboration, as it were, going on between people who think they can block Brexit in Parliament and our European friends'.[80] While some might suggest that the most significant reason why the UK did not leave the EU as scheduled in March 2019 was because those who professed themselves in favour of Brexit voted against the Withdrawal Agreement in Parliament on several occasions, the sort of statements that Johnson has come out with still ring quite true for large numbers of people in a deeply divided country. They feel that the obstacles to Brexit being 'delivered' were not its inherent complexity or the very substantial difficulties reconciling leaving the EU with maintaining an open border between Northern Ireland and Ireland, but rather the opposition of 'Remainers' who refused to admit defeat.[81]

It is clear, therefore, that the populist framing of the pre- and post-referendum debate raises many questions about constituent power and sovereignty in the UK, which are central to the understanding of constitutional citizenship. In the context of the UK's constitution, it would seem that constitutional proprieties may be vulnerable to mismanagement by populists in power, with relatively weak checks and balances. There may be few constitutional certainties against which to set a standard for appropriate political behaviour, and the emergence of a clarion call for popular sovereignty in a country that has long adhered to the principle of parliamentary sovereignty makes for uncomfortable watching. At the time of writing, nothing could be said with certainty with regard to the likely long-term impact of the Brexit on the UK constitution, or even – indeed – what its short-term impact has already been. It would seem that Brexit is the gift that keeps giving, when it comes to politicians reaching for the populists' playbook. Many fear that this may lead to constitutional and democratic destabilization going far beyond mere rhetoric.

It remains exceptionally tricky to pin down 'constitutional citizenship' as a status and body of rights in the UK, as the periodic references to UK citizenship law across the book have demonstrated (Dummett and Nicol 1990). Citizenship is now a creature of statute in the UK, and the common law principle of *ius soli*, which may perhaps once have been regarded as constitutional in nature, has long gone. We have only occasional references to the citizen as a constitutional actor from the

---

[80] R. Mason (2019) 'Johnson accuses MPs and EU of "terrible collaboration" over Brexit', *The Guardian*, 14 August (www.theguardian.com/politics/2019/aug/14/johnson-hits-out-at-terrible-collaboration-of-mps-and-eu-trying-to-block-brexit).
[81] For an iconoclastic approach to the question of sovereignty and democracy in the UK after the Brexit referendum, see Copus (2018).

judiciary, as with the quotation from the case of *G1* featured in Chapter 1. However, the impact of Brexit is not directly on national citizenship, but rather on *EU citizenship*, which is a constitutional status within the context of the EU legal order, and which was given a form of constitutional status in the UK by the foundational legislative enactment of the UK's EU membership, namely the European Communities Act 1972, which was repealed on the date of Brexit. As EU citizens have that status by virtue of their national citizenship, and there is an iterative relationship between the two statuses (Shaw 2019a), this makes the case for understanding Brexit as having a *direct* impact on EU citizenship and an *indirect* impact on national citizenship. This is because the UK leaving the EU means that citizens from the EU27 Member States will no longer be treated as EU citizens in the UK, and because UK citizens will no longer be EU citizens when resident, or travelling, in the EU27.[82] Brexit has rendered the UK a 'third country' *vis-à-vis* the EU, subject only to transition. EU citizens are losing their rights as well as the protection of the non-discrimination principle under EU law.[83] For all of these reasons, Brexit must be seen as bringing about fundamental changes in relation to 'constitutional citizenship', understood in this context as a multilevel concept, for those affected. But unlike some of the other moves driven by populism and a desire to reinterpret the notion of the national people and close down the discursive space of constitutional citizenship, it will not render anyone stateless,[84] at least in the short term. The changes can, none the less, cause considerable harm to individuals and groups.

In one sense, little changed in the three+ years after the referendum, as the UK was still an EU Member State right into 2020, and EU law has still applied right through the transitional period; and yet, everything has changed. While those coming and going between the UK and the other Member States still benefited from the various dimensions of free

---

[82] As the focus here is on populism in the UK, the treatment of UK citizens in the EU27 either under a Withdrawal Agreement or in the event of 'no deal' lies beyond the scope of this chapter, but falls within the scope of Chapter 7.

[83] The issue of voting rights for EU citizens before (for example, during the referendum itself and during the unexpected 2019 European Parliament elections, where many experienced the loss of the right to vote because of registration complexities) and after the departure of the UK from the EU is an important topic that is not discussed for lack of space.

[84] It is conceivable, however, that the long term effects of the EU Settlement Scheme – as with the Windrush scandal – could lead to child statelessness.

movement,[85] there were regular announcements that free movement 'must end' as soon as Brexit happens. It must always feel like the sword of Damocles is hanging nearby, especially since there were regular references to the EU citizens affected by Brexit on both sides (that is, the UK citizens in the EU27 as well) being ideal 'bargaining chips' in the context of the Withdrawal Agreement negotiations that concluded in November 2018. It was no surprise to well-informed observers that the woman who became Prime Minister, after six years as the Home Secretary who had significantly ramped up the UK's 'hostile environment' for irregular immigrants, was fully in tune with giving effect to one of the main themes of the successful Leave campaign, which was that British people wanted to take back control of their borders.[86] Yet there has been no firm policy or law on 'what comes next' in terms of immigration control, so that crowd-pleasing announcements that free movement must end on the day of a 'no deal' Brexit[87] have to be rapidly followed by U-turns based on legal advice that this simply is not possible at this stage.[88] But the effects of such twists and turns on people's daily lives are enormous, as people do not know whether they will be able to go about their normal business after a certain date, especially if that includes any cross-border activity.

---

[85] Anecdotal evidence in early 2020 suggested that those EU citizens unable to prove their rights under the EU Settlement Scheme may already be experiencing discrimination in relation to employment and housing (www.independent.co.uk/news/uk/home-news/eu-nationals-settled-status-brexit-employers-landlords-housing-rights-a9289186.html).

[86] K. McCann (2018) 'Theresa May says ending freedom of movement is top priority after Brexit', Sky News, 30 November (https://news.sky.com/story/theresa-may-says-ending-freedom-of-movement-is-top-priority-after-brexit-11568339).

[87] R. Merrick (2019) 'UK to end freedom of movement for EU citizens on day one of Brexit, under new government plan', *The Independent*, 18 August (www.independent.co.uk/news/uk/politics/uk-eu-brexit-freedom-of-movement-ends-november-boris-johnson-priti-patel-home-office-a9064376.html).

[88] L. O'Carroll (2019) 'U-turn over plan to end freedom of movement on 31 October', *The Guardian*, 1 September (www.theguardian.com/politics/2019/sep/01/government-to-scrap-plans-for-henry-viii-power-to-end-free-movement); see also House of Commons Library (2019c). In February 2020, it became clear that the UK government intended to enact no special preferences for EU migrants post Brexit: see Home Office (2020) 'The UK's points-based immigration system: Policy statement', 19 February (www.gov.uk/government/publications/the-uks-points-based-immigration-system-policy-statement). Furthermore, in order to end free movement at the end of the transitional period, the Immigration and Social Security Co-Ordination (EU Withdrawal) Bill was published in March 2020 (www.gov.uk/government/publications/immigration-bill-2020-overarching-documents).

One thing is certain: such headlines have clearly provoked spikes in the number of applications to the EU Settlement Scheme, discussed below.[89]

This illustrates that the legal and political management of the situation of those who were already in the UK on the date of the referendum, or who have arrived in the meantime under EU law, has involved a series of populist missteps and half-hearted reassurance for those affected. The UK designed and implemented the European Union Settlement Scheme (EUSS), under which (up to the end of 2019[90]) more than 2.5 million people out of the estimated 3 to 4 million EU citizens plus family members resident in the UK had applied for the right to stay in the UK.[91] Not all those who applied have been given 'settled status', or even its less secure shadow 'pre-settled status', and deep concerns have been expressed about how it is working,[92] and whether the figures given by the government are 'double-counting' repeat applications and follow-up applications by those with pre-settled status for settled status.[93] By the middle of November 2019, it had become obvious that a growing percentage of applicants were being given pre-settled status.[94] Settled status supersedes EU law and is intended to be concordant with the UK's commitments under the Withdrawal Agreement. Legally, the EUSS rests on a new Appendix to the UK's Immigration Rules, put in place from March 2019.[95]

---

[89] Statistics on the EU Settlement Scheme are released monthly, with more detailed analysis quarterly (www.gov.uk/government/collections/eu-settlement-scheme-statistics).

[90] See G. Sturge and O. Hawkins (2020) 'The progress of the EU Settlement Scheme so far', House of Commons Library, 14 February (https://commonslibrary.parliament.uk/home-affairs/immigration/the-progress-of-the-eu-settlement-scheme-so-far/).

[91] Ibid.

[92] Jablonowski (2019); see also A. Gentleman (2019) 'Rise in EU citizens not getting UK settled status causes alarm', *The Guardian*, 30 August (www.theguardian.com/politics/2019/aug/30/eu-citizens-uk-settled-status-alarm).

[93] 'Double counting could make UK settled status statistics "meaningless"', *Financial Times*, 27 October 2019 (www.ft.com/content/46616b84-f74e-11e9-a79c-bc9acae3b654).

[94] A. Gentleman (2019) 'Rising proportion of EU citizens in UK given temporary "pre-settled status"', *The Guardian*, 14 November (www.theguardian.com/politics/2019/nov/14/rising-proportion-of-eu-citizens-being-granted-presettled-status).

[95] Immigration Rules, Appendix EU (www.gov.uk/guidance/immigration-rules/immigration-rules-appendix-eu), as amended in September 2019 (www.gov.uk/government/publications/statement-of-changes-to-the-immigration-rules-hc-2631-9-september-2019) (for the Settlement Scheme application, see www.gov.uk/settled-status-eu-citizens-families). See House of Commons Library (2019b).

The other adjustments that EU27 citizens can make include applying for naturalization within the UK,[96] which may be a suitable (if rather expensive) option for some but complicated for others if it means losing an existing citizenship. Alternatively, EU citizens may choose to leave the UK, either returning to the state of origin or moving to another Member State. It would seem that there has still been net (if lower) positive migration from the EU27 to the UK after June 2016,[97] but anecdotal evidence points to recruitment difficulties in specific industries as a result of both departures and non-arrivals.[98] Whichever response is made, the effects of change are undoubtedly disruptive (Sigona 2019). In that context, having to deal with a xenophobic press and a recorded rise in hostility and racist incidents after the referendum[99] can be anticipated to have caused increased stress levels and raised the question as to whether EU27 citizens can truly feel 'at home' in the UK any more (Ranta and Nancheva 2019).

The issues around Brexit, free movement, residence and welfare are not isolated from a wider environment around immigration policy and immigration policy in the UK (Shaw 2019b). Increasingly, immigration and the politics of the UK border have become racialized and criminalized, with populist anxieties clustering around a variety of figures of fear: the Muslim terrorist, the foreign national prisoner, the Polish plumber, the Romanian fruit-picker. It was inevitable, given the parallels in relation to the involuntary change of legal status and the continued rise of the documentary and securitized state, that comparisons would be drawn between the treatment of the 'Windrush generation', previously discussed in Chapters 2 and 5, and the treatment of EU citizens in the context of Brexit. Much has been said about the potential for things to go seriously wrong with the change of legal status of such a large number of resident EU27 citizens and their families (up to 4 million people), some of whom are third country national family members of EU citizens. This latter

---

[96] D'Oliveira (2018) and Sigona and Godin (2019).

[97] 'Has there been a 'Brexodus' of EU citizens since the referendum?', *Full Fact*, 19 December 2018 (https://fullfact.org/immigration/eu-citizens-brexodus/).

[98] 'Large drop in the number of new nurses coming from the EU to work in the UK', The Health Foundation (www.health.org.uk/chart/chart-large-drop-in-the-number-of-new-nurses-coming-from-the-eu-to-work-in-the-uk); D. Campbell (2019) 'NHS nursing crisis worsened by Brexit exodus', *The Guardian*, 8 May (www.theguardian.com/society/2019/may/08/nhs-nursing-crisis-worsened-by-brexit-exodus).

[99] See Guma and Jones (2019) and Rzepnikowska (2019). For a preliminary report on ongoing research on perceptions of EU citizens of life in the UK after the Brexit referendum, see 'EU nationals feeling unwelcome in the UK', 28 November 2019 (https://ukandeu.ac.uk/eu-nationals-feeling-unwelcome-in-the-uk/).

group would ordinarily already be subject to the strictures of the 'hostile environment' were they not protected by the 'cloak' of EU law. Amongst these groups of EU citizens and their families are highly vulnerable and social excluded individuals, such as care-experienced children and young people (Barnard et al 2019). The parallels between Windrush and Brexit have been drawn by Home Affairs Select Committee in a report on the EUSS,[100] by media commentators,[101] and by other writers.[102] What provokes the parallels is the extraordinarily poor handling of the Windrush issue up to the present day, given that many charities and advocates for migrants' rights were already arguing many years ago about the impact of the imposition of documentary requirements on older and often vulnerable groups,. And yet so many individuals to whom harm has been caused have yet to receive effective redress.[103]

However, the parallels are limited, in the sense that Windrush is a product not so much of 'migration' in the usual sense, but of the complex and unresolved politics of decolonialization in the UK (O. Khan 2019). At the time when those we now characterize as the 'Windrush generation' migrated to the UK, they were most likely still British subjects (depending on precisely when this occurred and where they came from). Successive pieces of UK legislation stripped away their rights and many were not aware that their status changed if and when the country from which they moved achieved independence from the UK. There were steps put in place to regularize their situation and to deem them to be present lawfully in the UK after the Immigration Act 1971 came into force, but many of those affected by the scandal lacked the documentation to prove that they were covered by this (White 2019). The full horror of Windrush, and its specific constitutional resonance, legally speaking, is therefore the harsh and unacceptable treatment of co-citizens. From a political point of view, the realization of this fact has belatedly achieved a certain degree of traction within public opinion, in as much as this group of people, many from the Caribbean, fall within the UK's imaginary of 'who we are', not least because so many have worked for many years in the public services, especially the National Health Service. The extension of the 'co-citizen'

---

[100] House of Commons Home Affairs Committee (2019).

[101] 'EU migrants must not become Brexit bargaining chips. Ending free movement under a no-deal exit risks a repeat of the Windrush scandal', *The FT View*, *Financial Times*, 20 August 2019 (www.ft.com/content/9d71373a-c33a-11e9-a8e9-296ca66511c9).

[102] See Grant (2018), Smismans (2019) and Yeo et al (2019).

[103] B. Smith (2019) 'Just 13 Windrush victims given emergency support, Javid reveals', *Civil Service World*, 11 June (www.civilserviceworld.com/articles/news/just-13-windrush-victims-given-emergency-support-javid-reveals).

argument to the level of EU citizenship, drawing attention to the stripping of that status, is likely to have much less traction on the public sense of 'who we are' in the UK (Grant 2018), not least as one of the objectives of the Leave campaign at various points was to try to drive a wedge between different groups of migrants and to foster the characterization of EU immigrants as lucky immigrants and thus less deserving.

Drawing the parallel may even be thought of as tendentious. For some who have spent decades contesting the racialized character of UK immigration, it can feel like a potential 'colonization' of the space that Windrush has been afforded as a scandal that requires redress, if the question of the treatment of EU citizens is characterized in the same way.[104] In that sense, the closing of the discursive space by the populist rhetorics of Brexit and immigration may have the effect of setting two subaltern peoples against each other, as two 'superfluous populations' (Snow and Bernatzky 2019). This is one of the many reasons why the Brexit issue has such profound implications for understandings of constitutional citizenship in the UK.

Hungary

In recent years, Hungary has seen a substantial rise in authoritarianism, accompanied by an intensified populist politics. But perhaps the most remarkable feature has been the accelerated and intensified 'constitutional revolution', undertaken 'in the name of the people', which has set the scene for the closing down of political space for opposition to the current government. The opportunities for consensus building around constitutional politics have been abandoned in favour of building a singular edifice that reinforces the power of one governing elite, again in the name of the people.

Hungary's delayed 'constitutional revolution' was briefly presented in Chapter 3, where we saw the shifting and narrowing 'constitutional identity' of the state and its impact on constitutional citizenship. We also discussed the extension of external citizenship in Chapter 4, engaging with the argument that Hungary's extension of the boundaries of its citizenship

---

[104] At the same time, it is important to acknowledge research that contests the 'whiteness' of free movement: see Benson and Lewis (2019). In that sense, the gulf between the 'free movement' and 'immigration from third countries' may not be so great as it is sometimes seems to be. On the other hand, the anecdotal evidence of lack of migrant solidarity from some groups of UK citizens residing in other Member States is legion: see Parnell-Berry (2018).

regime can have a destabilizing effect on other states and represents a problematic and over-extensive approach to descent and ethnic-based citizenship, which pays little account to the actual connection between the person receiving citizenship and the target state. The adoption of a new constitution has been followed by a series of further amendments to the 2011 Fundamental Law, pushed through whenever Viktor Orbán's government has had the necessary two-thirds majority support for these changes in the Hungarian Parliament. This aggressive constitutional politics has gone hand in hand with many other manoeuvres, justified on populist grounds, to limit the space for opposition, such as packing the courts with supporters after imposing a retirement age on existing judges to clear out those with liberal tendencies, limiting media freedom by bringing much of the ostensibly free media under government control or ownership, dismantling many parts of civil society, especially by mounting a strong attack on the US/Hungarian billionaire and philanthropist George Soros (involving thinly veiled anti-Semitism), and undermining liberal educational institutions by forcing the Soros-funded Central European University out of Budapest as well as banning 'gender studies' as a subject.[105] All of these measures, and more, have been enabled by laws adopted in Parliament, but subject to ever-weaker constitutional scrutiny because of the effects of the Fundamental Law. This amounts to a prescription for an authoritarianism that claims a veneer of legality, leaving Hungarian constitutional democracy in grave danger, despite its membership of the EU.[106]

It is important to note that these changes have been driven by a party – *Fidesz* – that started in the liberal mainstream of politics. Much of this shift resulted because the leader of the party and Prime Minister since 2010, Viktor Orbán, calculated that it was on the nationalist right that there was political space where he could gain – and then cement – more political power. Indeed, *Fidesz* won its electoral victories in 2010, 2014 and 2018 as the result of 'an economic crisis in combination with a syndrome of nationalistic ideologies, antisemitism and historical revisionism' (Pichl 2019, 251). As an illiberal force, *Fidesz* emerged not as a reaction to liberalism, but 'from the structures of liberalism itself' (Pichl 2019, 251).

---

[105] This reflects a wider global attack on gender and feminism by authoritarians, discussed by Paternotte and Kuhar (2018).

[106] See Scheppele (2019). Some might suggest that this danger exists *because of* its membership of the EU, as the Hungarian and Polish cases have shown that the EU possesses very few tools to ensure that a Member State continues to comply with the high standards in relation to the rule of law and democratic constitutionalism against which it can be held, according to the Copenhagen criteria, during the pre-accession negotiation process.

Now Orbán champions the argument that Christian democracy (as *Fidesz* still belongs to that European 'party family', albeit under suspension) is necessarily 'illiberal' because it is anti-immigration (Scheppele 2019, 322). Orbán and similar central and eastern European 'democratic backsliders' in Poland and Romania have been described as opportunists using election victories in order to ensure that they maintain an 'eternal hold on power' (Scheppele 2019, 331). Overall, the EU is both an enemy (with the Hungarian government refusing to fly the EU flag) and a cash cow to be milked, with high levels of corruption uncovered in dealings with the Common Agricultural Policy.[107] The EU has also proved to be remarkably tolerant of an emergent authoritarian regime in its midst, lacking the political resources to contest most of the steps that the Orbán government has taken. Furthermore, free movement provides a safety valve, as the emigration of younger and more educated people to other EU Member States has accelerated since the election of *Fidesz*, depleting the ranks of the opposition and providing a source of remittances to offset economic decline (Kelemen 2019).

Hungary's 'new constitutionalism' has been driven by both populism and authoritarianism. For example, the Fourth Amendment to the Constitution, passed in 2013, repealed all Constitutional Court decisions prior to the coming into force of the Fundamental Law, reinforcing the sense of a brand new constitutional regime being created for a new Hungary. This move, according to Gabór Halmai, removed 'decisions that defined and protected constitutional rights and harmonized domestic rights protection to comply with European human rights law' (Halmai 2018, 89). Throughout this period, there have been weak and generally ineffectual efforts by the European Commission to 'persuade' Orbán to drop his authoritarian programme of reform. However, as *Fidesz* has continued until recently to be a full member of the supranational European People's Party, this has undermined efforts to bring effective EU-level pressure to bear (Scheppele and Pech 2018).

The shadow of populist politics has been clearly visible in the measures that have been taken in Hungary after the 2015 refugee crisis. This was a period that saw substantial numbers of asylum-seekers from countries such as Syria, Iraq and Libya arriving in the EU Member States. A stark Islamophobia marked the responses in Hungary and its neighbours in the so-called Višegrad group (Poland, Czech Republic and Slovakia),

---

[107] '"It's an absolutely corrupt system": How EU farm subsidies are abused by oligarchs and populists', *The Independent*, 4 November 2019 (www.independent.co.uk/news/world/europe/eu-farm-subsidies-central-eastern-europe-hungary-viktor-orban-populist-oligarch-a9183911.html).

in some ways replicating and in other ways going beyond the reactions visible in other Member States.[108] Those four countries have all fought back against any mandatory refugee relocation schemes that the EU has sought to develop and impose, pursuant to its pre-existing policies on burden sharing in this field. The consequences of these rejections are working their way through the EU legal order, as various enforcement actions to force compliance have been commenced by the European Commission and have now reached the CJEU.[109] Our particular interest is with the Hungarian approach, including the manner in which it has been legitimated internally by reference to a populist mandate.

Hungary has implemented a whole raft of laws effectively walling the country off legally, in order to complement the physical actions of putting razor wire at the border, detaining those asylum-seekers who reach its territory, and criminalizing the facilitation of 'illegal immigration' (including humanitarian actions to save life and protect health). The anti-immigrant measures were part of a wider package of laws dubbed 'Stop Soros', aimed at undermining the work of many NGOs in the country. In February 2019, the Hungarian Constitutional Court ruled that these provisions did not violate the Constitution, in a case brought by Amnesty International Hungary. It gave a restrictive reading to the most problematic provisions of the Law, thus making it possible to find them to be concordant with the Constitution (Kazai 2019). Doubtless this case will be used by the government to justify its resistance to the enforcement proceedings started by the European Commission, using an argument based on the supremacy of the Hungarian Constitution *vis-à-vis* EU law. At the same time, the Hungarian Court expressed approval of some of the most problematic amendments to the Hungarian Constitution, introduced in 2018, as part of the seventh round of amendments. The Preamble was amended to impose an obligation on organs of the state to uphold the 'identity' of Hungary, and Article XIV(1) of the Fundamental Law was amended to provide that:

> No foreign population shall be settled in Hungary. A foreign national, not including persons who have the right to free movement and residence, may only live in the territory of Hungary under an application individually examined by the Hungarian authorities.

---

[108] Goździak and Márton (2018) and Kalmar (2018).

[109] See the trenchant criticism of the rejection of burden-sharing in an Opinion issued by Advocate General Sharpston on 31 October 2019 in Joined Cases C-715/17, C-718/17 and C-719/17 *Commission v Poland, Hungary and Czech Republic*, ECLI:EU:C:2019:917.

The Constitutional Court expressed its approval of this populist move, noting that it provided the legal basis for the legislation that it then went on to hold did not infringe any other principles in the Constitution. It is clear that these amendments provide not only the *post hoc* populist legitimation for the previous measures taken in relation to the refugee crisis, but also offer a prospectus for future action that reinforces a vision of Hungary in opposition to outsiders.

One of the most remarkable aspects of Orbán's populist moves has been his capacity to reconstruct these actions as being 'European' rather than just 'national', a point that finds an echo in the next chapter, where we will discuss the idea of the 'European way of life'. Robert Csehi makes the point very effectively, reconstructing the argument using Orbán's own words, as uttered in his so-called 'state of the nation' speeches each year:

> The greatest shift in Orbán's (re)construction of "the people," ... came with the migration crisis. Instead of simply associating the Hungarians with "the people," Orbán elevated "the people" into the European sphere of action. Hence, he identified "the people" first as "the European people" ..., "we, Europeans" ..., and "we, the peoples of Europe". (Csehi 2019, 1017).

It is clear that an aggressive constitutional politics, as in the case of Hungary, can effectively transform the character of the constitutional system – and the space it allows for debate and contestation over issues such as international responsibilities for asylum-seekers – very quickly indeed. The refugee is characterized as an 'invasive other' (Ignatieff 2017), implicitly never capable of inclusion within 'the nation'. This has significant implications not only for those excluded, but also for the character of citizenship itself. The moves have not changed the formal boundaries of national citizenship as such, but none the less constitutional citizenship in Hungary has thereby been altered – perhaps irreversibly. But even more remarkably, the populist rhetoric in which these moves are couched poses a threat to established definitions of what it means in that context to be 'European'. We shall return to those questions in the next chapter.

India

In India, by way of contrast, the formal constitutional set-up remains untouched by populist governments thus far, but in this relatively fragile democracy, citizenship is becoming an increasingly significant battleground for those who want to redefine the essence of the polity. The human costs of these policies may be very high indeed.

Earlier chapters have referred to the mix of constitutional and statutory regulation of citizenship in India, with a trend latterly towards statutory regulation. This has seen the historic *ius soli* approach, which was included in the 1949 Constitution and the 1955 Citizenship Act, move towards a *ius sanguinis* approach. This solidified with the 1986 amendment to the 1955 Citizenship Act, which, along with later amendments, has emphasized the importance of being Indian by descent. Much of the constitutional controversy over citizenship in India has been and indeed continues to be related to the delimitation of the borders of the state. The shadow of Partition in 1947 dominated many of the provisions of the 1949 Constitution related to citizenship, because of the urgency of reacting to large numbers of people moving across borders. However, India's constitutional founders also wanted to make an offer of citizenship to the large numbers of often poor emigrants, who then got the chance to obtain Indian citizenship provided they had not voluntarily acquired the citizenship of another state (Rodrigues 2008).

These preoccupations were also reflected in much of the early case law of the Supreme Court on the Constitution.[110] The Constitution itself was determinedly secular, and the notion of using it to enshrine a religious divide was firmly rejected by those responsible for its drafting. All nations and religions were to be accepted equally in modern India, and Article 14 of the Constitution articulates the principle of equality before the law. But in such a complex federal country, citizenship itself has inevitably been a multi-layered concept, reflecting the historical and current dividing lines within the state and society and between the state and the outside, as well as the enormous challenges of holding this type of country together using a conception of 'nationhood'.[111] Fear of the outsider has always been present, and is now greater than ever. One noticeable shift has been the extent to which, over time, migration has come to be associated with 'illegality' in a manner that has sought to close off the informal, 'paper citizenship' routes highlighted by Kamal Sadiq (2009), and to create the conditions for the rejection of all 'illegal' 'foreigners', regardless of how long they have been present in India.

In recent years, India has had a Hindu nationalist party (Bharatiya Janata Party [BJP]) in (national) government. It was re-elected in 2019 for a

---

[110] For analysis, see Jayal (2016) and Ashesh and Thiruvengadam (2018).

[111] This has been extensively analysed in works such as Jayal (2013, 2016, 2019a, b) and Shani (2010).

further five-year term. Under the leadership of Prime Minister Narendra Modi, the Indian Government has been pursuing a number of policies that seem to be shifting India's nearly 200 million Muslims towards the status of second-class citizens, regardless of their formal legal status. A close adviser to Modi described Muslims as 'termites',[112] and politicians speak regularly of 'Bangladeshi infiltrators' as a catch-all phrase (Shamshad 2017). Concern focuses on the fact that members of these groups are often on the electoral register, and thus may affect electoral outcomes, reviving pride about how India managed to compile the largest ever voting register and hold its first general election in 1952 (Shani 2016), and raising fears that the authenticity of future elections may be compromised by these 'foreigners'. There has been an increase in hate crimes in recent years.[113] There is a close affinity between the negative tropes around 'illegality' and those around Muslims. Yet clearly Modi is popular, not just with the general public who vote for him, but also with many Indian elites (including the diaspora), who believe that he is effectively triangulating the many disparate identities that make up India, and thereby modernizing citizenship, strengthening democracy and creating the conditions for a more prosperous and more market-oriented India.[114]

Inevitably, therefore, citizenship has been and remains a battleground. While some of the moves adopted by governments at both the level of the states and of the Union (that is, the federal level) appear to be procedural and administrative in nature, at their heart lies the constitutional conception of citizenship in India. Is it truly secular and equal? Or has there been a slippage into a vision based on ethnicity and religion?

One such process, which appears at first sight to be administrative in character, is the rebuilding of the National Register of Citizens (NRC). This has been ongoing for some years in the state of Assam, which lies on the India/Bangladesh border.[115] The background to this process lies

---

[112] 'Bangladeshi migrants are "termites", will be removed from voters' list: Shah', *The Economic Times*, 22 September 2018 (https://economictimes.indiatimes.com/news/politics-and-nation/bangladeshi-migrants-are-termites-will-be-removed-from-voters-list-shah/articleshow/65912140.cms).

[113] 'India's Muslims fear for their future under Narendra Modi', *BBC News*, 16 May 2019 (www.bbc.co.uk/news/world-asia-india-48278441); *Violent Cow Protection in India Vigilante Groups Attack Minorities, Human Rights Watch Report, 18* February 2019 (www.hrw.org/report/2019/02/18/violent-cow-protection-india/vigilante-groups-attack-minorities).

[114] 'Election gives Modi a huge mandate in India. Now what will he do?', *New York Times*, 25 May 2019.

[115] For a clear statement of the background historical and legal issues, see Paulose (2019).

in heightened anxieties in that state about 'Bangladeshi infiltrators', mobilized as a threat to a Hindu Assamese majority within populist politics (Mookerjee 2019). It digs into a long history of migration between Bengal (part of which is now in the sovereign state of Bangladesh) and the state of Assam, dating back well over a century. These migrations have involved both Muslims and Hindus. The roots of Assamese political nationalism, which is often focused on linguistic distinctiveness, lie in colonial times. On a number of occasions, before and after Indian independence, the nationalist movement has spilled over into violence and massacres.[116] An Accord was signed in 1985, which hardened the position as regards 'foreigners' and what to do about them.[117]

For several years, the state authorities in Assam have been working on a new draft of the NRC, under the supervision of the Indian Supreme Court. Based on the obligation of each person to prove she is a citizen, this register is supposed to provide a definitive statement of who are Indian citizens and who are not, based on a cut-off date of 24 March 1971. Only those who can provide documentation relating to presence on the territory as at date can be considered citizens. Yet because so many people in the state lack documentation, and because the bureaucratic structures are weak and also subject to corruption, millions of people were left off the 2018 'final draft' who may, in fact, have a legitimate claim to Indian citizenship based on the existing law and the 1971 cut-off date (which is itself contested anyway). Critics of the process extend their concerns to the role of the Supreme Court, which has been described as a 'prelude to ethnic cleansing'.[118] The process of requiring those left off the 2018 register to prove their citizenship before special Foreigners' Tribunals continued until the end of August 2019, when a further 'final draft' was issued, although this still may not be the last. Around 1.9 million residents of Assam seem to have been left without citizenship. From the perspective of the populists at the national (that is, Union of India) level, one problem is that the NRC is not effectively distinguishing between the 'genuine Indians' (that is, Hindus) and the 'foreigners' (that is, Muslims), but catching the former as well as the latter in the net. The specific Assamese concern is around Bengali speakers, whether Hindu or Muslim, as Assamese nationalism is particularly focused on language.

---

[116] Dev (2019).

[117] Pillai (2019).

[118] S. Hegde and P. Kishore (2019) 'NRC: Why the Supreme Court ruling could be a prelude to ethnic cleansing', *Business Standard*, 6 August (www.business-standard.com/article/economy-policy/nrc-why-the-supreme-court-ruling-could-be-a-prelude-to-ethnic-cleansing-118080600363_1.html).

Meanwhile, global attention has now focused on the risk that the process may give rise to a mass denationalization and an outcome that might even parallel the treatment of the Rohingya in Myanmar.[119] Western newspapers and news outlets began to carry stories about the developing issue.[120] Human rights organizations have taken note, and 125 civil society organizations signed a statement condemning the mass disenfranchisement.[121] What lies in store for those who do not make the final cut raises profound concerns from a human rights perspective, as those who are still trying to prove their Indian citizenship are finding themselves in huge detention camps (often cut off from members of the same family who have passed the scrutiny test) and at apparent risk of deportation, generally to a place they have never been to. However, India has been at pains to assure Bangladesh that deportations are not on the cards, so there seems to be a risk of long-term incarceration in these camps. Those who cannot prove their Indian citizenship face a future of statelessness, which they will pass to their children. Quite a number of suicides have been recorded of people caught up in the process – they are unwanted people.

While the NRC update process is currently confined to Assam, where it has particularly complex resonances given the interaction between Assamese nationalism and a Hindu-dominated Indian nationalism, things may become even more problematic if the updating process is rolled out across the entire country, affecting 1.3 billion or more people, rather than just 30 million. The prospect in that case would be of tens or even hundreds of millions of people caught up in a process that has been constitutionally and politically legitimated as the logical consequence of drawing a bright line between citizens and foreigners, in a way that makes no legal distinction based on ethnicity or religion. Critics, of course, contend that the arbitrary nature of the process ought to make it constitutionally suspect, as it is misusing the law to make minorities stateless, as Muslims and other minorities will be particularly vulnerable.[122] The prospect of a cross-India roll-out was mooted by the BJP during the

---

[119] 'No papers, no rights: How Modi plans to oust millions of "foreigners" who have lived in India all their lives', *The Times*, 29 August 2019 (www.thetimes.co.uk/article/no-papers-no-rights-how-modi-plans-to-oust-millions-of-foreigners-who-have-lived-in-india-all-their-lives-qfsvk5750).

[120] Extended coverage of the issue can also be found on the independent Indian English language new website Scroll.in (https://scroll.in/topic/56205/the-final-count).

[121] '125 civil society organisations condemn mass-disenfranchisement in Assam', Institute on Statelessness and Inclusion, 31 August 2019 (www.institutesi.org/news/cso-joint-statement-on-assam-nrc).

[122] See Gogoi et al (2018).

2019 election campaign and afterwards. Such a move would undoubtedly be anti-Muslim in its motivation, given the strong anti-Muslim rhetoric of the governing party. But it also has to be seen in the light of the Citizenship Amendment Bill that the BJP government brought before the Indian Parliament in 2016 and again in 2019 after the election.

What is now the Citizenship Amendment Act, 2019 (CAA), which came into force in January 2020, facilitates the acquisition of Indian citizenship by six identified minority communities, namely Hindus, Sikhs, Jains, Buddhists, Christians and Parsees, from Afghanistan, Pakistan and Bangladesh. The CAA applies to those who came to India before 31 December 2014. At the same time, it excludes Muslims and also arrivals of any faith from two other neighbouring countries, Sri Lanka and Nepal. Ostensibly the purpose of the CAA, which removes these groups from the category of 'illegal migrant', is to recognize these groups because of their minority and potentially persecuted status in their countries of origin. Critics have understood this initiative to be one driven by a Hindu-focused populism, and have argued that it is set to introduce a distinction based on religion into the scheme of Indian citizenship for the first time. They argue that this is contrary to Article 14 of the Constitution[123] and several Indian States have refused to apply the legislation and brought constitutional challenges against it, which will be heard early in 2020 (see Mustafa and Mohammed 2020). Issues of equality, secularism and arbitrariness will be at the heart of all legal challenges (Ahmed 2020; Chandrachud 2020). The measure has been condemned as 'fundamentally discriminatory' by the UN's fundamental rights body, the OHCHR.[124] The CAA is also politically salient. Huge and often violent protests erupted across India against the Act, which has been treated as a symptom of a bigger challenge to India's secular and democratic character (Subramaniam 2019).

---

[123] For early criticism, see Poddar (2018), Bhat (2019) and Jayal (2019a, b).

[124] See UN News (2019) 'New citizenship law in India "fundamentally discriminatory": UN human rights office', 13 December (https://news.un.org/en/story/2019/12/1053511). The UN High Commissioner for Human Rights, Michelle Bachelet, has also taken the unusual step of seeking to intervene in the Indian Supreme Court proceedings through an *amicus* brief, arguing that the measures contravene the Indian Constitution as well as international human rights laws. This intervention has been condemned by the Indian government as an unwarranted interference in domestic affairs and represents an unusual interaction between international institutions and national constitutional law; see A. Withnall (2020) 'UN human rights chief launches unprecedented legal action against Indian government over citizenship protests', *The Independent*, 3 March (www.independent.co.uk/news/world/asia/delhi-riots-indian-un-human-rights-supreme-court-modi-a9372966.html).

However, it is the combination of the CAA and an NRC process rolled out across the whole of India that particularly alarms many observers. They argue that Muslims in India, who make up around 13 per cent of the population, may find themselves in a pincer movement threatening them with a substantial deprivation of status and rights. Such a move would contest the very basis of constitutional citizenship as it has existed hitherto in India. Such developments would undoubtedly lead to further legal challenges before the Supreme Court. At that point, the question would be raised whether the Supreme Court would stick with the approach that it adopted when it took on the task of monitoring the NRC, in a judgment of December 2014.[125] This approach has categorized the NRC process as being part of a larger and perfectly proper task for state authorities to undertake, which is that of sorting citizens from foreigners. Such a process seems legitimate under the Indian Constitution when it is taken at face value. Alternatively, it is possible that the Court might accept the argument that a wider roll-out of the NRC process in conjunction with the CAA, would be arbitrary, discriminatory and therefore unconstitutional.

It is therefore of interest to take as a reference point for such a potential challenge to the constitutionality of citizenship-related measures the Supreme Court's own recent judgment in a different sort of citizenship-related matter. This, however, is an issue that does not relate to external borders but to the question of 'full membership' for different groups within the borders. In a unanimous judgment in September 2018, the Supreme Court declared portions of the Indian criminal code dating back to colonial times that criminalized consensual sexual acts between adults of the same sex to be unconstitutional.[126] The *Johar* judgment is couched in the language of citizenship and dignity, taking us back to our earlier reflections on Jeremy Waldron's argument about citizenship as a dignity, and the role of human dignity as a baseline for the right to have rights. For Tarun Khaitan (2018), the judgment correctly reflects the 'inclusive, pluralist, liberal, democratic, egalitarian India' of the 1950 Constitution, with the Court openly declaring 'its unambiguous partisan support for inclusive pluralism and against majoritarian nationalism' (and doing so at a dangerous point in India's history, which Khaitan classes as being a crossroads for democracy). It will, of course, be open to the Supreme

---

[125] *All Assam Ahom Association & Ors v Union of India* Writ Petition (Civil) No 876 of 2014, judgment of 17 December 2014.

[126] *Navtej Singh Johar and Others v Union of India through Secretary Ministry of Law and Justice*, Writ Petition No 76 of 2016, judgment of 6 September 2019. For analysis, see McGoldrick (2019).

Court to draw a distinction between its pluralist and inclusive case law on LGB rights and its approach to the bordering of the state and the citizenry and to the protection of the state against the alleged threat of 'foreigners'. The omens are not good. It did not stand up to majoritarian pressure when it refused to stay the government's action of deporting Rohingya refugees, despite clear indications that this would be contrary to the international law principle of *non-refoulement*.[127] In the future, the Supreme Court may be faced with cases of people with long residence whose only 'fault' is not to be able to prove their citizenship according to modern standards of documentation, or cases of child statelessness caused by the NRC process. It will be interesting, at that point, to see which way the Court faces in relation to its interpretation of constitutional citizenship.

Conclusions

This chapter has explored the relationship between 'constitutional citizenship' and the rise of populism within political discourse and political practices in terms of understandings of 'the people' in relation to democracy and constitutionalism operating in a variety of national settings. We are at one of the 'populist moments' about which Rogers Brubaker (2017a) has warned us to be 'vigilant', which may represent the 'dark side' of stories of peoplehood.

We need to reflect on whether what we have observed is leading to the erosion of modern citizenship as an ideal of equality and self-rule. In the case studies discussed here, we have seen examples of 'superfluous peoples'[128] whose dignity and equal access to citizenship and citizenship rights have been brought into question as a result of the invocation of populism. The significance of protecting 'constitutional citizenship' via judicially enforced constitutional rights was referred to on several occasions across the chapter, raising once more that large question which has hung over this book about the relationship between majoritarian and non-majoritarian institutions as regards the constitutive qualities of citizenship. Furthermore, our conceptual reflections led us to question whether populism was inherently anti-pluralist, and thus presumptively hostile to the claims of minorities, outsiders and subaltern groups.

The rise of populism across the globe is one of a number of trends bringing constitutional democracy and especially liberal democracy, and thus the ideal of citizens as self-ruling equals, into question. The

---

[127] Samtani (2018).
[128] See Snow and Bernatzky (2019).

cases we have looked at show the variety of different challenges to the separation of powers and the rule of law, with the precise interplay between the executive, legislature and judiciary varying according to the specificities of national conditions. There have been few, if any, flashes of the promised re-invigoration of democracy through the people, which some say populism can bring amongst us. What we have observed throughout has been the generally inward-looking nature of the populist argument, focusing on the *national* dimensions of the *national* people. It is noteworthy that this point is further vindicated by preliminary research that has highlighted backlashes against international courts in the age of populism[129] and documented a decline in the numbers of citations made to international law where populism prevails.[130] These points go to the heart of the discussion in the next chapter, which acknowledges the paradox that alongside populism many dimensions of globalization still continue to flourish.

---

[129] See Voeten (2019).
[130] See Brandes (2019).

7

Shifting Spatialities
of Citizenship

Introduction

In Part I of the book, I emphasized that international law starts from the premise that the regulation of 'nationality' (in the technical sense of the link between a person and a state) is a matter of state sovereignty. It seems, then, counterintuitive that we should now embark on exploring the issue of citizenship 'beyond the state'. How can this be? In fact, while examining the regulation of citizenship under *national* constitutional law, in every chapter we have already seen multiple examples highlighting that national citizenship regimes do not exist in isolation. Any attempt to present citizenship regimes as islands in a sea of international law, which limits itself to dealing only with frictions between the regulatory systems of separate islands, presents an incomplete picture of membership in the 21st century. At many points, the outside has 'leaked in', with references throughout the book to various international and supranational legal regimes that directly impact on national citizenship or set up complementary and sometimes competing membership frameworks. In fact, through the historical examples we have pursued, especially the ones based on colonialism, we have seen that there has never been a time, since the rise of the 'modern citizen' after the first 18th-century revolutions, when the regulation of citizenship has not had to contend with the leaky and blurred boundaries of states.

Nowadays, we undoubtedly need to focus on the importance of a 'global governance' approach to regulating citizenship. The incidents of globalization are already intense, and growing more so, even if we only limit ourselves to territorial transgressions of borders. The allocated and often imposed boundaries of states have only ever imperfectly reflected other human communities and affinities such as 'nations' in the cultural or ethnic sense, or religious or linguistically based communities (Glenn 2013). The Westphalian ideal of each and every person being assigned to just one state in respect of every aspect of their lives was never realistic, and certainly in no way represents the reality of life at the present time. People move, and form families across borders. Try as they might, states have been unable to pigeonhole the citizenship affiliations of those who move or who, like children, are affected by movement driven by others into closed boxes. The human agency of these groups forces states to develop norms that ensure, through unilateral, bilateral or multilateral action, that their citizenship regimes interact reasonably smoothly as regards the effects they have on individuals. In fact, states' interests have changed over time, as a result of their participation in differing ways in the global migration system, as states of immigration, emigration or both (Bauböck 2018b, 499).

Aside from participating in the global system of states via engagement with international law and diplomacy, states also form voluntary alliances with each other establishing new legal orders that can have implications for citizenship, as in the case of the EU or global or regional human rights treaties. In addition, states change internally, federalizing or creating new frameworks for the devolution of powers, which reshape the territorial politics of state citizenship. Boundaries move, and new states are born or old states die. States may retain a dominant role in relation to the governance of the membership relation (and in that sense we do not live in a 'postnational' world), but they are not privileged and insulated from the impact of a range of pressures that stretch both the established norms around the territorial state and settled concepts of membership. In sum, it is now widely accepted that since the Second World War there has been a reconfiguration or transformation of the character of citizenship (Shaw 2007; Soysal 2012a).

Authors differ, of course, in relation to their understanding of the intensity and significance of these changes, and in their interpretation of the new norms of conduct that are emerging at the subnational, national, regional and international levels. It is, perhaps, no coincidence that the revival of interest in citizenship as a status and in developing theories of citizenship coincided in time with the creation of EU citizenship, which has been called, perhaps generously, 'the world's first example of fully institutionalised trans, or post-national political rights going beyond the nation state' (Favell 2010, 187). Yet, as the case of the UK's decision to leave the EU (and thus to unravel the implications of EU citizenship) will show in some of the examples below, centrifugal as well as centripetal forces can come into play in the fragmented governance of citizenship. Unscrambling the eggs of a regional union may be a legitimate exercise of national sovereignty, but, from a citizenship perspective, it is a complex task that is impossible to achieve without substantial negative impacts on groups and individuals, including those who have not actually moved across borders. This chapter will endeavour to offer an interpretative mapping of this terrain and some critical thoughts on the multilevel governance of citizenship.

It is tricky to find an effective analytical frame that would cover all of the issues which fall within the scope of the broad heuristic of the 'shifting spatialities of citizenship'. Some authors have tried to appeal to the concept of 'transnational citizenship', and in so doing they evoke the 'cross-border' dimension of practices of globalization from below, often involving the claiming rights across borders and/or the construction of political communities. However, without running the risk of excessive concept stretching, it is hard to find a sufficiently precise definition of what transnational citizenship actually is for it to be a useful analytical frame (Fox 2005).

Another possible candidate is the idea of 'citizenship constellations'. Where citizenship regimes intersect, various forms of dual and multiple membership come into play, horizontally across and between states, as well as vertically between states and their subnational units and supranational entities such as the EU. Rainer Bauböck defines 'citizenship constellations' as 'structure(s) in which individuals are simultaneously linked to several political entities, so that their legal rights and duties are determined not only by one political authority, but by several' (2010b, 848).

How useful is this concept as an analytical frame? It is certainly very helpful for understanding situations where those who migrate are connected to the citizenship regimes of both the home and destination states. It can also be deployed when we shift from thinking about the attachments of individuals, and focus instead on how states or polities respond to the challenges that stem from the plurality of legal orders. For example, how do states deal with the citizenship of others? Within the EU, discrimination on grounds of the nationality of the Member States is prohibited. Beyond that case, states can clearly make sovereign choices to favour citizens of some states over others, for example by demanding visas for entry from some and not others or even banning the entry of citizens from some states, although in so doing they may contravene their own norms of constitutional law (Ahmad 2014). Citizenship constellations also work well as an analytic frame in the case of federal citizenship, where there is a split between the federal and state levels. This is, of course, somewhat analogous to the situation of the EU as a regional union with a concept of 'citizenship of the Union' for the nationals of the Member States, which also belongs nicely within the construct of citizenship constellations. In such cases, there may well be triangular relations involving individuals, home and host states, as well as EU law. Finally, it provides a good reference point for understanding the citizenship consequences of the break-up of states and the creation of new states (Bauböck 2019b). These are all cases where dual and multiple attachments between individuals and polities may exist or be generated.

But the idea of citizenship constellations is not quite as good at capturing some other elements of the *beyond the state* dynamic, namely those that do not involve a duality of memberships, but simply the interpenetration of multiple legal orders. This would be a situation, for example, where national law is amended in order to comply with a voluntarily adopted norm of international law, but without any form of 'membership' relation emerging at the international level. We can see this scenario in cases where international organizations and international civil society mount campaigns, using global legal norms, to combat statelessness. It may express the aspiration to deliver a legally cognisable outcome stemming from the recognition of our common humanity, by ensuring that each and every one of us has effective access to Arendt's 'right to have rights', but it is hard to argue that this makes us somehow 'members' within a legally framed global compact. The idea of citizenship constellations is thus not a useful device when we consider the question of whether there ought to be an international law of citizenship that could provide a more detailed normative framework than the one we have at present. Finally, it should be noted that the concept of citizenship constellations has not yet been widely used for the empirical study of interactions between citizenship regimes in regions of the world beyond Europe.

For all these reasons, I will not try to identify any single all-encompassing analytical frame for understanding 'shifting spatialities', although I will use the terms 'transnational citizenship' and 'citizenship constellations' where appropriate in what follows. The aim of this discussion is to figure out what meaning there is to the concept of constitutional citizenship in the scenario of citizenship and constitutionalism *beyond the state*, and this focus influences the choice of which questions to address.[1] In each

---

[1] There are other meanings to 'beyond the state' that more directly place the notion of 'authority' in question than can be achieved in this book. This would demand more of a focus on actors affecting citizenship frameworks such as cities, third sector organizations, international NGOs, and other 'private' actors. For a discussion of some of the issues the 'citizenship agendas' of these actors could raise, see de Koning et al (2015).

section, I will provide a brief sketch of different types of *beyond the state* scenarios where citizenship is put in question, with the discussion mainly inspired by the types of questions about the character of constitutional citizenship that formed the reference points for Part II of the book (ideals and identities of citizenship, conditions for the acquisition and loss of citizenship as a status, and nature and scope of citizenship rights). The first three substantive sections focus on 'splintering states', interconnected national citizenship regimes and citizenship in the context of regional unions (mainly with a focus on EU law). The discussion is topped off with a broader enquiry into the role of international law in relation to citizenship. Each of the sections could be thought of as a mirror image of discussions that have already been developed in the preceding chapters, but reflecting explicitly the point made throughout the book that there simply is no language in which we can discuss citizenship as a hermetically sealed national construct. National citizenship regimes, far from being insulated or isolated from each other, are nested within complex matrices of overlapping and interlocking norms.

Splintering states: substate and secessionist pressures on national citizenship

Under the umbrella concept of 'splintering states' can be gathered a number of challenges to the unity and integrity of the 'national' state and its citizenship regime, some of which involve consensual change and some of which do not. All pose a challenge to the ideas and practices of *national* constitutional citizenship at the state level. The focus here is on territorial pressures on the state, but the concept could also be widened to encompass claims by non-territorial entities or groups, such as the Roma, who themselves may also be affected by territorial rescaling.[2]

Across a longer sweep of history, beyond the purview of democratic practices as we recognize these today, the changing of state boundaries, with consequential citizenship impacts, has been quite a common phenomenon. Examples include the absorption of territories into empires or expansionist states, often by conquest or dynastic alliance, sometimes by purchase and occasionally by consent, and their subsequent departure. The nature of departure has also varied: often under conditions of decolonialization (for example, much of the British and French empires), sometimes after uprisings (for example, Spanish and Portuguese Latin America), continental scale wars (for example, the break-up of Austria-

---

[2] See Sardelić (2017, 2019b).

Hungary and the Ottoman Empire) or wars of independence (for example, Algeria, North American colonies), and sometimes after UN-mandated acts of self-determination intended to resolve long-standing conflicts (for example, Timor-Leste, South Sudan). Many of these examples, involving the reconstruction of polity and citizenry along new territorial boundaries, reflect internationally recognized self-determination rights, even though international law contains no explicit right to unilateral secession. We can also cite the break-up of federal states (notably in Europe after the end of the Cold War: USSR, Czechoslovakia, Yugoslavia). In almost all cases, new citizenship regimes have been profoundly impacted by those of the 'old states', by those of neighbouring states and by international norms that are intended to guide state practice.[3] Some boundary changes are more uncertain, such as those that have resulted in the creation of semi-recognized entities, or so-called 'liminal states' (Krasniqi 2019) (for example, Kosovo, Taiwan), whose citizens cannot, by definition, be fully recognized citizens within the international states system, even if internally the citizenship regime performs most, if not all, of the normal functions.

The concept of the splintering state can also encompass vertically nested citizenship regimes, with constellations of citizenship regimes that remain rather stable, although there may be ongoing contestation of the permissible scope of local or regional autonomy. Within states, regions – whether or not pressing for secession – often seek greater powers and autonomy in relation to aspects of citizenship. This is confined, most often, to the spheres of social citizenship and fiscal powers,[4] but some (con)federal regions have considerable powers in relation to immigration (for example, Québec) or, as in Switzerland, jealously (but not always successfully) guard their competences relating to citizenship acquisition through naturalization against encroachment by the federal legislator. For some regions, such as Québec, Scotland and Catalonia, the search for greater autonomy has led to demands for secession, and the holding of referendums, in the first two cases in concert with the legal requirements of the 'parent' state, and in the latter case, in circumstances of contested legality. None have so far led to secession. In fact, as Rainer Bauböck notes, secessions under conditions of democracy are actually rather rare events (2019b).

The direct and obvious challenge of a splintering state to the integrity of constitutional citizenship is through the rupture of constituent power, sovereignty and constitutional identity, as discussed in Chapter 3. The

---

[3] For discussion of examples, see Štiks and Shaw (2012) on the former Yugoslavia and Manby (2018) on Africa.

[4] For an analysis of the complex impacts, see Piccoli (2019).

process of reconstruction raises issues of law, politics and political theory.[5] In some cases, the contestations over independence have been effectively 'constitutionally contained', as in Québec and Scotland. In Scotland, the independence referendum took place because the Westminster Parliament approved an Order under s. 30 of the Scotland Act 1998, which gave a legal basis to holding such a referendum, as it would normally have been a matter 'reserved' for the Westminster Parliament. In 1998, at the request of the Canadian government, the Canadian Supreme Court was asked to consider whether and under what terms Québec might have a right to unilateral secession under the Canadian Constitution or under international law.[6] The Court concluded unanimously that it did not have such a right, and only a constitutional amendment would make secession legal. However, it added that if Québec held a referendum, and then, given a clear question and a clear majority in favour, requested secession, the rest of Canada would be under a duty to negotiate in good faith over the terms of a putative departure. Some have argued that the Québec secession reference approach, and the manner in which it was subsequently reflected in Canadian legislation concerning Québec's autonomy, influenced the decision-making of the UK government in this matter (Tierney 2013).

Among the matters to be negotiated in any secession would be issues of citizenship. Would it be an option, as was proposed by the Scottish government in 2014 but not accepted as a principle by the UK government, that those resident in the seceding region could choose to take the citizenship of the new state and/or retain the old state citizenship, as they wished? The Scottish proposal was anchored in the long-standing acceptance of dual citizenship in the UK and in the idea of 'soft secession' pursued by the Scottish government. Moreover, it recognized, in the form of a legal proposal, the success of an ongoing self-determination campaign, largely driven by democratically elected political elites, which had re-worked ideas of national identity in Scotland. Over time, more and more people in Scotland have come to define themselves as solely Scottish, and no longer Scottish and British, or British and Scottish. But the proposed duality of citizenship would have recognized the complexity of those affiliations.[7] An ambiguous duality of citizenship may also be used

---

[5] See Shaw (2017a) on law, Arrighi (2019) on politics and Bauböck (2019) on political theory.

[6] Secession of Québec, Re, Reference to Supreme Court [1998] 2 SCR 217, [1998] 161 DLR (4th) 385.

[7] Scottish Government (2013) *Scotland's Future*, White Paper, November (www2.gov. scot/resource/0043/00439021.pdf).

by two states in respect of territories in which they both have strong and distinctive interests. The case of Northern Ireland, where people born in the territory can identify as British, or Irish, or both, under the so-called Good Friday Agreement, provides a good illustration of this rather unusual scenario.[8] Jean-Thomas Arrighi's case studies of Scotland and Catalonia highlight that in such cases the inclusive definitions put forward by the subnational governments as the baseline for the citizenry of the putative new state may help to reinforce a sense that these governments are pursuing an 'independence-lite' strategy, which emphasizes continuity with the previous state rather than a radical break with the past (Arrighi 2019). He argues that this applies both to the definition of the franchise for the purposes of the independence referendum, and also to the initial definition of the new citizenry.[9]

No citizenship regime is an island!

States are connected to each other as regards their citizenship regimes, as a result not only of human mobility but also of the mobility of borders. Indeed, the logical consequence of the splintering state, such as it was presented in the previous section, is often to produce two closely horizontally interconnected (state) citizenship regimes.

If we mark one of the starting points of *modern* citizenship as being the late 18th-century revolution in the North American colonies, then one of the first recognizable examples of a citizenship constellation must involve the conflicts that arose as a result of the movements of people from sending states and to the newly independent state (that is, the US). The sending states (which included, in the case of Great Britain, the spurned imperial power) asserted the doctrine of perpetual allegiance in order to argue that those leaving the metropole could not switch allegiance to the newly sovereign host state and thus escape obligations such as military service.[10] The doctrine of perpetual allegiance also sat neatly with historic opposition to the idea of dual citizenship, as discussed in Chapter 4. These exclusionary approaches reflect the techniques that the Atlantic empires endeavoured to use in relation to citizenship within their empires. While applying increasingly liberal regimes of rights within the metropole, reflecting the emergence of the idea of the sovereign

---

[8] For further discussion, see Chapter 3.
[9] See also Stjepanović and Tierney (2019) on fixing the franchise for substate referendums, as discussed in Chapter 3, and Shaw (2017a), in relation to Scotland.
[10] See Chapter 4.

citizen, they continued to impose exclusionary laws within the colonies (Fradera 2018).

Nowadays, we can collect a wide variety of practices under the umbrella of the 'citizenship constellations' that link (and sometimes divide) states, especially where there have been, over a longer period of time, larger migration flows. Bauböck (2010b) develops the case of interactions between Germany and Turkey as an example of such a constellation, in order to highlight these practices. The important interactions here engage not only the interconnected immigration, integration and citizenship policies of host states, but also the diaspora and emigration policies of home states, as well as the transnational political and citizenship practices of the migrants themselves. Voting rights for non-resident citizens and non-citizen residents, as discussed in Chapter 5, represent a particularly important area of contestation. These types of developments can be seen within the Global North, between the Global North and the Global South, and also on a South–South basis.

The intensifying of these connections is generally sustained by increased tolerance of dual citizenship, alongside acceptance of descent-based external citizenship. Data collected by Maastricht University for the case of naturalizations indicate that around 75 per cent of countries in the world allow dual citizenship for some groups, and only 25 per cent have provisions restricting both immigrants and emigrants retaining or gaining a second nationality.[11] This trend towards dual citizenship in turn creates additional pressures on those states that are still 'hold-outs' on this point, although there remain parts of the world, especially on the African and Asian continents, where dual citizenship is more an exception than the general norm. Even where dual citizenship is not currently an option (for example, India), a form of soft external citizenship has been created to foster relations with the diaspora, which gives the right to live and work in India (the Overseas Citizenship of India).

It is important to remember that these 'constellations' do not all point in the direction of greater inclusivity. For example, as discussed in Chapter 5, in many countries there has been an intensification of restrictive deportation and securitization policies aimed at immigrants, representing a noticeable 'thickening' of citizenship and a renewed vision of what counts as the 'best' kind of citizen or immigrant (Ahmad 2014). International migration has always been closely linked with issues of security for sending and receiving states (Adamson 2006). The resilience of state interests in the closure of national citizenship has been remarkable. As we have seen in this book, states and state citizenship have reinvented

---

[11] See Vink et al (2015, 2019).

themselves in countless ways such as to ensure continued relevance in the globalizing world.

Another substantial area of interest for research on transnational citizenship practices concerns the relationships between states linked by the redrawing of boundaries, giving rise to minorities in the 'host' state linked to majorities in the so-called 'kin state'. This can be the logical consequence of the dynamic of 'splintering' discussed in the previous section. In the context of the various nationalisms at play here, Rogers Brubaker has identified a crucial triadic nexus 'linking national minorities, the newly nationalizing states in which they live, and the external national "homelands" to which they belong, or can be construed as belonging, by ethnocultural affinity though not by legal citizenship' (1996, 4). In fact, as we have seen in Chapter 4, kin state external citizenship has been on the rise, especially in central and eastern Europe and the area of the former Soviet Union (Waterbury 2014), so the final comment is often not applicable. As with the immigration/emigration-related constellations, the increased tolerance of dual citizenship is crucial. However, kin state activism by the 'home' state is rarely without repercussions, and may have significant security implications if it gives rise to friction between different groups of states (Liebich 2017). Costica Dumbrava (2019) has also drawn attention to the 'ethno-demographic' effects of such policies.

Scholars unsurprisingly link the minority/kin state-related citizenship constellations in which states are gathered to processes of nation-building. This remains especially important in regions such as the former Yugoslavia, where states remain unconsolidated and the boundaries of countries are still contested (Džankič 2017). These intersections between citizenship regimes cannot, moreover, be seen in isolation from the ongoing processes of Europeanization (Waterbury 2017). These have been particularly significant even before or in the absence of accession of the relevant states to the EU.[12] Paradoxically, Europeanization effects on citizenship seem to be weaker after accession (Shaw and Štiks 2012). In fact, as Myra Waterbury (2018) has shown, Europe represents an interesting test case where two or perhaps three dimensions of 'citizenship constellations' intersect. This is because of the prevalence of east–west emigration among central and eastern European states during recent decades alongside widespread kin state policies, all within the framework of European integration and the additional tensions that this imports into the citizenship universe, in particular through the provision of free movement rights after EU accession.

---

[12] This is the case for most of the new states of south east Europe: see Džankić and Keil (2019).

In so far as the focus in this section has been on the normal incidents of the citizenship policies of states, the implications of the sorts of interactions across borders that we have observed for the case of constitutional citizenship have already appeared in previous chapters, where we have drawn attention, for example, to the constitutional dimensions of external citizenship policies and how these may also reshape issues of constitutional identity by changing the meaning of who are 'we, the people'. One point deserves particular reinforcement and that is the question of what impact the 'stretching' of national citizenship across borders has on the equality principle. To what extent can those whose lives are connected to two or more citizenship regimes claim equality with those who remain 'static', both in the home state and in the host state? Or, to look at the issue the other way around, are those with a duality or plurality of memberships or attachments inherently privileged over those whose lives remain bounded by a single state polity? We will return to this point in the following section, once we have added to the mix the additional dimension that may operate as a supplement to horizontal constellations of citizenship regimes, namely the case of 'supranational citizenship.'

Citizenship in voluntary alliances of states and regional unions: the emerging constitutional dimension

At least three related questions emerge as we shift attention away from 'horizontal' interactions between national citizenship policies towards the vertical 'nesting' of citizenship regimes in voluntary and regional alliances of states in unions. The first question relates to the extent to which those developments can be seen as 'constitutional', thus allowing us to 'read up' some of the issues that constitutional citizenship raises to the supranational level. The second question is closely related: what follows from that 'reading up' to a constitutional principle of citizenship *beyond the state*, in terms of rights to non-discrimination and recognition across not only the supranational legal order but also the component national legal orders? Following on from this, the third question concerns the impact on national constitutional citizenship of what may in some circumstances be regarded as a superior source of law (as with EU law). How are national citizenship regimes remade in the light of supranational law?

EU citizenship offers, of course, by far the most well-known and well-developed case of such a 'supranational' citizenship, but some elements of the pioneer approach of EU law have also been picked up in other regional integration organizations such as the Association of Southeast

Asian Nations (ASEAN), the Economic Community of West African States (ECOWAS) and the Southern Common Market (Mercosur), even though these cases are much more intergovernmental than supranational in terms of their legal orders.[13] Had it not been killed stone dead by British immigration control, this might also have been the place to discuss some form of 'citizenship' shared across the Commonwealth of Nations.[14] While recognizing that there are a number of examples of people-oriented measures within regional integration organizations, and that it is wrong simply to conflate EU citizenship with supranational citizenship,[15] in what follows I will focus on EU citizenship alone, as it is the example that is most closely associated with the types of constitutional shifts that allow us to reflect on the questions posed above.

I have argued elsewhere that:

> EU citizenship is paradoxical in nature: formally constitutionalised in the Union's treaty framework, yet dependent upon national citizenship to provide the gateway to membership. Its fate remains intimately tied to the broader question of the trajectory of European integration, as well as to changing perspectives about the character of citizenship as a membership status. (Shaw 2019a, 1)

EU citizenship builds on the free movement of persons, which dates back to the original Treaty of Rome, which entered into force in 1958. In its earliest form, free movement largely focused on economic actors such as workers, the self-employed and service providers, although from the very beginning it extended to cover their family members, so the worker was never seen solely as a factor of production. But in that early sense, it was certainly not conceived as a link between a community of citizens and a political authority. The inklings of such an idea came about gradually over time, notably in combination with direct elections to the European Parliament from 1979 onwards. EU citizenship as a status was eventually inaugurated in the Treaty of Maastricht, or Treaty on European Union (TEU), as of 1993 and it is now firmly installed in both the TEU and the Treaty on the Functioning of the European Union (TFEU). It still comprises the right of residence, free movement, non-discrimination on grounds of nationality and a limited set of political rights to be exercised on the basis of residence, not nationality (Shaw 2019a).

---

[13] For detailed analysis, see Neuvonen (2019).

[14] Fransman (2009) and Bloom (2011).

[15] Strumia (2017).

EU citizens are those who are the nationals of the Member States, so the status is derivative from national citizenship. The EU does not, and cannot regulate national citizenship, although we discussed some areas where this conclusion must be tempered in Chapter 4, since Member States are obliged to interpret and apply their national laws so as not to contradict or frustrate the principles of EU law. These are indeed important constraints on national sovereignty that flow from the constitutionalization of EU law, although the case law thus far has focused on issues of loss of citizenship, and the consequential loss of the benefits of EU citizenship.[16] The other question that needs to be considered is whether the same principles apply to the acquisition of national citizenship and thus all of the benefits of EU citizenship.

One area that has given rise to particular concern in the European institutions, especially in the European Parliament and the European Commission, has been so-called 'investor citizenship' (Džankić 2019a). In early 2019, the European Commission issued a communication on this topic.[17] Based on detailed research[18] on the substantial numbers of schemes across the Member States according to which citizenship may be granted on a discretionary basis in return for an investment of some sort, and often with minimal, if any, residence requirements, the Commission's report is largely confined to the task of re-iterating the existing principles regarding the extent to which Member States must have due regard to the requirements of EU law when regulating matters of citizenship. It draws these from the CJEU's case law on the relationship between EU citizenship and national law. It makes the point that other Member States are impacted by the actions of one of them in relation to acquisition of citizenship, because the new national/EU citizen gains rights under EU law *vis-à-vis* all the other Member States. The report also contains analysis of other areas of EU law that could be undermined by investor citizenship schemes, such as measures relating to financial transparency and money laundering.

Where it has attracted some controversy is in relation to its analysis of the centrality of the 'genuine link' to citizenship (Kochenov 2019b). It

---

[16] Case C-135/08 *Rottmann v Freistaat Bayern*, ECLI:EU:C:2010:104; Case 221/17 *Tjebbes and Others v Minister van Buitenlandse Zaken*, ECLI:EU:C:2019:189. For an extended analysis of the relationship between nationality, EU citizenship and migration in the EU, see Oosterom-Staples (2018).

[17] Commission Report, *Investor Citizenship and Residence Schemes in the European Union*, COM/2019/12 final, 23 January 2019. See Džankić (2019c).

[18] Commission Staff Working Document accompanying the Report on Investor Citizenship and Residence Schemes in the European Union, SWD(2019) 5 final, 23 January 2019.

does this not only by reference to international law and the *Nottebohm* case,[19] but also by inferring from the types of measures that Member States have in place for cases such as ordinary naturalization, including residence and integration requirements, that this is a principle to which they also cleave. This represents quite a bold step by the Commission, and one for which it has been criticized (Spiro 2019). *A fortiori*, the Commission seems to doubt that a monetary payment alone could be a 'genuine link'. There is also more than a grain of truth to the criticism that the Commission may be somewhat hypocritical in focusing attention on investor citizenship and how it attracts the bees around the honey pot of EU citizenship, since quite a few Member States (among them Hungary, Italy and Romania) have generous descent- or kin-based external citizenship rules that impact in exactly the same way on all the other Member States by creating new EU citizens. Yet these arrangements have not faced the same level of scrutiny, even though they have been very widely used to obtain EU citizenship,[20] arguably as part of a process of 'trading up' in a global hierarchy of citizenship (Harpaz 2019b). In fact, the numbers involved are much larger than those involved in investor citizenship, yet these schemes have not received similar levels of attention from supranational policy-makers, in terms of arguments about the need for security and due diligence. This is despite the fact that the point about (unjustified mass) naturalizations in one state impacting all of the other states has been widely made in the literature[21] and by Advocate General Maduro in the *Rottmann* case.[22]

These cases highlight that there are some curious multilevel constitutional conversations taking place here. For example, it is arguable that the Commission, as the guardian of the EU treaties, is making an argument that would elevate the idea of the 'genuine link' towards a quasi-constitutional status in the context of the EU's legal order (van den Brink 2020), yet this would be in total contrast to our earlier survey of constitutional citizenship at the level of states. Whatever its status in international law or even its desirability as a normative principle, states have by no means internalized the genuine link principle. Moreover, it seems doubtful that states generally see investor citizens as members of the 'constitutional citizenry', as they are not resident, cannot generally vote and do not pay tax on their worldwide income, under the vast majority

---

[19] Judgment of the International Court of Justice of 6 April 1955, *Nottebohm*, ICJ Reports 1955, p 4.

[20] See Harpaz (2015) and Tintori (2016).

[21] The original source is de Groot (1998, 123, 128).

[22] See *Rottmann* above, note 16, AG Opinion, ECLI:EU:C:2009:588, para 30.

of the applicable schemes.[23] In invoking the significance of the 'genuine link' principle, what is the Commission seeking to do? Is the European Commission now inviting Member States not to recognize the investor citizens of other states on the grounds that they lack a 'genuine link'? If so, this would run contrary to the fundamental principles of the free movement of persons.

So what precisely is this EU citizenship that investors (and others) are so keen to acquire? EU citizens have the right to reside and to work, study or conduct their lives however they wish in another Member State, subject only to certain conditions around self-sufficiency (at least initially) and the propriety of their conduct. These are regulated in a 2004 Directive, which created a right of permanent residence for long-term residents (5+ years).[24] This is very clearly a 'citizenship-lite' status based on rights, with enhanced protection against deportation and a package of electoral rights enshrined in the treaties (Shaw 2007). These rights also benefit EU citizens' family members who are third country nationals. Several elements of a fully functioning concept of citizenship are missing including the issues of identity and community affiliation discussed in Chapter 3, and any obvious reference to duties, which many would argue are the necessary corollary of any concept of citizenship (Bellamy 2015).[25]

Despite those limitations, the CJEU has not hesitated to offer a constitutional gloss on EU citizenship, coming out with the oft-repeated statement that it is 'destined to be the fundamental status of the nationals of the Member States'.[26] The resonance of this constitutional call to arms has led some observers to conclude that EU citizenship is already fully constitutionalized. At the same time, both the EU as a whole (Grimm 2015) and EU citizenship in particular (Schmidt 2017) have been said to be 'over-constitutionalized', which is a shorthand for criticizing an excessive reliance on judicial interventions to shore up and develop the provisions in the treaties or the limited actions of the legislature. It is unsurprising, therefore, that some scholars would take a critical perspective and argue that EU citizenship should be seen as a form of 'personal status' under EU law, which builds not so much on the EU's arrested constitutional

---

[23] For detailed analysis, see Džankić (2019a). The starkest example of 'investor citizens' not being 'constitutional citizens' is provided by the mass purchase of passports of the Union of Comoros, a small volcanic island group in the Indian Ocean, for otherwise stateless Bidoons, by the governments of the United Arab Emirates and Kuwait. Although carrying Comorian passports, the Bidoons are not permitted to enter the territory of which they ostensibly citizens. See Džankić (2019b).

[24] Directive 2004/38/EC (ECLI http://data.europa.eu/eli/dir/2004/38/oj).

[25] See Bauböck (2019c, Part III).

[26] Case C-184/99 *Grzelczyk*, ECLI:EU:C:2001:458, para 31. See Shaw (2019a).

evolution as on its successes as a legal framework within which individuals are able to exercise personal freedoms based on a framework of mutual recognition and non–discrimination.[27] One proposition underpinning this view is that investing too much constitutional weight in EU citizenship itself can undermine the constitutional objectives of the Member States in relation to the social and democratic aspects of citizenship, and that view has been articulated as justifying the UK's vote to leave the EU (Shaw 2019b).

A different view of EU citizenship, driven by a conception of fundamental rights protection as central to the EU legal order, comes from scholars who defend the view that EU citizenship could be given an autonomous status that is independent of the nationality of the Member States, such that it could be preserved as an 'associate status' to which UK citizens reluctant to lose the protection of EU law after the UK's withdrawal from the EU could opt in, even on payment of a fee.[28] In similar terms, Dora Kostakopoulou (2018) argues for EU citizenship to be seen as a special status protecting the nationals of the Member States, which should be protected after Brexit.[29] But any analogy to the loss of citizenship case law (*Rottmann, Tjebbes*) is harder to sustain when a country ceases to be a Member State under EU law and under international law, given the prominence of national sovereignty. The better view, developed by Martijn van den Brink and Dimitry Kochenov, is that it would be more consistent with EU law itself, and its constitutional respect for the autonomy and democracy of the Member States' systems (as well as the right to withdraw from the EU enshrined in Article 50 TEU), for such an idea to be rejected (van den Brink and Kochenov 2019; van den Brink 2020). The Court of Justice in the *Wightman* case confirmed this scenario implicitly by noting that:

> ... since citizenship of the Union is intended to be the fundamental status of nationals of the Member States any withdrawal of a Member State from the European Union is liable to have a considerable impact on the rights of all Union citizens, including, inter alia, their right to free movement,

---

[27] For an example of such an argument, see Menéndez and Olsen (2019); *contra*, see Favell (2019).

[28] See, for example, Roeben et al (2018).

[29] See also Garner (2018).

as regards both nationals of the Member State concerned and nationals of other Member States.[30]

The weakness of the argument for the stickiness of EU citizenship in legal terms should not, however, detract from the extraordinarily effective mobilization that has been undertaken by and on behalf of those EU citizens most directly affected by the Brexit decision, in order to draw attention to the impact of that decision on their lives and the fact that they were not (for the most part) able to take part in the deliberations and voting that gave rise to it.[31] Nor does it detract from the obligations under *international and European human rights law* that Member States, and the UK once it has withdrawn, may have to protect resident non-national citizens who lose the protective cloak of EU citizenship at the moment of withdrawal.[32]

In sum, the constitutional effects of EU citizenship are somewhat limited at the present time, when one looks for answers to the three questions posed at the beginning of this section. At this stage, arguments about the emergence of a determinable concept of constituent power[33] (and associated issues around sovereignty) in the EU context are aspirational rather than realistic. Democratic representation at the supranational level is limited and, in some respects, rather ineffective, and requires the complementarity of the democratic systems of the Member States in order to deliver legitimate policy and legislative outcomes. The EU remains a regional union among states, underpinned by a hesitant and arrested process of polity-building, which lacks the effective politicization of the key issues over which citizens divide, which characterizes the Member States as democracies.[34] Its law has limited impact on the legal orders of the Member States, within the spheres of competence of the EU, albeit in those areas it takes precedence over national law, based on a substantial constitutionalization of the treaties driven by the CJEU. EU citizenship is not comparable to national citizenship, but it is a meaningful bundle

---

[30] Case C-621/18 *Wightman and Others v Secretary of State for Exiting the European Union*, ECLI:EU:C:2018:999, at para 64. The CJEU made this statement in order to buttress the argument that the decision to leave the EU must be a voluntary sovereign act, so that it followed that a Member State is in a position to withdraw its Article 50 TEU notification unilaterally, subject to the condition that this notice should be unequivocal and unconditional.

[31] See Brändle et al (2018) and Shaw (2019b).

[32] See Shaw (2019b: 27). *Kurić and Others v Slovenia*, No 26828/06 [2013] 56 EHRR 20.

[33] See Patberg (2017).

[34] See Bellamy (2019), but compare Wolkenstein (2019b).

of rights that offers significant benefits in terms of enhanced personal freedom for those who benefit from it, and the previous paragraphs have highlighted some areas where EU law may develop further in the future in relation to the impact on the national constitutional systems, perhaps under the guidance of norms of international law.

At the same time, we need to look at the implications for those who do not benefit from EU citizenship. They experience the sharp edges of EU free movement law, and find their situations governed either by the emerging body of EU immigration law or national immigration law (which is largely responsible for issues around the first admission of migrants and, of course, matters such as the acquisition of national citizenship). They do not benefit from the 'freedoms' of 'Europeans'. Their perspective is that of looking at a so-called Fortress Europe, even if they are already on the inside. This is, it would seem, precisely the position that UK citizens will find themselves in, now that Brexit has gone ahead.

There are many who would argue that the weaknesses of the EU as a polity relate to the absence of an effective politicization of issues such as immigration over which citizens disagree within a so far largely non-existent European public sphere. Additional politicization may not, however, necessarily secure the fundamentals of a liberal society. In September 2019, when announcing the names and portfolios of her new 'Commission designate', European Commission President-elect Ursula von der Leyen designated one of the portfolios as being for the purpose of 'protecting our European way of life'.[35] It turned out that this portfolio included, among other matters, migration (into the EU).[36] Eyebrows were raised at the potentially xenophobic implication that migration into the EU might be threatening 'our way of life', and opposition within the European Parliament was one reason why this title came under rapid

---

[35] 'The von der Leyen Commission: for a Union that strives for more', European Commission, Press Release, IP/19/5542, 10 September 2019 (https://ec.europa.eu/commission/presscorner/detail/en/ip_19_5542).

[36] 'President-elect von der Leyen's Mission Letter to Margaritis Schinas', 10 September 2019 (https://ec.europa.eu/commission/files/margaritis-schinas-mission-letter_en). An updated version of the Mission Letter referring to '*promoting* our way of life' (with an updated title for the Commissioner) was published on 1 December 2019, the day the new Commission took office (https://ec.europa.eu/commission/commissioners/2019-2024/schinas_en).

attack, given the Parliament's role in approving the Commission before it takes office.[37]

This language has travelled some distance in order to reach the designation of one new Commissioner's portfolio. 'Protecting our European way of life' was one of 'six headline ambitions' included in von der Leyen's *Political Guidelines for the Next European Commission 2019–2024*, put before the European Parliament when she was still a candidate for election as Commission President.[38] In turn, the 'way of life' phrase was drawn from the manifesto for the 2019 European Parliament elections put forward by the European People's Party (to which von der Leyen belongs as a German Christian Democratic Party member). One of the headline commitments of the manifesto was to ensure 'A Europe that preserves our way of life', and the text went on to specify this by reference to 'common Judeo-Christian roots', a rider not included in von der Leyen's political guidelines.[39] This framing of a threat (presumably from non-Judeo-Christian sources) is, in turn, borrowed directly from populist radical-right agendas, although these often come with the 'Judeo' bit dropped. This language has seeped into the political communications of an ostensibly mainstream Christian Democrat political group (Mudde 2019).[40] A good example of the radical right discourse comes from Hungarian Prime Minister Viktor Orbán's own pitch for the 2019 European Parliament elections on behalf of his *Fidesz* party, which, in 2019, was still nominally a member of the European People's Party, albeit suspended for the time being. This explicitly and stridently

---

[37] J. Rankin (2019) 'MEPs damn "protecting European way of life" job title', *The Guardian* 11 September (www.theguardian.com/world/2019/sep/11/meps-damn-insulting-protecting-our-european-way-of-life-job-title).

[38] U. von der Leyen (no date) *A Union that Strives for More: My Agenda for Europe* (https://ec.europa.eu/commission/sites/beta-political/files/political-guidelines-next-commission_en.pdf). In November 2019, it was announced that the title of the portfolio would be changed to 'promoting' our way of life, thus still preserving one tendentious element: 'way of life'; M. Mc Mahon (2019) 'The brief: Von der Leyen changes controversial portfolio', *EuroNews*, 14 November (www.euronews.com/2019/11/14/von-der-leyen-changes-controversial-portfolio).

[39] EPP (European People's Party) (2019) *Let's Open the Next Chapter for Europe Together*, EPP Manifesto, March (www.epp.eu/files/uploads/2019/05/EPP-MANIFESTO-2019.pdf).

[40] I am grateful to Cas Mudde for drawing my attention to this connection on Twitter (https://twitter.com/CasMudde/status/1171771515370496000), and for giving me early sight of Mudde (2019).

promised a defence of 'Christian Europe',[41] reflecting Orbán's invocation of the idea of a 'European' 'us', discussed in Chapter 6 as one of the elements of his populist defence of Hungarian constitutional identity. It is not clear whether von der Leyen's intention, through her use of a variant of this language, which was eventually adjusted to read 'promoting our way of life', was to co-opt some of the resonance of the far-right approach or to distance herself from the far right.[42] What is clear is that exclusivist 'stories of peoplehood' can also be developed at the level of the EU, in such a way as to offer a narrow and culturally inspired reading of 'the people'. The challenge posed by populism to constitutional citizenship is not confined to the national level.

Towards international norms governing citizenship

The final substantive section of this chapter will look at whether and how international norms impact on some of those dimensions of constitutional citizenship that we have been discussing in this book. It picks up on earlier discussions of the nature of the international law contribution to citizenship law in previous chapters. It starts from the proposition that international law is a *context* in which the national regulation of constitutional citizenship occurs. Despite the principle of the sovereignty of states in relation to nationality, international law does impact on the freedom of choice that states have in relation to principles of the acquisition and loss of citizenship, and, of course, state practice itself has always been highly influential in determining the character of international legal norms. They do not emerge from thin air, even though other actors such as international courts, international organizations and non-governmental actors have also contributed to the development of international law. Compared to the case of a regional union such as the EU, however, there is a much weaker case for arguing that there is an emergent 'constitutionalized' framing of citizenship practice at the global level as a result of the effects of international law or a decisive 'global' reframing of constitutional citizenship. The idea of 'global constitutionalism', although a useful heuristic device to understand the emergence of intensified networks of international norms precisely in

---

[41] 'Hungary's Orban vows defence of "Christian" Europe', *France24*, 10 February 2019 (www.france24.com/en/20190210-hungarys-orban-vows-defence-christian-europe).
[42] C. Mortera-Martinez, C. (2019) 'New Commission bows to the populists', *Politico*, 12 September (www.politico.eu/article/ursula-von-der-leyen-new-commission-bows-to-the-populists-agenda/).

fields such as citizenship and nationality, still needs to be treated with some caution. Moreover, even if where there may be said to be an emergent constitutional framework under the rubric of 'global constitutionalism', for example in the area of international human rights law (which does have limited impact on citizenship), it is much harder to argue that along with this comes an incipient form of 'membership' at the global level. Rights, as such, do not provide a sufficient basis for some sort of community of affinity or attachment. They represent a thin strand of belonging, and their legitimation relies primarily on outputs rather than inputs. The global citizen – the 'citizen of the world' – may be an appealing idea and it is one that is sometimes invoked rhetorically, but it is not (yet?) a legal reality, just as the concept of global constitutionalism remains more aspirational than real. None the less, some of these ideas represent emergent heuristic devices which help us to make sense of the multilevel governance of citizenship.

The precise manner in which international law does, or does not, take effect within the municipal legal order will vary according to a number of factors. These include the nature of the international norm in question, the type of compliance mechanisms in place for any given legal instrument, and the reception of international law according to the domestic constitutional set-up. In some countries, international law is self-executing, and does not require domestic implementing measures. In other cases, international norms do require implementing measures. The only exception in the latter so-called 'dualist countries' concerns the so-called peremptory norms of international law, from which no derogation will be permitted and which do not require implementation to be enforceable. This contested category includes rules like the prohibitions of torture or slavery, or the *non-refoulement* of refugees,[43] so there is some scope for the applicability of such norms in the broad field of citizenship law. The wider but vague field of customary international law, identified by reference to the general practice of states and what states have accepted as law, is generally regarded – by scholars at least– as including the commitment to eliminating statelessness, especially in relation to children (Edwards 2014, 29).

Back in Chapter 1, I noted that international law appears much more frequently as a frame of reference in scholarly work on citizenship – especially work that takes a comparative approach – than constitutional

---

[43] *Non-refoulement* is the guarantee that refugees have under international law that they will not be sent back to a country where they will face persecution. See the UNESCO glossary (www.unesco.org/new/en/social-and-human-sciences/themes/ international-migration/glossary/refoulement/).

law. One reason for this is that there now exists a substantial volume of benchmarking material within international law. A good example is external citizenship. In Chapter 4, we discussed some cases where the principle of *ius sanguinis* as the basis for citizenship attribution may be overstretched by states, when looked at from the perspective on constitutional citizenship. An alternative perspective on these issues can be gained by examining the same issue from the perspective of compliance with the mandates of international law. Anne Peters (2010) judges such approaches to citizenship attribution to be problematic, based on a review of the relevant sources of international law.

Quite a number of scholars offer synoptic approaches to international law's coverage of the field of citizenship. For example, Peter Spiro (2011) takes both a historical and contemporary perspective, and Barbara von Rütte (2018) seeks to identify the contours of an international 'right to citizenship'. Both Spiro and von Rütte adopt an individual rights focus in their analysis, leaving behind the traditional sovereignty focus of the idea of nationality in international law (epitomized by the various conventions agreed in the earlier parts of the 20th century focused on the elimination of dual nationality) in order to zoom in on the ways in which individuals do or do not benefit from access to citizenship and its associated rights under currently applicable international law rules. In both cases the argument is normative. Spiro is making the case that there exists, or soon will exist, a 'rights-oriented' international law of citizenship, which – he acknowledges – would contribute to the fragmentation of citizenship governance and undermine the liberal state. Von Rütte's claim is for the recognition of an international right to citizenship resting on the ethical foundation of *ius nexi*, or the principle of the genuine link or connection.

As Bauböck makes clear (2018b), rights protection is only one of several goals that can be attributed to international law in relation to citizenship. International law is also concerned with the resolution of conflicts between states in relation to matters of nationality and jurisdiction, and with the setting of minimum standards against which states can benchmark themselves, as well as – in appropriate circumstances – be judged (de Groot and Vonk 2016). These include the European Convention on Nationality[44] and soft law measures such as the International Law Commission's Draft Articles on Nationality of Natural Persons in Relation to the Succession of States and, more recently, the Global Compact on

---

[44] All of the international treaties referred to in this section are available at the GLOBALCIT International Legal Norms database (http://globalcit.eu/international_legal_norms/).

Migration.[45] Previous 'standards' such as the 1930 Convention on Certain Questions Relating to the Conflict of Nationality Laws, intended to eliminate statelessness *and* dual nationality, have largely fallen into abeyance. Furthermore, so far as concerns the 'toolbox' that would need to be assembled for there to be such a set of international norms, it is clear that these must go way beyond the field of public law and must draw on materials in all fields of law, including civil law, family law and inheritance law, and their international cognates (de Groot 2016). Overall, despite the growing abundance of international law sources, I would argue that the totality still falls well short of providing the groundwork for some sort of international law of citizenship, or even a regional (for example, European) nationality law.[46]

Two short and interconnected case studies will assist in highlighting both the potential and the weaknesses of the international law optic on constitutional citizenship: the international regulation of statelessness (with a view to its elimination) and the effects of regional human rights regimes on citizenship norms. With statelessness, we are returning to a topic also addressed in several sections of Chapter 4, and many of the topics to be discussed under the headline of regional human rights regimes will, as promised at the beginning of this chapter, find a counterparty elsewhere in the book.

More than 10 million people worldwide are stateless today, perhaps many more. By definition, these numbers are based on estimates, and while many stateless people are to be found in parts of the world where documentary evidence of their existence is sometimes sparse, many others are 'hiding in plain sight' in so-called western countries. The causes of statelessness are multiple, and include conflicts of nationality laws, individualized or group-based deprivations of citizenship, forced displacement of populations, the creation of new states, weak bureaucracies, and the exclusion of and discrimination against minorities. Statelessness can be passed down across generations. The effects of statelessness are substantial, especially in a world where proving identity and belonging has become an ever-more important part of gaining access to employment, healthcare, education and welfare, as well as – obviously – mobility and travel. The prevention of statelessness is not widely accepted as a peremptory norm of international law, despite the inclusion of the right to a nationality in the Universal Declaration of Human Rights and the conclusion of the 1954 Convention relating to the Status of Stateless Persons and the 1961 Convention on

---

[45] UN Global Compact for Safe, Orderly and Regular Migration, December 2018 (https://refugeesmigrants.un.org/migration-compact).

[46] But compare the arguments mounted by de Groot (2004) and Orgad (2019).

the Reduction of Statelessness. The latter are examples of multilateral international treaties that relatively large numbers of states have signed up to, including substantial numbers of recent accessions, but they lack an effective enforcement procedure, so that compliance remains largely a matter for each contracting party that may use different definitions of the key terms, such as 'stateless person' (Bianchini 2017). Indeed, for many years, statelessness was largely regarded as a technical issue that needed technical solutions, even after the recognition of 'nationality' as a human right in the Universal Declaration.

According to Laura van Waas, it was the incidence of statelessness in Europe caused by the break-up of Yugoslavia and the Soviet Union after the end of the Cold War that catalysed a revival of interest in statelessness as legal issue (van Waas 2014, 344). Alongside this, the UNHCR (UN High Commissioner for Refugees, which amounts to the UN's Refugee Agency) was given a broader global mandate to take the lead on endeavours to eradicate statelessness, and an associated budget. UNHCR's campaigns on this have involved pushing for accessions by states to the statelessness conventions and drawing up interpretative advice for the implementation of those conventions, and, from 2014, an ambitious global campaign based on a Global Action Plan[47] to eradicate statelessness worldwide within 10 years.[48] Good practice codes and guidance notes have been developed, and regular reports are issued. Many more resources are now available in the area of statelessness,[49] and these have come from civil society organizations[50] and from academic scholars, as well as from national and international public bodies. Effective work on the ground also needs detailed local knowledge, and often occurs in tandem with the efforts of development donors and NGOs. Despite this, progress is hard to quantify except in respect of obvious indicators such as accessions to the statelessness treaties.

There are other legal building blocks involved in efforts to combat statelessness. Many of these are to be found in the extensive network of human rights treaties adopted under the aegis of the UN since 1945. The relevant norms include Article 7 of the Convention on the Rights of the Child, Article 24(3) of the International Covenant on Civil and Political Rights, Article 9 of the Convention on the Elimination of All

---

[47] See UNHCR, Global Action Plan to End Statelessness, 2014–2024 (www.unhcr. org/ibelong/global-action-plan-2014-2024/).

[48] See the #ibelong website (www.unhcr.org/ibelong/).

[49] Many of these resources are gathered together on the UNHCR's Refworld website (www.refworld.org/statelessness.html).

[50] For example, the Institute on Statelessness and Inclusion (www.institutesi.org/) and the European Network on Statelessness (www.statelessness.eu/).

Forms of Discrimination against Women and Article 5 of the Convention on the Elimination of All Forms of Racial Discrimination, all of which directly address the 'right to a nationality'. Under the umbrella of the UN's Office of the High Commissioner for Human Rights (OHCHR), there are a variety of quasi-judicial charter- and treaty-based bodies that have developed bodies of 'case law' addressing the meaning and effects of some of these norms in specific situations at the national level. Such implementation mechanisms lie more on the political rather than the legal side. The legal applicability of norms guaranteeing the right to a nationality at the domestic level depends, as noted above, on how the contracting parties go about implementing international law at the municipal level. In addition, work continues to be done to engage with 'stopping statelessness at source'[51] by looking at the way that rules on acquisition of citizenship may restrict the opportunities of children or women in particular to gain an effective nationality. As Vlieks et al (2017) note, statelessness is not just about a formal answer to the question of whether a person has 'a nationality', but rather about ensuring that such nationality is meaningful and allows that person to enjoy all the rights that are associated with it.

In this context, it is also important to note the contribution of regional human rights treaties to the task of combating statelessness. In Chapter 4, we discussed the interventions of the Inter-American Human Rights Court (IAHRCt) in relation to the denial of access to nationality by Haitians, and consequential statelessness, in the Dominican Republic. In the two cases that have come before the IAHRCt, it found numerous violations of provisions of the American Convention on Human Rights, including Article 20 that establishes the right to a nationality. In particular, the IAHRCt held that the right to a nationality could not be limited for discriminatory purposes.[52] This was not the Court's first foray into the field of citizenship law. It had already scrutinized the right to nationality in an advisory opinion on proposed amendments to the naturalization provisions of the Constitution of Costa Rica in 1984, where it held that it was not a violation of Article 20 or other provisions of the Convention for Costa Rica to impose differential naturalization requirements, which distinguished between native-born Central Americans, Spaniards and Ibero-Americans, who were required to have five years of official residence in Costa Rica and others, who were required to have seven

---

[51] This phrase is attributed to Guy Goodwin-Gill, cited in Foster and Lambert (2016: 572).

[52] *Case of the Yean and Bosico Girls v Dominican Republic*, 8 September 2005 (full judgment at www.corteidh.or.cr/docs/casos/articulos/seriec_130_%20ing.pdf).

years of residence.[53] It was acceptable for the law to take into account cultural differences between the two groups and to recognize their closer historical, cultural and spiritual bonds with Costa Rica, highlighting a deferential approach to the cultural definition of constitutional citizenship in that state. Since then, the Court has also held Peru in violation of Article 20 for arbitrarily depriving a naturalized citizen of his nationality, failing to follow national procedures.[54] The case law of the IAHRCt in this and other areas has contributed to triggering threatened and actual denunciations of the Inter-American Human Rights system (IAHR), inter alia by the Dominican Republic and Peru.[55] Despite the backlash, the IAHR system is widely judged to be reasonably resilient, and it can be said to have made important contributions to the development of constitutional citizenship in the region via the case law of the IAHRCt.

The regional human rights institutions in Africa have also delivered a number of key rulings on matters of nationality and statelessness. Following a number of cases that had come before the African Commission on Human and Peoples' Rights and the African Committee of Experts on the Rights and Welfare of the Child, in 2018 the African Court on Human and Peoples' Rights decided the *Anudo* case on the right to a nationality.[56] The applicant was born in Tanzania and had Tanzanian citizenship and identity documents until 2012, at which point doubts were cast by the relevant authorities as to whether he was a citizen. He was subsequently expelled to Kenya, but Kenya refused to accept him, and he spent several years living in 'no man's land' between the two states, without access to any services. The African Court found that he had been denied his right to a nationality contrary to Article 15 of the Universal Declaration of Human Rights. It needed to refer to the Declaration as there is no express right to a nationality in the African Charter on Human and Peoples' Rights. As the Court concluded that Article 15 of the Declaration amounts to customary international law, it could then use this provision in order to fill the gap left in the African Charter. It further concluded that Tanzania was also in multiple violation of other treaties by which it was bound and which the Court is empowered to interpret, including failure to take steps to ensure the applicant was not in a situation

---

[53] *Proposed Amendments to the Naturalization Provision of the Constitution of Costa Rica*, Advisory opinion OC-4/84 (IACtHR), 19 January 1984.

[54] *Case of Ivcher Bronstein v Peru*, IACHR Series C No 74, IHRL 1457 (IACHR 2001), 6 February 2001.

[55] On this practice, see Soley and Steininger (2018).

[56] *Anudo v United Republic of Tanzania* (Application No 012/2015) [2018] AfCHPR 5 (22 March 2018) (https://africanlii.org/node/1806).

of statelessness contrary to Article 13 of the International Covenant on Civil and Political Rights. Bronwen Manby has noted that the number of cases on nationality previously coming before the African Commission 'reflects the fact that contested rights to belong to the national community have been at the basis of many of the most intractable political and military conflicts in the continent' (2019c, 174). This was not such a case, but it provided an important opportunity for the Court to establish that in cases of contested citizenship – which are not rare in Africa – the burden of proof lies on the state that has previously issued documentation, not on the person whose citizenship is contested, and that the person must be accorded due process before an independent tribunal. The powers of the Court are such that it can order a state to change its citizenship law, as it did with Tanzania, but this does not necessarily mean that change will occur (Daly and Wiebusch 2018).

Finally, we turn to the European Convention on Human Rights and Fundamental Freedoms (ECHR), and the case law of its Court (ECtHR). In its work, the ECtHR has drawn on a wider range of sources of international law in order to indicate how human rights norms have developed, referring in particular to the general principles of international law that provide the broader environment in which the ECHR operates (Dzehtsiarou 2017/18), but it has not done this in such a way as to fill gaps, such as the lack of an explicit guarantee of the right to a nationality. To address issues of citizenship, the ECtHR has had to be creative in its interpretation of the provisions of the Convention. Its leading judgment on national citizenship is the case of *Genovese v Malta*,[57] where the Court recognized social identity as an intrinsic part of nationality, and held that as such it was protected as an element of private life under Article 8 ECHR. It concluded that Maltese citizenship law was discriminatory and in violation of human rights (by reading Article 14 on non-discrimination in conjunction with Article 8), because it denied Maltese citizenship to an illegitimate child born of a non-Maltese mother and a Maltese father. The case came before the ECtHR after a failed constitutional complaint before the Maltese constitutional court. The latter court found that the national provisions were compatible with the Constitution of Malta. Consequently, when the ECtHR interpreted the provisions of the ECHR to cover nationality as social identity, it did so in a way that explicitly ran counter to the applicable Maltese conception of constitutional citizenship, which had permitted the distinction to be drawn in respect of the parentage of an illegitimate child.

---

[57] *Genovese v Malta* App No 53124/09 (ECtHR, 11 October 2011).

The ECtHR has also ruled on issues related to statelessness, in particular in the context of the consequences of the dissolution of the former Yugoslavia (SFRY). In *Kurić*, the ECtHR was faced with the consequences of the 'erasure' from the public records by Slovenia of certain citizens of SFRY who did not become citizens of the new state of Slovenia after independence in 1991, despite long residence.[58] By the erasures that took place in 1992, some of the applicants were left stateless. The Grand Chamber held that it was a violation of Article 8 for Slovenia not to make provision for the legal situation of such people to be regulated, for example, via the register of foreign nationals and the law on aliens. For many years, they faced considerable difficulties and hardship in relation to residence permits, housing, healthcare, employment and other matters, and some faced deportation although they had resided as co-citizens of SFRY before Slovenia's independence. Although the original erasure took place before Slovenia acceded to the ECHR, the failure to regulate their situation was ongoing until at least 2010 (that is, long after the accession). It is notable that this state of affairs persisted in Slovenia even after the Constitutional Court had ruled that the relevant provisions of the Aliens Act of 1991 were unconstitutional because they failed to deal with the situation of the Erased. The *Kurić* case thus highlights an ongoing conflict over the meaning of constitutional citizenship in Slovenia, which the ECtHR settled in favour of better inclusion of those threatened with a vulnerable outsider status.

Most recently, in the case of *Hoti*[59] the ECtHR directly engaged with the issue of statelessness. The Court adjudged that the applicant in that case was stateless. He was born in Kosovo, in what was then SFRY, of parents who were political refugees from Albania. He moved to Croatia in 1979, 13 years before Croatia became an independent state, and had remained there ever since. It seems that he may have been stateless from birth. From shortly after the independence of Croatia, during which time he did military service, Hoti attempted to regularize his residence either by becoming a citizen of Croatia or by obtaining a residence permit on some other basis. The ECtHR judged that Croatia had failed in:

> ... its positive obligation to provide an effective and accessible procedure or a combination of procedures enabling the applicant to have the issues of his further stay and status in Croatia determined with due regard to his private-life interests under Article 8 of the Convention. (para 141)

---

[58] *Kurić and Others v Slovenia* No 26828/06, [2013] 56 EHRR 20.
[59] *Hoti v Croatia* No 63311/14 26, 26 April 2018.

According to Katja Swider (2019), one significant part of the judgment lies in the ECtHR's determination that the applicant was indeed stateless, and that what followed from this was a violation of the Convention because of the failure of Croatia to make provision for him to regularize his residence. It was not that he somehow had the right to become a citizen; this was something he had earlier sought and been refused. Ironically, much earlier in his life he had declined to become a citizen of SFRY when this had been possible. Swider concludes from the judgment that the ECHR can be said to place an obligation on its contracting parties to put in place mechanisms for determining statelessness and thereafter for regularizing residence, in accordance with their international obligations, and that furthermore, 'access to human rights cannot be made dependent on whether, when and how a stateless person may choose to invoke their right to a nationality' (2019, 190). This seems to turn Arendt's 'right to have rights' on its head, by explicitly prioritizing human rights over the right to a nationality, rather than the assumption that it is the right to a nationality that must come first for effective rights protection.

Conclusion

This chapter has explored just a few of the many dimensions of the simple proposition that in today's world, citizenship is best understood not in unitary terms, but as a set of relationships nested within multilevel and plural sources of legal authority, where different norms apply in different contexts. It has thereby opened up a new optic on the contestation of citizenship as a relational concept, in the context of constitutionalism 'beyond the state'. Alongside discussions of splintering states, horizontal constellations of citizenship regimes and citizenship in voluntary alliances, I have only been able to give a tiny selection of examples of how international norms relating to citizenship are evolving, leaving many issues thus far untouched. For instance, we have not had space to consider the role of 'soft' institutions of international law in Europe, such as the Venice Commission of the Council of Europe (European Commission for Democracy through Law), which has issued many reports and opinions contesting developments in countries such Hungary from the perspective of standards of democracy and the rule of law, sometimes with success and more often – especially since Hungary's populist turn – without. Even so, the themes covered have been very diverse. In some cases, we can see overlapping and often competing instances of membership relations, with implications for those who are dual citizens, or a citizen of one state and (permanent) resident in another. In those contexts, the question of the genuine link or *ius nexi* has come to the fore, at least as an aspiration for a more equitable allocation of the benefits of citizenship, despite the neglect of this principle by states in the context of those arenas of constitutional citizenship surveyed in Part II of the book. In other circumstances, especially those relating to international law, and in some respects in areas covered by EU law, the fragmentation of citizenship governance is best understood in terms of overlapping legal orders, with consequent issues arising over the hierarchy of norms. Which one should take precedence? It seems clear that international law has stepped well beyond its Westphalian core of simply oiling the wheels between states and establishing standards relating to jurisdiction, conflicts of laws and diplomacy. If nothing else, the human rights revolution since the Second World War as well as the rise of regional integration organizations have opened up many new possibilities for law beyond the state. The international law dimension of citizenship has both global justice and individual rights elements.

While globalization clearly has impacts on citizenship norms, so too does the creation of multiple potentially competing legal orders, as the examples from Latin America, Africa and Europe have shown. With examples – however contested – of citizenship *and constitutionalism* beyond the state, the idea of a single insulated national concept of constitutional citizenship simply cannot hold. While there is (thus far) no single European, or African, or global nationality law (or even model law), any more than there is a global citizen, there are increasing numbers of internationally engaged norms, and it may well be that international courts will increasingly learn from each other about creative interpretations that can fill the gaps in the normative structure. In that sense, while the populism we studied in Chapter 6 stood for the closing of discursive space, what we have seen in this chapter has been the opening of new discursive spaces, and the testing out of new potentialities for the membership relation and for constitutional citizenship. But at the same time, the neat triptychs of identity, status and rights do not sit comfortably together, even less than they do at the national level. The supranational and international spheres currently largely depend on measures of output legitimacy (that is, the quality and acceptability of the decisions of international legislatures, executives and courts) to secure consent, in the absence of effective public spheres and deliberation among 'citizens' or recognized democratic structures at those levels. These things may change in the future. For now, we stand, perhaps, at a moment of transition.

8

Conclusions

I embarked on the task of exploring *The People in Question* by embracing a widely shared intuition, namely that constitutions and citizenship are closely related in modern states. I then took it into an intellectual space that seemed to be surprisingly sparsely occupied. Hitherto, there have been few in-depth attempts to make sense of the interactions between citizenship and constitutions, or to place those interactions in a wider context. This was a puzzle, which demanded an answer. A second puzzle also formed part of my motivations. Why is it that citizenship is so rarely regulated, in substantive terms, within constitutions themselves? Why is it, as we have seen throughout Part II, that the constitutional substance of citizenship so often reveals itself in ways that are indirect or that present a fragmented picture, so that the pieces need to be assembled from different sources in order construct an intelligible picture? Is citizenship really such a taken-for-granted element of the typical constitutional set-up that it is sufficient for constitution-makers just to refer to it glancingly in the text of the constitution, delegating the task of settling the detailed terms of membership to the various majoritarian or non-majoritarian institutions of the state? And if the latter, how do we choose who should decide? If the task is one of fixing the people, then who but 'the people' can complete the task? The problem seems circular in nature.

This unresolved dilemma reinforces one insight that has emerged from pursuing these puzzles about citizenship and constitutions. There is no such thing as a purely descriptive approach to examining the interactions of citizenship and constitutions. This is what I intended to imply by choosing the book title of *The People in Question*. Even if we treat state membership largely as an artefact of government, the task of describing citizenship and constitutions in the same space remains an exercise in understanding and interpreting those interactions in the context of the claims of citizenship and of constitutionalism as idealized practices. Such a task involves ethical choices, which inevitably have distributional, social and political effects.

It has not been my primary intention at any point to impose my own view about what citizenship ought to encompass and how it should be dealt with by constitutions, about who ought to belong and who ought not, or about who should determine the answers to questions such as these. But in order to pursue my project, I have had to develop and apply concepts that are not somehow innocent bystanders in the world, such as the idea of 'constitutional citizenship'. This combination of constitutions and citizenship (two contested concepts) is itself also a contested concept. I have endeavoured to keep that contestation at the forefront of our attention by drawing attention to important historical factors, such as the legacy of colonialism, which are central to our understanding modern citizenship but sometimes downplayed. However, in a world of Westphalian states which universally adopt constitutions as their basic operating systems, constitutional citizenship has been a useful starting point for reflection. Yet the process of studying modern citizenship and modern constitutions, in combination, also reconstructs those concepts. It does not leave them untouched. In that sense, the enquiry in this book has been – as I put it in Chapter 1 – both interpretative and critical.

As the work progressed, a number of thematic conclusions about constitutional citizenship have emerged. Many elaborate on the inevitable tensions between the symbolic role of the citizen at the heart of constitutionalism and the instrumental behaviour of states and governments in relation to citizenship status and citizenship rights. One major theme concerns the role of different institutions in setting the limits and scope of citizenship and citizenship rights. While many constitutions delegate most of this function to legislatures and executives, this has not prevented courts from intervening in this sphere. This, in turn, raises some interesting questions about how and why courts should intervene, if asked, and what legitimacy they have when intervening. This question is especially interesting in cases where those interventions are not merely procedural, in so far as they review the limits of the powers or discretion delegated to other institutions, but also substantive, in so far as they claim to discover the constitutional 'essence' of the polity, in particular via the concept of the people. Throughout Chapters 3 to 5 of the book we have seen numerous examples of this, from the Greek Council of State asserting the central importance of the concept of descent to the idea of citizenship in Greece, via the Constitutional Court of the Philippines decreeing that a foundling is a 'natural-born citizen', to the Constitutional Court of post-apartheid South Africa asserting that the right to vote is a facet of the dignity of the citizen. These institutional questions, and the foundational ethical dilemmas they conceal, clearly deserve further research.

A second theme relates to the, also as yet incomplete, search for those elements that could elevate the idea of constitutional citizenship into something more substantial than a simple procedural expression of the place of citizenship in any given constitutional scheme. In this book, we have paid particular attention to the principles of dignity and equality. Throughout Part II of the book these ideas kept returning to our attention in various guises, and within a variety of different institutional frameworks. Placing human rights at the centre of the account would certainly reveal many gaps in relation to what states do, but we lack a full picture of how citizenship relates to the ubiquity of rights (citizenship rights, constitutional rights, human rights) in state constitutions. States – or perhaps better, 'governments' – often fail when they endeavour to recognize and give heft to the notion of equal citizenship, but a legal concept of equality has emerged as an important tool for those who challenge 'unequal' outcomes, reminding us of the centrality of struggles to our contested concept of citizenship. In addition, it is arguable that states could do more to recognize the 'proximity' of putative citizens by developing a specific mode of citizenship acquisition that some have called *ius nexi*. Or, turning to the political content of citizenship, states could also acknowledge the centrality of certain 'stakeholders' as the basis for democratic legitimacy. On the other side of the coin, some of the examples explored in Part II of the book raise the question of whether all of those who possess the formal badges of citizenship (such as a passport), as with those who become citizens 'by investment', are actually 'constitutional citizens' in a substantive sense. Once again, we could see the need for more research in this area, but not in the form of a vain search for a single answer to the question 'what makes a constitutional citizen?' Rather, the question should be an open one: 'what are the elements that shape the development of the discursive space within which the citizenship/constitution interaction plays out?'

Third, close attention has been paid in the book to issues of citizenship and non-citizenship. Some states announce the right to a nationality grandly in their constitutions, but do not necessarily provide all of the means to assure that the right is actually observed. And much is hidden by the badge of citizenship, for in the absence of systematic birth registration in many countries, many people are denied all of the benefits of being 'citizens'. However, this book has not given a systematic treatment of the issue of non-citizenship, so this is another topic within the broad field of 'constitutional citizenship' that still remains to be researched in full. For example, we have paid attention across the book to many of the ways in which mobility has reconstructed the notion of citizenship, while offering little analysis of the extent to which it has enhanced the spread of non-citizenship (in the state of residence) with larger numbers of foreign-born residents not all of whom naturalize in the host state or whose children (easily) acquire citizenship. In any event, rates of naturalization remain hard to measure with any certainty, so to some extent the scale of this problem – if it is one – is unknown (Janoski 2013).

On the other hand, while constitutional citizenship remains an important analytical category in some places and at some times, it cannot be asserted that it offers a complete picture of citizenship. Even where the constitutional citizen represents an important legal construct in any given country, it can still be an elusive figure to 'capture' and describe. It is useful to highlight an important point made by Jim Tully (1995), namely that there is no single universal 'language of citizenship', but rather a multiplicity. Constitutions, as well as citizenships, are a 'strange multiplicity'. It is thus the deception of 'modern citizenship' that it masquerades as universal, thereby concealing from view other plausible ways of being and relating to each other (Seubert 2014). As the survey of constitutional citizenship has sought to show, the blending of – and where necessary the distinction between – practice and status is thus crucial to understanding the complex interrelationships between citizenship and constitutional law.

The aim of this book was not simply to map the terrain of constitutional citizenship, challenging as that task has proved to be on its own. I also wanted to focus on the pressure points of the citizenship/constitution interaction by exploring the implications of the turn to populist politics at the national level and the increasingly dense network of citizenship-related norms and practices 'beyond the state'. Although its topic is populism, Chapter 6 also provides us with many examples of 'the return of the state' (not that it had ever left the building), and Chapter 7 articulates the continuing challenges that the state faces from many different angles. Neither of these arenas of struggle is likely to disappear any time soon. In an era of populism, as the discursive space for citizenship is closed down by reference to a restrictive conception of 'the people', statelessness, citizenship deprivation, and so on, are back, with a vengeance. Groups such as the Roma in Europe or refugees throughout the world struggle to gain a foothold within the states in which they find themselves, as many forms of mobility becoming increasingly securitized in moves that may also be supported by international actors. David Owen (2018) shows that at present neither international society nor states themselves effectively guarantee the right to a nationality, or right to have rights, and the main reason for this lies in defects within the international political order whereby 'free statehood' is not secured across the board. Westphalian states are not 'free' states, in the republican sense of non-domination. But states still possess relatively high degrees of autonomy, at least in the Global North. While the state is continually put in question by developments such as subnational claims for autonomy and voluntary and involuntary engagement with international norms, the state may also be strengthened if the international consensus on how to control certain 'disturbances' of the status quo such as political violence is shifted in a more restrictive direction.

There are constant interactions between the two challenges to constitutional citizenship examined in Part III. For example, international norms are commonly instrumentalized by actors such as national and international public and civil society organizations to contest egregious human rights-denying or liberal institution-trashing measures at the national level that flow from the populist reconstruction of 'the people'.[1] At the same time, the non-majoritarian nature of almost all international norms renders them vulnerable to the riposte that they may be liberal, but they are not democratic, but rather the product of internationalized elites who ignore the specificities of local circumstances.[2] As populist governments and parties, including some in the EU such as Hungary and Poland, explicitly and happily embrace the branding of 'illiberalism',[3] liberal international institutions face unprecedented challenges to their survival. Sometimes, the claims of illiberal governments are picked up at the supranational level, as the case of the European Commissioner for (previously defending, now promoting) 'our European way of life', discussed in Chapter 7, makes clear. European autocrats such as Viktor Orbán do not so much reject European institutions as try to remake them in their own image, as can be seen by the co-optation of ideas of legal pluralism to justify *national* constitutional supremacy in the name of the people.[4] There is, then, a curious parallelism between the issues covered in Chapters 6 and 7, in the sense that both populism and globalism struggle with democracy *and* rights. Clearly, neither offers a panacea. Moreover, the situation we are describing should not, however, be characterized as being simply a contest between 'authoritarian illiberal national' and 'undemocratic liberal international' norms, as there is evidence of democratic decay, not just in the authoritarian states, but throughout the world. It is easy to overgeneralize when using terms such as these, but the magisterial survey edited by Graber et al (2018) of the state of

---

[1] For fuller accounts of recent examples, see Pech and Scheppele (2017) and Gyollai and Amatrudo (2019).

[2] Chryssogelos (2018).

[3] Fekete (2016).

[4] For a vehement critique of legal pluralism, see Pech and Kelemen (2018).

constitutional democracy contains much worrying material drawn from across the globe.

In the transition between Parts II and III of the book, I drew on Jean Cohen's (1999) contribution to reconciling the different elements of the citizenship principle. We need to return to these points now. There are conflicts, she argues, within both liberal democratic constitutionalism, with its focus on limited powers, and civic republican constitutionalism, with its focus on popular sovereignty. Each misses the opportunities that can come from viewing citizenship no longer in a singular national optic, but rather from the pluralist perspective of many citizenships. But the task is by no means easy, which is why Jürgen Habermas has invoked the idea of the 'Janus face' of the modern nation: acting in the name of universal principles but within the particularistic and legal contexts of specific communities of citizens (Habermas 2001, 101–2). Other scholars have developed a multitude of conceptual vehicles for trying to overcome those gaps in such a way as to deliver on the promise of citizenship to offer equality, democracy and recognition both within and across states, such as 'post-sovereign citizenship' (Murphy and Harty 2003) and 'post-Westphalian citizenship' (Falk 2000). Pluralism has received a negative press in recent times, because it is perceived to have been an enabling force in relation to populism and authoritarianism in central and eastern Europe. Despite that cautionary note, it still has potential. It remains plausible to suggest that somewhere in the discursive resources of pluralism lie the means by which we can effectively reconcile those countervailing tendencies produced within our complex heterogeneous political communities, in ways that both respect the democratic authenticity of communities organized as states or similar polities and tap the as-yet unfulfilled potential of a world of freely associating communities, based on a variety of territorial and other affinities. If this step could be taken, it would involve a decisive reworking of the concept of 'constitutional citizenship'. This is the work to be done in the future.

References

Abbas, M.-S. (2019) 'Conflating the Muslim refugee and the terror suspect: Responses to the Syrian refugee "crisis" in Brexit Britain', *Ethnic and Racial Studies*, 42(14), 2450–69. doi:10.1080/01419870.2019.1588339.

Achermann, A., Achermann, C., D'Amato, G., Kamm, M. and von Rütte, B. (2013) *Report on Citizenship Law: Switzerland*, Country Report, San Domenico di Fiesole: Global Citizenship Observatory (GLOBALCIT), Robert Schuman Centre for Advanced Studies, European University Institute, 2010/25 (https://cadmus.eui.eu/handle/1814/19639).

ACHPR (African Commission on Human and Peoples' Rights) (2015) *The Right to Nationality in Africa*, Banjul (www.refworld.org/docid/54cb3c8f4.html).

ACJR (African Criminal Justice Reform) (2019) *The Right of Prisoners to Vote in Africa: An Update*, May (https://acjr.org.za/resource-centre/fact-sheet-17-prisoners-vote.pdf).

Acosta, D. (2016) *Regional Report on Citizenship: The South American and Mexican Cases*, Comparative Report 2016/01, San Domenico di Fiesole: Global Citizenship Observatory (GLOBALCIT), Robert Schuman Centre for Advanced Studies, European University Institute (http://hdl.handle.net/1814/43325).

Acosta, D. (2018) *The National versus the Foreigner in South America: 200 Years of Migration and Citizenship Law*, Cambridge: Cambridge University Press.

Adams, M. (2016) *Who Belongs? Race, Resources, and Tribal Citizenship in the Native South*, Oxford: Oxford University Press.

Adamson, F. (2006) 'Crossing borders: International migration and national security', *International Security*, 31(1), 165–99.

Addis, A. (2018) 'Constitutional preambles as narratives of peoplehood', *International Constitutional Law Journal*, 12(2), 125–81.

Aguilar Jr, F.V. (2018) 'Political love: Affect, instrumentalism and dual citizenship legislation in the Philippines', *Citizenship Studies*, 22(8), 829–54. doi:10.1080/13621025.2018.1538317.

Ahmad, M. (2014) 'The citizenship of others', *Fordham Law Review*, 82(5), 2041–67.

Ahmed, F. (2020) *Arbitrariness, Subordination and Unequal Citizenship* (https://papers.ssrn.com/sol3/papers.cfm?abstract_id=3515056).

Ajanovic, E., Mayer, S. and Sauer, B. (2015) 'Natural enemies: Articulations of racism in right-wing Populism in Austria', *Časopis za kritiko znanosti, domišljijo in novo antropologijo*, 260, 203–14.

Ajanovic, E., Mayer, S. and Sauer, B. (2018) 'Constructing "the people": An intersectional analysis of right-wing concepts of democracy and citizenship in Austria', *Journal of Language and Politics*, 17 (5), 636–54. doi:https://doi.org/10.1075/jlp.18013.may.

Albarazi, Z. (2017) *Regional Report on Citizenship: The Middle East and North Africa (MENA)*, Comparative Report 2017/03, San Domenico di Fiesole: Global Citizenship Observatory (GLOBALCIT), Robert Schuman Centre for Advanced Studies, European University Institute, (http://hdl.handle.net/1814/50046).

Aleinikoff, T.A. (2000) 'Between Principles and Policies: US Citizenship Policy', in T.A. Aleinikoff and D. Klusmeyer (eds) *From Migrants to Citizens. Membership in a Changing World*, Washington, DC: Carnegie Endowment for International Peace, 119–72.

Aleinikoff, T.A. (2002) *Semblances of Sovereignty: The Constitution, the State, and American Citizenship*, Cambridge, MA: Harvard University Press.

Alexopoulos, G. (2006) 'Soviet citizenship, more or less: Rights, emotions, and states of civic belonging', *Kritika: Explorations in Russian and Eurasian History*, 7(3), 487–528.

Alviar García, H. and Frankenberg, G. (eds) (2019) *Authoritarian Constitutionalism: Comparative Analysis and Critique*, Cheltenham/ Northampton, MA: Edward Elgar Publishing. doi:https://doi.org/ 10.4337/9781788117852.

Anagnostou, D. (2016) 'Judicial activism in the name of the nation: Reneging on the integration of immigrants in Greece', *Journal of Law and Society*, 43(4), 596–618.

Angus Reid Institute (2019) 'Birthright citizenship: Plurality of Canadians see it as good policy, but also say some changes are needed', 14 March (http://angusreid.org/birthright-citizenship-birth-tourism/).

Annoni, A. and Forlati, S. (eds) (2013) *The Changing Role of Nationality in International Law*, London: Routledge and Taylor & Francis.

Appelbaum, N., Macpherson, A. and Rosemblatt, K. (2003) 'Introduction. Racial Nations', in N. Appelbaum, A. Macpherson and K. Rosemblatt (eds) *Race and Nation in Modern Latin America*, Chapel Hill, NC and London: University of North Carolina Press, 1–31.

Arcioni, E. (2014) 'Democracy and the Constitution: The People Deciding the Identity of "the People"', in G. Patmore and K. Rubenstein (eds) *Law and Democracy: Contemporary Questions*, Canberra, ACT: Australian National University Press, 11–25.

Arcioni, E. (2015) 'Tracing the ethno-cultural or racial identity of the Australian constitutional people', *Oxford University Commonwealth Law Journal*, 15(2), 173–95. doi: https://doi.org/10.1080/14729342.2016. 1173350.

Arcioni, E. (2018) 'Citizenship', in C. Saunders and A. Stone (eds) *The Oxford Handbook of the Australian Constitution*, Oxford: Oxford University Press, 339–56.

Arcioni, E. and Irving, H. (2017) 'Form over substance? Foreign citizenship and the Australian Parliament', GLOBALCIT Blog, 16 October (http:// globalcit.eu/dual-citizenship-and-eligibility-to-serve-as-a-member-of-parliament-the-evolving-story-in-australia/).

Arcioni, E. and Thwaites, R. (2020) 'Australian Aboriginals are not vulnerable to deportation', GLOBALCIT Blog, 17 February (http:// globalcit.eu/aboriginal-australians-not-vulnerable-to-deportation/).

Arendt, H. (1986) *The Origins of Totalitarianism*, London: Andre Deutsch.

Arrighi, J.-T. (2019) '"The people, year zero": Secessionism and citizenship in Scotland and Catalonia', *Ethnopolitics*, 18(3), 278–97. doi:10.1080/1 7449057.2019.1585091.

Arrighi, J.-T. and Bauböck, R. (2017) 'A multilevel puzzle: Migrants' voting rights in national and local elections', *European Journal of Political Research*, 56(3), 619–39. doi:10.1111/1475-6765.12176.

Arrighi, J.-T., Bauböck, R., Hutcheson, D., Ostling, A. and Piccoli, L. (2019) *Conditions for Electoral Rights 2019*, San Domenico di Fiesole: European University Institute (http://globalcit.eu/conditions-for-electoral-rights/).

Ashesh, A. and Thiruvengadam, A. (2018) 'India', in O. Vonk (ed) *Nationality Law in the Eastern Hemisphere: Acquisition and Loss of Citizenship in Asian Perspective*, Oisterwijk: Wolf Legal Publishers, 153–74.

Backer, L.C. (2006) 'Theocratic constitutionalism: An introduction to a new global legal ordering', *Indiana Journal of Global Legal Studies*, 16(1) (www.repository.law.indiana.edu/ijgls/vol16/iss1/5).

Baer, S. (2012) 'Equality', in M. Rosenfeld and A. Sajó (eds) *Oxford Handbook of Comparative Constitutional Law*, Oxford: Oxford University Press, 982–1001.

Baer, S. (2018) 'The rule of – and not by any – Law. On constitutionalism', *Current Legal Problems*, 71(1), 335–368. doi: https://doi.org/10.1093/ clp/cuy010.

Balibar, E. (2012) 'The "impossible" community of the citizens: Past and present problems', *Environment and Planning D: Society and Space*, 30(3), 437–449. doi: https://doi.org/10.1068/d19310.

Ballin, E.H. (2016) 'Citizenship at Home and Across Borders', in M. Kuijer and W. Werner (eds) *Netherlands Yearbook of International Law*, 47, 245–60. doi:10.1007/978-94-6265-207-1_10.

Balot, R. (2017) 'Revisiting the Classical Ideal of Citizenship', in A. Shachar, R. Bauböck, I. Bloemraad and M. Vink (eds) *The Oxford Handbook of Citizenship*, Oxford: Oxford University Press, 17–35.

Banting, K. and Kymlicka, W. (eds) (2017) *The Strains of Commitment: The Political Sources of Solidarity in Diverse Societies*, Oxford: Oxford University Press.

Barber, N.W. (2018) *The Principles of Constitutionalism*, Oxford: Oxford University Press.

Barker, V. (2013) 'Nordic exceptionalism revisited: Explaining the paradox of a Janus-faced penal regime', *Theoretical Criminology*, 17(1), 5–25. doi: https://doi.org/10.1177/1362480612468935.

Barker, V. (2017a) 'Nordic vagabonds: The Roma and the logic of benevolent violence in the Swedish welfare state', *European Journal of Criminology*, 14(1), 120–39. doi: https://doi.org/10.1177/1477370816640141.

Barker, V. (2017b) 'Penal power at the border: Realigning state and nation', *Theoretical Criminology*, 21(4), 441–57. doi: https://doi.org/10.1177/1362480617724827.

Barnard, C. (2019) 'So long, farewell, Auf Wiedersehen, adieu: Brexit and the Charter of Fundamental Rights', *Modern Law Review*, 82(2), 350–66.

Barnard, C., Fraser-Butler, S. and Costello, F. (2019) 'Unsettled status? Vulnerable EU citizens may lose their UK residence overnight', LSE Brexit Blog, 27 November (https://blogs.lse.ac.uk/brexit/2019/11/27/long-read-unsettled-status-vulnerable-eu-citizens-may-lose-their-uk-residence-overnight/).

Barras, A. (2017) 'France citizenship in the aftermath of 2015: Officializing a two-tier system?', *Citizenship Studies*, 21(8), 918–36. doi:10.1080/13621025.2017.1380647.

Bast, J. and Orgad, L. (2017) 'Constitutional identity in the age of global migration', *German Law Journal*, 18(7), 1587–94. doi:10.1017/S2071832200022446.

Batory, A. (2010) 'Kin-state identity in the European context: Citizenship, nationalism and constitutionalism in Hungary', *Nations and Nationalism*, 16(1), 31–48. doi:10.1111/j.1469-8129.2010.00433.x.

Bauböck, R. (2001) 'Recombinant Citizenship', in M. Kohli and A. Woodward (eds) *Inclusions and Exclusions in European Societies*, London: Routledge, 38–58.

Bauböck, R. (2005) 'Expansive citizenship – Voting beyond territory and membership', *PS: Political Science & Politics*, 38(4), 683–7.

Bauböck, R. (ed) (2010a) *Dual Citizenship for Transborder Minorities? How to Respond to the Hungarian-Slovak Tit-for-Tat*, EUI RSCAS, 2010/75, San Domenico di Fiesole: Global Citizenship Observatory (GLOBALCIT), Robert Schuman Centre for Advanced Studies, European University Institute (http://hdl.handle.net/1814/14625).

Bauböck, R. (2010b) 'Studying citizenship constellations', *Journal of Ethnic and Migration Studies*, 36(5), 847–59. doi:10.1080/13691831003764375.

Bauböck, R. (2017) 'Political Membership and Democratic Boundaries', in A. Shachar, R. Bauböck, I. Bloemraad and M. Vink (eds) *The Oxford Handbook of Citizenship*, Oxford: Oxford University Press, 60–82.

Bauböck, R. (2018a) *Democratic Inclusion*, Manchester: Manchester University Press.

Bauböck, R. (2018b) 'Epilogue: International norms for nationality: An elusive goal?', *Netherlands International Law Review*, 65, 497–506. doi: https://doi.org/10.1007/s40802-018-0126-5.

Bauböck, R. (2019a) 'Genuine links and useful passports: Evaluating strategic uses of citizenship', *Journal of Ethnic and Migration Studies*, 45(6), 1015–26. doi:10.1080/1369183X.2018.1440495.

Bauböck, R. (2019b) 'A multilevel theory of democratic secession', *Ethnopolitics*, 18(3), 227–46. doi:10.1080/17449057.2019.1585088.

Bauböck, R. (ed) (2019c) *Debating European Citizenship*, IMISCOE Research Series, Cham, Switzerland: Springer.

Bauböck, R. and Paskalev, V. (2015) 'Cutting genuine links: A normative analysis of citizenship deprivation', *Georgetown Immigration Law Journal*, 30(1), 47–104 (http://hdl.handle.net/1814/42964).

Bauböck, R., Perchinig, B. and Sievers, W. (eds) (2009) *Citizenship Policies in the New Europe*, IMISCOE Research, Amsterdam: Amsterdam University Press.

Bauböck, R., Carens, J.H., Gray, S.W.D., Rubenstein, J.C. and Williams, M.S. (2019) 'Critical exchange: Democratic inclusion beyond the state?' *Contemporary Political Theory*, 18, 88–114. doi: https://doi.org/10.1057/s41296-018-0262-z.

Beckman, L. (2018) 'Democratic legitimacy does not require constitutional referendum. On "the constitution" in theories of constituent power', *European Constitutional Law Review*, 14(3), 567–83, doi:10.1017/S1574019618000287.

Beckman, L. (2019) 'Deciding the demos: Three conceptions of democratic legitimacy', *Critical Review of International Social and Political Philosophy*, 22(4), 412–31. doi:10.1080/13698230.2017.1390661.

Béland, D. (2019) 'Right-wing populism and the politics of insecurity: How President Trump frames migrants as collective threats', *Political Studies Review.* doi: https://doi.org/10.1177/1478929919865131.

Bellamy, R. (2001) 'Constitutive Citizenship versus Constitutional Rights: Republican Reflections on the EU Charter and the Human Rights Act', in T. Campbell, K. Ewing and A. Tomkins (eds) *Sceptical Essays on Human Rights*, Oxford: Oxford University Press, 15–39.

Bellamy, R. (2004) 'Introduction: The Making of Modern Citizenship,' in R. Bellamy, D. Castiglione and E. Santoro (eds) *Lineages of European Citizenship: Rights, Belonging and Participation in Eleven Nation-States*, London: Palgrave, 1–21.

Bellamy, R. (2015) 'A duty-free Europe?', *European Law Journal*, 21(4), 558–65. doi:10.1111/eulj.12142.

Bellamy, R. (2019) *A Republican Europe of States: Cosmopolitanism, Intergovernmentalism and Democracy in the EU*, Cambridge: Cambridge University Press. doi:10.1017/9781139136303.

Ben-Youssef, N. and Tamari, SS (2018) 'Enshrining discrimination: Israel's Nation-State Law', *Journal of Palestine Studies*, 48(1), 73–87. doi:10.1525/jps.2018.48.1.73.

Benhabib, S. (1999) 'Citizens, residents, and aliens in a changing world: Political membership in the global era', *Social Research*, 66(3), 709–44.

Benhabib, S. (2004) *The Rights of Others: Aliens, Residents and Citizens*, Cambridge: Cambridge University Press.

Benson, M. and Lewis, L. (2019) 'Brexit, British people of colour in the EU-27 and everyday racism in Britain and Europe', *Ethnic and Racial Studies*, 42(13), 2211–28. doi:10.1080/01419870.2019.1599134.

Berg, M. and Fiddian-Qasmiyeh, E. (2018) 'Hospitality and hostility towards migrants: Global perspectives – An introduction', *Migration and Society*, 1(1), 1–6. doi:10.3167/arms.2018.010102.

Beydoun, L. (2013) 'The complexities of citizenship among Lebanese immigrants in Sierra Leone', *African Conflict and Peacebuilding Review*, 3(1), 112–43. doi:10.2979/africonfpeacrevi.3.1.112.

Bhambra, G.K. (2017) 'Locating Brexit in the Pragmatics of Race, Citizenship and Empire', in W. Outhwaite (ed) *Brexit: Sociological Responses*, London: Anthem Press, 91–100.

Bhambra, G.K. (2018) 'The State: Postcolonial Histories of the Concept', in O. Rutazibwa and R. Shilliam (eds) *Routledge Handbook of Postcolonial Politics*, Abingdon: Routledge, 200–9.

Bhat, M. (2019) 'The constitutional case against the Citizenship Amendment Bill', *Economic and Political Weekly*, lIV(3), (https://ssrn.com/abstract=3367310).

Bhatta, N. and Morch, M. (2019) 'Citizenship, identity and Nepal's contested 2015 Constitution', *The Diplomat*, 19 September (https://thediplomat.com/2019/09/citizenship-identity-and-nepals-contested-2015-constitution/).

Bianchini, K. (2017) 'The "stateless person" definition in selected EU Member States: Variations of interpretation and application', *Refugee Survey Quarterly*, 36(3), 81–107. doi: https://doi.org/10.1093/rsq/hdx006.

Bijl, P. and van Klinken, G. (2019) 'Citizenship in Asian history', *Citizenship Studies*, 23(3), 189–205. doi:10.1080/13621025.2019.1603268.

Black, H.C. (2004 [1891]) *A Dictionary of Law* (11th edn), Clark, NJ: The Lawbook Exchange.

Blauberger, M. and Kelemen, R.D. (2017) 'Can courts rescue national democracy? Judicial safeguards against democratic backsliding in the EU', *Journal of European Public Policy*, 24(3), 321–36. doi:10.1080/13501763.2016.1229357.

Bloch, N. and Rubenstein, K. (2018) 'Reading down Section 44(i) of the Australian Constitution as a method of affirming Australian Citizenship in the 21st century', *Denning Law Journal*, 30(2), 79–99.

Bloemraad, I. (2015) 'Theorizing and analyzing citizenship in multicultural societies', *The Sociological Quarterly*, 56(4), 591–606. doi:10.1111/tsq.12095.

Bloemraad, I. (2018) 'Theorising the power of citizenship as claims-making', *Journal of Ethnic and Migration Studies*, 44(1), 4–26. doi:10.1080/1369183X.2018.1396108.

Bloemraad, I. and Sheares, A. (2017) 'Understanding membership in a world of global migration: (How) does citizenship matter?', *International Migration Review*, 51(4), 823–67. doi:10.1111/imre.12354.

Blokker, P. (2017) 'Introduction: Constitutional Challenges, Reform, and Acceleration', in P. Blokker (ed) *Constitutional Acceleration within the European Union and Beyond*, London: Routledge, 1–21.

Blokker, P. (2019) 'Populism as a constitutional project', *International Journal of Constitutional Law*, 17(2), 536–53, Available at: https://doi.org/10.1093/icon/moz028.

Blokker, P., Bugarić, B. and Halmai, G. (2019) 'Introduction: Populist constitutionalism: Varieties, complexities, and contradictions', *German Law Journal*, 20(3), 291–5. doi:10.1017/glj.2019.24.

Bloom, T. (2011) 'Contradictions in formal Commonwealth citizenship rights in Commonwealth countries', *The Round Table*, 100(417), 639–54. doi:10.1080/00358533.2011.633381.

Bloom, T. (2017) 'Members of Colonised Groups, Statelessness and the Right to Have Rights', in T. Bloom, K. Tonkiss and P. Cole (eds) *Understanding Statelessness*, Abingdon: Routledge, 153–72.

Bloom, T. (2018) 'Citizenship and colonialism: Liberal concepts of citizenship are not adequate for understanding contemporary individual-state relationships', *Soundings: A Journal of Politics and Culture*, 67, 114–27.

Bloom, T., Manby, B. and Bhadri, K. (2019) 'Why Citizenship is Relevant to Sustainable Development: Considerations for the 2019 High Level Political Forum', Policy Brief, May, European Network on Statelessness (www.statelessness.eu/resources/why-citizenship-relevant-sustainable-development-considerations-2019-high-level-political).

Boll, A.M. (2007) *Multiple Nationality and International Law*, Leiden/Boston, MA: Martinus Nijhoff Publishers.

Bonikowski, B., Halikiopoulou, D., Kaufmann, E. and Rooduijn, M. (2019) 'Populism and nationalism in a comparative perspective: A scholarly exchange', *Nations and Nationalism*, 25(1), 58–81. doi: https://doi.org/10.1111/nana.12480.

Bosniak, L. (2006) *The Citizen and the Alien: Dilemmas of Contemporary Membership*, Princeton, NJ: Princeton University Press.

Bosniak, L. (2007) 'Being here: Ethical territoriality and the rights of immigrants', *Theoretical Inquiries in Law*, 8(2), 389–410.

Bosniak, L. (2010) 'Persons and citizens in constitutional thought', *International Journal of Constitutional Law*, 8(1), 9–29. doi: https://doi.org/10.1093/icon/mop031.

Bosworth, M., Franko, K. and Pickering, S. (2018) 'Punishment, globalization and migration control: "Get them the hell out of here"', *Punishment & Society*, 20(1), 34–53. doi: https://doi.org/10.1177/1462474517738984.

Brandes, T.H. (2018a) 'Law, citizenship and social solidarity: Israel's "loyalty-citizenship" laws as a test case', *Politics, Groups, and Identities*, 6, 39–58. doi:10.1080/21565503.2017.1318758.

Brandes, T.H. (2018b) 'Israel's nation-state law – What now for equality, self-determination, and social solidarity?', Verfassungsblog, 9 November (https://verfassungsblog.de/israels-nation-state-law-what-now-for-equality-self-determination-and-social-solidarity/).

Brandes, T.H. (2019) 'International law in domestic courts in an era of populism', *International Journal of Constitutional Law*, 17(2), 576–96. doi: https://doi.org/10.1093/icon/moz031.

Brändle, V., Galpin, C. and Trenz, H.-J. (2018) 'Marching for Europe? Enacting European citizenship as justice during Brexit', *Citizenship Studies*, 22(8), 810–28. doi:10.1080/13621025.2018.1531825.

Brems, E. (2014) 'Introduction to the Volume', in E. Brems (ed) *The Experiences of Face Veil Wearers in Europe and the Law*, Cambridge: Cambridge University Press, 1–16. doi:10.1017/CBO9781107415591.001.

Brennan, M. and Cohen, M. (2018) 'Citizenship by descent: How Canada's one-generation rule fails to comply with international legal norms', *International Journal of Human Rights*, 22(10), 1302–17. doi:10.1080/13642987.2018.1480095.

Brubaker, R. (1992) *Citizenship and Nationhood in France and Germany*, Cambridge, MA: Harvard University Press.

Brubaker, R. (1996) *Nationalism Reframed*, Cambridge: Cambridge University Press.

Brubaker, R. (1998) 'Myths and Misconceptions in the Study of Nationalism,' in J. Hall (ed) *The State of the Nation*, Cambridge: Cambridge University Press, 272–306.

Brubaker, R. (2011) 'Nationalizing states revisited: Projects and processes of nationalization in post-Soviet states', *Ethnic and Racial Studies*, 34(11), 1785–814. doi:10.1080/01419870.2011.579137.

Brubaker, R. (2017a) '*Political Peoplehood: The Roles of Values, Interests, and Identities* by Rogers M. Smith. Chicago: University of Chicago Press, 2015', *Perspectives on Politics*, 15, 796–7. doi:10.1017/S1537592717001050.

Brubaker, R. (2017b) 'Why populism?', *Theory and Society*, 46, 357–85. doi: https://doi.org/10.1007/s11186-017-9301-7.

Bugarić, B. (2019) 'Could populism be good for constitutional democracy?', *Annual Review of Law and Social Science*, 15, 41–58. doi: https://doi.org/10.1146/annurev-lawsocsci-101518-042927.

Buratti, A. (2019) *Western Constitutionalism: History, Institutions, Comparative Law* (2nd edn), Cham, Switzerland: Springer.

Burchardt, M. and Griera, M. (2019) 'To see or not to see: Explaining intolerance against the "Burqa" in European public space', *Ethnic and Racial Studies*, 42(5), 726–44. doi:10.1080/01419870.2018.1448100.

Burke Wood, P. and Gilmartin, M. (2018) 'Irish enough: Changing narratives of citizenship and national identity in the context of Brexit', *Space and Polity*, 22(2), 224–37. doi:10.1080/13562576.2018.1543824.

Burtenshaw, R. and Jäger, A. (2018) '*The Guardian*'s populism panic', *Jacobin Magazine*, 5 December (https://jacobinmag.com/2018/12/guardian-populism-europe-cas-mudde-hillary-clinton-immigration-tony-blair).

Burton, S. (2019) 'Ambassadors or outsiders? The constitutionality of non-resident voting in *Frank v Canada (Attorney General)*', *International Journal of Constitutional Law* Blog, 31 January (www.iconnectblog.com/2019/01/ambassadors-or-outsiders?-the-constitutionality-of-non-resident-voting-in-frank-v-canada-(attorney-general)).

Caggiano, S. (2018) 'Blood ties: Migrations, state transnationalism and automatic nationality', *Ethnic and Racial Studies*, 41(2), 267–84. doi:10.1080/01419870.2017.1341990.

Calvo, J. (2016) 'Morales-Santana before the US Supreme Court: Gender discrimination in derivative citizenship with consequences for gender equity, parental responsibility and children's well being', *City University of New York Law Review Forum*, 20(1), 1–13.

Cambien, N. (2018) 'Residence rights for EU citizens and their family members: Navigating the new normal', *European Papers*, 3(3), 1333–52. doi:10.15166/2499-8249/273.

Canovan, M. (1999) 'Trust the people! Populism and the two faces of democracy', *Political Studies*, 47(1), 2–16.

Canovan, M. (2005) *The People*, Cambridge: Polity.

Caramani, D. (2017) 'Will vs reason: The populist and technocratic forms of political representation and their critique to party government', *American Political Science Review*, 111(1), 54–67. doi:10.1017/S0003055416000538.

Caramani, D. and Grotz, F. (2015) 'Beyond citizenship and residence? Exploring the extension of voting rights in the age of globalization', *Democratization*, 22(5), 799–819.

Carden, J. (2019) 'The Pompeo Commission is weaponizing human rights', *The Nation*, 30 July (www.thenation.com/article/mike-pompeo-human-rights-mary-ann-glendon/).

Carens, J. (2013) *The Ethics of Immigration*, Oxford: Oxford University Press.

Carens, J. (2016) 'In Defense of Birthright Citizenship', in S. Fine and L. Ypi (eds) *Migration in Political Theory: The Ethics of Movement and Membership*, Oxford: Oxford University Press, 205–24.

Carlaw, J. (2017) 'Authoritarian populism and Canada's conservative decade (2006–2015) in citizenship and immigration: The politics and practices of Kenneyism and neo-conservative multiculturalism', *Journal of Canadian Studies/Revue d'études canadiennes*, 51(3), 782–816. doi: https://doi.org/10.3138/jcs.2017-0054.

Castro, A. (2020) 'Three important lessons from the recent decision of the Colombian Constitutional Court', GLOBALCIT Blog, 19 February (http://globalcit.eu/three-important-lessons-from-the-recent-decision-of-the-colombian-constitutional-court/).

Celikates, R. (2019) 'Constituent power beyond exceptionalism: Irregular migration, disobedience, and (re-)constitution', *Journal of International Political Theory*, 15(1), 67–81. doi: https://doi.org/10.1177/1755088218808311.

Chacón, J.M. (2018) 'Citizenship matters: Conceptualizing belonging in an era of fragile inclusions', *University of California at Davis Law Review*, 52(1), 1–80.

Chacón, R. (2001) *Pueblos Indígenas de Costa Rica: 10 Años de Jurisprudencia Constitucional*, San José, Costa Rica: Serie Normativa y Jurisprudencia Indígena (http://unpan1.un.org/intradoc/groups/public/documents/icap/unpan046677.pdf).

Chandrachud, A. (2020) *Secularism and the Citizenship Amendment Act* (https://papers.ssrn.com/sol3/papers.cfm?abstract_id=3513828).

Chang, W.-C. (2019) 'Back into the political? Rethinking judicial, legal, and transnational constitutionalism', *International Journal of Constitutional Law*, 17(2), 453–60. doi: https://doi.org/10.1093/icon/moz055.

Chaudhuri, B. and König, L. (2018) 'The Aadhaar scheme: A cornerstone of a new citizenship regime in India?', *Contemporary South Asia*, 26(2), 127–42. doi:10.1080/09584935.2017.1369934.

Chilton, A. and Versteeg, M. (2018) 'Courts' limited ability to protect constitutional rights', *The University of Chicago Law Review*, 85(2), 293–336.

Christopoulos, D. (2017) 'An unexpected reform in the maelstrom of the crisis: Greek nationality in the times of the memoranda (2010–2015)', *Citizenship Studies*, 21(4), 483–94. doi:10.1080/13621025.2017.1307604.

Christopoulos, D. (2019) 'At last, a law on expatriate vote in Greece', GLOBALCIT Blog, 16 December (http://globalcit.eu/at-last-a-law-on-expatriate-vote-in-greece/).

Chryssogelos, A. (2018) 'State transformation and populism: From the internationalized to the neo-sovereign state?', *Politics*. doi: https://doi.org/10.1177/0263395718803830.

Chung, E. (2017) 'Citizenship in non-western contexts', in A. Shachar, R. Bauböck, I. Bloemraad and M. Vink (eds) *The Oxford Handbook of Citizenship*, Oxford: Oxford University Press, 431–52.

Chung, E. and Kim, D. (2012) 'Citizenship and marriage in a globalizing world: Multicultural families and monocultural nationality laws in Korea and Japan', *Indiana Journal of Global Legal Studies*, 19, 195–219.

Cloots, E. (2017) 'The legal limits of citizenship deprivation as a counterterror strategy', *European Public Law*, 23(1), 57–92.

Cobb, J. (2019) 'Donald Trump's idea of selective citizenship', *The New Yorker*, 21 July (www.newyorker.com/magazine/2019/07/29/donald-trumps-idea-of-selective-citizenship).

Coca-Vila, I. (2019) 'Our "barbarians" at the gate: On the undercriminalized citizenship deprivation as a counterterrorism tool', *Criminal Law and Philosophy*. doi: https://doi.org/10.1007/s11572-019-09517-5.

Coetzee, A. (2019) 'Revisiting citizenship in the South African postcolony: Empire, white romance and the (continued) abjection of the black woman', *Postcolonial Studies*, 22(3), 345–61. doi:10.1080/13688790.2019.1638520.

Cohen, E. (2009) *Semi-Citizenship in Democratic Politics*, Cambridge, Cambridge University Press.

Cohen, E. (2010) '*Jus tempus* in the Magna Carta: The sovereignty of time in modern politics and citizenship', *PS: Political Science & Politics*, 43(3), 463–66. doi: https://doi.org/10.1017/S1049096510000582.

Cohen, E. (2018) *The Political Value of Time: Citizenship, Duration, and Democratic Justice*, Cambridge: Cambridge University Press.

Cohen, J. (1999) 'Changing paradigms of citizenship and the exclusiveness of the demos', *International Sociology*, 14(3), 245–68.

Cohen, J. (2019) 'Populism and the politics of resentment' *Jus Cogens*, 1, 5–39. doi: https://doi.org/10.1007/s42439-019-00009-7.

Cold-Ravnkilde, S.M. (2019) 'Contested norms in fragmented institutions: Gender equality in South Africa's development cooperation', *Progress in Development Studies*, 19(3), 211–31. doi: https://doi.org/10.1177/1464993419853444.

Cole, D. (2007) 'Against citizenship as a predicate for basic rights', *Fordham Law Review*, 75, 2541–8.

Collins, K. (2014) 'Illegitimate borders: *Jus sanguinis* citizenship and the legal construction of family, race, and nation', *Yale Law Journal*, 123(7), 2134–235.

Collyer, M. (2013) *Emigration Nations: Policies and Ideologies of Emigrant Engagement*, Basingstoke: Palgrave Macmillan.

Collyer, M. (2014) 'A geography of extra-territorial citizenship: Explanations of external voting', *Migration Studies*, 2(1), 55–72.

Colón-Ríos, J. (2014) 'Constituent power, the rights of nature, and universal jurisdiction', *McGill Law Journal/Revue de droit de McGill*, 60(1), 127–72.

Conway, G. and Katyal, N. (2018) 'Trump's proposal to end birthright citizenship is unconstitutional', *Washington Post*, 30 October.

Copus, C. (2018) 'The Brexit referendum: Testing the support of *elites* and their allies for democracy; or, racists, bigots and xenophobes, oh my!', *British Politics*, 13, 90–104. doi: https://doi.org/10.1057/s41293-018-0070-3.

Cotterrell, R. (1998) 'Why must legal ideas be interpreted sociologically?', *Journal of Law and Society*, 25(2), 171–92.

Corrias, L. (2016) 'Populism in a constitutional key: Constituent power, popular sovereignty and constitutional identity', *European Constitutional Law Review*, 12(1), 6–26. doi:10.1017/S1574019616000031.

Craig, P. (2019) The Supreme Court, Prorogation and Constitutional Principle, *Public Law*, Oxford Legal Studies Research Paper No 57/2019 (https://ssrn.com/abstract=3477487).

Crenshaw, K. (1989) 'Demarginalizing the intersection of race and sex: A black feminist critique of antidiscrimination doctrine, feminist theory and antiracist politics', *University of Chicago Legal Forum*, 1(8) (http://chicagounbound.uchicago.edu/uclf/vol1989/iss1/8).

Crenshaw, K. (1991) 'Mapping the margins: Intersectionality, identity politics, and violence against women of color', *Stanford Law Review*, 43(6), 1241–99.

Crewe, I. (2020) 'Authoritarian Populism and Brexit in the UK in Historical Perspective', in I. Crewe and D. Sanders (eds) *Authoritarian Populism and Liberal Democracy*, Cham, Switzerland: Palgrave Macmillan, 15–31. doi: https://doi.org/10.1007/978-3-030-17997-7_2.

Csehi, R. (2019) 'Neither episodic, nor destined to failure? The endurance of Hungarian populism after 2010', *Democratization*, 26(6), 1011–27. doi: 10.1080/13510347.2019.1590814.

Culliton-González, K. (2012) 'Born in the Americas: Birthright citizenship and human rights', *Harvard Human Rights Journal*, 25, 127–82.

D'Angelo, A. and Kofman, E. (2018) 'From mobile workers to fellow citizens and back again? The future status of EU citizens in the UK', *Social Policy and Society*, 17(2), 331–43. doi:10.1017/S1474746417000495.

D'Oliveira, H.U.J. (2018) *Brexit, Nationality and Union Citizenship: Bottom Up*, Working Paper, EUI RSCAS, 2018/49, Global Governance Programme-317, GLOBALCIT, San Domenico di Fiesole: Global Citizenship Observatory (GLOBALCIT), Robert Schuman Centre for Advanced Studies, European University Institute (http://hdl.handle.net/1814/59115).

Daly, T.G. and Wiebusch, M. (2018) 'The African Court on Human and Peoples' Rights: Mapping resistance against a young court', *International Journal of Law in Context*, 14(2), 294–313. doi: https://doi.org/10.1017/S1744552318000083.

Dann, P., Riegner, M. and Bönnemann, M. (eds) (2020) *The Global South and Comparative Constitutional Law*, Oxford: Oxford University Press.

Dauvergne, C. (2007) 'Citizenship with a vengeance', *Theoretical Inquiries in Law*, 8(2), 489–507.

Dauvergne, C. (2013) 'How the charter has failed non-citizens in Canada: Reviewing thirty years of Supreme Court of Canada jurisprudence', *McGill Law Journal/Revue de droit de McGill*, 58(3), 663–728. doi: https://doi.org/10.7202/1018393ar.

Dauvergne, C. (2019) 'Gendering Islamophobia to better understand immigration laws', *Journal of Ethnic and Migration Studies*. doi:10.1080/1369183X.2018.1561066.

Day, S. and Shaw, J. (2003) 'The boundaries of suffrage and external conditionality: Estonia as an applicant member of the EU', *European Public Law*, 9(2), 211–36.

de Groot, D. (2017) '(Dual national) politicians – between "pure-bloods" and "half-bloods"', NCCR on the move blog, 14 November (http://blog.nccr-onthemove.ch/dual-national-politicians-between-pure-bloods-and-half-bloods/).

de Groot, G.-R. (1989) *Staatsangehörigkeitsrecht im Wandel: Eine Rechtsvergleichende Studie über Erwerbs- und Verlustgründe der Staatsangehörigkeit*, Köln: Carl Heymans Verlag.

de Groot, G.-R. (1998) 'The Relationship between Nationality Legislation of the Member States of the European Union and European Citizenship', in M. La Torre (ed) *European Citizenship: An Institutional Challenge*, The Hague/London: Kluwer Law International, 115–35.

de Groot, G.-R. (2004) 'Towards a European nationality law', *Electronic Journal of Comparative Law*, 8(3), October.

de Groot, G.-R. (2012) 'Nationality Law', in J.M. Smits (ed) *Elgar Encyclopedia of Comparative Law*, Cheltenham: Edward Elgar (2nd edn), 600–19.

de Groot, G.-R. (2016) 'Towards a Toolbox for Nationality Legislation', Text of the Valedictory Lecture as Professor of Comparative Law and Private International Law at Maastricht University, 14 October.

de Groot, G.-R. and Vonk, O. (2016) *International Standards on Nationality Law*, Oisterwijk: Wolf Legal Publishers.

de Groot, G.-R. and Vonk, O. (2018) 'Acquisition of nationality by birth on a particular territory or establishment of parentage: Global trends regarding *ius sanguinis* and *ius soli*', *Netherlands International Law Review*, 65, 319–35. doi: https://doi.org/10.1007/s40802-018-0118-5.

de Koning, A., Jaffe, R. and Koster, M. (2015) 'Citizenship agendas in and beyond the nation-state: (En)countering framings of the good citizen', *Citizenship Studies*, 19(2), 121–7. doi:10.1080/13621025.2015.1005940.

de la Torre, C. (2017a) 'Populism in Latin America', in C.R. Kaltwasser, P. Taggart, P. Espejo and P. Ostiguy (eds) *The Oxford Handbook of Populism*, Oxford: Oxford University Press, 195–213.

de la Torre, C. (2017b) 'Populist citizenship in the Bolivarian revolutions', *Middle Atlantic Review of Latin American Studies*, 1(1), 4–29. doi: http://doi.org/10.23870/marlasv1n1ct.

Denza, E. (2018) 'Nationality and diplomatic protection', *Netherlands International Law Review*, 65, 463–80. doi: https://doi.org/10.1007/s40802-018-0119-4.

Dev, A. (2019) 'India is testing the bounds of citizenship', *The Atlantic*, 31 August (www.theatlantic.com/international/archive/2019/08/india-citizenship-assam-nrc/597208/).

Diamond, L. (2002) 'Elections without democracy: Thinking about hybrid regimes', *Journal of Democracy*, 13(2), 21–35.

Diamond, P., Nedergaard, P. and Rosamond, B. (eds) (2018) *Routledge Handbook of the Politics of Brexit*, Abingdon: Routledge.

Dobrowolsky, A. (2017) 'Bad versus Big Canada: State imaginaries of immigration and citizenship', *Studies in Political Economy*, 98(3), 197–222. doi:10.1080/07078552.2017.1343001.

Dommett, K. and Pearce, W. (2019) 'What do we know about public attitudes towards experts? Reviewing survey data in the United Kingdom and European Union', *Public Understanding of Science*, 28(6), 669–78. doi: https://doi.org/10.1177/0963662519852038.

Donnan, S. (2019) '"Imposed citizenship": How Brexit is already quietly affecting Northern Ireland's Irish citizens', *Prospect Magazine*, 8 May (www.prospectmagazine.co.uk/other/emma-de-souza-northern-ireland-citizenship-brexit-irish-british).

Dörr, O. (2006) 'Nationality', in *Max Planck Encyclopedia of Public International Law*, Oxford: Oxford University Press.

Dowdle, M. and Wilkinson, M. (eds) (2017) *Constitutionalism beyond Liberalism*, Cambridge: Cambridge University Press.

Doyle, O. (2019) 'Populist constitutionalism and constituent power', *German Law Journal*, 20(2), 161–80. doi:10.1017/glj.2019.11.

Dumbrava, C. (2014a) *Nationality, Citizenship and Ethno-National Belonging: Preferential Membership Policies in Europe*, Basingstoke: Palgrave Macmillan.

Dumbrava, C. (2014b) 'External citizenship in EU countries', *Ethnic and Racial Studies*, 37(13), 2340–60. doi:10.1080/01419870.2013.826812.

Dumbrava, C. (2015) 'Super-foreigners and sub-citizens: Mapping ethno-national hierarchies of foreignness and citizenship in Europe', *Ethnopolitics*, 14(3), 296–310. doi:10.1080/17449057.2014.994883.

Dumbrava, C. (2018) 'Bloodlines and Belonging: Time to Abandon *Jus Sanguinis?*', in R. Bauböck (ed) *Debating Transformations of National Citizenship*, Cham, Switzerland: Springer, 73–81.

Dumbrava, C. (2019) 'The ethno-demographic impact of co-ethnic citizenship in Central and Eastern Europe', *Journal of Ethnic and Migration Studies*, 45(6), 958–74. doi:10.1080/1369183X.2018.1440490.

Dummett, A. (2006) 'United Kingdom', in R. Bauböck, E. Ersbøll, K. Groenendijk and H. Waldrauch (eds) *Acquisition and Loss of Nationality: Policies and Trends in 15 European States. Volume 2: Country Analyses*, Amsterdam: Amsterdam University Press, 551–85.

Dummett, A. and Nicol, A. (1990) *Subjects, Citizens and Aliens: Nationality and Immigration Law*, London: Weidenfeld & Nicolson.

Džankić, J. (2017) 'Dimensions of citizenship policy in the post-Yugoslav space: Divergent paths', *Central and Eastern European Migration Review*, 6(1), 31–48. doi:10.17467/ceemr.2017.05.

Džankić, J. (2019a) *The Global Market for Investor Citizenship*, Cham, Switzerland: Palgrave Macmillan/Springer.

Džankić, J. (2019b) 'Investor citizenship and refusal as political practice of states and non-citizens', GLOBALCIT Blog, 11 February (http://globalcit.eu/investor-citizenship-and-refusal-as-political-practice-for-states-and-non-citizens/).

Džankić, J. (2019c) 'What's in the EC's report on investor citizenship?', GLOBALCIT Blog, 23 January (http://globalcit.eu/whats-in-the-ecs-report-on-investor-citizenship/).

Džankić, J. and Keil, S. (2019) 'The Europeanisation of Contested States: Comparing Bosnia and Herzegovina, Macedonia and Montenegro', in J. Džankić, S. Keil and M. Kmezić (eds) *The Europeanisation of the Western Balkans: A Failure of EU Conditionality?*, Cham, Switzerland: Palgrave Macmillan/Springer, 181–206. doi: https://doi.org/10.1007/978-3-319-91412-1_9.

Dzehtsiarou, K. (2017/18) 'What is law for the European Court of Human Rights?', *Georgetown Journal of International Law*, 49(1), 89–134.

Edwards, A. (2014) 'The Meaning of Nationality in International Law in an Era of Human Rights', in A. Edwards and L. van Waas (eds) *Nationality and Statelessness under International Law*, Cambridge: Cambridge University Press, 11–43. doi:10.1017/CBO9781139506007.002.

Edwards, S. (2016) 'Targeting Muslims through Women's Dress: The Niqab and the Psychological War against Muslims', in J. Scutt (ed) *Women, Law and Culture*, Cham, Switzerland: Palgrave Macmillan, 51–68.

Eisenberg, A. and Lenard, P.T. (2018) 'The theory and politics of the second-class citizenship', *Politics, Groups, and Identities*. doi:10.1080/21565503.2017.1420618.

Elkins, Z., Ginsburg, T. and Melton, J. (2009) *The Endurance of National Constitutions*, Cambridge: Cambridge University Press. doi:10.1017/CBO9780511817595.

Ellermann, A. (2019) 'Discrimination in migration and citizenship', *Journal of Ethnic and Migration Studies*. doi:10.1080/1369183X.2018.1561053.

Epps, G. (2019) 'A Supreme Court case that will affect every aspect of national life', *The Atlantic*, 21 April (www.theatlantic.com/ideas/archive/2019/04/can-census-ask-about-citizenship/587503/).

Escobar, C. (2015a) *Report on Citizenship Law: Colombia*, San Domenico di Fiesole: Global Citizenship Observatory (GLOBALCIT), Robert Schuman Centre for Advanced Studies, European University Institute (http://hdl.handle.net/1814/35997).

Escobar, C. (2015b) 'Immigrant enfranchisement in Latin America: From strongmen to universal citizenship', *Democratization*, 22(5), 927–50. doi:10.1080/13510347.2014.979322.

Espejo, P. (2017) 'Populism and the Idea of the People', in C.R. Kaltwasser, P. Taggart, P. Espejo and P. Ostiguy (eds) *The Oxford Handbook of Populism*, Oxford: Oxford University Press, 607–28.

Fabbrini, F. and Sajó, A. (2019) 'The dangers of constitutional identity', *European Law Journal*. doi: https://doi.org/10.1111/eulj.12332.

Falk, R. (2000) 'The decline of citizenship in an era of globalization', *Citizenship Studies*, 4(1), 5–17. doi:10.1080/136210200109997.

Farahat, A. (2019) 'Recent changes in German citizenship law', GLOBALCIT News Item, 23 July (http://globalcit.eu/recent-changes-in-german-citizenship-law/).

Fargues, E. (2017) 'The revival of citizenship deprivation in France and the UK as an instance of citizenship renationalisation', *Citizenship Studies*, 21(8), 984–98. doi:10.1080/13621025.2017.1377152.

Fargues, E. (2019) 'Simply a matter of compliance with the rules? The moralising and responsibilising function of fraud-based citizenship deprivation in France and the UK', *Citizenship Studies*, 23(4), 356–71. doi:10.1080/13621025.2019.1616451.

Farnsworth, K. and Irving, K. (2012) 'Fiscal crisis, financial crisis, and the great recession', in B. Greve (ed) *The Routledge Handbook of the Welfare State*, Abingdon: Routledge, 307–18.

Farr, J. (2005) 'Point: The Westphalia legacy and the modern nation-state', *International Social Science Review*, 80(3/4), 156–9.

Favell, A. (2010) 'European identity and European citizenship in three "Eurocities": A sociological approach to the European Union', *Politique Européenne*, 30, 187–224. doi:10.3917/poeu.030.0187.

Favell, A. (2019) 'Brexit: A requiem for the post-national society?', *Global Discourse: An Interdisciplinary Journal of Current Affairs*, 9(1), 157–68. doi: https://doi.org/10.1332/204378918X15453934506021.

Fekete, L. (2016) 'Hungary: Power, punishment and the "Christian-national idea"', *Race and Class*, 57(4), 39–53. doi: https://doi.org/10.1177/0306396815624607.

Fernández, C. (2019) 'The unbearable lightness of being Swedish? On the ideological thinness of a liberal citizenship regime', *Ethnicities*, 19(4), 674–92. doi: https://doi.org/10.1177/1468796819843531.

Finck, M. (2015) 'Towards an ever closer union between residents and citizens?', *European Constitutional Law Review*, 11(1), 78–98.

Fine, S. and Ypi, L. (eds) (2016) *Migration in Political Theory: The Ethics of Movement and Membership*, Oxford: Oxford University Press.

Fitzgerald, D. and Cook-Martín, D. (2014) *Culling the Masses*, Cambridge, MA: Harvard University Press.

Font, N., Graziano, P. and Tsakatika, M. (2019) 'Varieties of inclusionary populism? SYRIZA, Podemos and the Five Star Movement', *Government and Opposition*. doi:10.1017/gov.2019.17.

Forst, R. (2014) 'Toleration and democracy', *Journal of Social Philosophy*, 45(1), 65–75. doi:10.1111/josp.12046.

Foster, M. (2009) '"An alien" by the barest of threads' – The legality of the deportation of long-term residents from Australia', *Melbourne University Law Review*, 33(2), 483–541.

Foster, M. and Lambert, H. (2016) 'Statelessness as a human rights issue: A concept whose time has come', *International Journal of Refugee Law*, 28(4), 564–84. doi: https://doi.org/10.1093/ijrl/eew044.

Fowkes, J. and Hailbronner, M. (2019) 'Decolonizing Eastern Europe: A global perspective on 1989 and the world it made', *International Journal of Constitutional Law*, 17(2), 497–509. doi: https://doi.org/10.1093/icon/moz040.

Fox, J. (2005) 'Unpacking "transnational citizenship"', *Annual Review of Political Science*, 8, 171–201. doi: https://doi.org/10.1146/annurev.polisci.7.012003.104851.

Fox, J. and Vermeersch, P. (2010) 'Backdoor nationalism', *European Journal of Sociology*, 51(2), 325–57. doi:10.1017/S0003975610000159.

Fradera, J. (2018) *The Imperial Nation: Citizens and Subjects in the British, French, Spanish, and American Empires*, Princeton, NJ: Princeton University Press.

Fransman, L. (2009) 'Commonwealth, Subjects and Nationality Rules', in *Max Planck Encyclopedia of Public International Law*, Oxford: Oxford University Press.

Fraser, N. (1995) 'From redistribution to recognition? Dilemmas of justice in a "post-socialist" age', *New Left Review*, 212, 68–93.

Fraser, N. (2016) 'Progressive neoliberalism versus reactionary populism: A choice that feminists should refuse', *NORA – Nordic Journal of Feminist and Gender Research*, 24(4), 281–4. doi:10.1080/08038740.2016.1278263.

Freeden, M. (2017) 'After the Brexit referendum: revisiting populism as an ideology', *Journal of Political Ideologies*, 22:1, 1-11, doi:10.1080/135 69317.2016.1260813.

Freyburg, T., Huber, R. and Mohrenberg, S. (2019) 'Do populist-leaning citizens support direct democracy?', *Democratic Audit*, 18 August (www.democraticaudit.com/2019/08/18/do-populist-leaning-citizens-support-direct-democracy/).

Fripp, E. (2015) *The Law and Practice of Expulsion and Exclusion from the United Kingdom: Deportation, Removal, Exclusion and Deprivation of Citizenship*, Oxford: Hart Publishing.

Fripp, E. (2016) *Nationality and Statelessness in the International Law of Refugee Status*, Oxford: Hart Publishing.

Frost, A. (2019) 'The revival of denaturalisation under the Trump administration', GLOBALCIT Blog, 29 January (http://globalcit.eu/the-revival-of-denaturalisation-under-the-trump-administration/).

Fuchs, A. (2019) 'The nation-state law, one year later: What has changed?', *The Times of Israel*, 31 July (https://blogs.timesofisrael.com/the-nation-state-law-one-year-later-what-has-changed).

Fukuyama, F. (1992) *The End of History and the Last Man*, London: Penguin.

Gallagher-Teske, K. and Giesing, Y. (2017) 'Dual citizenship in the EU', *ifo DICE Report*, 3/2017, September, 15, 43–7.

Galligan, D.J. (2013a) 'The sovereignty deficit of modern constitutions', *Oxford Journal of Legal Studies*, 33(4), 703–32. doi: https://doi.org/10.1093/ojls/gqt025.

Galligan, D.J. (2013b) 'The People, the Constitution, and the Idea of Representation', in D.J. Galligan and M. Versteeg (eds) *Social and Political Foundations of Constitutions*, Cambridge: Cambridge University Press, 134–56. doi:10.1017/CBO9781139507509.008.

Galligan, D.J. and Versteeg, M. (2013a) 'Theoretical Perspectives on the Social and Political Foundations of Constitutions', in D.J. Galligan and M. Versteeg (eds) *Social and Political Foundations of Constitutions*, Cambridge: Cambridge University Press, 3–48. doi:10.1017/CBO9781139507509.003.

Galligan, D.J. and Versteeg, M. (eds) (2013b) *Social and Political Foundations of Constitutions*, Cambridge: Cambridge University Press.

Gammerl, B. (2009) 'Subjects, citizens and others: The handling of ethnic differences in the British and the Habsburg Empires (late nineteenth and early twentieth century)', *European Review of History – Revue européenne d'histoire*, 16(4), 523–49. doi:10.1080/13507480903063829.

Gans, C. (2017) 'Citizenship and Nationhood', in A. Shachar, R. Bauböck, I. Bloemraad and M. Vink (eds) *The Oxford Handbook of Citizenship*, Oxford: Oxford University Press, 107–28.

Gardbaum, S. (2011) 'The Structure and Scope of Constitutional Rights', in T. Ginsburg and R. Dixon (eds) *Comparative Constitutional Law*, Cheltenham: Edward Elgar, 387–405.

Gardbaum, S. (2019) *The Counter-Playbook: Resisting the Populist Assault on Separation of Powers*, UCLA School of Law, Public Law Research Paper No 19-45 (https://ssrn.com/abstract=3485761).

Gardner, J.P. (ed) (1997) *Citizenship: The White Paper*, London: Institute for Citizenship Studies/The British Institute of International and Comparative Law.

Garner, B.A. and Black, H.C. (2009) *Black's Law Dictionary* (9th edn), St Paul, MN: West.

Garner, O. (2018) 'The existential crisis of citizenship of the European Union: The argument for an autonomous status', *Cambridge Yearbook of European Legal Studies*, 20, 116–46. doi: https://doi.org/10.1017/cel.2018.6.

Gearty, C. (2019) 'States of denial. What the search for a UK Bill of Rights tell us about human rights protection today', *European Human Rights Law Review*, 5, 415–21.

Gentleman, A. (2018) 'Perspectives on the *Windrush* generation scandal: An account by Amelia Gentleman', British Library Windrush Stories, 4 October (www.bl.uk/windrush/articles/perspectives-on-the-windrush-generation-scandal-an-account-by-amelia-gentleman).

Gentleman, A. (2019) *The Windrush Betrayal: Exposing the Hostile Environment*, London: Guardian/Faber Publishing.

Gibney, M.J. (2013) 'Should citizenship be conditional? The ethics of denationalization', *The Journal of Politics*, 75(3), 646–58.

Gibney, M.J. (2017) 'Denationalisation', in A. Shachar, R. Bauböck, I. Bloemraad and M. Vink (eds) *The Oxford Handbook of Citizenship*, Oxford: Oxford University Press, 358–82.

Gibney, M.J. (2019) 'Denationalisation and discrimination', *Journal of Ethnic and Migration Studies*. doi:10.1080/1369183X.2018.1561065.

Ginsburg, T. and Dixon, R. (2011) 'Introduction', in T. Ginsburg and R. Dixon (eds) *Comparative Constitutional Law*, Cheltenham: Edward Elgar, 1–15.

Ginsburg, T. and Simpser, A. (eds) (2013) *Constitutions in Authoritarian Regimes*, Cambridge: Cambridge University Press. doi:10.1017/CBO9781107252523.

Ginsburg, T., Elkins, Z. and Melton, J. (2009) 'The Lifespan of Written Constitutions', The University of Chicago Law School, 15 October (www.law.uchicago.edu/news/lifespan-written-constitutions).

Gitelman, Z. (1982) 'Exiting from the Soviet Union: Emigrés or refugees?', *Michigan Journal of International Law*, 39(1), 43–61 (https://repository.law.umich.edu/mjil/vol3/iss1/3).

Glen, P.J. (2007) 'Wong Kim Ark and Sentencia que Declara Constitucional la Ley General de Migración 285-04 in comparative perspective: Constitutional interpretation, jus soli principles, and political morality', *University of Miami Inter-American Law Review*, 39, 67–109.

Glenn, H.P. (2013) *The Cosmopolitan State*, Oxford: Oxford University Press.

GLOBALCIT (2016) 'Citizenship Law Indicators', Version 2.0, San Domenico di Fiesole: Global Citizenship Observatory, Robert Schuman Centre for Advanced Studies, European University Institute (http://globalcit.eu/citizenship-law-indicators/).

GLOBALCIT (2017a) 'Global Database on Modes of Acquisition of Citizenship', Version 1.0, San Domenico di Fiesole: Global Citizenship Observatory, Robert Schuman Centre for Advanced Studies, European University Institute (http://globalcit.eu/acquisition-citizenship/).

GLOBALCIT (2017b) 'Global Database on Modes of Loss of Citizenship', Version 1.0, San Domenico di Fiesole: Global Citizenship Observatory, Robert Schuman Centre for Advanced Studies, European University Institute (http://globalcit.eu/loss-of-citizenship/).

GLOBALCIT (2019) 'Global Birthright Indicators', San Domenico di Fiesole: Global Citizenship Observatory, Robert Schuman Centre for Advanced Studies, European University Institute (http://globalcit.eu/databases/global-birthright-indicators/).

Gogoi, S., Chakraborty, G. and Saikia, P.J. (2018) 'Assam against itself: A reply to Sanjib Baruah', South Asia @ LSE Blog, 21 March (https://blogs.lse.ac.uk/southasia/2018/03/21/assam-against-itself-a-reply-to-sanjib-baruah/).

Gorman, D. (2007) *Imperial Citizenship: Empire and the Question of Belonging*, Manchester: Manchester University Press.

Górny, A. and Pudzianowska, D. (2013) *Report on Citizenship Law: Poland*, Country Report 2013/26, San Domenico di Fiesole: Global Citizenship Observatory (GLOBALCIT), Robert Schuman Centre for Advanced Studies, European University Institute (http://hdl.handle.net/1814/19631).

Gosewinkel, D. (2001) 'Citizenship, Subjecthood, Nationality: Concepts of Belonging in the Age of Modern Nation States', in K. Eder and B. Giesen (eds) *European Citizenship between National Legacies and Postnational Projects*, Oxford: Oxford University Press, 17–35.

Gosewinkel, D. (2008) 'The dominance of nationality? Nation and citizenship from the late nineteenth century onwards: A comparative European perspective', *German History*, 26(1), 92–108. doi: https://doi.org/10.1093/gerhis/ghm005.

Gosewinkel, D. (2009) 'Introduction: Neither East nor West – New approaches to citizenship in modern European history', *European Review of History – Revue européenne d'histoire*, 16, 499–501. doi:10.1080/13507480903063738.

Gosewinkel, D. (2017) 'Citizenship as Political Membership: A Fundamental Strand of Twentieth- and Twenty-first-Century European History', in J. Mackert and B. Turner (eds) *The Transformation of Citizenship. Volume 2: Boundaries of Inclusion and Exclusion*, London/New York: Routledge, 15–34.

Gover, K. (2017) 'Indigenous Citizenship in Settler States', in A. Shachar, R. Bauböck, I. Bloemraad and M. Vink (eds) *The Oxford Handbook of Citizenship*, Oxford: Oxford University Press, 453–77.

Goździak, E.M. and Márton, P. (2018) 'Where the wild things are: Fear of Islam and the anti-refugee rhetoric in Hungary and in Poland', *Central and Eastern European Migration Review*, 7(2), 125–51. doi:10.17467/ceemr.2018.04.

Graber, M., Levinson, S. and Tushnet, M. (eds) (2018) *Constitutional Democracy in Crisis?*, Oxford: Oxford University Press.

Grant, M. (2018) 'The Windrush Generation have been treated appallingly. EU migrants may expect an even worse deal', LSE Brexit Blog, 20 April (https://blogs.lse.ac.uk/brexit/2018/04/20/the-windrush-generation-have-been-treated-appallingly-eu-migrants-may-expect-an-even-worse-deal/).

Graves, F. and Valpy, M. (2018) 'Canada is a tinderbox for populism. The 2019 election could spark it', *Maclean's*, 3 December (www.macleans.ca/politics/canada-is-a-tinderbox-for-populism-the-2019-election-could-spark-it/).

Gray, B. (2011) 'From exile of citizens to deportation of non-citizens: Ancient Greece as a mirror to illuminate a modern transition', *Citizenship Studies*, 15(5), 565–82. doi:10.1080/13621025.2011.583788.

Green, H.D. (2014) 'The quasi-constitutional right to vote in the United Kingdom', *Election Law Journal: Rules, Politics, and Policy*, 13(4), 493–516. doi: https://doi.org/10.1089/elj.2013.0193.

Green, H.D. (2018) 'Article 3, First Protocol: The Right to Free Elections', in D. Harris, M. O'Boyle, E. Bates and C. Buckley (eds) *Law of the European Convention on Human Rights* (4th edn), Oxford: Oxford University Press, Chapter 22.

Green, N.L. (2009) 'Expatriation, expatriates, and expats: The American transformation of a concept', *The American Historical Review*, 114(2), 307–28. doi: https://doi.org/10.1086/ahr.114.2.307.

Greve, B. (2012) 'Future of the welfare state?', in B. Greve (ed) *The Routledge Handbook of the Welfare State*, Abingdon: Routledge, 433–9.

Grigera, J. (2017) 'Populism in Latin America: Old and new populisms in Argentina and Brazil', *International Political Science Review*, 38(4), 441–55. doi: https://doi.org/10.1177/0192512117701510.

Grimm, D. (2012) 'Types of Constitutions', in M. Rosenfeld and A. Sajó (eds) *Oxford Handbook of Comparative Constitutional Law*, Oxford: Oxford University Press, 98–132.

Grimm, D. (2015) 'The democratic costs of constitutionalisation: The European case', *European Law Journal*, 21(4), 460–73.

Gross, A. and de la Fuente, A. (2019), 'Citizenship once meant whiteness. Here's how that changed', *The Washington Post*, 18 July (www.washingtonpost.com/outlook/2019/07/18/citizenship-once-meant-whiteness-heres-how-that-changed/).

Grote, R. (2018) 'Definition of Constitutions', in R. Grote, F. Lachenmann and R. Wolfrum (eds) *Max Planck Encyclopedia of Comparative Constitutional Law*, Oxford: Oxford University Press (https://global.oup.com).

Guma, T. and Jones, R.D. (2019) '"Where are we going to go now?" European Union migrants' experiences of hostility, anxiety, and (non-)belonging during Brexit', *Population, Space and Place*, 25(1), e2198. doi: https://doi.org/10.1002/psp.2198.

Gustavsson, G. (2019) 'Liberal national identity: Thinner than conservative, thicker than civic?', *Ethnicities*, 19(4), 693–711. doi: https://doi.org/10.1177/1468796819843542.

Gyollai, D. and Amatrudo, A. (2019) 'Controlling irregular migration: International human rights standards and the Hungarian legal framework', *European Journal of Criminology*, 16(4), 432–51. doi: https://doi.org/10.1177/1477370818772776.

Habermas, J. (2001) *The Postnational Constellation: Political Essays*, Cambridge: Polity.

Hahm, C. and Kim, S.H. (2010) 'To make "We the People": Constitutional founding in postwar Japan and South Korea', *International Journal of Constitutional Law*, 8(4), 800–48. doi: https://doi.org/10.1093/icon/mor007.

Hailbronner, K. and Farahat, A. (2015) *Country Report on Citizenship Law: Germany*, San Domenico di Fiesole: Global Citizenship Observatory (GLOBALCIT), Robert Schuman Centre for Advanced Studies, European University Institute (http://hdl.handle.net/1814/34478).

Hajjat, A. (2010a) 'Port du hijab et "défaut d'assimilation": Étude d'un cas problématique pour l'acquisition de la nationalité française', *Sociologie*, 1(4), 439–55.

Hajjat, A. (2010b) '"Bons" et "mauvais" musulmans', *Cultures & Conflits*, 139–59 (http://journals.openedition.org/conflits/18066).

Hałas, E. (2005) 'Constructing the identity of a nation-state: Symbolic conflict over the preamble to the Constitution of the Third Republic of Poland', *Polish Sociological Review*, 149, 49–67.

Hale, A. and M'Cormack-Hale, F. (2018) 'Statelessness, nationality, and citizenship in Sierra Leone', *Journal of Global South Studies*, 35(2), 311–45. doi:10.1353/gss.2018.0029.

Halmai, G. (2018) 'Illiberal Constitutionalism? The Hungarian Constitution in a European Perspective', in S. Kadelbach (ed) *Verfassungskrisen in der Europäischen Union*, Baden-Baden: Nomos, 85–104.

Hansen, R. (2009) 'The poverty of postnationalism: Citizenship, immigration, and the new Europe', *Theory and Society*, 38(1),1–24. doi:10.1007/s11186-008-9074-0.

Harel, A. (2018) 'Shifting towards a democratic-authoritarian state: Israel's new Nation-State Law,' *Verfassungsblog*, 31 July (https://verfassungsblog.de/shifting-towards-a-democratic-authoritarian-state-israels-new-nation-state-law/).

Harpaz, Y. (2015) 'Ancestry into opportunity: How global inequality drives demand for long-distance European Union citizenship', *Journal of Ethnic and Migration Studies*, 41(13), 2081–104. doi:10.1080/1369183X.2015.1037258.

Harpaz, Y. (2019) 'Compensatory citizenship: Dual nationality as a strategy of global upward mobility', *Journal of Ethnic and Migration Studies*, 45(6), 897–916. doi:10.1080/1369183X.2018.1440486.

Harpaz, Y. and Herzog, B. (2018) *Report on Citizenship Law: Israel*, Country Report 2018/02, San Domenico di Fiesole: Global Citizenship Observatory (GLOBALCIT), Robert Schuman Centre for Advanced Studies, European University Institute (http://hdl.handle.net/1814/56024).

Harpaz, Y. and Mateos, P. (2019) 'Strategic citizenship: Negotiating membership in the age of dual nationality', *Journal of Ethnic and Migration Studies*, 45(6), 843–57. doi:10.1080/1369183X.2018.1440482.

Hartmann, C. (2015) 'Expatriates as voters? The new dynamics of external voting in Sub-Saharan Africa', *Democratization*, 22(5), 906–26. doi:10.1 080/13510347.2014.979800.

Harvey, C. (2018) 'Mutual respect? Interrogating human rights in a fractured union', *King's Law Journal*, 19(2), 216–41. doi:10.1080/0961 5768.2018.1502060.

Hayden, R. (1992) 'Constitutional nationalism in the formerly Yugoslav Republics', *Slavic Review*, 51(4), 654–73. doi:10.2307/2500130.

Helmke, G. and Ríos-Figueroa, J. (2011) Introduction', in G. Helmke and J. Ríos-Figueroa (eds) *Courts in Latin America*, Cambridge: Cambridge University Press, 1–26. doi:10.1017/CBO9780511976520.001.

Henrard, K. (2018) 'The shifting parameters of nationality', *Netherlands International Law Review*, 65, 269–97. doi: https://doi.org/10.1007/s40802-018-0117-6.

Hernández, T. (2014) *Racial Subordination in Latin America: The Role of the State, Customary Law, and the New Civil Rights Response*, Cambridge: Cambridge University Press.

Herzog, B. (2012) 'The paradoxes of citizenship removal: Soviet and post-Soviet citizenship', *East European Politics and Societies*, 26(4), 792–810. doi: https://doi.org/10.1177/0888325412453482.

Herzog, T. (2007) 'Communities becoming a nation: Spain and Spanish America in the wake of modernity (and thereafter)', *Citizenship Studies*, 11(2), 151–72. doi:10.1080/13621020701262487.

Hewitt, S. (2019) 'Why the UK could regret angering Canada by stripping IS suspect Jack Letts of British citizenship', *The Conversation*, 20 August (https://theconversation.com/why-the-uk-could-regret-angering-canada-by-stripping-is-suspect-jack-letts-of-british-citizenship-122081).

Hindess, B. (2002) 'Neo-liberal citizenship', *Citizenship Studies*, 6(2), 127–43. doi:10.1080/13621020220142932.

Hindess, B. (2004) 'Citizenship for all', *Citizenship Studies*, 23(8), 305–15. doi:10.1080/1362102042000257023.

Hirschl, R. (2011) 'The Nordic counternarrative: Democracy, human development, and judicial review', *International Journal of Constitutional Law*, 9(2), 449–69. doi: https://doi.org/10.1093/icon/mor034.

Ho, J.C. (2006) 'Defining "American": Birthright citizenship and the original understanding of the 14th Amendment', *Green Bag*, 9(4), 367–78.

Hobden, C. (2018) *Report on Citizenship Law: South Africa*, Country Report 2018/01, San Domenico di Fiesole: Global Citizenship Observatory (GLOBALCIT), Robert Schuman Centre for Advanced Studies, European University Institute (http://hdl.handle.net/1814/51447).

Honohan, I. (2019) 'Just what's wrong with losing citizenship? Examining revocation of citizenship from a non-domination perspective', *Citizenship Studies*, 16(2), 135–51. doi:10.1080/13621025.2019.1700045.

Honohan, I. and Hutcheson, D. (2015) 'Transnational Citizenship and Access to Electoral Rights: Defining the Demos in European States', in J. Elkink and D.M. Farrell (eds) *The Act of Voting: Identities, Institutions and Locale*, Abingdon: Routledge, 59–79.

Hopgood, S. (2014) 'Challenges to the global human rights regime: Are human rights still an effective language for social change?', *SUR – International Journal on Human Rights*, 11(20), June/December, 67–75 (https://ssrn.com/abstract=2550279).

Hopgood, S., Snyder, J. and Vinjamuri, L. (2017) 'Introduction: Human Rights Past, Present, and Future,' in S. Hopgood, J. Snyder and L. Vinjamuri (eds) *Human Rights Futures*, Cambridge: Cambridge University Press, 1–23. doi:10.1017/9781108147767.001.

Horsley, T. (2018) *The Court of Justice of the European Union as an Institutional Actor: Judicial Lawmaking and its Limits*, Cambridge: Cambridge University Press.

Horváth, E. and Rubio-Marín, R. (2010) '"Alles oder Nichts"? The outer boundaries of the German citizenship debate', *International Journal of Constitutional Law*, 8(1), 72–93.

House of Commons Home Affairs Committee (2019) *EU Settlement Scheme*, 15th Report, Session 207-2019, HC 1945, 14 May.

House of Commons Library (2017) 'Deprivation of British Citizenship and Withdrawal of Passport Facilities', House of Commons Library Briefing, Number 6820, 9 June.

House of Commons Library (2019a) 'Northern Ireland, Citizenship and the Belfast/Good Friday Agreement', House of Commons Library Briefing, Number 8571, 23 May.

House of Commons Library (2019b) 'EU Settlement Scheme', House of Commons Library Briefing, Number 8584, 19 September.

House of Commons Library (2019c) 'Post-Brexit EU immigration policy in the event of a no-deal', Policy Insight, 10 September (https://commonslibrary.parliament.uk/home-affairs/immigration/post-brexit-eu-immigration-policy-in-the-event-of-a-no-deal/).

House of Commons Library (2020) 'The progress of the EU Settlement Scheme so far', Policy Insight, 17 January (https://commonslibrary.parliament.uk/home-affairs/immigration/the-progress-of-the-eu-settlement-scheme-so-far).

Howard, E. (2012) 'Banning Islamic veils: Is gender equality a valid argument?', *International Journal of Discrimination and the Law*, 12(3), 147–65. doi: https://doi.org/10.1177/1358229112464450.

Howse, R. (2019) 'Epilogue: In defense of disruptive democracy – A critique of anti-populism', *International Journal of Constitutional Law*, 17(2), 641–60. doi: https://doi.org/10.1093/icon/moz051.

Huneeus, A. and Urueña, R. (2017) 'Treaty exit and Latin America's constitutional courts', *AJIL Unbound*, 111, 456–60. doi:10.1017/aju.2017.101.

Hunter, W. (2019) *Undocumented Nationals: Between Statelessness and Citizenship*, Cambridge: Cambridge University Press.

Hunter, W. and Brill, R. (2016) '"Documents, please": Advances in social protection and birth certification in the developing world', *World Politics*, 68(2), 191–228. doi:10.1017/S0043887115000465.

Hunter, W. and Sugiyama, N.B. (2014) 'Transforming subjects into citizens: Insights from Brazil's Bolsa Família', *Perspectives on Politics*, 12(4), 829–45. doi:10.1017/S1537592714002151.

Hunter, W. and Sugiyama, N.B. (2018) 'Making the newest citizens: Achieving universal birth registration in contemporary Brazil', *Journal of Development Studies*, 54(3), 397–412. doi:10.1080/00220388.2017.1316378.

Hutcheson, D.S. and Arrighi, J.-T. (2015) '"Keeping Pandora's (ballot) box half-shut": A comparative inquiry into the institutional limits of external voting in EU Member States', *Democratization*, 22(5), 884–905. doi:10.1080/13510347.2014.979161.

IDEA (ed) (2007) *Voting from Abroad: The International IDEA Handbook*, Stockholm: IDEA.

Ignatieff, M. (2017) 'The refugee as invasive other', *Social Research: An International Quarterly*, 84(1), 223–31.

Iordachi, C. (2019) *Liberalism, Constitutional Nationalism, and Minorities: The Making of Romanian Citizenship, c.1750–1918*, Leiden/Boston, MA: Brill.

Irving, H. (2008) 'Still call Australia home: The Constitution and the citizen's right of abode', *Sydney Law Review*, 30(1), 133–53.

Irving, H. (2016) *Citizenship, Alienage, and the Modern Constitutional State*, Cambridge: Cambridge University Press.

Irving, H. (2019) 'The concept of allegiance in citizenship law and revocation: An Australian study', *Citizenship Studies*, 23(4), 372–87. doi:10.1080/13621025.2019.1616452.

Isin, E.F. (2008) 'Theorizing Acts of Citizenship', in E.F. Isin and G. Nielsen (eds) *Acts of Citizenship*, London: Zed Books, 15–43.

Isin, E.F. (2009) 'Citizenship in flux: The figure of the activist citizen', *Subjectivity*, 29, 367–88. doi: https://doi.org/10.1057/sub.2009.25.

Isin, E.F. (2015) 'Citizenship's Empire', in E.F. Isin (ed) *Citizenship after Orientalism: Transforming Political Theory*, London: Palgrave Macmillan, 263–81.

Isin, E.F. (2017) 'Performative Citizenship', in A. Shachar, R. Bauböck, I. Bloemraad and M. Vink (eds) *The Oxford Handbook of Citizenship*, Oxford: Oxford University Press, 500–23.

Isin, E.F. and Nielsen, G. (2008) 'Introduction: Acts of Citizenship', in E.F. Isin and G. Nielsen (eds) *Acts of Citizenship*, London: Zed Books, 1–12.

Israel Democracy Institute, The (2018) 'Q&A about the Nation-State Law', 9 August (https://en.idi.org.il/articles/24378).

Jabareen, H. and Bishara, S. (2019) 'The Jewish Nation-State Law', *Journal of Palestine Studies*, 48(2), 43–57. doi:10.1525/jps.2019.48.2.43.

Jablonowski, K. (2019) 'Is the EU Settlement Scheme working? Not as well as the Home Office pretends', LSE Brexit Blog, 4 September (https://blogs.lse.ac.uk/brexit/2019/09/04/eu-settlement-scheme-is-it-working/).

Jacobsohn, G. (2011) 'The Formation of Constitutional Identities', in T. Ginsburg and R. Dixon (eds) *Comparative Constitutional Law*, Cheltenham: Edward Elgar, 129–42.

Jacobson, D.A. (1997) *Rights across Borders: Immigration and the Decline of Citizenship*, Baltimore, MD: Johns Hopkins University Press.

Jakab, A. (2016) *European Constitutional Language*, Cambridge: Cambridge University Press.

Janoski, T. (2013) 'The complexities of measuring naturalization rates in advanced industrialized countries', *Comparative European Politics*, 11, 649–70. doi: https://doi.org/10.1057/cep.2013.15.

Jayal, N.G. (2013) *Citizenship and Its Discontents: An Indian History*, Cambridge, MA: Harvard University Press.

Jayal, N.G. (2016) 'Citizenship', in S. Choudhry, M. Khosla and P. Mehta (eds) *The Oxford Handbook of the Indian Constitution*, Oxford: Oxford University Press, 163–79.

Jayal, N.G. (2019a) 'Faith-based citizenship: The dangerous path India is choosing', *The India Forum*, 1 November (www.theindiaforum.in/article/faith-criterion-citizenship).

Jayal, N.G. (2019b) 'Reconfiguring citizenship in contemporary India', *South Asia: Journal of South Asian Studies*, 42(1), 33–50. doi:10.1080/00856401.2019.1555874.

Jenkins, F., Nolan, M. and Rubenstein, K. (2014) 'Introduction: Allegiance and Identity in a Globalised World', in F. Jenkins, M. Nolan and K. Rubenstein (eds) *Allegiance and Identity in a Globalised World*, Cambridge: Cambridge University Press, Chapter 1.

Jennings, R. and Watts, A. (eds) (2008) *Oppenheim's International Law: Volume 1: Peace*, Oxford: Oxford University Press (9th edn, 'Nationality of individuals').

Jensen, K.K., Fernández, C. and Brochmann, G. (2017) 'Nationhood and Scandinavian naturalization politics: Varieties of the civic turn', *Citizenship Studies*, 21(5), 606–24. doi:10.1080/13621025.2017.1330 399.

Jerónimo, P. (2018) 'East Timor (Timor Leste)', in O. Vonk (ed) *Nationality Law in the Eastern Hemisphere: Acquisition and Loss of Citizenship in Asian Perspective*, Oisterwijk: Wolf Legal Publishers, 413–60.

Jones, G. (2016) 'What is new about Dutch populism? Dutch colonialism, hierarchical citizenship and contemporary populist debates and policies in the Netherlands', *Journal of Intercultural Studies*, 37(6), 605–20. doi: 10.1080/07256868.2016.1235025.

Joppke, C. (2003) 'Citizenship between de- and re-ethnicization', *European Journal of Sociology/Archives européennes de sociologie*, 44(3), 429–58. doi: https://doi.org/10.1017/S0003975603001346.

Joppke, C. (2007) 'Transformation of citizenship: Status, rights, identity', *Citizenship Studies*, 11(1), 37–48. doi:10.1080/13621020601099831.

Joppke, C. (2019) 'The instrumental turn of citizenship', *Journal of Ethnic and Migration Studies*, 45(6), 858–78. doi:10.1080/136918 3X.2018.1440484.

Kabeer, N. (2006) 'Citizenship, affiliation and exclusion: Perspectives from the South', *IDS Bulletin*, 37, 91–101. doi:10.1111/j.1759-5436.2006. tb00291.x

Kalmar, I. (2018) '"The battlefield is in Brussels": Islamophobia in the Visegrád Four in its global context', *Patterns of Prejudice*, 52(5), 406–19. doi:10.1080/0031322X.2018.1512473.

Kaltwasser, C.R., Taggart, P., Espejo, P. and Ostiguy, P. (2017a) 'Populism: An Overview of the Concept and the State of the Art', in C.R. Kaltwasser, P. Taggart, P. Espejo and P. Ostiguy (eds) *The Oxford Handbook of Populism*, Oxford: Oxford University Press, 1–24.

Kaltwasser, C.R., Taggart, P., Espejo, P. and Ostiguy, P. (eds) (2017b) *The Oxford Handbook of Populism*, Oxford: Oxford University Press.

Kapur, R. (2016) 'Gender Equality', in S. Choudhry, M. Khosla and P. Mehta (eds) *The Oxford Handbook of the Indian Constitution*, Oxford: Oxford University Press, 742–55.

Kassem, R. (2014) 'Passport revocation as proxy denaturalization: Examining the Yemen cases', *Fordham Law Review*, 82(5), 2099–113.

Kay, R.S. (2011) 'Constituent authority', *American Journal of Comparative Law*, 59(3), 715–61. doi: https://doi.org/10.5131/AJCL.2010.0027.

Kazai, V.Z. (2019) 'Stop Soros Law left on the books – The return of the "Red Tail"?', Verfassungsblog, 5 March (https://verfassungsblog.de/ stop-soros-law-left-on-the-books-the-return-of-the-red-tail/).

Kelemen, R. (2019) 'The European Union's authoritarian equilibrium', *Journal of European Public Policy* (https://ssrn.com/abstract=3450716).

Kennett, P. and Lendvai-Bainton, N. (eds) (2017) *Handbook of European Social Policy*, Cheltenham: Edward Elgar.

Kerber, L. (1997) 'The meanings of citizenship', *The Journal of American History*, 84(3), 833–54. doi:10.2307/2953082.

Kesby, A. (2012) *The Right to Have Rights: Citizenship, Humanity and International Law*, Oxford: Oxford University Press.

Ketola, M. and Nordensvard, J. (2018a) 'Reviewing the relationship between social policy and the contemporary populist radical right: Welfare chauvinism, welfare nation state and social citizenship', *Journal of International and Comparative Social Policy*, 34(3), 172–87. doi:10.1080/21699763.2018.1521863.

Ketola, M. and Nordensvard, J. (2018b) 'Social Policy and Populism: Welfare Nationalism as the New Narrative of Social Citizenship', in C. Needham, E. Heins and J. Rees (eds) *Social Policy Review 30: Analysis and Debate in Social Policy*, Bristol: Policy Press, 161–80.

Khaitan, T. (2018) 'Indian democracy at a crossroads', Verfassungsblog, 22 October (https://verfassungsblog.de/indian-democracy-at-a-crossroads/).

Khan, O. (2019) 'Reply: Can a post-national vision better tackle racial discrimination than a national one? Response to Adrian Favell: "Brexit: A requiem for a post-national society?"', *Global Discourse: An Interdisciplinary Journal of Current Affairs*, 9(1), 169–73. doi: https://doi.org/10.1332/204378919X15470487645466.

Khan, S. (2019) 'Revoking IS fighters' UK citizenship may be lawful – But it's irresponsible', RightsInfo Blog, 9 August (https://rightsinfo.org/revoking-isis-fighters-uk-citizenship-may-be-lawful-but-its-irresponsible/).

Kicinger, A. and Koryś, I. (2011) 'The Case of Poland', in G. Zincone, M. Borkert and R. Penninx (eds) *Migration Policymaking in Europe: The Dynamics of Actors and Contexts in Past and Present*, Amsterdam: Amsterdam University Press, 347–76.

Kim, K. (2000) *Aliens in Medieval Law: The Origins of Modern Citizenship*, Cambridge: Cambridge University Press.

King, J. (2016) 'On the proposal for a UK constitutional court', UCL European Institute Blog, 16 February (www.ucl.ac.uk/european-institute/news/2016/feb/proposal-uk-constitutional-court).

Kingston, L. (2019) 'Conceptualizing statelessness as a human rights challenge: Framing, visual representation, and (partial) issue emergence', *Journal of Human Rights Practice*, 11(1), 52–72. doi: https://doi.org/10.1093/jhuman/huz010.

Kirsch, A. (2011) 'The loss of citizenship by revocation of naturalization or ex lege: Overview of German case law and legislative changes of 2009', *German Law Journal*, 12(8), 1659–80. doi:10.1017/S207183220001748X.

Klaaren, J. (2010) 'Constitutional citizenship in South Africa', *International Journal of Constitutional Law*, 8(1), 94–110. doi: https://doi.org/10.1093/icon/mop033.

Knop, K. (2001) 'Relational Nationality: On Gender and Nationality in International Law', in T.A. Aleinikoff and D. Klusmeyer (eds) *Citizenship Today: Global Perspectives and Practices*, Washington, DC: Carnegie Endowment for International Peace, 89–124.

Kochenov, D. (2014) 'EU citizenship without duties', *European Law Journal*, 20(4), 482–98. doi:10.1111/eulj.12095.

Kochenov, D. (2019a) *Citizenship*, Cambridge, MA: MIT Press.

Kochenov, D. (2019b) 'Investor citizenship and residence: The EU Commission's incompetent case for blood and soil', Verfassungsblog, 23 January (https://verfassungsblog.de/investor-citizenship-and-residence-the-eu-commissions-incompetent-case-for-blood-and-soil/).

Koessler, M. (1946) '"Subject", "citizen", "national", and "permanent allegiance"', *Yale Law Journal*, 56, 58–76.

Komarek, J. (2018) 'EU Citizens' Duties: Preventing Barriers to the Exercise of Citizens' Rights', in S. Seubert, O. Eberl and F. van Waarden (eds) *Reconsidering EU Citizenship: Contradictions and Constraints*, Cheltenham/Northampton: Edward Elgar, 64–86. doi: https://doi.org/10.4337/9781788113540.00011.

Koopmans, R. (2012) 'The post-nationalization of immigrant rights: A theory in search of evidence', *British Journal of Sociology*, 63(1), 22–30. doi:10.1111/j.1468-4446.2011.01401.x.

Koppel, M. and Kontorovich, E. (2018) 'Why all the outrage over Israel's Nation-State Law?', *Mosaic Magazine*, 8 October (https://mosaicmagazine.com/essay/israel-zionism/2018/10/why-all-the-outrage-over-israels-nation-state-law/).

Körtvélyesi, Z. (2012) 'From "We the People" to "We the Nation"', in G. Tóth (ed) *Constitution for a Disunited Nation: On Hungary's 2011 Fundamental Law*, Budapest: Central European University Press, 111–40.

Körtvélyesi, Z. and Majtényi, B. (2017) 'Game of values: The threat of exclusive constitutional identity, the EU and Hungary', *German Law Journal*, 18(7), 1721–44. doi:10.1017/S2071832200022513.

Kosinski, S. (2009) 'State of uncertainty: Citizenship, statelessness and discrimination in the Dominican Republic', *Boston College International and Comparative Law Review*, 32(2), 377–98.

Kostakopoulou, D. (2018) 'Scala civium: Citizenship templates post-Brexit and the European Union's duty to protect EU citizens', *Journal of Common Market Studies*, 56(4), 854–69.

Kovács, K. (2017) 'The rise of an ethnocultural constitutional identity in the jurisprudence of the East Central European Courts', *German Law Journal*, 18(7), 1703–20. doi:10.1017/S2071832200022501.

Krasniqi, G. (2019) 'Contested states as liminal spaces of citizenship: Comparing Kosovo and the Turkish Republic of Northern Cyprus', *Ethnopolitics*, 18(3), 298–314. doi:10.1080/17449057.2019.1585092.

Kremnitzer, M. (2018) 'In grand debut, Israel's Nation-State Law reveals its ugly true colors', *The Israel Democracy Institute*, 20 September (https://en.idi.org.il/articles/24542).

Kristol, A. and Dahinden, J. (2020) 'Becoming a citizen through marriage: How gender, ethnicity and class shape the nation', *Citizenship Studies*, 24(1), 40–56. doi:10.1080/13621025.2019.169115.

Kröger, S. (2019) 'The democratic legitimacy of the 2016 British Referendum on EU membership', *Journal of Contemporary European Research*, 15(3), 284–98. doi: https://doi.org/10.30950/jcer.v15i3.1052.

Krunke, H. and Thorarensen, B. (2018) 'Concluding Thoughts', in H. Krunke and B. Thorarensen (eds) *The Nordic Constitutions: A Comparative and Contextual Study*, Oxford: Hart Publishing, 203–18. doi:10.5040/9781509910960.ch-008.

Krygier, M. (2017) 'Tempering Power,' in M. Adams, A. Meuwese and E.H. Ballin (eds) *Constitutionalism and the Rule of Law: Bridging Idealism and Realism*, Cambridge: Cambridge University Press, 34–59. doi:10.1017/9781316585221.002.

Kunz, S. (2016) 'Privileged mobilities: Locating the expatriate in migration scholarship', *Geography Compass*, 10(3), 89–101. doi:10.1111/gec3.12253.

Kusa, D. (2010) *Report on Citizenship Law: Slovakia*, Country Report, San Domenico di Fiesole: Global Citizenship Observatory (GLOBALCIT), Robert Schuman Centre for Advanced Studies, European University Institute (http://hdl.handle.net/1814/19635).

Kymlicka, W. and Norman, W. (1994) 'Return of the citizen: A survey of recent work on citizenship theory', *Ethics*, 104(2), 352–81.

Kymlicka, W. and Norman, W. (2000) 'Citizenship in Culturally Diverse Societies: Issues, Contexts, Concepts', in W. Kymlicka and W. Norman (eds) *Citizenship in Diverse Societies*, Oxford: Oxford University Press, 1–41.

La Vina, A., Martin, N. and Garcia, J. (2017) 'High noon in the Supreme Court: The Poe-Llamanzares decision and its impact on substantive and procedural jurisprudence', *Philippine Law Journal*, 90, 218–77.

Lacey, N. (2019) 'Populism and the rule of law', *Annual Review of Law and Social Science*, 15(1), 79–96. doi: https://doi.org/10.1146/annurev-lawsocsci-101518-042919.

Ładykowski, P. (2018) '"National belonging" in legal and diplomatic formulas: The Pole's card as a legacy of Poland's colonial history', *Baltic Journal of European Studies*, 8(2), 92–120. doi: https://doi.org/10.1515/bjes-2018-0017.

Lang, A. and Wiener, A. (2017) *Handbook on Global Constitutionalism*, Cheltenham/Northampton, MA: Edward Elgar.

Lasso, M. (2019) 'Why birthright citizenship is crucial to democratic governance', *The Washington Post*, 14 June (www.washingtonpost.com/outlook/2019/06/14/why-birthright-citizenship-is-crucial-democratic-governance/).

Law, D. and Versteeg, M. (2013) 'Sham constitutions', *California Law Review*, 101(4), 863–952.

Law, I., Easat-Daas, A., Merali, A. and Sayyid, S. (eds) (2019) *Countering Islamophobia in Europe: Mapping Global Racisms*, Cham, Switzerland: Palgrave Macmillan.

Lawrence, B. and Stevens, J. (eds) (2017) *Citizenship in Question: Evidentiary Birthright and Statelessness*, Durham, NC: Duke University Press.

Laycock, D. (2006) 'Populism', in *The Canadian Encyclopedia* (www.thecanadianencyclopedia.ca/en/article/populism).

Lee, C.T. (2014) 'Decolonizing global citizenship', in E.F. Isin and P. Nyers (eds) *Routledge Handbook of Global Citizenship Studies*, Abingdon: Routledge, 75–85.

Legomsky, S. (1994) 'Why citizenship?', *Virginia Journal of International Law*, 35, 279–300.

Lenard, P.T. (2018a) 'Democratic citizenship and denationalization', *American Political Science Review*, 112(1), 99–111. doi:10.1017/S0003055417000442.

Lenard, P.T. (2018b) 'Whither the Canadian Model? Evaluating the New Canadian Nationalism (2006–2015)', in J. Fossum, R. Kastoryano and B. Siim (eds) *Diversity and Contestations over Nationalism in Europe and Canada*, London: Palgrave, 211–36.

Lepoutre, J. (2019) 'Ius Soli: A French constitutional principle?', GLOBALCIT Blog, 1 February (http://globalcit.eu/ius-soli-a-french-constitutional-principle/).

Lewans, M. (2010) 'Roncarelli's green card: The role of citizenship in Randian constitutionalism', *McGill Law Journal/Revue de droit de McGill*, 55(3), 537–62. doi: https://doi.org/10.7202/1000623ar.

Lichtenberger, A. (2018) 'Undocumented citizens of the United States: The repercussions of denying birth certificates', *St Mary's Law Journal*, 49(2), 435–59.

Liebich, A. (2017) 'The "boomerang effect" of kin-state activism: Cross-border ties and the securitization of kin minorities', *Journal of Borderlands Studies*, 34(5), 665–84. doi:10.1080/08865655.2017.1402202.

Liu, L. (2017) 'An assault on the fundamental right to parenthood and birthright citizenship: An equal protection analysis of the recent ban of the Matrícula Consular in Texas's birth certificate application policy', *Columbia Journal of Law and Social Problems*, 50(4), 619–63.

Llanque, M. (2010) 'On Constitutional Membership', in P. Dobner and M. Loughlin (eds) *The Twilight of Constitutionalism?*, Oxford: Oxford University Press, 162–78.

Lokrantz Bernitz, H. (2012) *Report on Citizenship Law: Sweden*, Country Report, San Domenico di Fiesole: Global Citizenship Observatory (GLOBALCIT), Robert Schuman Centre for Advanced Studies, European University Institute (http://hdl.handle.net/1814/60231).

Lopez, I.H. (2006) *White by Law*, New York: New York University Press.

Lori, N. (2017) 'Statelessness, "in-between" statuses, and precarious citizenship', in A. Shachar, R. Bauböck, I. Bloemraad and M. Vink (eds) *The Oxford Handbook of Citizenship*, Oxford: Oxford University Press, 743–66.

Lori, N. (2019) *Offshore Citizens: Permanent Temporary Status in the Gulf*, Cambridge: Cambridge University Press.

Loughlin, M. (2017) 'On Constituent Power', in M. Dowdle and M. Wilkinson (eds) *Constitutionalism beyond Liberalism*, Cambridge: Cambridge University Press, 151–75.

Low, C.C. (2016) 'The politics of emigration and expatriation: Ethnicisation of citizenship in Imperial Germany and China', *Journal of Historical Sociology*, 29(3), 385–412. doi:10.1111/johs.12085.

Low, C.C. (2017) *Report on Citizenship Law: Malaysia and Singapore*, Country Report 2017/03, San Domenico di Fiesole: Global Citizenship Observatory (GLOBALCIT), Robert Schuman Centre for Advanced Studies, European University Institute (https://cadmus.eui.eu/bitstream/handle/1814/45371/GLOBALCIT_CR_2017_03.pdf?sequence=1).

Low, C.C. (2018) 'MyOverseasVote: Liberalism and extraterritorial citizenship', *Citizenship Studies*, 22(7), 745–68. doi:10.1080/1362102 5.2018.1508416.

MacKinnon, C. (2006) 'Sex equality under the Constitution of India: Problems, prospects, and "personal laws"', *International Journal of Constitutional Law*, 4(2), 181–202. doi: https://doi.org/10.1093/icon/mol001.

MacKinnon, C. (2012) 'Gender in Constitutions', in M. Rosenfeld and A. Sajó (eds) *Oxford Handbook of Comparative Constitutional Law*, Oxford: Oxford University Press, 397–416.

Macklin, A. (2007) 'Who is the citizen's other? Considering the heft of citizenship', *Theoretical Inquiries in Law*, 8(2), 333–66.

Macklin, A. (2014) 'Citizenship revocation, the privilege to have rights and the production of the alien', *Queen's Law Journal*, Fall, 1–54.

Macklin, A. (2017a) 'From Settler Society to Warrior Nation and Back Again', in J. Mann (ed) *Citizenship in Transnational Perspective: Politics of Citizenship and Migration*, New York: Palgrave Macmillan, 285–313.

Macklin, A. (2017b) 'Is it time to retire Nottebohm?', *AJIL Unbound*, 111, 492–7. doi:10.1017/aju.2018.5.

Macklin, A. (2019) '"Jihadi Jack" and the folly of revoking citizenship', *The Conversation*, 20 August (https://theconversation.com/jihadi-jack-and-the-folly-of-revoking-citizenship-122155).

Macmillan, K. (2017) 'From "the Commonwealth's Most Dutiful Daughter" to "Young Multicultural Nation": Non-citizen Voting Rights and New Zealand's Citizenship Regime', in J. Mann (ed) *Citizenship in Transnational Perspective, Politics of Citizenship and Migration*, New York: Palgrave Macmillan, 117–38.

Majtényi, B., Nagy, A. and Kállai, P. (2018) '"Only Fidesz" – Minority electoral law in Hungary', Verfassungsblog, 31 March (https://verfassungsblog.de/only-fidesz-electoral-law-in-hungary/).

Malki, I. (2017) 'The competing ontologies of belonging: Race, class, citizenship, and Sierra Leone's "Lebanese Question"', *Dialectical Anthropology*, 41, 343–66. doi:10.1007/s10624-017-9470-9.

Manby, B. (2018) *Citizenship in Africa: The Law of Belonging*, Oxford: Bloomsbury/Hart.

Manby, B. (2019a) 'Citizenship law as the foundation for political participation in Africa', *Oxford Research Encyclopedia of Politics* (https://oxfordre.com/politics/view/10.1093/acrefore/9780190228637.001.0001/acrefore-9780190228637-e-736).

Manby, B. (2019b) *Report on Citizenship Law: Zimbabwe*, Country Report 2019/01, San Domenico di Fiesole: Global Citizenship Observatory (GLOBALCIT), Robert Schuman Centre for Advanced Studies, European University Institute (https://cadmus.eui.eu/handle/1814/60436).

Manby, B. (2019c) '*Anudo Ochieng Anudo vs Tanzania (Judgment) (African Court on Human and Peoples' Rights*, Application No 012/2015, 22 March 2018)', *The Statelessness and Citizenship Review*, 1, 170–6.

Mantu, S. (2018) '"Terrorist" citizens and the human right to nationality', *Journal of Contemporary European Studies*, 26(1), 28–41. doi:10.1080/14 782804.2017.1397503.

Marcus, R. (2019a) 'Is Trudeau's multi-cultural idyll in danger?', *Qantara. de*, 15 July (https://en.qantara.de/node/36348).

Marcus, R. (2019b) 'Islamophobia festers in Canada's Francophone heart', *Qantara.de*, 26 August (https://en.qantara.de/node/36961).

Markakis, M. (2018) 'Brexit and the EU Charter of Fundamental Rights', *Public Law*, January, 82–101.

Marsh, D. (2020) 'Populism and Brexit', in I. Crewe and D. Sanders (eds) *Authoritarian Populism and Liberal Democracy*, Cham, Switzerland: Palgrave Macmillan, 73–86. doi: https://doi.org/10.1007/978-3-030-17997-7_5.

Marshall, P. (2018) 'Voting from prison: against the democratic case for disenfranchisement', *Ethics and Global Politics*, 11(3), 1–16. doi:10.1080 /16544951.2018.1498696.

Marshall, T.H. (1992 [1950]) 'Citizenship and Social Class,' in T.H. Marshall and T. Bottomore (eds) *Citizenship and Social Class*, London: Pluto Press, 1–51.

Martí, J.L. (2013) 'Two Different Ideas of Constitutional Identity: Identity of the Constitution v Identity of the People', in A. Sáiz Arnáiz and C. Alcoberro (eds) *National Constitutional Identity and European Integration*, Antwerp: Intersentia, 17–36.

Martin, D.A. (1985) 'Membership and consent: Abstract or organic?', *Yale Journal of International Law*, 11(1), 278–96.

Masri, M. (2013) 'Love suspended: Demography, comparative law and Palestinian couples in the Israeli Supreme Court', *Social and Legal Studies*, 22(3), 309–34.

Masri, M. (2017) *The Dynamics of Exclusionary Constitutionalism: Israel as a Jewish and Democratic State*, Oxford: Bloomsbury/Hart Publishing.

Mavrommatis, G. (2018) 'Greek citizenship tradition in flux? Investigating contemporary tensions between ethnic and civic elements of nationality', *Nationalities Papers*, 46(3), 484–500.

McCrea, R. (2013) 'The ban on the veil and European Law', *Human Rights Law Review*, 13(1), 57–97. doi: https://doi.org/10.1093/hrlr/ngs035.

McCrone, D. and Kiely, R. (2000) 'Nationalism and citizenship', *Sociology*, 34(1), 19–34.

McGinnis, B.L. (2018) 'Beyond disenfranchisement: Collateral consequences and equal citizenship', *Politics, Groups, and Identities*, 6(1), 59–76. doi:10.1080/21565503.2017.1318759.

McGoldrick, D. (2019) 'Challenging the constitutionality of restrictions on same-sex sexual relations: Lessons from India', *Human Rights Law Review*, 19(1), 173–85. doi: https://doi.org/10.1093/hrlr/ngy041.

McGranahan, C. (2018) 'Refusal as political practice: Citizenship, sovereignty, and Tibetan refugee status,' *American Ethnologist*, 45(3), 367–79. doi: https://doi.org/10.1111/amet.12671.

McIntyre, J. (2017) 'The dual citizenship saga shows our Constitution must be changed, and now', *The Conversation*, 16 November (https://theconversation.com/the-dual-citizenship-saga-shows-our-constitution-must-be-changed-and-now-87330).

McKinney, C.J. (2019) 'Good Friday Agreement doesn't stop Northern Irish people being born automatically British', Free Movement Blog, 25 November (www.freemovement.org.uk/desouza-case-good-friday-agreement/).

Mechoulan, S. (2018) 'The case against the face-veil: A European perspective', *International Journal of Constitutional Law*, 16(4), 1267–92. doi: https://doi.org/10.1093/icon/moy099.

Menand, L. (2018) 'Francis Fukuyama postpones the end of history', *The New Yorker*, 3 September (www.newyorker.com/magazine/2018/09/03/francis-fukuyama-postpones-the-end-of-history).

Menéndez, A.J. and Olsen, E.D.H. (2019) *Challenging European Citizenship: Ideas and Realities in Contrast*, Cham, Switzerland: Palgrave Macmillan/Springer. doi: https://doi.org/10.1007/978-3-030-22281-9.

Michaels, R. (2018) 'Banning Burqas: The perspective of postsecular comparative law', *Duke Journal of Comparative & International Law*, 28, 213–45.

Midtbøen, A. (2019) 'No longer the "last man standing": Norway decides to allow dual citizenship', GLOBALCIT Blog, 9 January (http://globalcit.eu/no-longer-the-last-man-standing-norway-decides-to-allow-dual-citizenship/).

Miklóssy, K. and Nyyssönen, H. (2018) 'Defining the new polity: Constitutional memory in Hungary and beyond', *Journal of Contemporary European Studies*, 26(3), 322–33. doi:10.1080/14782804.2018.1498775.

Miller, D. (1993) 'In defence of nationality', *Journal of Applied Philosophy*, 10(1), 3–16.

Miller, R. (2019) '(Un)settling home during the Brexit process', *Population, Space and Place*, 25(1). doi:10.1002/psp.2203.

Mindus, P. (2014) 'Dimensions of citizenship', *German Law Journal*, 15(5), 735–49, Available at: https://doi.org/10.1017/S2071832200019118.

Möller, K. (2018) 'Populism, democracy and popular sovereignty', *Philosophical Inquiry*, 1–2, 14–36.

Mookerjee, A.S. (2019) 'How the National Citizenship Registration in Assam is shaping a new national identity in India', *The Conversation*, 29 August (https://theconversation.com/how-the-national-citizenship-registration-in-assam-is-shaping-a-new-national-identity-in-india-121152).

Moran, M. (2020) 'Populism and Social Citizenship: An Anglo-American Comparison', in I. Crewe and D. Sanders (eds) *Authoritarian Populism and Liberal Democracy*, Cham, Switzerland: Palgrave Macmillan, 211–25. doi: https://doi.org/10.1007/978-3-030-17997-7_14.

Moret, J., Andrikopoulos, A. and Dahinden, J. (2019) 'Contesting categories: Cross-border marriages from the perspectives of the state, spouses and researchers', *Journal of Ethnic and Migration Studies*. doi:10.1080/1369183X.2019.1625124.

Mouffe, C. (2018) *For a Left Populism*, London: Verso.

Mouritsen, P., Faas, D., Meer, N. and de Witte, N. (2019) '*Leitkultur* debates as civic integration in North-Western Europe: The nationalism of "values" and "good citizenship"', *Ethnicities*, 19, 632–53. doi: https://doi.org/10.1177/1468796819843538.

Moyn, S. (2014) 'The future of human rights', *SUR – International Journal on Human Rights*, 11, 57–64 (https://ssrn.com/abstract=2550376).

Moyn, S. (2019) 'Can Pompeo redefine human rights for the Trump era?', *The American Prospect*, 12 July (https://prospect.org/article/can-pompeo-redefine-human-rights-trump-era).

Mudde, C. (2019) 'The 2019 EU elections: Moving the center', *Journal of Democracy*, 30(4), 20–34.

Mudde, C. and Kaltwasser, C.R. (2017) *Populism: A Very Short Introduction*, Oxford: Oxford University Press.

Mudde, C. and Kaltwasser, C.R. (2018) 'Studying populism in comparative perspective: Reflections on the contemporary and future research agenda', *Comparative Political Studies*, 51(13), 1667–93. doi: https://doi.org/10.1177/0010414018789490.

Müller, J.-W. (2007) 'Is Europe converging on constitutional patriotism? (And if so: Is it justified?)', *Critical Review of International Social and Political Philosophy*, 10(3), 377–87. doi:10.1080/13698230701400429.

Müller, J.-W. (2017) 'Populism and Constitutionalism', in C.R. Kaltwasser, P. Taggart, P. Espejo and P. Ostiguy (eds) *The Oxford Handbook of Populism*, Oxford: Oxford University Press, 590–606.

Müller, J.-W. (2019) 'What spaces does democracy need?', *Soundings: An Interdisciplinary Journal*, 102(2), 203–16.

Mulmi, S. and Shneiderman, S. (2017) 'Citizenship, gender and statelessness in Nepal Before and after the 2015 Constitution', in T. Bloom, K. Tonkiss and P. Cole (eds) *Understanding Statelessness*, London: Routledge, 135–52.

Murphy, J. (2018) 'Citizens, aliens and Aboriginal Australians – An uncertain constitutional community', Blog of the International Journal of Constitutional Law, 19 October (www.iconnectblog.com/2018/10/citizens-aliens-and-aboriginal-australians-an-uncertain-constitutional-community).

Murphy, M. and Harty, S. (2003) 'Post-sovereign citizenship', *Citizenship Studies*, 7(2), 181–97. doi:10.1080/1362102032000065964.

Mustafa, F. and Mohammed, A. (2020) 'The great Indian citizenship mess', *The Hindu*, 21 January (www.thehindu.com/opinion/op-ed/the-great-indian-citizenship-mess/article30609610.ece).

Nadler, A. (2019) 'Populist communication and media environments', *Sociology Compass*, 13(8), 13:e12718. doi: https://doi.org/10.1111/soc4.12718.

Navot, S. (2018) 'A new chapter in Israel's "constitution": Israel as the Nation State of the Jewish People', Verfassungsblog, 27 July (https://verfassungsblog.de/a-new-chapter-in-israels-constitution-israel-as-the-nation-state-of-the-jewish-people/).

Neuman, G. (2015) 'Citizenship', in M. Tushnet, M. Graber and S. Levinson (eds) *The Oxford Handbook of the US Constitution*, Oxford: Oxford University Press, 587–606.

Neuman, K. (2019) 'Canadian public opinion on immigration and refugees', Environics Institute, 30 April (www.environicsinstitute.org).

Neuvonen, P.J. (2019) 'Transforming membership? Citizenship, identity and the problem of belonging in regional integration organizations', *European Journal of International Law*, 30(1), 229–55. doi: https://doi.org/10.1093/ejil/chz007.

Ng'weno, B. and Aloo, L.O. (2019) 'Irony of citizenship: Descent, national belonging, and constitutions in the postcolonial African state', *Law and Society Review*, 53(1), 141–72. doi:10.1111/lasr.12395.

Nienhusser, H.K. and Oshio, T. (2019) 'Awakened hatred and heightened fears: "The Trump effect" on the lives of mixed-status families', *Cultural Studies – Critical Methodologies*, 19(3), 173–83. doi: https://doi.org/10.1177/1532708618817872.

Norris, P. and Inglehart, R. (2019) *Cultural Backlash: Trump, Brexit, and Authoritarian Populism*, Cambridge: Cambridge University Press. doi:10.1017/9781108595841.

Nyyssönen, H. and Metsälä, J. (2019) 'Dual citizenship as power politics: The case of the Carpathian Basin', *Europa Ethnica*, 1/2, 50–6.

O'Byrne, D. (2019) 'The rise of populism, the demise of the neoliberal and neoconservative globalist projects, and the war on human rights', *International Critical Thought*, 9(2), 254–68. doi:10.1080/21598282.20 19.1613917.

O'Neill, O. (2005) 'The dark side of human rights', *International Affairs*, 81(2), 427–39. doi: https://doi.org/10.1111/j.1468-2346.2005.00459.x.

O'Regan, K and Friedman, N. (2011) 'Equality', in T. Ginsburg and R. Dixon (eds) *Comparative Constitutional Law*, Cheltenham: Edward Elgar, 473–503.

O'Sullivan, D. (2020) 'The human right to belong: Indigenous rights and sovereignty in Australia', 20 February (https://news.csu.edu.au/opinion/the-human-right-to-belong-indigenous-rights-and-sovereignty-in-australia).

Oberman, K. (2016) 'Immigration as a Human Right', in S. Fine and L. Ypi (eds) *Migration in Political Theory: The Ethics of Movement and Membership*, Oxford: Oxford University Press, 32–56.

Oosterom-Staples, H. (2018) 'The triangular relationship between nationality, EU citizenship and migration in EU law: A tale of competing competences', *Netherlands International Law Review*, 65(3), 431–61.

Open Society Justice Initiative (2019) *Unmaking Americans: Insecure Citizenship in the United States*, Open Society Justice Initiative Report, September (www.justiceinitiative.org/publications/unmaking-americans).

Orgad, L. (2014) 'Liberalism, allegiance, and obedience: The inappropriateness of loyalty oaths in a liberal democracy', *Canadian Journal of Law and Jurisprudence*, 27(1), 99–122. doi:10.1017/S084182090000624X.

Orgad, L. (2017) 'Naturalization', in A. Shachar, R. Bauböck, I. Bloemraad and M. Vink (eds) *The Oxford Handbook of Citizenship*, Oxford: Oxford University Press, 337–57.

Orgad, L. (2018) 'Review of *At Home in Two Countries: The Past and Future of Dual Citizenship* by Peter J. Spiro', *American Journal of International Law*, 112(4), 789–95. doi:10.1017/ajil.2018.80.

Orgad, L. (2019) 'The citizen-makers: Ethical dilemmas in immigrant integration', *European Law Journal*, 25(6), 524–43. doi: https://doi.org/10.1111/eulj.12338.

Orr, G. (2017) 'Dual citizen MPs in Australia's National Parliament – The barriers bite', GLOBALCIT Blog, 16 October (http://globalcit.eu/dual-citizen-mps-in-australias-national-parliament-the-barriers-bite/).

Orr, G. (2018) 'Fertilising a thicket: Section 44, MP qualifications and the High Court', *Public Law Review*, 29, 3.

Owen, D. (2013) 'Citizenship and the marginalities of migrants', *Critical Review of International Social and Political Philosophy*, 16(3), 326–43. doi: https://doi.org/10.1080/13698230.2013.795702.

Owen, D. (2018) 'On the right to have nationality rights: Statelessness, citizenship and human rights', *Netherlands International Law Review*, 65, 299–317. doi: https://doi.org/10.1007/s40802-018-0116-7.

Pailey, R. (2018) 'Between rootedness and rootlessness: How sedentarist and nomadic metaphysics simultaneously challenge and reinforce (dual) citizenship claims for Liberia', *Migration Studies*, 6(3), 400–19. doi: https://doi.org/10.1093/migration/mnx056.

Pailey, R. (2019) 'Women, equality, and citizenship in contemporary Africa', *Oxford Research Encyclopedia of Politics* (https://oxfordre.com/politics/view/10.1093/acrefore/9780190228637.001.0001/acrefore-9780190228637-e-852).

Palop-García, P. and Pedroza, L. (2019) 'Passed, regulated, or applied? The different stages of emigrant enfranchisement in Latin America and the Caribbean', *Democratization*, 26(3), 401–21. doi:10.1080/1351034 7.2018.1534827.

Panagiotidis, J. (2018) 'Tainted Law? Why History Cannot Provide the Justification for Abandoning Ius Sanguinis', in R. Bauböck (ed) *Debating Transformations of National Citizenship*, Cham, Switzerland: Springer, 91–5.

Parashar, A. and Alam, J. (2019) 'The national laws of Myanmar: Making of statelessness for the Rohingya', *International Migration*, 57(1), 94–108. doi:10.1111/imig.12532.

Paris, M.-L., Foulon, J., Pouillaude, H.-B. and Sterck, J. (2019) *Constitutional Law in France*, The Hague: Kluwer Law International.

Parnell-Berry, B. (2018) '"Silence is not allyship": Migrant solidarity is lacking from Brits abroad panicking about Brexit', *gal-dem*, 2 October (http://gal-dem.com/silence-allyship-lacking-migrant-solidarity-brits-abroad/).

Parolin, G. (2009) *Citizenship in the Arab World*, Amsterdam: Amsterdam University Press.

Patberg, M. (2017) 'The levelling up of constituent power in the European Union', JCMS: *Journal of Common Market Studies*, 55(2), 203–12. doi:10.1111/jcms.12520.

Paternotte, D. and Kuhar, R. (2018) 'Disentangling and locating the "Global Right": Anti-gender campaigns in Europe', *Politics and Governance*, 6(3), 6-19. doi:10.17645/pag.v6i3.1557.

Patrignani, E. (2018) '"Overcoming essentialisation: A comparative study of "living-together" conceptions', *International Journal of Law in Context*, 14(3), 374–95. doi:10.1017/S1744552317000210.

Paulose, R. (2019) 'A new dawn? Statelessness and Assam', *Groningen Journal of International Law*, 7(1), 99–111. doi:10.21827/5d5141d9ebe6a.

Pech, L. and Kelemen, R.D. (2018) *Why Autocrats Love Constitutional Identity and Constitutional Pluralism: Lessons from Hungary and Poland*, RECONNECT, Working Paper No 2, September (https://reconnect-europe.eu/wp-content/uploads/2018/10/RECONNECT-WorkingPaper2-Kelemen-Pech-LP-KO.pdf).

Pech, L. and Scheppele, K.L. (2017) 'Illiberalism within: Rule of law backsliding in the EU', *Cambridge Yearbook of European Legal Studies*, 19, 3–47. doi:10.1017/cel.2017.9.

Pedroza, L. and Palop-García, P. (2017) 'The grey area between nationality and citizenship: An analysis of external citizenship policies in Latin America and the Caribbean', *Citizenship Studies*, 21(5), 587–605. doi:10.1080/13621025.2017.1316701.

Perez, L.M. (2008) 'Citizenship denied: The "insular cases" and the Fourteenth Amendment', *Virginia Law Review*, 94(4), 1029–81.

Peters, A. (2010) 'Extraterritorial naturalizations: Between the human right to nationality, state sovereignty and fair principles of jurisdiction', *German Yearbook of International Law*, 53, 623–725.

Petrozziello, A.J. (2019a) 'Bringing the border to baby: Birth registration as bordering practice for migrant women's children', *Gender and Development*, 27(1), 31–47. doi:10.1080/13552074.2019.1570724.

Petrozziello, A.J. (2019b) '(Re)producing statelessness via indirect gender discrimination: Descendants of Haitian migrants in the Dominican Republic', *International Migration*, 57(1), 213–28. doi:10.1111/imig.12527.

Pfeifer, G. (2020) 'Balibar, citizenship, and the return of right populism', *Philosophy & Social Criticism*, 46(3), 323–41 (https://doi.org/10.1177/0191453719860228).

Piccoli, L. (2019) 'The regional battleground: Partisanship as a key driver of the subnational contestation of citizenship', *Ethnopolitics*, 18(4), 340–61. doi:10.1080/17449057.2019.1584494.

Pichl, M. (2019) 'Constitution of False Prophecies: The Illiberal Transformation of Hungary', in H. Alviar García and G. Frankenberg (eds) *Authoritarian Constitutionalism*, Cheltenham/Northampton, MA: Edward Elgar Publishing, 240–64.

Pillai, P. (2019) 'Of statelessness, detention camps and deportations: India and the "National Register of Citizens" in Assam', Opinio Juris Blog, 12 July (http://opiniojuris.org/2019/07/12/of-statelessness-detention-camps-and-deportations-india-and-the-national-register-of-citizens-in-assam/).

Pillai, S. (2014) 'Non-immigrants, non-aliens and people of the Commonwealth: Australian constitutional citizenship revisited', *Monash University Law Review*, 39, 568–609.

Pincock, H. (2018) 'Can democratic states justify restricting the rights of persons with mental illness? Presumption of competence, voting, and gun rights', *Politics, Groups, and Identities*, 6(1), 20–38. doi:10.1080/21 565503.2017.1318757.

Pitts, J. (2010) 'Political theory of empire and imperialism', *Annual Review of Political Science*, 13, 211–35. doi: https://doi.org/10.1146/annurev. polisci.051508.214538.

Pocock, J.G.A. (1992) 'The ideal of citizenship since classical times', *Queen's Quarterly*, 99(1), 33–55.

Poddar, M. (2018) 'The Citizenship (Amendment) Bill, 2016: International law on religion-based discrimination and naturalisation law', *Indian Law Review*, 2(1), 108–18. doi:10.1080/24730580.2018.1512290.

Pogonyi, S. (2017) *Extra-Territorial Ethnic Politics, Discourses and Identities in Hungary*, New York: Palgrave Macmillan.

Pogonyi, S. (2019) 'The passport as means of identity management: Making and unmaking ethnic boundaries through citizenship', *Journal of Ethnic and Migration Studies*, 45(6), 975–93. doi:10.1080/136918 3X.2018.1440493.

Polese, A., Morris, J. and Kovács, B. (2014) 'Introduction: The failure and future of the welfare state in post-socialism', *Journal of Eurasian Studies*, 6(1), 1–5. doi: https://doi.org/10.1016/j.euras.2014.11.001.

Polzin, M. (2016) 'Constitutional identity, unconstitutional amendments and the idea of constituent power: The development of the doctrine of constitutional identity in German constitutional law', *International Journal of Constitutional Law*, 14(2), 411–38. doi: https://doi.org/10.1093/icon/ mow035.

Polzin, M. (2017) 'Constitutional identity as a constructed reality and a restless soul', *German Law Journal*, 18(7), 1595–616. doi:10.1017/ S2071832200022458.

Pompeo, M. (2019) 'Unalienable rights and US foreign policy; The Founders' principles can help revitalize liberal democracy world-wide', *The Wall Street Journal*, 7 July.

Popławska, E. (2011) 'Preamble to the constitution as an expression of the new axiology of the Republic of Poland', *Acta Juridica Hungarica*, 52(1), 40–53.

Prabhat, D. (2018) *Britishness, Belonging and Citizenship: Experiencing Nationality Law*, Bristol: Policy Press.

Prak, M. (2018) *Citizens without Nations: Urban Citizenship in Europe and the World, c.1000–1789*, Cambridge: Cambridge University Press.

Prandini, R. (2013) 'The future of societal constitutionalism in the age of acceleration', *Indiana Journal of Global Legal Studies*, 20(2), 731–76.

Price, P. (1997) 'Natural law and birthright citizenship in Calvin's case 1608', *Yale Journal of Law and Humanities*, 9(1), 73–145.

Przeworski, A. (2009) 'Conquered or granted? A history of suffrage extensions', *British Journal of Political Science*, 39(2), 291–321. doi:10.1017/S0007123408000434.

Puzzo, C. (2016) 'UK citizenship in the early 21st century: Earning and losing the right to stay', *Revue Française de civilisation Britannique/French Journal of British Studies*, XXI-1. doi:10.4000/rfcb.750.

Quesada, P. (2015) *Report on Citizenship Law: Costa Rica*, Country Report 2015/20, San Domenico di Fiesole: Global Citizenship Observatory (GLOBALCIT), Robert Schuman Centre for Advanced Studies, European University Institute (http://hdl.handle.net/1814/38288).

Ramirez, F.O., Soysal, Y. and Shanahan, S. (1997) 'The changing logic of political citizenship: Cross-national acquisition of women's suffrage rights, 1890 to 1990', *American Sociological Review*, 62(5), 735–45. doi:10.2307/2657357.

Ramsay, R. (2013) 'Voters should not be in prison! The rights of prisoners in a democracy', *Critical Review of International Social and Political Philosophy*, 16(3), 421–38, Available at: https://doi.org/10.1080/1369 8230.2013.795706.

Ranta, R. and Nancheva, N. (2019) 'Unsettled: Brexit and European Union nationals' sense of belonging', *Population, Space and Place*, 25(1), e2199. doi: https://doi.org/10.1002/psp.2199.

Reynolds, S. (2017) 'May We Stay? Assessing the Security of Residence for EU Citizens Living in the UK', in M. Dougan (ed) *The UK after Brexit: Legal and Policy Challenges*, Cambridge: Intersentia, 181–202. doi:10.1017/9781780685953.010.

Richez, E. and Manfredi, C. (2015) 'Citizenship and the Canadian Charter', in K. Sarkowsky, R.O. Schultze and S. Schwarze (eds) *Migration, Regionalization, Citizenship*, Wiesbaden: Springer VS, 127–50.

Riesenberg, P. (1992) *Citizenship in the Western Tradition: Plato to Rousseau*, Chapel Hill, NC: University of North Carolina Press.

Roberts, K. (2017) 'Populism and Political Parties', in C.R. Kaltwasser, P. Taggart, P. Espejo and P. Ostiguy (eds) *The Oxford Handbook of Populism*, Oxford: Oxford University Press, 287–304.

Robertson, C. and Manta, I. (2019) '(Un)civil denaturalization', *New York University Law Review*, 94, 402–71.

Rodrigues, V. (2008) 'Citizenship and the Indian Constitution', in R. Bhargava (ed) *Politics and Ethics of the Indian Constitution*, New Delhi: Oxford University Press, 164–88.

Rodríguez, C.M. (2010) 'Noncitizen voting and the extraconstitutional construction of the polity', *International Journal of Constitutional Law*, 8(1), 30–49. doi: https://doi.org/10.1093/icon/mop032.

Rodrik, D. (2018) 'Populism and the economics of globalization', *Journal of International Business Policy*, 1, 12–33.

Roeben, V., Minnerop, P., Snell, J. and Telles, P. (2018) 'Revisiting Union citizenship from a fundamental rights perspective in the time of Brexit', *European Human Rights Law Review*, 5, 450–73.

Roone Miller, C. (2001) *Taylored Citizenship: State Institutions and Subjectivity*, Westport, CT: Praeger Publishers.

Rosenfeld, M. (2009) *The Identity of the Constitutional Subject: Selfhood, Citizenship, Culture and Community*, Abingdon: Routledge.

Rosenfeld, M. (2012) 'Constitutional Identity', in M. Rosenfeld and A. Sajó (eds) *Oxford Handbook of Comparative Constitutional Law*, Oxford: Oxford University Press, 756–75.

Rosenfeld, M. (2014) 'Is global constitutionalism meaningful or desirable?', *European Journal of International Law*, 25(1), 177–99. doi: https://doi.org/10.1093/ejil/cht083.

Roy, A. (2016) *Citizenship in India*, Oxford: Oxford University Press.

Rubenstein, K. (2017) *Australian Citizenship Law* (2nd edn), Sydney, NSW: Lawbook Company of Australia/Thomson Reuters.

Rubenstein, K. (2018) 'Power, control and citizenship: The Uluru statement from the heart as active citizenship', *Bond Law Review*, 30, 19–30.

Rubenstein, K. (2020) 'A surprise judgment from a conservative court', *The Canberra Times*, 12 February (www.canberratimes.com.au/story/6625520/a-surprise-judgment-from-a-conservative-court/).

Rubenstein, K. with Field, J. (2017) 'What is a "Real" Australian Citizen? Insights from Papua New Guinea and Mr Amos Ame', in B. Lawrance and J. Stevens (eds) *Citizenship in Question: Evidentiary Birthright and Statelessness*, Durham, NC/London: Duke University Press, 100–13.

Rubenstein, K. and Lenagh-Maguire, N. (2011) 'Citizenship and the Boundaries of the Constitution', in T. Ginsburg and R. Dixon (eds) *Comparative Constitutional Law*, Cheltenham: Edward Elgar, 143–69.

Rubio-Marín, R. (1998) 'National limits of democratic citizenship', *Ratio Juris*, 11(1), 51–66.

Rubio-Marín, R. (2015) 'The (dis)establishment of gender: Care and gender roles in the family as a constitutional matter', *International Journal of Constitutional Law*, 13(4), 787–818. doi: https://doi.org/10.1093/icon/mov059.

Ruškytė, R. (2015) *UPDATE: Recent Changes in Citizenship Law and Policy May 2010–January 2015 Lithuania* (http://eudo-citizenship.eu/admin/?p=file&appl=countryProfiles&f=Lithuania_citizenship_update_January2015.pdf).

Rytter, M. (2011) 'Semi-legal family life: Pakistani couples in the borderlands of Denmark and Sweden', *Journal of Transnational Affair*, 12(1), 91–108.

Rzepnikowska, A. (2019) 'Racism and xenophobia experienced by Polish migrants in the UK before and after Brexit vote', *Journal of Ethnic and Migration Studies*, 45(1), 61–77. doi:10.1080/1369183X.2018.1451308.

Sadiq, K. (2009) *Paper Citizens*, New York: Oxford University Press.

Sadiq, K. (2017) 'Post-Colonial Citizenship', in A. Shachar, R. Bauböck, I. Bloemraad and M. Vink (eds) *The Oxford Handbook of Citizenship*, Oxford: Oxford University Press, 178–99.

Sadurski, W. (2019) *Poland's Constitutional Breakdown*, Oxford: Oxford University Press.

Sagas, E. (2017) *Report on Citizenship Law: Dominican Republic*, Country Report 2017/16, San Domenico di Fiesole: Global Citizenship Observatory (GLOBALCIT), Robert Schuman Centre for Advanced Studies, European University Institute (http://hdl.handle.net/1814/50045).

Samtani, S. (2018) 'Deporting Rohingya refugees: Indian Supreme Court violates principle of non-refoulement', Oxford Human Rights Hub Blog, 18 October (http://ohrh.law.ox.ac.uk/deporting-rohingya-refugees-indian-supreme-court-violates-principle-of-non-refoulement/).

Santini, R. (2018) *Limited Statehood in Post-Revolutionary Tunisia: Citizenship, Economy and Security*, Cham, Switzerland: Palgrave/Springer.

Sarajlić, E. (2012) 'Conceptualising citizenship regime(s) in post-Dayton Bosnia and Herzegovina', *Citizenship Studies*, 16(3–4), 367–81. doi: http://dx.doi.org/10.1080/13621025.2012.683247.

Sarajlić, E. (2013) 'Multilevel Citizenship and the Contested Statehood of Bosnia and Herzegovina', in W. Maas (ed) *Multilevel Citizenship*, Philadelphia, PA: University of Pennsylvania Press, 168–83.

Sardelić, J. (2017) 'The position and agency of the "irregularized": Romani migrants as European semi-citizens', *Politics*, 37(3), 332–46. doi: https://doi.org/10.1177/0263395716668537.

Sardelić, J. (2019a) 'Does stripping people of citizenship lead to security and justice?', GLOBALCIT blog, 1 April (http://globalcit.eu/does-stripping-people-of-citizenship-lead-to-security-and-justice/).

Sardelić, J. (2019b) 'Roma in times of territorial rescaling: An inquiry into the margins of European citizenship', *Ethnopolitics*, 18(4), 325–39. doi:10.1080/17449057.2019.1584495.

Saucedo, L. and Cuison-Villazor, R. (2019) *Illegitimate Citizenship Rules*, UC Davis Legal Studies Research Paper (https://ssrn.com/abstract=3396786).

Scheppele, K.L. (2004) 'Constitutional ethnography: An introduction', *Law and Society Review*, 38, 389–406.

Scheppele, K.L. (2017) 'The Social Lives of Constitutions', in P. Blokker and C. Thornhill (eds) *Sociological Constitutionalism*, Cambridge: Cambridge University Press, 35–66. doi:10.1017/9781316403808.002.

Scheppele, K.L. (2019) 'The opportunism of populists and the defense of constitutional liberalism', *German Law*, 20(3), 314–31. doi:10.1017/glj.2019.25.

Scheppele, K.L. and Pech, L. (2018) 'Is there a better way forward?', Verfassungsblog, 10 March (https://verfassungsblog.de/is-there-a-better-way-forward/).

Schmid, S.D., Piccoli, L. and Arrighi, J.T. (2019) 'Non-universal suffrage: Measuring electoral inclusion in contemporary democracies', *European Political Science*, 18(4), 695–713. doi: https://doi.org/10.1057/s41304-019-00202-8.

Schmidt, G. (2013) 'Troubled by law: The subjunctivizing effects of Danish marriage reunification laws', *International Migration* 52(3), 129–43. doi:10.1111/imig.12132.

Schmidt, S. (2017) 'Extending Citizenship Rights and Losing it All: Brexit and the Perils of "Over-Constitutionalisation"', in D. Thym (ed) *Questioning EU Citizenship: Judges and the Limits of Free Movement and Solidarity in the EU*, Oxford: Hart Publishing, 17–36.

Scholtes, J. (2019) 'The complacency of legality: Constitutionalist vulnerabilities to populist constituent power,' *German Law Journal*, 20(3), 351–61. doi:10.1017/glj.2019.26.

Scholz, K.-A. (2017) 'What is German Leitkultur?', *German Issues in a Nutshell*, Deutsche Welle, 3 May (www.dw.com/en/what-is-german-leitkultur/a-38684973).

Schuck, P. and Smith, R. (1985) *Citizenship without Consent: Illegal Aliens in the American Polity*, New Haven, CT: Yale University Press.

Scott, J. (1998) *Seeing Like a State: How Certain Schemes to Improve the Human Condition Have Failed*, New Haven, CT/London: Yale University Press.

Sekulic, D., Massey, G. and Hodson, R. (1994) 'Who were the Yugoslavs? Failed sources of a common identity in the Former Yugoslavia', *American Sociological Review*, 59(1), 83–97.

Sendhardt, B. (2017) 'Theorizing the *Karta Polaka*', *The Journal of Power Institutions in Post-Soviet Societies*, 18. doi:10.4000/pipss.4348.

Seubert, S. (2014) 'Dynamics of modern citizenship democracy and peopleness in a global era', *Constellations*, 21(4), 547–59.

Shachar, A. (2009) *The Birthright Lottery: Citizenship and Global Inequality*, Cambridge, MA: Harvard University Press.

Shachar, A. (2011) 'Earned citizenship: Property lessons for immigration reform', *Yale Journal of Law the Humanities*, 23(1), 110–58.

Shachar, A. (2012) 'Citizenship', in M. Rosenfeld and A. Sajó (eds) *Oxford Handbook of Comparative Constitutional Law*, Oxford: Oxford University Press, 1002–19.

Shachar, A. (2017) 'Citizenship for Sale', in A. Shachar, R. Bauböck, I. Bloemraad and M. Vink (eds) *The Oxford Handbook of Citizenship*, Oxford: Oxford University Press, 789–816.

Shachar, A., Bauböck, R., Bloemraad, I. and Vink, M. (eds) (2017) *The Oxford Handbook of Citizenship*, Oxford: Oxford University Press.

Shamshad, R. (2017) *Bangladeshi Migrants in India: Foreigners, Refugees, or Infiltrators?*, New Delhi: Oxford University Press.

Shani, O. (2010) 'Conceptions of citizenship in India and the "Muslim question"', *Modern Asian Studies*, 44(1), 145–73. doi:10.1017/S0026749X09990102.

Shani, O. (2016) 'Making India's democracy: Rewriting the bureaucratic colonial imagination in the preparation of the first elections', *Comparative Studies of South Asia, Africa and the Middle East*, 36(1), 83–101. doi:10.1215/1089201x-3482135.

Shattuck, J., Huangand, A. and Thoreson-Green, E. (2019) *The War on Voting Rights*, CCDP 2019-003, February.

Shaw, J. (2007) *The Transformation of Citizenship in the European Union: Electoral Rights and the Restructuring of European Political Space*, Cambridge: Cambridge University Press.

Shaw, J. (2009) 'Citizenship and Electoral Rights in the Multi-Level "Euro-Polity": The Case of the United Kingdom', in H. Lindahl (ed) *A Right to Inclusion and Exclusion? Normative Fault Lines of the EU's Area of Freedom, Security and Justice*, Oxford: Hart Publishing, 241–53.

Shaw, J. (2011) 'The Constitutional Mosaic across the Boundaries of the European Union: Citizenship Regimes in the New States of South Eastern Europe', in N. Walker, S. Tierney and J. Shaw (eds) *Europe's Constitutional Mosaic*, Oxford: Hart Publishing, 137–70.

Shaw, J. (2017a) 'Unions and Citizens: Membership Status and Political Rights in Scotland, the UK and the EU', in C. Closa (ed) *Secession from a Member State and Withdrawal from the European Union: Troubled Membership*, Cambridge: Cambridge University Press, 153–86. doi: https://doi.org/10.1017/9781316771464.009.

Shaw, J. (2017b) 'The quintessentially democratic act? Democracy, political community and citizenship in and after the UK's EU referendum of June 2016', *Journal of European Integration*, 39(5), 559–74. doi:10.1080/0703 6337.2017.1333119.

Shaw, J. (2017c) 'Citizenship and the Franchise', in A. Shachar, R. Bauböck, I. Bloemraad and M. Vink (eds) *The Oxford Handbook of Citizenship*, Oxford: Oxford University Press, 290–312.

Shaw, J. (2018) 'Citizenship and Free Movement in a Changing EU: Navigating an Archipelago of Contradictions', in B. Martill and U. Staiger (eds) *Brexit and Beyond: Rethinking the Future of Europe*, London: UCL Press, 156–64.

Shaw, J. (2019a) 'EU Citizenship: Still a Fundamental Status?', in R. Bauböck (ed) *Debating European Citizenship*, IMISCO Research Series, Cham, Switzerland: Springer, 1–17.

Shaw, J. '(2019b) '"Shunning" and "seeking" membership: Rethinking citizenship regimes in the European constitutional space', *Global Constitutionalism*, 8(3), 425–69. doi: https://doi.org/10.1017/ S2045381719000133.

Shaw, J. (2019c) 'The UK constitution after the General Election 2019: big challenges ahead', 14 December (https://medium.com/@userjoshaw/ the-uk-constitution-after-the-general-election-2019-bigchallenges- ahead-b3d8331c0adc).

Shaw, J. and Štiks, I. (2012) 'Introduction: Citizenship in the New States of South Eastern Europe', in J. Shaw and I. Štiks (eds) *Citizenship after Yugoslavia*, Abingdon: Routledge, 1–13.

Shaw, J. and Wiener, A. (2000) 'The Paradox of the "European Polity"', in M.G. Cowles and M. Smith (eds) *The State of the European Union, V: Risks, Reform, Resistance, and Revival*, Oxford: Oxford University Press, 64–89.

Shevel, O. (2009) 'The politics of citizenship policy in new states', *Comparative Politics*, 41(3), 273–91. doi: https://doi.org/10.5129/0010 41509X12911362972197.

Sigona, N. (2019) 'How EU families in Britain are coping with Brexit uncertainty', *The Conversation*, 31 August (https://theconversation. com/how-eu-families-in-britain-are-coping-with-brexit- uncertainty-122659).

Sigona, N. and Godin, M. (2019) *Naturalisation and (Dis)integration for EU Families in Brexiting Britain*, EU Families and Eurochildren in Brexiting Britain Brief Series, No 6, Birmingham: University of Birmingham (https://eurochildren.info/publications/).

Sitapati, V. (2016) 'Reservations', in S. Choudhry, M. Khosla and P. Mehta (eds) *The Oxford Handbook of the Indian Constitution*, Oxford: Oxford University Press, 720–41.

Śledzińska-Simon, A. (2015) 'Constitutional identity in 3D: A model of individual, relational, and collective self and its application in Poland', *International Journal of Constitutional Law*, 13(1), 124–55. doi: https://doi.org/10.1093/icon/mov007.

Sloane, R. (2009) 'Breaking the genuine link: The contemporary international legal regulation of nationality', *Harvard International Law Journal*, 50, 1–60.

Smismans, S. (2019) *Protecting EU Citizens in the UK from a Brexit 'Windrush on Steroids': A Legislative Proposal for a Declaratory Registration System*, 6 August, DCU Brexit Institute – Working Paper No 8 (https://ssrn.com/abstract=3433055).

Smith, R.M. (2001) 'Citizenship and the politics of people-building', *Citizenship Studies*, 5(1), 73–96. doi:10.1080/13621020020025204.

Smith, R.M. (2010) 'The Strangers in Ourselves: The Rights of Suspect Citizens in the Age of Terrorism', in A. Sarat, L. Douglas and M. Umphrey (eds) *Law and the Stranger*, Stanford, CA: Stanford University Press, 65–95.

Smith, R.M. (2015) *Political Peoplehood: The Roles of Values, Interests, and Identities*, Chicago, IL: University of Chicago Press.

Snow, D. and Bernatzky, C. (2019) 'The Coterminous Rise of Right-Wing Populism and Superfluous Populations', in G. Fitzi, J. Mackert and B. Turner (eds) *Populism and the Crisis of Democracy, Volume 1: Concepts and Theory*, London/New York: Routledge, 130–46.

Sobel, N. (2015) 'A typology of the changing narratives of Canadian citizens through time', *Canadian Ethnic Studies*, 47(1), 11–39. doi: https://doi.org/10.1353/ces.2015.0003.

Södersten, A. (2017) 'The (dis)establishment of gender: Care and gender roles in the family as a constitutional matter: A reply to Ruth Rubio-Marín', *International Journal of Constitutional Law*, 15(4), 1178–83. doi: https://doi.org/10.1093/icon/mox082.

Soley, X. and Steininger, S. (2018) 'Parting ways or lashing back? Withdrawals, backlash and the Inter-American Court of Human Rights', *International Journal of Law in Context*, 14, 237–57. doi:10.1017/S1744552318000058.

Somers, M.R. (1993) 'Citizenship and the place of the public sphere: Law, community and political culture in the transition to democracy', *American Sociological Review*, 58(5), 587–620.

Somers, M.R. (1994) 'Rights, relationality, and membership: Rethinking the making and meaning of citizenship', *Law and Social Inquiry*, 19(1), 63–112.

Somers, M.R. (2008) *Genealogies of Citizenship: Markets, Statelessness and the Right to Have Rights*, Cambridge: Cambridge University Press.

Somers, M.R. and Roberts, C.N.J. (2008) Toward a new sociology of rights: A genealogy of "buried bodies" of citizenship and human rights', *Annual Review of Law and Social Science*, 4(1), 385–425.

Soros, J. (2013) 'The missing right: A constitutional right to vote', *Democracy: A Journal of Ideas*, Spring, No 28 (https://democracyjournal. org/magazine/28/the-missing-right-a-constitutional-right-to-vote/).

Soysal, Y. (1994) *Limits of Citizenship: Migrants and Postnational Membership in Europe*, Chicago, IL and London: University of Chicago Press.

Soysal, Y. (2012a) 'Post-National Citizenship: Rights and Obligations of Individuality', in E. Amenta, K. Nash and A. Scott (eds) *The Wiley-Blackwell Companion to Political Sociology*, Chichester: Wiley-Blackwell, 383–93.

Soysal, Y. (2012b) 'Citizenship, immigration, and the European social project: Rights and obligations of individuality', *The British Journal of Sociology*, 63(1), 1–21. doi:10.1111/j.1468-4446.2011.01404.x.

Soysal, Y. (2012c) 'Individuality, sociological institutionalism, and continuing inequalities: A response to commentators', *The British Journal of Sociology*, 63(1), 47–53. doi:10.1111/j.1468-4446.2012.01405.x.

Spiro, P.J. (2008) 'Multiple Nationality', in *Max Planck Encyclopedia of Public International Law*, Oxford: Oxford University Press.

Spiro, P.J. (2011) 'A new international law of citizenship', *American Journal of International Law*, 105, 694–746. doi:10.5305/amerjintelaw.105.4.0694.

Spiro, P.J. (2017) 'Multiple Citizenship', in A. Shachar, R. Bauböck, I. Bloemraad and M. Vink (eds) *The Oxford Handbook of Citizenship*, Oxford: Oxford University Press, 623–43.

Spiro, P.J. (2018) 'Stakeholder citizenship won't save citizenship', in R. Bauböck (ed) *Democratic Inclusion*, Manchester: Manchester University Press, 204–24.

Spiro, P.J. (2019) *Nottebohm and 'Genuine Link': Anatomy of a Jurisprudential Illusion*, Working Paper, IMC-RP 2019/1, Investment Migration Council (https://investmentmigration.org/download/nottebohm-genuine-link-anatomy-jurisprudential-illusion-imc-rp-2019-1/).

Steinbeis, M. (2019) 'Our own people', Verfassungsblog, 2 February. doi: https://doi.org/10.17176/20190324-210141-0.

Stern, J. and Valchars, G. (2013) *Report on Citizenship Law: Austria*, Country Report 2013/28, San Domenico di Fiesole: Global Citizenship Observatory (GLOBALCIT), Robert Schuman Centre for Advanced Studies, European University Institute (http://hdl.handle.net/1814/60232).

Štiks, I. (2015) *Nations and Citizens in Yugoslavia and the Post-Yugoslav States: One Hundred Years of Citizenship*, London: Bloomsbury.

Štiks, I. and Shaw, J. (2014) 'Citizenship rights: Statuses, challenges and struggles', *Belgrade Journal of Media and Communications*, 18(6), 73–90 (www.ceeol.com/search/article-detail?id=79153).

Stjepanović, D. (2019) 'Self-Determination Constellations: Sub-State Regions and Citizenship in Europe', in J. Jordana, M. Keating, A. Marx and J. Wouters (eds) *Borders, Sovereignty and Self-Determination in Contemporary Europe*, Abingdon: Routledge, 95–109.

Stjepanović, D. and Tierney, S. (2019) 'The right to vote: Constitutive referendums and regional citizenship', *Ethnopolitics*, 18(3), 264–77. doi: 10.1080/17449057.2019.1585090.

Stockemer, D. (ed) (2019) *Populism Around the World: A Comparative Perspective*, Cham, Switzerland: Springer. doi: https://doi.org/10.1007/978-3-319-96758-5.

Stolcke, V. (1997) 'The "Nature" of Nationality', in V. Bader (ed) *Citizenship and Exclusion*, London: Palgrave Macmillan, 61–80.

Strumia, F. (2017) 'Supranational Citizenship', in A. Shachar, R. Bauböck, I. Bloemraad and M. Vink (eds) *The Oxford Handbook of Citizenship*, Oxford: Oxford University Press, 669–93.

Strumia, F. (2018) 'From alternative triggers to shifting links: Social integration and protection of supranational citizenship in the context of Brexit and beyond', *European Papers*, 3(2), 733–59. doi:10.15166/2499-8249/253.

Suárez-Krabbe, J. and Lindberg, A. (2019) 'Enforcing apartheid? The politics of "intolerability" in the Danish migration and integration regimes', *Migration and Society: Advances in Research*, 2(1), 90–7. doi:10.3167/arms.2019.020109.

Subramaniam, S. (2019) 'Indian democracy is fighting back', *The Atlantic*, 24 December (www.theatlantic.com/ideas/archive/2019/12/indian-democracy-fighting-back/604129/).

Sullivan, M. (2018) 'Beyond allegiance: Toward a right to Canadian citizenship status', *American Review of Canadian Studies*, 48(3), 327–43. doi:10.1080/02722011.2018.1503608.

Swider, K. (2019) '*Hoti v Croatia*', *Statelessness and Citizenship Review*, 1, 184–90.

Tabachnik, M. (2019) 'Defining the nation in Russia's buffer zone: The politics of citizenship by birth on territory (*jus soli*) in Moldova, Azerbaijan, and Georgia', *Post-Soviet Affairs*, 35(3), 223–39. doi:10.108 0/1060586X.2018.1542868.

Teague, P. (2019) 'Brexit, the Belfast Agreement and Northern Ireland: Imperilling a fragile political bargain', *The Political Quarterly*, 90(4), 690–704. doi:10.1111/1467-923X.12766.

Teubner, G. (2017) 'Societal Constitutionalism', in P. Blokker and C. Thornhill (eds) *Sociological Constitutionalism*, Cambridge: Cambridge University Press, 313–40. doi:10.1017/9781316403808.010.

Thio, L.A. (2012) 'Constitutionalism in Illiberal Polities', in M. Rosenfeld and A. Sajó (eds) *Oxford Handbook of Comparative Constitutional Law*, Oxford: Oxford University Press, 133–52.

Thio, L.A. (2019) 'Singapore's relational constitutionalism: The living institution and the project of religious harmony', *Singapore Journal of Legal Studies*, 204–34.

Thomas, E. (2002) 'Who belongs? Competing conceptions of political membership', *European Journal of Social Theory*, 5(3), 323–49.

Thornhill, C. (2017) 'The sociology of constitutions', *Annual Review of Law and Social Science*, 13, 493–513. doi: https://doi.org/10.1146/annurev-lawsocsci-110316-113518.

Thornhill, C. (2018) 'The citizen of many worlds: Societal constitutionalism and the antinomies of democracy', *Journal of Law and Society*, 45, S73–S93. doi:10.1111/jols.12104.

Thwaites, R. (2017) *Report on Citizenship Law: Australia*, Country Report 2017/11, San Domenico di Fiesole: Global Citizenship Observatory (GLOBALCIT), Robert Schuman Centre for Advanced Studies, European University Institute (http://hdl.handle.net/1814/46449).

Thwaites, R. (2018) 'The life and times of the genuine link', *Victoria University of Wellington Law Review*, 49(4), 645–70. doi: https://doi.org/10.26686/vuwlr.v49i4.5345.

Tierney, S. (2013) 'Legal issues surrounding the referendum on independence for Scotland', *European Constitutional Law Review*, 9(3), 359–90. doi:10.1017/S1574019612001216.

Tintori, G. (2016) 'Italian Mobilities and the Demos', in R. Ben-Ghiat and S. Hom (eds) *Italian Mobilities*, London: Routledge, 111–32.

Tóth, J. (2018) 'The curious case of Hungary: Why the naturalisation rate does not always show how inclusive a country is', GLOBALCIT Blog, 3 January (http://globalcit.eu/the-curious-case-of-hungary-why-the-naturalisation-rate-does-not-always-show-how-inclusive-a-country-is/).

Tripković, M. (2019) *Punishment and Citizenship: A Theory of Criminal Disenfranchisement*, Oxford: Oxford University Press.

Trispiotis, I (2016) 'Two interpretations of "living together" in European Human Rights Law', *Cambridge Law Journal*, 75(3), 580–607.

Troper, M. (1998) 'The Concept of Citizenship in the Period of the French Revolution', in M. La Torre (ed) *European Citizenship: An Institutional Challenge*, The Hague/London: Kluwer Law International, 29–45.

Troper, M. (2010) 'Behind the Constitution? The Principle of Constitutional Identity in France', in A. Sajó and R. Uitz (eds) *Constitutional Topography: Values and Constitutions*, The Hague: Eleven Publishing, 201–30.

Troy, D. (2019) 'Governing imperial citizenship: a historical account of citizenship revocation', *Citizenship Studies*, 23(4), 304–19. doi:10.1080 /13621025.2019.1616447.

Tully, J. (1995) *Strange Multiplicity: Constitutionalism in an Age of Diversity*, Cambridge: Cambridge University Press.

Tully, J. (2008) 'Two Meanings of Global Citizenship: Modern and Diverse', in M. Peters, A. Britton and H. Blee (eds) *Global Citizenship Education: Philosophy, Theory and Pedagogy*, Rotterdam: Sense Publishers, 15–39.

Tushnet, M. (2017) *Comparative Constitutional Law*, Edward Elgar Research Review in Law, Cheltenham/Northampton, MA: Edward Elgar. doi:10.4337/9781785362705.

Twomey, A. (2020) 'High Court decision in Love and Thoms case reflects Aboriginal connection to the land', ABC News, 12 February (www. abc.net.au/news/2020-02-12/high-court-love-and-thoms-aboriginal-connection-to-land/11954662).

Uggen, C. and Manza, J. (2002) 'Democratic contraction? Political consequences of felon disenfranchisement in the United States', *American Sociological Review*, 67(6), 777–803.

UN Women (2017) 'Why and how constitutions matter for advancing gender equality: Gains, gaps and policy implications', UN Women Policy Brief Series, B. Duncan (www.unwomen.org/en/digital-library/publications/2017/2/why-and-how-constitutions-matter-for-advancing-gender-equality).

Vakulenko, A. (2009) 'Gender equality as an essential French value: The case of *Mme M*', *Human Rights Law Review*, 9(1), 143–50. doi: https:// doi.org/10.1093/hrlr/ngn034.

Valle, A.J. (2019) 'Race and the empire-state: Puerto Ricans' unequal US citizenship', *Sociology of Race and Ethnicity*, 5(1), 26–40. doi: https://doi. org/10.1177/2332649218776031.

van den Brink, M. (2020) 'A qualified defence of the primacy of nationality over European Union citizenship', *International and Comparative Law Quarterly*, 69(1), 177–202. doi:10.1017/S0020589319000538.

van den Brink, M. and Kochenov, D. (2019) 'Against associate EU citizenship', *JCMS: Journal of Common Market Studies*, 57(6), 1366–82. doi: https://doi.org/10.1111/jcms.12898.

van der Schyff, E. and Callies, D.L. (eds) (2019) *Constitutional Identity in a Europe of Multilevel Constitutionalism*, Cambridge: Cambridge University Press.

van Steenbergen, B. (ed) (1994) *The Condition of Citizenship*, London, Thousand Oaks, CA and New Delhi: Sage.

van Waas, L. (2014) '"Are we there yet?" The emergence of statelessness on the international human rights agenda', *Netherlands Quarterly of Human Rights*, 32(4), 342–6.

van Waas, L. and Jaghai, S. (2018) 'All citizens are created equal, but some are more equal than others', *Netherlands International Law Review*, 65, 413–30.

Vink, M. (2017) 'Comparing Citizenship Regimes', in A. Shachar, R. Bauböck, I. Bloemraad and M. Vink (eds) *The Oxford Handbook of Citizenship*, Oxford: Oxford University Press, 221–44.

Vink, M. and Bauböck, R. (2013) 'Citizenship configurations: Analysing the multiple purposes of citizenship regimes in Europe', *Comparative European Politics*, 11, 621–48.

Vink, M., Bauböck, R. and Shaw, J. (2016) 'A Short History of Comparative Research on Citizenship', in O. Vonk (ed) *Grootboek: Opstellen aangeboden aan Prof.mr. Gerard-René de Groot ter gelegenheid van zijn afscheid als hoogleraar rechtsvergelijking en internationaal privaatrecht aan de Universiteit Maastricht*, Alphen aan den Rijn: Wolters Kluwer, 409–22.

Vink, M., de Groot, G.-R. and Luk, N.C. (2015) 'MACIMIDE Global Expatriate Dual Citizenship Dataset'. doi:10.7910/DVN/TTMZ08, Harvard Dataverse, V3.

Vink, M., Honohan, I. and Bauböck, R. (no date) 'Varieties of citizenship regimes: Birthright models, individual rights and arbitrary state power around the world'.

Vink, M., Schakel, A., Reichel, D., Luk, N.C. and de Groot, G.-R. (2019) 'The international diffusion of expatriate dual citizenship', *Migration Studies*, 7(3), 362–83. doi: https://doi.org/10.1093/migration/mnz011.

Vlieks, C. (2019) '*Tjebbes and Others v Minister van Buitenlandse Zaken*: A next step in European Union case law on nationality matters?', *Tilburg Law Review*, 24, 142–6. doi: http://doi.org/10.5334/tilr.149.

Vlieks, C., Ballin, E.H. and Vela, M.J.R. (2017) 'Solving statelessness: Interpreting the right to nationality', *Netherlands Quarterly of Human Rights*, 35(3), 158–75. doi: https://doi.org/10.1177/0924051917722222.

Voeten, E. (2019) 'Populism and backlashes against international courts', *Perspectives on Politics*, 1–16. doi:10.1017/S1537592719000975.

Volpp, L. (2015) 'The indigenous as alien', *Immigration and Nationality Law Review*, 36, 773–814.

Volpp, L. (2017) 'Feminist, Sexual and Queer Citizenship', in A. Shachar, R. Bauböck, I. Bloemraad and M. Vink (eds) *The Oxford Handbook of Citizenship*, Oxford: Oxford University Press, 153–77.

Vonk, O. (2015) *Nationality Law in the Western Hemisphere: A Study on Grounds for Acquisition and Loss of Citizenship in the Americas and the Caribbean*, Boston, MA/Leiden: Brill.

Vonk, O. (2018a) 'Citizenship Law in Asia', in O. Vonk (ed) *Nationality Law in the Eastern Hemisphere: Acquisition and Loss of Citizenship in Asian Perspective*, Oisterwijk: Wolf Legal Publishers, 1–34.

Vonk, O. (ed) (2018b) *Nationality Law in the Eastern Hemisphere. Acquisition and Loss of Citizenship in Asian Perspective*, Oisterwijk: Wolf Legal Publishers.

von Rütte, B. (2018) 'From State Privilege to Right – A Proposal for Reinterpreting the Right to Citizenship', Paper delivered to the GLOBALCIT Conference 'Rights and Status: The Role of Citizenship in Immigrant Integration and Diaspora Building', 29–30 November, European University Institute, Florence.

Waldrauch, H. (2006a) 'Methodology for Comparing Acquisition and Loss of Nationality', in R. Bauböck, E. Ersbøll, K. Groenendijk and H. Waldrauch (eds) *Acquisition and Loss of Nationality: Volume I: Comparative Analysis*, Amsterdam: Amsterdam University Press, 105–19.

Waldrauch, H. (2006b) 'Acquisition of Nationality', in R. Bauböck, E. Ersbøll, K. Groenendijk and H. Waldrauch (eds) *Acquisition and Loss of Nationality: Volume I: Comparative Analysis*, Amsterdam: Amsterdam University Press, 121–82.

Waldrauch, H. (2006c) 'Loss of Nationality', in R. Bauböck, E. Ersbøll, K. Groenendijk and H. Waldrauch (eds) *Acquisition and Loss of Nationality: Volume I: Comparative Analysis*, Amsterdam: Amsterdam University Press, 182–220.

Waldron, J. (2013) 'Citizenship and Dignity', in C. McCrudden and British Academy (eds) *Understanding Human Dignity*, Oxford: Oxford University Press, 327–43.

Walker, N. (2010) 'Rosenfeld's plural constitutionalism', *International Journal of Constitutional Law*, 8(3), 677–84.

Walker, N. (2017) 'The Place of Territory in Citizenship', in A. Shachar, R. Bauböck, I. Bloemraad and M. Vink (eds) *The Oxford Handbook of Citizenship*, Oxford: Oxford University Press, 553–75.

Walker, N. (2019a) 'When Sovereigns Stir', in B. Leijssenaar and N. Walker (eds) *Sovereignty in Action*, Cambridge: Cambridge University Press, 31–64. doi:10.1017/9781108692502.003.

Walker, N. (2019b) 'Populism and constitutional tension', *International Journal of Constitutional Law*, 17(2), 515–35. doi: https://doi.org/10.1093/icon/moz027.

Wallace Goodman, S. (2019) 'Liberal democracy, national identity boundaries, and populist entry points', *Critical Review: A Journal of Politics and Society*. doi:10.1080/08913811.2019.1647679.

Wandan, S. (2015) 'Nothing out of the ordinary: Constitution making as representative politics', *Constellations*, 22(1), 44–58. doi:10.1111/1467-8675.12139.

Waterbury, M.A. (2014) 'Making citizens beyond the borders', *Problems of Post-Communism*, 61(4), 36–49. doi:10.2753/PPC1075-8216610403.

Waterbury, M.A. (2017) 'National minorities in an era of externalization', *Problems of Post-Communism*, 64(5), 228–41. doi:10.1080/10758216.2016.1251825.

Waterbury, M.A. (2018) 'Caught between nationalism and transnationalism: How Central and East European states respond to East–West emigration', *International Political Science Review*, 39(3), 338–52. doi: https://doi.org/10.1177/0192512117753613.

Wautelet, P. (2018) 'The next frontier: Dual nationality as a multi-layered concept', *Netherlands International Law Review*, 65, 391–412. doi: https://doi.org/10.1007/s40802-018-0125-6.

Waylen, G. (2006) 'Constitutional engineering: What opportunities for the enhancement of gender rights?', *Third World Quarterly*, 27(7), 1209–21. doi: https://doi.org/10.1080/01436590600933305.

Weale, A. (2017) 'The democratic duty to oppose Brexit', *The Political Quarterly*, 88(2), 170–81. doi:10.1111/1467-923X.12338.

Weale, A. (2018) *The Will of the People: A Modern Myth*, Cambridge: Polity Press.

Webber, F. (2018) *The Embedding of State Hostility: A Background Paper on the Windrush Scandal*, Institute for Race Relations (www.irr.org.uk/publications/issues/the-embedding-of-state-hostility-a-background-paper-on-the-windrush-scandal/).

Weil, P. (2008) *How To Be French: Nationality in the Making since 1789*, Porter, Durham NC: Duke University Press.

Weil, P. (2012) *The Sovereign Citizen: Denaturalization and the Origins of the American Republic*, Philadelphia, PA: University of Pennsylvania Press.

Weil, P. (2014) 'Citizenship, passports, and the legal identity of Americans: Edward Snowden and others have a case in the courts', *Yale Law Journal Forum*, 123, 565–85.

Weil, P. (2017a) 'Denaturalization and denationalization in comparison (France, the United Kingdom, the United States)', *Philosophy & Social Criticism*, 43(4–5), 417–29. doi: https://doi.org/10.1177/0191453717704133.

Weil, P. (2017b) 'Can a citizen be sovereign?', *Humanity: An International Journal of Human Rights, Humanitarianism, and Development*, 8(1), 1–27 (https://muse.jhu.edu/article/650941).

White, J. and Ypi, L. (2017) 'The politics of peoplehood', *Political Theory*, 45(4), 439–65. doi: https://doi.org/10.1177/0090591715608899.

White, R. (2019) 'The nationality and immigration status of the "Windrush Generation" and the perils of lawful presence in a "hostile environment"', *Journal of Immigration Asylum and National Law*, 33, 218–39.

Whitehouse, R. (2019) 'The fight to get citizenship for descendants of German Jews', BBC News, 18 November (www.bbc.co.uk/news/stories-50398227).

Wiener, A. (1997) 'Making sense of the new geography of citizenship: Fragmented citizenship in the European Union', *Theory and Society*, 26(4), 529–60. doi: https://doi.org/10.1023/A:1006809913519.

Wiesner, C., Björk, A., Kivistö, H.-M. and Mäkinen, K. (2018) 'Introduction: Shaping Citizenship as a Political Concept', in C. Wiesner, A. Björk, H.-M. Kivistö and K. Mäkinen (eds) *Shaping Citizenship*, New York: Routledge, 1–16.

Williams, M. (2007) 'Nonterritorial Boundaries of Citizenship', in S. Benhabib, I. Shapiro and D. Petranovich (eds) *Identities, Affiliation, and Allegiances*, Cambridge: Cambridge University Press, 226–56.

Wilson, B. (2011) 'Enforcing Rights and Exercising an Accountability Function', in G. Helmke and J. Ríos-Figueroa (eds) *Courts in Latin America*, Cambridge: Cambridge University Press, 55–80. doi:10.1017/CBO9780511976520.003.

Wimmer, A. (2013) *Ethnic Boundary Making: Institutions, Power, Networks*, Oxford: Oxford University Press.

Winter, E. (2015) *Report on Citizenship Law: Canada*, Country Report 2015/18, San Domenico di Fiesole: Global Citizenship Observatory (GLOBALCIT), Robert Schuman Centre for Advanced Studies, European University Institute (http://hdl.handle.net/1814/38289).

Winter, E. and Previsic, I. (2019) 'The politics of un-belonging: lessons from Canada's experiment with citizenship revocation', *Citizenship Studies*, 23(4), 338–55. doi:10.1080/13621025.2019.1616450.

Wodak, R. (2019) 'Entering the "post-shame era": The rise of illiberal democracy, populism and neo-authoritarianism in Europe', *Global Discourse: An Interdisciplinary Journal of Current Affairs*, 9(1), 195–213. doi: https://doi.org/10.1332/204378919X15470487645420.

Wolf, T. and Cea, B. (2019a) 'A critical history of the United States Census and citizenship questions', *Georgetown Law Journal Online*, 108 (https://www.law.georgetown.edu/georgetown-law-journal/glj-online/108-online/a-critical-history-of-the-united-states-census-and-citizenship-questions/).

Wolf, T. and Cea, B. (2019b) 'How the Supreme Court messed up the Census case', *The Atlantic*, 1 July (www.theatlantic.com/ideas/archive/2019/07/citizenship-questions-are-not-historically-normal/593014/).

Wolkenstein, F. (2019a) 'Populism, liberal democracy and the ethics of peoplehood', *European Journal of Political Theory*, 18(3), 330–48. doi: https://doi.org/10.1177/1474885116677901.

Wolkenstein, F. (2019b) 'The revival of democratic intergovernmentalism, first principles and the case for a contest-based account of democracy in the European Union', *Political Studies*. doi: https://doi.org/10.1177/0032321719850690.

Wooding, B. (2008) 'Contesting Dominican discrimination and statelessness', *Peace Review*, 20(3), 366–75. doi:10.1080/10402650802330279.

Wooding, B. (2018) 'Haitian Immigrants and Their Descendants Born in the Dominican Republic', in *Oxford Research Encyclopedia of Latin American History*, Oxford: Oxford University Press (https://oxfordre.com/latinamericanhistory/view/10.1093/acrefore/9780199366439.001.0001/acrefore-9780199366439-e-474).

World Bank (2017) *Governance and Law*, World Development Report 2017, Washington, DC: World Bank Group.

Xavier, C. (2011) 'Experimenting with diasporic incorporation: The overseas citizenship of India', *Nationalism and Ethnic Politics*, 17(1), 34–53. doi:10.1080/13537113.2011.550545.

Yashar, D.J. (2005) *Contesting Citizenship in Latin America: The Rise of Indigenous Movements and the Postliberal Challenge*, New York: Cambridge University Press.

Yeo, C. (2019) 'The Rise of Modern Banishment: Deprivation and Nullification of British Citizenship', in D. Prabhat (ed) *Citizenship in Times of Turmoil? Theory, Practice and Policy*, Cheltenham: Edward Elgar Publishing Limited, 134–50.

Yeo, C., Sigona, N. and Godin, M. (2019) *Parallels and Differences between Ending Commonwealth and EU Citizen Free Movement*, EU Familes and Eurochildren in Brexiting Britain Brief Series, No 4, Birmingham: University of Birmingham (https://eurochildren.info/publications/).

Yılmaz, F. (2012) 'Right-wing hegemony and immigration: How the populist far-right achieved hegemony through the immigration debate in Europe', *Current Sociology*, 60(3), 368–81. doi: https://doi.org/10.1177/0011392111426192.

Young, I.M. (1989) 'Polity and group difference: A critique of the ideal of universal citizenship', *Ethics*, 99(2), 250–74.

Young, K. (2016) 'On what matters in comparative constitutional law: A comment on Hirschl', *Boston University Law Review*, 96(4), 1375–92.

Ypi, L. (2013) 'What's wrong with colonialism', *Philosophy and Public Affairs*, 41(2), 158–91. doi:10.1111/papa.12014.

Zedner, L. (2016) 'Citizenship deprivation, security and human rights', *European Journal of Migration and Law*, 18, 222–42.

Zedner, L. (2019) 'The hostile border: Crimmigration, counter-terrorism, or crossing the line on rights?', *New Criminal Law Review*, 22(3), 318–45. doi:10.1525/nclr.2019.22.3.318.

Ziegler, R., Shaw, J. and Bauböck, R. (eds) (2014) *Independence Referendums: Who Should Vote and Who Should Be Offered Citizenship?*, Research Paper No 90, Florence: Robert Schuman Centre for Advanced Studies and European University Institute.

Ziemele, I. (2014) 'State Succession and Issues of Nationality and Statelessness', in A. Edwards and L. van Waas (eds) *Nationality and Statelessness under International Law*, Cambridge: Cambridge University Press, 217–246. doi:10.1017/CBO9781139506007.010.

Žilović, M. (2012) *Citizenship, Ethnicity, and Territory: The Politics of Selecting by Origin in Post-Communist Southeast Europe*, CITSEE Working Paper 2012/20 (www.citsee.ed.ac.uk).

Zincone, G. and Basili, M. (2009) *Report on Citizenship Law: Italy*, Country Report, San Domenico di Fiesole: Global Citizenship Observatory (GLOBALCIT), Robert Schuman Centre for Advanced Studies, European University Institute, Country Report, Italy (http://hdl.handle.net/1814/19619).

Zubrzycki, G. (2001) '"We, the Polish nation": Ethnic and civic visions of nationhood in post-communist constitutional debates', *Theory and Society*, 30, 629–68. doi: https://doi.org/10.1023/A:1013024707150.

Index

CPSIA information can be obtained
at www.ICGtesting.com
Printed in the USA
BVHW041952051021
618210BV00005B/17